Farbrengen
Hasidic Gatherings with Rabbi Steinsaltz

RABBI ADIN EVEN-ISRAEL STEINSALTZ

FARBRENGEN

HASIDIC GATHERINGS WITH RABBI STEINSALTZ

Rabbi Adin Even-Israel Steinsaltz
translated by Rabbi Joshua Schreier

Steinsaltz Center
Maggid Books

Farbrengen
Hasidic Gatherings with Rabbi Steinsaltz

First English Edition, 2026

Maggid Books
An imprint of Koren Publishers Jerusalem Ltd.

POB 8531, New Milford, CT 06776-8531, USA
& POB 4044, Jerusalem 9104001, Israel
www.korenpub.com

The book was published with the participation of the Steinsaltz Center.

Originally published as *Ad Bli Dai* (Hebrew)

Cover Design: Eliyahu Misgav
Cover Drawing: Shaḥar Gesundheit
Cover Photo: © Portrait of Rabbi Steinsaltz, Erik Tischler
Typesetting: Taly Hahn
Project Manager: Fruma Holland
Editor-in-Chief: Elḥanan Yisraeli
Editors: Elad Schlesinger, Yedidya Aviner, and Aharon Billet
Translation editor: Gaya Aranoff Bernstein
Copy Editor: Suri Brand
Writing of the Prefaces: Yisrael Malkiel
Consultation and Assistance in Editing: Sara Friedland Ben-Arza

Special thanks to Rabbi Steinsaltz's students who recorded and invested many hours in listening and transcribing matters for the book.

With deep gratitude, we acknowledge the support of our friend Rabbi Dr. Yosef Wosk for bringing this series to publication.

The publication of this book was made possible through the generous support of the Jewish Book Trust.

Please send corrections to: tikunim@steinsaltz-center.org

ISBN 978-1-59264-749-1, *hardcover*

Printed and bound in United States

This volume is dedicated with gratitude to the memory of
the rare soul known to this world as

***Rabbi Adin Steinsaltz** z"l*

His life's work uplifted humanity through the study
of his spiritual teachings.

This volume is also dedicated to the memory of

***Marvin P. Cohen** z"l*

a devotee of truth and lifelong learning.

His ongoing study of Torah and Talmud led to his continual
growth until his final breath.

Dedicated by the Burton G. and Anne C. Greenblatt Foundation

Reading a book of farbrengens isn't like reading and studying any other book.

A farbrengen must be experienced through hearing the voice of the speaker, through connecting with the burning of his soul, and by cleaving to his great spirit.

Consequently, the publication of these farbrengens is dedicated to the elevation of the soul of our master and our teacher

***Rabbi Adin Even-Israel Steinsaltz** zt"l*

who hewed the words of this book from the fire of his soul, and over the course of dozens of years and hundreds of farbrengens illuminated the souls of tens of thousands of listeners and students.

Our intent in the writing and editing of this book is to keep the flame of his soul burning.

May it serve as a flaming torch that will illuminate the souls of those who read it, wherever they may be.

Contents

Preface

A good farbrengen is one that can't be summarized in writing.

– Rabbi Adin Even-Israel Steinsaltz

This book is a collection of ideas that Rabbi Steinsaltz discussed at hasidic gatherings, or farbrengens, with his students and others who came to hear what he had to say.

"Farbrengen" in hasidic jargon is a gathering of hasidim for the purpose of spiritual elevation and strengthening. At a farbrengen, they eat, drink *leḥayim*, sing, and talk about serving God. There is no preset program at a farbrengen. It develops organically from the proceedings depending on those present and the time and place.

It's hard to describe what transpired at a farbrengen led by Rabbi Steinsaltz. For many of those listening to him speak, these farbrengens contained moments of the kind that a person remembers and experiences throughout his life. He repeatedly emphasized that the farbrengen is not an occasion for Torah insights, nor, on a totally different plane, idle talk. A farbrengen is a time for speaking truth, for shedding the veneer to allow something to enter so that something will penetrate the heart and mind and spur a person to make a change. The change could be major or minor, a minuscule step or a great leap. The main thing is that it be genuine and true, not imaginary and not an ephemeral spiritual experience.

Rabbi Steinsaltz was fully present at these farbrengen with his entire being. This wasn't merely a speech or lecture, but it was an unvarnished, fervent, and sometimes acerbic talk aimed at those present in the room in general and in particular. Rabbi Steinsaltz would lead every stage of the farbrengen: the preamble to the farbrengen, the *leḥayim*, the joyous dancing and longing melodies, the general talks about "what is a farbrengen" or "what is the essence of the day that we are commemorating," and the emphatic discussions on the essence of a thing and other matters.

At times, Rabbi Steinsaltz's words would assume the form of a long, coherent progression, and at times he would present several disparate ideas. He would explain the point in a concrete manner, analyze it thoroughly, and describe its various facets, cite parables, and tell stories until the ideas received color and form. He paid close attention to what was going on in the room and responded to the questions and statements of those present, the melodies that were sung, and the degree of enthusiasm of the attendees. He would frequently direct questions to the listeners, students, or incidental visitors, asking about their lives and how they intended to "do something" with the things that were said.

The farbrengens often continued until the small hours of the night, when Rabbi Steinsaltz's words would converge and reach their conclusion. On many occasions, before he left the farbrengen, he would say, "I need to go, but you – stay and continue to *farbreng* until the morning."

Over the years, Rabbi Steinsaltz conducted farbrengens in Israel and abroad, in institutions over which he presided, at public events, at official events, and at small, private gatherings. Most of the farbrengens that appear in this book took place in the Tekoa Yeshiva, some of them at Mekor Ḥayim Yeshiva, and a few in other places. Typically he held these farbrengens on certain occasions throughout the year. Most of these dates were days on which Lubavitch hasidim were accustomed to hold farbrengens, and accordingly, the content of most of the gatherings was tied to some extent to the Lubavitcher Rebbes and the history of Chabad Hasidism. The exceptions were the farbrengen held on the *yartzeit* of the Kotzker Rebbe and the farbrengen held on Rabbi Steinsaltz's birthday.

This book is divided according to these dates, and in each section, the farbrengens that took place on that date are presented.

It's not a simple challenge to commit to writing down that which was said orally, especially when the matter at hand is an organic, evolving event like a farbrengen. We sought to preserve Rabbi Steinsaltz's beautiful, invigorating language and sharp, direct speech, while suiting his words to the form and style of a printed book.

Since the book was edited after Rabbi Steinsaltz's passing and he did not review it, it's possible that there are some errors or inaccuracies that cropped up in the transfer of his words to written form. It goes without saying that responsibility for this is ours alone.

In editing the book, we related to each farbrengen as an independent unit, as a complete event that is a sum of its parts. Each farbrengen in the book stands by itself, and it's therefore possible that there will be ideas or stories that are repeated. Though we did attempt to limit redundancy, we allowed for repetition that contributes to the development of the farbrengen.

Despite all this, this book is not an attempt to summarize the content of Rabbi Steinsaltz's farbrengens. Any such attempt would be futile and also misses the point. It is futile because it's impossible to transmit in writing all the components of a farbrengen – the vitality of the event, the timing, the place, the participants, the atmosphere, the melodies, the togetherness, and especially Rabbi Steinsaltz's direct way of addressing his listeners. It misses the point because the main component of a farbrengen, as Rabbi Steinsaltz himself often told us, is not the content, but what one absorbs, what remains in the heart of the listeners long after the event.

This book is therefore an attempt to transmit in writing the seeds of a farbrengen, so that they will be able to grow and come to life in the reader's heart. The objective of the book is like the objective of the farbrengens themselves, even if the path is different, and, perhaps, complex: to rouse the reader to change and move something in his life. If at the live farbrengen the attendees are required to lend their ears and open their hearts, the responsibility of the reader is much greater, because he is required to listen and place the matters in his heart even more, reading them as ideas directed to him personally.

The original book, printed in Hebrew, was published at the end of the year of mourning after Rabbi Steinsaltz's passing. But this is not a memorial volume, first of all because Rabbi Steinsaltz never asked that a monument be left for him nor sought to make a name for himself, and second, because "the righteous in their death are called living" and "a righteous man who passed is found in all the worlds more than during his lifetime." The book does not reflect Rabbi Steinsaltz's departure from us, but rather his enduring presence in the world and a life that continues to live on even now. The purpose of this book is not to evoke Rabbi Steinsaltz's memory in the hearts of the readers, but to inspire them to change and to move through his inspiration.

Part of the book deals with our connection to *tzaddikim* who have departed from the world but continue to live on in it. Likewise, one who searches will be able to find among the pages of this book a portal of connection to Rabbi Steinsaltz and the path he paved. This book, with its various ideas, reveals something of his internal life, his thoughts, his faith, and his focus on eternal life. Therefore, it contains a path and a way for us, not only to continue receiving guidance and spiritual vitality from Rabbi Steinsaltz, but also to connecting with him and ascending spiritually together with him.

Introduction

1

What Does One Do at a Farbrengen?

IDLE TALK VERSUS WORDS WITH SUBSTANCE

At this farbrengen, we will try not to speak idle talk. Whatever I said at last year's farbrengen was, without a doubt, idle talk. I know this because it accomplished nothing.

The definition of idle talk relates, not to its content, but to its effects. Speech that has no lasting effect is idle talk, regardless of what was said or how it was said. Simply put, words that accomplish nothing are idle talk; they become meaningless over time.

There is a very subtle, indiscernible difference between idle talk and speech that has substance. Batteries that are fully charged and batteries that are depleted may look the same, but only the former can activate appliances. Likewise, only words of substance contain a charge that will have an impact on the listener, while idle talk generates nothing.

There is no way to immediately determine whether a speech can be classified as idle talk because its outcome depends on the listener rather than the speaker. One would expect a meaningful speech to have an effect, but this is not always the case. Meaningful words can turn out, in retrospect, to be idle talk if they fall on deaf ears. From this perspective, even prominent Torah personalities can be guilty of engaging in idle talk if the words they say have no practical effect on their listeners.

Many years ago, when I was a young man, I attended a Yod Tet Kislev farbrengen that lasted an entire night. In the morning, I asked the *mashpia* (spiritual mentor) who was there, "What do I take with me from this farbrengen?"

The *mashpia*, an astute man, shared a pearl of wisdom: "What you take with you is what you remember."

If the listener doesn't take what was said to heart, the words become meaningless, no matter how sublime the topic. The loftiest matters will remain lofty and will never descend from on high; they will have no substantive effect on the world whatsoever. At a farbrengen, one must speak about what is important and relevant to those present. If I were to speak now about what is transpiring in the realm of *Malkhut* of *Ḥokhma* of the world of *Atzilut* – a matter that has no practical relevance to your life – my words, however significant, will not have any effect.

When the High Priest sprinkled ritual blood in the Temple, "he would neither intend to sprinkle upward nor downward, but rather like one who whips."[1] At a farbrengen, too, one must wield his words as one does a "whip" to ensure that they reach their target – so that they will enter and touch the heart. When one speaks "upward," and the words fly above the listeners' heads, or "downward," and the words fly below the radar, the speech does not enter the heart.

I don't want to speak to you now about colossal matters but rather to focus on the question: What does one do at a farbrengen?

Lubavitcher hasidim have a song: "What does one do in Lubavitch? One drinks whiskey, acts wild, and dances in a circle!" This song has a hasidic interpretation, but on its simplest level, it describes an experience and atmosphere. My question is the same as that of the song, and the answer, too, will describe an experience, an atmosphere.

So let us now address the question: What does one do at a farbrengen?

TOGETHER

At a farbrengen, Jews sit together. This simple feeling of togetherness is sublime and of unparalleled importance. This is actually one of the great

1. Mishna *Yoma* 5:3.

virtues of a synagogue. I'm not referring to the kind of synagogue where seats are purchased in advance or designated according to status. I'm referring to synagogues where people can sit wherever they want. And even though the atmosphere in those synagogues might not be noticeable, its power is exceptional. Not infrequently, a person who lost his way, who has been seeking something that has eluded him, enters such a synagogue and suddenly feels at home. He has finally found what he has been searching for after years of traveling to distant places.

What is it that makes the synagogue special? First and foremost, there is no place more democratic than the synagogue. Where else can a prominent wealthy man and a Jew who doesn't have the means to pay his grocery bill be treated as equals?

In a synagogue, both the prominent rabbi and the simplest of men count to make a *minyan*. As the saying goes, "It's impossible to make a *minyan* from nine rabbis, but ten shoemakers can make a *minyan*." In the synagogue, Jews of all types sit together, pray together, eat herring together at *seuda shelishit*, and sing songs off key together. In the synagogue, I can sit with people without concerning myself with how much money they have in the bank or whether they will appear in the newspaper tomorrow. I sit with a person, not his persona.

Does everyone in the synagogue actually like each other? Not necessarily. This unique atmosphere is not necessarily an outgrowth of love. But the feeling of togetherness is real; it stems from a sense of partnership, from being part of the *minyan*.

Hasidic synagogues consciously initiate the breaking of barriers. There are no designated seats; the most revered people sit next to the simplest. This emphasis on togetherness is actually fundamental to the synagogue by definition. In Hebrew, the term for synagogue is *beit knesset*, literally, "a house of gathering." *Beit knesset* is the conventional term, even though other terms, such as *beit tefilla*, "house of prayer," and *mikdash me'at*, "lesser sanctuary," appear in the sources. The terminology we use teaches us that the synagogue is essentially a place where people come together. Even the English word, "synagogue," from the Greek *sinagoga*, also means "people sitting together." So even though one person might be studying, another praying, a third belching, and a fourth yawning, all of the people sitting together in the synagogue comprise equal parts of a holy congregation.

A farbrengen must transcend even that, because at a farbrengen individuals do not study or pray. It's not an academic lecture where the learned and honored are seated in front and the rest of the audience sit in the back. A farbrengen is based on feeling comfortable together, on eating, drinking, and rejoicing together. I'm not saying that people need to embrace each other; that is already a higher level of love among Jews. I'm speaking of Jews feeling that they can live in peace with the person sitting next to them. This is the most basic level of love among Jews.

Fifty years ago, I experienced this type of togetherness, and I remember it to this day. At that time, the Belzer Rebbe would travel to Jerusalem for the High Holy Days. On Friday night, people would come to the *beit midrash* after they had finished their Shabbat meal and wait for the Rebbe to come out and conduct the *tisch*, which typically started very late.

A hundred people sat together and waited on one long bench in a rather plain hall. Since they had already eaten their Shabbat meal and were not studying Torah, they all naturally they began to doze. I remember the sight clearly: a row of one hundred men, all of them sleeping, each with his head resting on the shoulder of the man sitting next to him. I remember that experience to this day because it warmed my heart. I'm certain that sitting on that bench were wealthy men and poor men, members of the upper class and simple people. And despite the differences in status, they were all comfortable sitting together and reclining on one another because of their shared experience. I'm not speaking of a shared ideology, like democracy, equality, or brotherhood. I'm speaking of something much simpler: the experience of simply sitting side by side and feeling at ease together.

The sense of togetherness of the farbrengen is not based on a profound connection between people, like the intense love between David and Yonatan. It can be a much more basic connection. Often one will see strange groupings of very different people sitting together. This is what creates a farbrengen.

The sense of togetherness at a farbrengen is, to a large extent, similar to that of soldiers in a tank. The soldiers didn't choose each other, and they may have little in common. But after being together for a long time in extreme proximity, a connection is formed; an experience is shared.

At a farbrengen, too, people draw close to one another until, from a random collection of individuals, a group with a sense of unity and togetherness is formed.

In the book of Malachi, it is written, "Then those who fear the Lord spoke one to another, and the Lord listened and heeded; a book of remembrance was written before Him."[2] The verse does not tell us what precisely those who fear God said to one another. Maybe one said to the other, "Do you know where I can get a discounted airline ticket to New York?" In truth, it doesn't matter. The point is that "the Lord listened and heeded; a book of remembrance was written before Him." God listens to two Jews who are sitting together peacefully, doing nothing more than speaking to one another openly and without reservation. That is sufficient for God to record it in the book of remembrance.

The foundation of a farbrengen is reaching such a state, that of "then they spoke with one another" – when individuals are able to sit together without consideration of status. When I attend a farbrengen, I must think about more than what I'm about to hear, whether I'll hear words that encourage, teach, or even insult me. I must also think about whether I'm capable of sitting with different kinds of people without feeling alienated, without feeling like I don't belong. I must ask myself: Am I able to be present without wondering what people think of me or what I think of them? Am I able to be one with everyone else at the farbrengen?

THE SOURCE OF SOULS

This togetherness may sound simple, but it is, in truth, a very sublime matter. There is a hasidic saying attributed to Rabbi Shneur Zalman of Liadi, the founder of Chabad Hasidism also known as the Baal HaTanya, that he might have said in the name of Rabbi Avraham HaMalakh, the son of the Maggid of Mezeritch: "What ten Jews can accomplish at a farbrengen, even the angel Mikhael is unable to accomplish." The blessings uttered by Jews sitting together at a farbrengen are more effective in achieving healing and salvation than those of the angel Mikhael himself.

2. Malachi 3:16.

What is the source of this special power? The answer is that the holy aspects of the togetherness experienced at a farbrengen can ascend to the highest of heights.

It is written in the teachings of Kabbala that the soul contains five levels. The most basic level, common to every Jew, is *nefesh*. A worthy person can attain the next level, *ruaḥ*. Above the level of *ruah* is *neshama*, which is usually the highest level that a person can achieve. Only the most extraordinarily virtuous person can reach the level of *neshama*. The level above *neshama* is *ḥaya*, which appears in Psalms as one of the names of the soul. It is revealed only rarely, and only to special people at very special times.

Many years ago, I studied with a Jew who had devotedly served as a rabbi in the Soviet Union for years. The rabbi told me that he had been privileged to sense the revelation of the *ḥaya* aspect of the soul. This happened after he had been apprehended by the government authorities due to his religious activities. At one point, they stood him against a wall and were about to execute him. Then, whatever happened, happened; somehow he was spared. He told me that after that incident, he could sense the *ḥaya* aspect of his soul. When he studied Torah and prayed, he had a clarity that he had never experienced in his entire life. The *ḥaya* level is latent within the soul, but it is revealed at rare times to rare people.

Above the level of *ḥaya* is *yeḥida*, also mentioned in the book of Psalms. This level is called *yeḥida*, literally, "a single unit," because at this level the soul reach its original source, the place where all the souls unite into a single point. My *yeḥida* and that of other people is the same exact *yeḥida*. At the *nefesh* or *ruaḥ* levels, there can be great differences between me and another Jew, but at the *yeḥida* level of the soul there are no differences. *Yeḥida* is the first spark, the original source of all the souls before they individuate and separate into the lower, distinct levels.

When Jewish people sit together at a farbrengen, having something to drink, possibly dozing, to a certain degree they reflect the mingling of souls that occurs at a level known as *Knesset Yisrael*. This is a level even higher than that of the upper level of Garden of Eden. At the level of *Knesset Yisrael*, souls are not seen as wealthy or poor, learned or ignorant, worthy of eternal life or headed for eternal disgrace. In the repository of souls that is the realm of *Knesset Yisrael*, there is no distinction between them.

Whether the farbrengen commemorates Yod Tet Kislev, Ḥai Elul, or the commemoration of one *tzaddik* or another, the essence of the farbrengen is Jews being together, seeing one another, connecting with one another, trying somehow, to the best of their abilities, to remove all veneers, all masks, most of which are false. The essence of the farbrengen is to exist in absolute brotherhood. In this way, perhaps, they can attain a sense of life at the level of *Knesset Yisrael*.

The Midrash states that God consulted with the souls of the righteous when He sought to create the world.[3] It's hard to fathom how it could be that there were souls that preceded the giving of the Torah, that preceded the Garden of Eden, Gehenna, even the very existence of the world. But these formless souls, having not yet been given an incarnation that would give them shape. Still, God consulted these souls whether it was worthwhile to create the world. He did not seek the counsel of angels regarding this matter, as they are similar to a group of intellectuals who don't stop bickering. He specifically asked the pure, unadulterated souls of the righteous whether it's worthwhile to create a world. These souls sat together, perhaps like Jews sitting in the *mikve* and conversing, and they determined whether there should be a world and what it would be like.

At a farbrengen, as we sit together and have something to eat and drink here in this lower world, we are actually able to reach a place of inherent sanctity, where everything exists at their source. We go back in time, past the generations, and exist together in a place where exalted souls extend a hand to one another.

In *mikva'ot* of old, it was possible to see a group of Jews sitting together in the water, just relaxing and talking to each other. That is precisely how a farbrengen begins – with a group of Jews relaxing together. From there, it's possible to reach great heights.

When a person comes to a farbrengen, he doesn't know whether he will hear words of Torah or, even if the does, whether he'll remember them. What he does know is that he'll be sitting with other Jews, eating,

3. *Bereshit Rabba* 8:7.

drinking, talking, possibly dancing, and sometimes just being silent together. A sense of togetherness suddenly becomes palpable, and everyone present find themselves in another state of being.

So what does one do at a farbrengen? The answer, first and foremost, is that one should internalize the togetherness, feel it, revel in it. Then it becomes possible to move on to the rest.

THE LIVING WILL TAKE IT TO HEART

Aside from this point, the aspect of togetherness, the essence of a farbrengen can be described by the words of the verse "The living will take it to heart."[4] At a farbrengen, people sit and talk, but most importantly, they open their hearts to the possibility of change. But in order for this to happen a person must be "alive" – fully present, conscious of his surroundings, with a genuine desire for the experience to enter his heart.

Sometimes a person contemplates the way he is living his life and it breaks his heart; it makes his soul shudder. Other times a person doesn't feel any particular distress, turmoil, or even great hopes when he thinks about his life. But as long as a person is truly alive and able to feel the pain of something missing in his life, he is compelled to change.

Rabbi Simḥa Bunim of Peshisḥa once came upon a group of people while walking with his hasidim. He asked his hasidim to approach the group in order to see how they were dressed. To their consternation, the hasidim saw that they were all wearing shrouds under their clothing. It turned out that these people were dead, each one living in the world of imagination.

The hasidim returned to the Rebbe, distraught. "Perhaps we too are dead!" they cried. "Could it be that our lives are also nothing more than figments of our imagination?"

The Rebbe answered, "As long as a person has an inkling of a desire to repent, he is clearly and unequivocally alive."

The ability to experience the pain of remorse distinguishes between a person being truly alive or dead.

4. Ecclesiastes 7:2.

The Rebbe also said that a person must always be conscious of his own mortality. He must see himself as if his head is on an anvil and someone above him is wielding a sword and about to decapitate him.

"Rebbe," one of his disciples asked, "what should I do if I can't see myself in that way?"

The Rebbe replied, "An inability to picture this scenario would indicate that one has already lost his head."

THE LIVING DOG

It is written in the book of Ecclesiastes, "A living dog is better than a dead lion, for the living know that they will die, but the dead do not know anything."[5] Why is a living dog better than a dead lion? Surely, in his lifetime, the "dead lion" was not just any lion. Surely, he was an exceedingly righteous, virtuous, important rabbi who accomplished wonderful things in heaven and on earth. When he was eulogized, he was most likely described as "our master and teacher, Rabbi Aryeh Leib, son of Rabbi Lavi, rabbi of such and such congregation, grandson of Rabbi Shaḥal, rabbi of such and such *beit midrash*...."[6] Wasn't Rabbi Aryeh Leib, a "dead lion," better than a living dog? All the praises in the world were written on his tombstone. Contrast this image to that of a living dog, possibly a mongrel whose father was a street dog, whose grandfather ran around who knows where.

The answer is that, lion or no, once dead it has reached the end of its path. Even if the dog is a wretched, lowly creature, it can still wag its tail. The dead lion can't move a hair on its mane, while the living dog is capable of movement. The dead lion's carcass decomposes, while the living dog must eat, drink, and find shelter, and these problems compel it to walk, seek, take action, and move forward. The dead lion is no longer troubled by these matters. The problems that define the life of a dog compel it to see the world around it and figure out how to navigate its way through it.

The dog's genealogy is irrelevant. The living dog, whoever it may be, is capable of considering its situation in life. Something could reach it

5. Ecclesiastes 9:4–5.

6. *Aryeh, lavi,* and *shaḥal* are all words that mean "lion."

and cause it to move from its place. This is the glory of the living dog. At best, a dead lion could be placed in a museum or have books written about it, while a living dog can move forward and accomplish something in this world.

Every farbrengen revolves around the living dog. At the farbrengen, I seize the living dog and say to it, "I don't know who you are. I don't know how talented you are, how many transgressions or how many *mitzvot* you have performed, but if you're already here – why are you standing still? Why don't you move forward? Why postpone the next step until tomorrow? Why don't you jump? Why don't you run?"

These questions can be posed only to the living dog. They are no longer relevant to the dead lion.

THE BOOKS OF LIONS

Dead lions have written wonderful books on all sorts of topics. Almost all of the Torah that people study is from the teachings of dead lions. The question is not how wonderful these books are, but rather what is the extent to which they have an impact on my life, whether or not they touch me personally.

I have said before that the old books on ethics are manuals for angels, and as manuals for angels, they are excellent. When I open *Chovot HaLevavot, Orḥot Tzaddikim*, or *Sefer HaYashar*, I find wonderful advice, but not for a person like me. I understand what these books are saying, but they were written by lions for lions who have never been burdened by a dog's problems.

I'm not a lion; I'm a living dog standing outside in the rain. I'm cold, and my stomach is rumbling. The living dog's problems will not be resolved by seeking answers from dead lions.

At a farbrengen, we don't sit and discuss the lofty ideas from this dead lion or that dead lion; we don't cite what is written in their books. We focus on the interests of the living dog: What does a person who lives in this world need to do? What can I do so that tomorrow will be better than today? It is for answers to these questions that one participates in a farbrengen.

The ideas internalized at a good farbrengen can't be summarized in writing. At every farbrengen, there are moments when the listeners take out their notebooks and write down the words of Torah and wisdom they have heard. After a certain number of farbrengens, a large collection of Torah insights has accrued. But those who are occupied with simply recording Torah insights have missed the point.

This phenomenon evokes what was said by a certain Jew who had written a doctorate about the revelation at Sinai. He spoke at a synagogue and asked the congregation whether God could reveal Himself today the way He revealed Himself at Sinai. "Of course," he answered. "God could reveal Himself in that way. But He doesn't reveal Himself in that way because He's afraid people would photograph Him and sell the pictures in tourist shops for small change."

The same can be said for those who sit at a farbrengen and record Torah insights. Those words of Torah ultimately have no effect because the purpose of the farbrengen is in the here and now. A farbrengen is not an event where one goes to learn sublime or profound subject matter to be studied later. It's an experience in which I open my heart in the moment so that I will be moved and affected in the present.

WHO ARE THEY SPEAKING TO?

When a person is in the proper frame of mind at a farbrengen, he can hear completely general statements and feel like they were said specifically to him. By contrast, when a person is in a normative frame of mind, he can be opaque, totally closed off, and unable to hear anything that is being said, even if it is explicitly directed toward him. For a person like that, any statement will automatically be understood as a general statement meant for others.

This often happens when a person recites the confession: "*Ashamnu*. We have been guilty of sin." The heart won't accept this burden. It would be much easier for a person to recite the confession about his neighbor, to beat the chest of the person standing next to him, rather than his own.

There is a terrible story about Hershele from Ostropoli, who served as the entertainer in the hasidic court of Rabbi Barukh of Medzhibozh. One day Rabbi Barukh asked Hershele if he had a new story to tell. "Some time ago," Hershele replied, "I met Satan. I asked him how he was. He said that he was fed up with his work. He was fed up sitting with all sorts of lowly people and inciting them to commit transgressions. He was fed up with his lot, with having to deal with repulsive people day and night.

"Sometime later, I met him again and saw that he was smiling and happy. I asked him what had happened, and he told me that he changed the description of the people he associated with. He now goes to the righteous, and he makes his living in peace and comfort."

Rabbi Barukh turned to Hershele and said to him, "You can't possibly be referring to me."

Hershele answered, "All the rabbis to whom I told this story said the same thing."

A good farbrengen is one where I understand that the words being spoken are directed toward me. The message relates, first and foremost, to me and only incidentally to others. It's of no help to me if others fulfill *mitzvot* and perform good deeds. It's of no help to me if so-and-so advances while I remain mired in my muck. What's the point of saying, "Leave the *mitzvot* for the dead lion," while I continue licking my piece of rotten meat? When a person is told to move, he shouldn't think that his parents, grandparents, friends, and neighbors need to move. He should realize that those words are directed toward him in the here and now.

WHAT HAPPENS NEXT?

When the farbrengen is over, after sitting together for several hours in brotherhood and friendship and after all that was said either penetrated or didn't, the only serious remaining question is, what now? All other questions are null and void and, like the dust of the earth, lack validity and relevance. After people have been sitting at a farbrengen for two hours or ten hours, after all the drinking and the singing, after all that was said and done, the question remains: What happens next?

It can't be that after the farbrengen a person will go home, cover himself with his blanket, and go to sleep, and that will be the sum total of his experience. The farbrengen should give him a jolt that won't allow him to sleep, that will leave a mark on him, that will leave him restless and unsettled. The farbrengen should be like a periodic booster shot, and its effects should be felt for at least several years to come.

Another big danger that occurs after the farbrengen is over is when a person makes the necessary change he must undergo contingent on matters that are external to him. He says to himself, "I'll do it later in life. Everything will be different then. Meanwhile, I'll continue to engage in my nonsense."

There are people who wait for the moment they retire to begin living. Some postpone the change they need to make in their lives until they get the promotion they want, while others decide they'll change when they marry. But I know several married people who, although they are certainly happy, didn't transform in any way just because there was a wedding. Even when change takes place, it is not always the comprehensive, absolute change that people envision.

The bottom line is that a person shouldn't postpone the actions he must take to transform his life to a later date when he'll supposedly be a new, wonderful person.

And so the most important question at every farbrengen remains: What happens tomorrow? The essence of every farbrengen is what a person takes from it. He should leave a farbrengen with at least one takeaway – one action that he intends to take on, one aspect that he intends to change. If he experiences farbrengen after farbrengen but never moves forward at all, perhaps he should travel back in time, return to the farbrengen, and effect the change he should have made.

ONE SMALL STEP FORWARD

One need not take on something significant in the wake of the farbrengen to progress in life. Taking just one small step forward is enough.

There are different ways of making a significant change in one's life. One can do it the way one blows up a mountain: by taking explosives and detonating them. Although this path can result in great change, it can also dismember a person, leaving him in small, useless fragments. Often, change needs to happen in a much more subtle, incremental manner.

I once drove in Sweden on a road that was hundreds of miles long. It ran through a huge forest for its entire length, and there were nothing but pine trees on either side. Mile after mile, all I saw were pine trees. This continued for hundreds of miles: only pine trees and more pine trees. The road was extraordinarily monotonous, but amazingly, after traversing all those miles, I was ultimately able to reach a different place.

Many people would prefer their internal change to take place in one big dramatic explosion. But when changes of that kind occur, they are frequently a passing delusion, a fleeting deception of the senses. By contrast, though the path of small, continuous changes might feel monotonous, it's ultimately the best way to progress. If a person follows the path assiduously, he can effect true change and reach a new place in his life.

When a person takes one small step at a time – say, he learns one mishna a day – he is a little further down the road than he was yesterday. Furthermore, the movement forward is more significant than the magnitude of the change, because it's not enough to make a significant change. Even if he walks out of a farbrengen with his entire face aglow, like Moses when he descended from Mount Sinai, and he feels like a different person, it isn't enough. As long as a person is alive, he must always be moving forward. In that respect, it hardly matters whether the change that was effected was big or small. What matters is whether the person took a step in the right direction.

Sometimes one is blessed with inspiration from on high. The gates are wide open, and he has the opportunity to make big, significant changes. But usually lasting change need to be made with steady persistence over time, in dark times and good ones, in sadness and in joy. If one truly wants to change the course of his life, he shouldn't expect one big explosion that will turn his life upside down. He should simply start moving forward, with small steps or big ones, as much and as often as he can. That's the only way to effect real change.

LENDING A HAND TO OTHERS

Sometimes a person comes to the conclusion that he can't change, and if that's the case, he can still help others to do so. They say that a horse, a soldier, and a hasid are useless when they're old. An old horse is no longer able to run, an old soldier is no longer able to fight, and as for the old hasid – if he's old, he should already have become a Rebbe.

Jokes aside, if a person feels that he is in the category of an old hasid, where he has reached a point where he feels he is no longer making progress, he can at least help others advance. When a person is no longer able to improve, if he feels like he is completely burnt out, he can still help others.

A lion that is about to die can at least contribute its mane for the benefit of others. A person can't help others attain a level beyond his own, but he is still capable of lending a hand to others within the parameters of his own level.

People today are becoming more divided, like islands scattered in the vast ocean, each in isolation, caring nothing about the existence of the others. Gathering together at the farbrengen is intended, among other things, to put an end to this tendency to isolate, to spur us to care about one another and extend a helping hand. At a farbrengen, people sit together, look for the good in each other, and this presents them with the opportunity to offer help to the others. Each person at the farbrengen must think, *Someone is standing here. What can I do for him? What can I say to him that will bolster him?* People are sitting together in brotherhood and fellowship, and each has the chance to look at a person to whom he had never previously given much thought and ask himself, *How I can lend him a hand?*

It's rarely possible to change someone's entire life with a few words, but sometimes a smile is enough to transform someone's day. I had a relative in Israel who was an Egged bus driver. After years of driving on a certain route, he was transferred to a different one. That very day letters began arriving at the Egged offices demanding that he be restored to his original route. One woman wrote, "I used to see him every morning, and he would always say 'good morning' to me. That would make my day! I miss him."

An Egged bus driver, while driving his regular route from Raanana to Tel Aviv, can brighten someone else's day.

The farbrengen doesn't deal with profound issues, but rather the stomachache of so-and-so, my neighbor. What does one do when someone has a stomachache? A great *tzaddik* could, perhaps, cure the stomachache by reaching out to Heaven. As for me, I can, at least, go to the person in pain, smile at him, and offer him comfort. I can't always elevate my own heavens, but I can help ease someone else's burden. When I do this, I have, in a certain sense, moved the world.

Our entire world is awaiting the end of days. We work, we pray, and we anticipate a time when all of a sudden the whole world will begin to shine. We're awaiting a time when God will bring about the great reform that we have not succeeded in achieving. We are waiting for the moment when He will decide that His small creations have allowed too much time to elapse. "I'm fed up with you, He will say. "You don't know how to finish this chapter of the story. Let us now agree that the current state of the world is over and done, and begin the next chapter."

We wait for this every day, for Him to decide that there's no choice but to send the Messiah, who will bring order to the world. Until that time comes, we can still attempt to do small things to improve the world, to remove the weeds from our little garden while trying to help our neighbor with his garden next door. Is the existence of the world dependent on the removal of those weeds? I'm not sure. But if we work on it, at least there will be fewer weeds.

Preparing the Receptacles

RINSING AND WASHING

To have a long-lasting effect, inspiration and ideas require a receptacle to contain them. A person can talk and talk, but the words don't necessarily remain with the listener, and even if an idea does penetrate, it goes in one ear and out the other. One can speak of profound matters, but the words can easily go to waste, and nothing will result from them. The reason for this is simple: they did not enter the receptacle.

When a person has a good thought or notion relating to repairing an aspect of his soul, there is nothing better he can do than to craft a receptacle for these ideas. When a person takes a thought and crafts a receptacle for it, even a small receptacle, something of that illumination, of the flow of inspiration that came to him, will remain with him and won't be wasted.

Beyond crafting a receptacle, one must also make sure that the receptacle is clean. When one pours wine into a dirty goblet, a chemical reaction is initiated between the wine and the dirt, resulting not in wine but rather in dirt with a certain percentage of alcohol, which is much worse than plain dirt. Plain dirt isn't very harmful, but when dirt is given potency, it is a much greater problem. Occasionally, whether at a farbrengen or elsewhere, a person hears ideas that not only do not benefit him, but they cause harm because his receptacle is dirty. As a result, the wine within is ruined.

According to the *halakha,* a cup for *Kiddush* requires washing and rinsing – washing on the outside and rinsing on the inside. If one cleans the goblet on only one side, it remains dirty on the other. That's why one must clean both sides of the goblet. How can one make certain that the person is clean from without and within? Just as one washes and rinses a material receptacle, the same is necessary with a spiritual receptacle. It requires washing on the outside and rinsing on the inside. At a farbrengen, one cleans the receptacle on both sides: he drinks, and sings a tune. The drink, though it enters the body, functions as the washing from without. The tune has the effect of rinsing from within.

When washing with drink and rinsing with song, one must do so properly. Sometimes one pours water on a stain, and the small stain spreads and becomes much larger. By the same token, sometimes a person who has a minor transgression in his head downs a shot of whiskey, and the transgression expands along with the drink. At a farbrengen, one must drink in a manner that will reduce the stain and work on it so that the stain will be eradicated.

By the same token, singing a tune once isn't enough. It may be enough to fulfill one's obligation, but in order to rinse the receptacle well, one must sing the tune again and again until the dirt begins to be cleansed.

There is a difference between the washing of the cup on the outside and rinsing it on the inside. If the outside of the cup is dirty, it's unpleasant to the touch, but this is nothing more than a matter of aesthetics. But if the cup is dirty on the inside, everything that enters it is sullied. The defect is liable to render other things defective. Drinking the shot is not so important, because it merely accomplishes a very superficial cleansing. For the cleansing to be internal, to have a significant effect, one must sing the melodies. At a farbrengen, much greater effort must be invested in singing, the internal rinsing, than in the drinking, the external cleansing.

One must sing the melody the way he washes a dish: washing it once and then a second time, scrubbing it again and again until all the dirt and residue is washed away. In the same manner, one should sing each song several times so the receptacle will be well scrubbed, so that another layer of dirt, will be washed away. One should repeat the melodies again and again and allow them to be internalized until the receptacle is rendered suitable.

THE SOUL'S PURIFICATION

The power of melody to purify the soul is related to its central characteristic: In contrast to other sacred matters, melody, in and of itself, has no content. If a person wishes to tell a story – for example, "I woke up this morning and ate breakfast" – he can relate it verbally in any language, or he can relate it in pantomime. But it's impossible to tell a story clearly with music alone. By its nature, music transmits the condition of the soul rather than content. In this sense, music can accomplish what words cannot.

When a person says that someone is happy, the words themselves can't transmit the actual feeling of happiness. It's even more difficult to do this with a drawing. But with singing, it's actually possible to transmit a feeling. Music is like the encompassing light discussed in books of Kabbala and Hasidism rather than the inner light, because it's impossible to internalize the melody and know exactly what the melody is saying. It's possible to understand something, to understand its process and where it is leading, but it's impossible to transmit or receive explicit content from it.

This characteristic of melody is connected to the concept of purity. We could say a lot about the purity of the soul, but those words don't engender purity itself. What is dirty remains dirty even after everything was said, after all the speeches and homilies. A person can pound his heart numerous times, but the heart remains as it was before. To achieve purity of the soul, one must employ something that doesn't function on the track of comprehending defined content, but rather, something that rouses the loftier powers of the soul.

I once read a story that, interestingly, I haven't found in any work of Chabad. It is a story about "*Arba Bavot*" (Four Gates), a well-known melody that was composed by the Baal HaTanya. He delivered many Torah discourses in his lifetime. The number of treatises we have in our possession is significant, and we know that the majority of them have been lost. Anyone who has read these treatises knows they can't be summarized with brief sayings or clever remarks, because they are so complex. The story goes that one day, after the Rebbe delivered one of his treatises, an elderly hasid, who had been his follower for many years, approached him and said, "Rebbe, what can I do? I'm not a Torah scholar, and when the Rebbe speaks, I don't understand a word. Can the Rebbe explain to me what he said in plain words that even I can understand?"

The Baal HaTanya gave it some thought and then said to the hasid, "I can't explain it to you in words, but I will sing you a melody that contains all of my Torah." And the Baal HaTanya promptly sang the "*Arba Bavot*" melody for the hasid.

As I said, this story isn't found in any of the Chabad works, perhaps because, in a certain sense, it's inconsistent with the Chabad approach, an approach that is based on internalization and intellectual comprehension. I don't know if the story took place precisely in this manner, but what is certainly true is that the one who related it heard the melody and thought it expressed the essence of the Baal HaTanya's teachings, even though it did not express it in words.

There are melodies you can sing while washing the floor or splitting logs. The Baal HaTanya's melody isn't one of them – not only because it wouldn't be suitable, but also because it transports a person to another world, a world without specific, defined content.

The melody isn't analogous to the actual drink that is poured into the cup, but it does at least flow into the cup and rinse it.

A MELODY THAT SPARES A PERSON FROM SIN

The melody can't convey everything it needs to say to me, because melodies don't know how to speak. It can't say, "Repent," but it can tell me that I'm not in a good place. It can tell me that the circumstances in which I am mired are tiresome. It can tell me that I'm not doing well. It can tell me that I'm not my true self. This is the power of melody.

But even after a person has heard a melody several times, he still doesn't know what he needs to do the next morning, but the melody might help him learn what not to do the next morning. When the melody reverberates in a person's mind, even if he doesn't understand what it's saying, it still places him in a certain frame of mind, and that frame of mind can, at times, affect him more than several homilies or profound ideas.

The Gemara states that *tzitzit* (ritual fringes) have saved people from serious transgressions. There are also many stories about melodies that have saved people from transgression. These people intended to commit a sin when suddenly a melody started playing inside them, and they were simply unable to carry it out. One can do many things with a good hasidic melody, but one can't eat pork with it. Imagine someone who plans to commit some indecent act, and suddenly something starts playing inside him. When a melody starts playing inside him, when it reverberates within his mind, it's impossible to stop it. And whether or not he understands it, it has a significant effect.

A melody must be heard more than once for it to reverberate within a person. At a concert, hearing a song once may certainly be enough. Really, how many times can they play the same melody? But the melody sung at a farbrengen is not a concert. It's more like a laundromat. Washing heavily soiled clothing one time isn't enough. One must wash it again and again before a change can be seen.

PURGING THE VESSEL IN BOILING WATER

There is a melody that rinses like cold water, and there is a melody that is more like scouring with hot water. And then there's a melody that has the power to purge. Just as there is no difference between cold or hot water at their essence, the difference between the types of melody described here is not about their content. Rather, the difference is in their effect.

As a rule, all the upbeat melodies that are sung at a farbrengen loudly, energetically, and while clapping hands are like a rinse in cold water. Even if these tunes can be sung enthusiastically, they are cold at their essence. For minor surface dirt, rinsing in cold water is sufficient.

Then there are melodies that are more like scouring in hot water. These melodies have more meaning, more content. They aren't necessarily louder, and at times might even be sung softly, but they penetrate more deeply. A melody of this kind can wash away more substantial dirt.

And then there are melodies that are deeply profound, melodies that have an impact similar to purging in boiling water. When a person immerses himself in a melody of that sort, he undergoes transformation. For one thing, forbidden and repulsive elements are cleansed from him. At the same time, he becomes a kosher vessel into which other, holy matters can be introduced. When a person isn't merely scalded with boiling water, but is immersed in it, it leaves a deep impression.

It is said in the name of the Baal Shem Tov that in the verse where God said to Noah, "Come you and your entire household into the ark,"[7] the word for "ark," *teiva,* also means "word." The Baal Shem Tov spoke of this in the context of prayer. One must enter the word one utters. One should not just say it and spit it out, but one should enter its essence. When a person enters the word, it can shield him and lead him through the "great waters," the turbulence and turmoil, that he will encounter in the world.

In the same manner, a person must completely enter the melody. In order to enter the word or the melody, one must go in all the way. When a person prays or sings a melody, all of him must be immersed in it. If he is only halfway in, it is tantamount to a person who purges a vessel with half the vessel outside the water, in which case the purge is ineffective. But if he enters it entirely, he becomes transformed, and when he emerges, he is a completely different person. At that moment, he can achieve reparation and purity.

7. Genesis 7:1.

Ḥai Elul
The Birthday of the Baal Shem Tov

On Ḥai Elul (the eighteenth day of the Hebrew month of Elul), Chabad hasidim mark the birthdays of two great *tzaddikim* who were leaders and central figures in the history of Hasidism. According to hasidic tradition, both the founder of Hasidism, Rabbi Yisrael Baal Shem Tov, and the founder of Chabad Hasidism, Rabbi Shneur Zalman of Liadi, the Alter Rebbe, were born on this day.

The Baal Shem Tov lived and was active in Podolia (in present-day Ukraine) during the first half of the eighteenth century. His disciples eventually expanded and developed the movement that he founded, and his teachings spread throughout Eastern Europe. The Baal Shem Tov created a new world of Judaism, one that was alive and meaningful for Jews of all strata of society, from simple Jews to Torah scholars. Even today his legacy is a source of inspiration for a life that is profound, relevant, and inspirational.

Rabbi Shneur Zalman, also known as Baal HaTanya (author of the *Tanya*), was the youngest of the disciples of the Maggid of Mezeritch. He was active as a rabbi and teacher during the closing decades of the eighteenth century and the beginning of the nineteenth century. Responsible for the flourishing of Hasidism throughout Belarus, and within the larger hasidic movement, he created a unique intellectual sect with a distinctive way of serving God. Through him, the Chabad dynasty began – a dynasty that led to the Chabad movement in Russia over the course of seven generations and in the United States for ten.

Because Ḥai Elul is identified with the personalities and activities of the Baal Shem Tov and the Baal HaTanya, it remains a day of inspiration and renewal for those who aspire to follow the path of Hasidism.

Ḥai Elul is also the day that Rabbi Yehuda Loew, also known as the Maharal of Prague, passed away. The Baal HaTanya was his descendant and in certain respects continued his philosophical approach. On the title page of the *Tanya*, he wrote that it was "compiled from the works and teachings of the holy masters." According to the Chabad tradition, the writings of the Maharal of Prague are included among those works. Rabbi Adin Even-Israel Steinsaltz, in many of his Ḥai Elul farbrengens, often spoke of the Maharal of Prague and cited his teachings.

It's no coincidence that two pioneers of Hasidism – the founder of the hasidic movement and the founder of its Chabad branch – were both born on the same day. Their lives overlapped by a few years: Hasidic tradition relates that when the Baal HaTanya was a child, he visited the Baal Shem Tov, who blessed him and foresaw his future as a leader.

In contrast to the widespread custom of marking the day on which great personalities passed away, it's unusual to mark the birthday of a *tzaddik*. In many of his farbrengens, Rabbi Steinsaltz's discourse revolved around this point.

A significant aspect of marking the eighteenth day of Elul is related to its numeric equivalent: the word *ḥai,* which means "life." The central motifs of life and vitality are emphasized on this day – vitality in the service of God, vitality in Hasidism, vitality in the process of repentance. Rabbi Steinsaltz's farbrengens commemorating these birthdays dovetailed with the fact that Ḥai Elul is a final waystation before the onset of the High Holy Days in the month of Tishrei. Thoughts about these personalities and their significance to our lives intertwine with thoughts related to repentance and spiritual preparation for the holidays. A Ḥai Elul farbrengen was always accompanied by a feeling of vitality and excitement that was enhanced by anticipation of the High Holy Days just around the corner.

2

The Innovation of the Baal Shem Tov

ENLIVENING THE MONTH OF ELUL

In recent generations, it has been said that the purpose of Ḥai Elul is to "enliven" the month of Elul. In previous generations, Elul had always been a heavy month, when people sat and contemplated repentance – not only people whose personal transgressions included the entire list that appears in *Al Ḥet*, but also to upright people and even full-fledged *tzaddikim*. Everyone alike was occupied with a review of their misdeeds. Even if a person had no transgressions, he would repent for neglecting *mitzvot*. Even someone who had no need to feel regret for violating the *halakha* according to this or that paragraph in the *Shulḥan Arukh* would ask himself, "Were my prayers worth anything this past year, or were they like Bialik's brief description of prayer: 'Wrapping, kissing, and spitting'?" The endless reckoning that characterized the month of Elul frequently created a kind of tension, an atmosphere of gloom, and sometimes even melancholy. That is why it was said that Elul needed to be "enlivened."

By contrast, people today go through the month of Elul nonchalantly. Even the sounding of the *shofar*, about which it is written, "Will the *shofar* be sounded in a city and the people not tremble?"[1] does not agitate

1. Amos 3:6.

anyone. At most, people might count the number of blasts that are blown, but that is the extent of their focus.

In the past, it was said that even the fish in the sea trembled during the month of Elul. Today, neither fish nor people tremble in Elul. So if the fish don't tremble and the people don't tremble, how can a person enliven Elul?

It remains necessary to celebrate Ḥai Elul and achieve at least a minimal elevation. The question is, what does one do on Ḥai Elul?

"AND LIVE BY THEM"

The Baal Shem Tov was born on Ḥai Elul. If one views matters objectively, from a historical perspective it becomes clear that there's nothing actually new in anything that the Baal Shem Tov said. Even sayings or actions that are specifically attributed to Hasidism, or are considered typical of Hasidism, are not unique to Hasidism. They had already been written or stated before the advent of Hasidism, but people were unfamiliar with them or failed to notice them. What, then, was so novel about the teachings of the Baal Shem Tov?

It was the element of "and live by them [*vaḥai bahem*],"[2] which is also the essence of Ḥai Elul.

The Baal Shem Tov sought to address a problem that we Jews have. We suffer from the fact that we have too many words, too many Torahs, too many books. There are words with which every observant Jew is familiar: love of God, fear of God, greatness of God. A religious Jew hears these words numerous times in the course of his lifetime, so much so that they can become nothing more than meaningless sounds to him, nothing more than part of his vocabulary. But do these words actually affect the person?

This problem existed in the time of the Baal Shem Tov, too. Jews read so many books, knew so much Torah, and read so much *mussar* literature, particularly in the month of Elul, but all of this knowledge had little effect because it lacked vitality. The Baal Shem Tov's innovation was something that was both very simple and quite complicated:

2. Leviticus 18:5.

to truly and authentically connect to these ideas and teachings – to take these matters seriously.

What does it mean to really take matters seriously? Imagine, for example, that I'm attempting to wake a person from a deep sleep. I say to him, "The alarm is ringing. It's time to wake up for prayers." But it doesn't work; he doesn't get up. So I say to him, "There's a poisonous snake under your pillow," and he leaps out of bed. Even if the person knows that he has an obligation to get to work on time or that it's a great *mitzva* to get out of bed to pray, it's the snake that causes him to jump up and take things seriously. How does the snake succeed in affecting the person more than the words I said to him? When a person sees a snake, the snake speaks to him. Perhaps it speaks without words, but it speaks very clearly and is easily understood.

I once had an experience of that kind. It happened one day when I was a child, home sick from school. Suddenly I felt something crawling inside my pajamas, and instinctively I swatted at it. It turned out that there were five small yellow scorpions there that didn't appreciate being struck! I think that my shriek was heard on the other side of the neighborhood.

There's a huge difference between feeling a scorpion crawling on one's skin and reading books on piety. The scorpion isn't articulate – not in Hebrew, not in French, and not in Russian – but I certainly hear it. It has an effect on me. If hearing words of Torah or praying doesn't result in that kind of experience, it's because a person doesn't take those matters with the same degree of seriousness.

A RENEWAL OF CUSTOMS

The Baal Shem Tov didn't try to get people to fulfill more *mitzvot* or to be more exacting about specific *halakhot* in the *Shulḥan Arukh*. His objective was to make the *mitzvot* come alive, in the spirit of "*vaḥai bahem*." Although there were certain practices that hasidim seemed to initiate, those too were laws and customs that had been in the holy books long before the advent of Hasidism, only they were neglected until that time, viewed as one does safety precautions or driving instructions to which no one pays any attention. All the Baal Shem Tov was trying to say was, "My fellow Jews, how about taking Judaism seriously?"

I'm not referring only to spiritual matters that are addressed in books of piety, but also to practical laws and customs that appear in the *Shulḥan Arukh*. For example, the *Shulḥan Arukh* states explicitly that before prayer one should put on a *gartel* (a kind of sash worn like a belt).[3] This is not a practice only for very pious people. If it appears in the *Shulḥan Arukh*, it's meant for everyone, hasid or not. Although the *Shulḥan Arukh* also states that many Jews have not taken on this practice, the hasidim came along and started wearing a *gartel* for prayers. The difference between hasidim and their predecessors is that when a hasid learns about a required action, he says to himself, *Perhaps this is meant for me. If it is written that one needs to wear a gartel, it is speaking to me, and I will wear a gartel.* That's how the *gartel* entered the world. It didn't happen because it was new idea, but rather because someone saw that it was a requirement and said to himself, *If I'm going to take Judaism seriously, I will do this, too.*

There are also demands of a different kind in the *Shulḥan Arukh*, illustrated by two paragraphs [*se'ifim*] to which the verse "For how long will you skip over two opinions [*se'ipim*]"[4] applies. The first paragraph states that when a person awakens in the morning, he must remind himself that God is standing over him, and as a result he should leap from his bed "in the service of his Creator."[5] In the other paragraph, one that is typically disregarded, it is written that when praying, a person must imagine that the Divine Presence is before him and that pious people and men of good deeds "would seclude themselves and concentrate on their prayers until they divested themselves of physicality... until they attained a level close to that of prophecy."[6] The *Shulḥan Arukh* is saying: How long will you disregard these two paragraphs? You don't take them seriously, and you don't fulfill them.

The fact that these paragraphs are in the *Shulḥan Arukh* and not in books of piety seems to make no difference. A person can even know them by heart and may also know that there are people who fulfill them.

3. *Shulḥan Arukh, Oraḥ Ḥayim* 91:2.
4. I Kings 18:21.
5. *Oraḥ Ḥayim* 1:1.
6. *Oraḥ Ḥayim* 98:1.

The question is whether he personally relates to these *halakhot* as he would to an advertisement or does he relate to it as he would to a binding directive that everyone must fulfill? Does he assume that it's addressed to his neighbor and not to him, or does he feel that it is directed toward him?

A person can know all 613 *mitzvot* and thousands upon thousands of detailed laws and still feel that they don't relate to him. The moment a person arrives at the conclusion that they actually do relate to him, he begins to consider that perhaps they are serious requirements, after all. The Baal Shem Tov's innovation was nothing more than this: One must study these matters, take them seriously, and carry them out.

WHY USE HARSH LANGUAGE?

The answer to this question – why use harsh language? – pertains to many instances in the *Tanakh* and can also explain a phenomenon in the book of Ezekiel that is difficult to understand. Anyone who studies Ezekiel will see that it contains more harsh language and coarse expressions than anywhere else in *Tanakh*. There are actually chapters in the book that schoolteachers make certain to skip. For a long time I wondered what led Ezekiel, prophet, priest, and scribe, to use language that is so harsh.

In truth, when Ezekiel spoke, people would come and listen because his words sounded like the song of a singer: "beautiful of voice and skillful of melody."[7] They surely said to one another, "Ezekiel is speaking at eight this evening. We must attend! How well he speaks! His vocabulary, his eloquence, his hand motions… You don't want to miss it!" Though Ezekiel's speech inevitably included serious topics, that wasn't what the audience came to hear, just as an audience doesn't attend a performance of *Othello* or *King Lear* in order to learn morality. The audience is entertained and returns home, tired but happy. After hearing Ezekiel, it's likely that people said to one another, "The prophet outdid himself today. What a speech! Wonderful! Simply wonderful!"

In order to put an end to attitudes and reactions of that kind, Ezekiel spoke to them using crude language, so that they wouldn't be left with

7. Ezekiel 33:32.

the same pleasant feeling they had when he spoke so beautifully. He wanted to shake them up, to move them. Were people really moved? Did his words actually penetrate? We don't know. But the harsh language he chose to employ stemmed precisely from this reason.

This used to be the case in the past, at least in the army. A commander would speak harshly to a soldier, and the soldier would listen. Sometimes the words would actually penetrate. But today every soldier has a cell phone. Everything that happens prompts a call to his mother. A sergeant can no longer speak to a soldier that way, and the soldier, in turn, learns nothing.

TAKING MATTERS SERIOUSLY

When Hasidism began, many different kinds of people became affiliated with the movement. Some were members of the elite, and some were simple people. This perhaps reflects the central message the Baal Shem Tov conveyed to them: Take it seriously. You all have enough Torah, enough wisdom, enough fear of God. The question is, do you take it seriously? If you don't, nothing will come of it. But if you do take it seriously, something could happen.

Although this formulation isn't written down in the great books of Hasidism, both the learned and less learned hasidim arrived at the same conclusion: Everyone reads too many books, knows too much, and thinks too much. And none of it leaves any impression because we don't take it seriously.

When a person makes this small change and understands that all these matters are to be taken seriously, his experience is completely transformed. It's like a person driving a car with warning lights flashing on the dashboard. As long as he ignores them, he continues to drive as if nothing is happening while the car keeps limping along. The moment he begins to understand that a flashing red light might mean that at any moment the engine will overheat, his entire experience changes. I'm speaking of that kind of experience – the feeling that all the matters about which we are speaking are to be taken seriously.

The impact that words can have if only we take them seriously is true even regarding a simple prayer like *Modeh Ani*, which contains no sacred names and nothing special. When someone says *Modeh Ani* with feeling, he won't remain the same person. *Modeh Ani* blurted out by rote, without intention, has absolutely no effect on the person saying it.

When Abraham came into the world and began "calling in the name of the Lord," it was nothing new to people. They were already familiar with what he was saying, but no one took it seriously. "We've heard it all," they said. "Our grandfathers said the same thing. There's no need to pay them any attention." But Abraham came along, and he decided to take matters seriously. When one makes that choice, his perspective, his way of life, and his entire world changes completely.

This experience can be replicated in a variety of areas. When a person receives instructions from a doctor, the most important question is, Will he take the advice seriously?

I'll tell you a story that relates to this.

Many years ago, I went to see a specialist, who served as the doctor for all the elite people in the State of Israel. As he examined me, I asked him, "What makes you such a famous doctor?" He could have said that it was because he was the best doctor in the country, but that wasn't his answer.

He said, "I'm a cardiologist. There are other cardiologists in the country who are no less capable than I am, and there are definitely some who are more capable. What's the difference between us? When a government minister or a high-ranking official comes to one of those doctors after suffering a heart attack, he'll say, 'You had a heart attack. You need to rest for a few weeks before returning to work. After that, you will gradually be able to resume your activities.'

"The patient proceeds to ignore the doctor's advice and returns to work right away because there's so much work to be done, and even though he suffered a heart attack, he's now feeling better. When nothing bad happens to him, he takes on more work. But he never fully recovers, and in all likelihood, he'll have another heart attack. When that happens, he'll say, 'That doctor isn't a very good doctor. He wasn't able to heal me.' When I treat a patient who has just had a heart attack, I tell him, 'You need to rest for three weeks. If you don't, I guarantee you'll be dead in six months.' The patient, of course, listens to me and recovers. That's how I've gotten such a good reputation."

The same is true regarding works of Torah. The more seriously they are taken, the greater the likelihood that they will have an impact. A simple person thinks, for example, that if he eats something without reciting a blessing, a stone will fall from the ceiling and crush his skull. That's why he recites a blessing. By contrast, a person who considers himself wise and clever isn't afraid that a stone will fall on his head, so he sometimes recites a blessing and sometimes he doesn't. Neither of them, though, take the matter of reciting blessings seriously, the former because he is doing it for the wrong reasons and the latter because he doesn't understand the enormity of reciting just one blessing.

It is this point that the Baal Shem Tov tried to drive home to others. He circulated from place to place and encountered many people, some of whom were very simple and some of whom were very learned, and he said to the simple just as he said to the wise, "Know that these are important matters and that they need to be taken seriously."

The Innovation of the Baal HaTanya

THE BASIC DEMANDS OF HASIDISM

The Baal HaTanya was born on the same date that the Baal Shem Tov was born: Ḥai Elul. The message of the Baal HaTanya is similar to that of the Baal Shem Tov, but it is less basic, less elementary. It brings another layer, built on the basic demands of Hasidism.

The basic expectation that Hasidism demands from a person is a practical one: Anything one takes upon himself must be taken seriously. Good intentions alone aren't enough, and performing a deed while rolling one's eyes is certainly not on the mark. Just as one who has a job must wake up and go to work, and one who has a small child must feed him, and one who is a yeshiva student must wake up and study, so too, says the Gemara, "One who wishes to be a hasid [literally, a pious person] should observe the matters of tractate *Nezikin,* the matters of tractate *Avot,* and matters of tractate *Berakhot.*"[8] This means that one who wishes to be a hasid must take action. In other words, he must fulfill the obligations written in tractate *Nezikin,* in tractate *Avot,* and those discussed in tractate *Berakhot.*

---

8. *Bava Kamma* 30a.

The Gemara does not say, "Let him wear a *gartel* and recite '*veyatzmaḥ purkanei*.'"[9] Doing those things don't make a person into a hasid. A person who wishes to be a hasid must take on certain obligations and carry them out. Sometimes he does things that relate to a swath of categories; sometimes he begins by being meticulous in only one area. Either way, it's liable to be hard. Being serious about the obligation to refrain from hurting one's neighbor can be more difficult than concentrating during prayers.

The basic ability to make a decision and execute it is an important skill. Simply put, a person who wants to tend his garden knows that he must work hard. He must cultivate a certain number of square yards today and a certain number of square yards tomorrow. His garden needs tending whether or not he is in an agricultural state of mind on any given day. Excuses make no difference.

Similarly, a yeshiva student must sit and study. He must do so seriously – not in order to withstand scrutiny, or to receive some sort of certification, but rather to ultimately know something, to acquire knowledge. Even a student who has studied one or two tractates must ask himself how much he understood, how much he retained. This is the fundamental expectation of Hasidism: When one does something, one must do it seriously. It's a matter of making a decision and taking action.

Yet even when a person meets this demand, another problem may arise. Very often, a person compares himself to his neighbor. He asks himself, for example, whether his study partner or the fellow sitting next to him studies more than he does. Since there is a reasonable chance that this is not the case, he feels satisfied that he has fulfilled his obligation. But the truth is that this comparison doesn't exempt him at all.

Imagine that a person is told that he is suffering from a certain illness. His doctors say to him, "You need to take these pills twice a day, morning and evening." Clearly, it makes no difference to the person that his neighbor doesn't have to take the pills. What his neighbor is doing is irrelevant. He takes the pills morning and evening because he knows that if he doesn't take them, he's playing with his life.

---

9. A phrase that hasidim add to the *Kaddish* prayer.

Similarly, every person is obligated to fulfill the *mitzva* of "You shall ponder it day and night."[10] This is in no way related to how much one's neighbor is studying. One who feels that his Torah study is satisfactory because he is no worse than others will perhaps be able to sleep at night, but obviously it's not enough. A person who exempts himself from study based on his neighbor's behavior is only deceiving himself.

THE DEMAND FOR VIGILANT CONSCIOUSNESS

To counter this problem, the Baal HaTanya added another layer to the fundamental requirements of Hasidism. Above and beyond the demand for action, for taking one's obligations seriously, the Baal HaTanya added the demand for vigilant consciousness.

A person who seeks to fulfill his obligations is liable to say to himself, "I'm okay. My wife isn't fighting with me, my parents aren't breaking dishes on my head, my life is more or less in order – everything is fine. Others don't study Torah at all. At least I study a little. I'm very fortunate."

To counter such complacence, the Baal HaTanya raises questions of consciousness: What, in essence, is a person's connections to his obligations? What is his attitude toward them? How can he improve personally?

When a person asks himself such questions, it is no longer a question of merely fulfilling an obligation. If it were merely about meeting standards, then it may be possible to meet a standard set by one's neighbor, and it's often possible to meet a standard set by one's wife. But meeting the standard set by God may seem impossible. The question, then, isn't merely how to fulfill an obligation, but rather, what is *my* obligation and how should I approach it.

The question of my attitude toward the obligation is a much more philosophical question. A person can carry out an obligation and feel comfortable and happy with himself, yet still wonder, *Is that it? Is this what I was supposed to do? Is this what I wanted? Is this what I dreamed of being?*

10. Joshua 1:8.

The *Tanya* contains no technical demands more exacting than any other work. It merely presents the background of those demands in much sharper resolution than the manner in which they are presented elsewhere. It doesn't ask a person whether he fulfilled his obligation. Rather, the question asked is whether, in the framework of his internal struggle, a person succeeded in reaching his maximum potential.

A BLOW TO THE BACK

Many people are happy with themselves. They feel comfortable with their lives, as if enveloped by a down blanket. But what happens when they start to question things, and this level of comfort begins to disappear? These questions are liable to be unsettling to them as well as to their relationship with their family.

These questions make life more difficult, more uncomfortable. But one is ultimately better off. Someone who asks these questions may feel that everything is not right in his world, but when he eventually arrives in the World to Come, he will be sent straight to the Garden of Eden. By contrast, one who lives in this world convinced that he has fulfilled all of his obligations, and that everything is fine and good, will not gain entry to the Garden of Eden. A small angel will be standing at the entrance to the garden, and when the person presents a note saying that he has been found meritorious and that he has the right to enter, the angel will ask him, "Did you do everything you possibly could?" If the answer is no, the angel will say, "Perhaps return to the first grade and begin studying from the beginning. You may have received a passing grade, and that may be good enough for you, but it's not sufficient to earn your place here. You must do more."

Excuses may be good for the police, but when a person is confronted with questions like "Why was a certain action that you performed ineffective? Why didn't it work?" excuses are of no use at all.

Sometimes it's good for a person to sustain a blow to the back. At first, he might rub his back and cry out, "Ouch, ouch, ouch!" But in the next moment he realizes that he is no longer in the same place that he was before. He was living in his limited world for ten years, and now someone gave him a kick. It's very unpleasant, not very nice, and a blow to his dignity, but at the end of the day, he's no longer the same person.

On Ḥai Elul, we try to kick ourselves so we can breach the limited boundaries of our consciousness.

The Baal HaTanya demanded that a person make more problems for himself. Beyond the choices one has already made, beyond actions already taken, the Baal HaTanya asks, "What is your state of mind? How do you relate to your choices and actions?" This is a whole other world of trouble and hardship. We celebrate Ḥai Elul so that a person will at least remember and think about those troubles.

Leḥayim!

3

Living Life

AS LONG AS ONE IS ALIVE, ONE MUST LIVE

I once met a Breslov hasid named Avraham who greatly impressed me. He was a grandson of Reb Noson of Breslov, Rabbi Naḥman's closest disciple. At ninety-five years old, he suffered terribly from a disease in his legs. I remember him standing at the *minyan* where he prayed and apologizing to the congregation: "Once I could serve as the prayer leader for all the prayers of Yom Kippur. Now I'm weak, and I can serve as prayer leader for only *Arvit, Mussaf,* and *Ne'ila....*"

One day someone met him while he was out walking. Due to his affliction, Reb Avraham could barely walk, and he was almost crawling. "Where are you going?" the passerby asked.

Reb Avraham said he was going to the *mikve*. The other man knew that the *mikve* was more than a mile away, and out of love and concern for the venerable hasid, he told him that perhaps going to the *mikve* wasn't so urgent. After all, he was no longer young and no longer needed to concern himself with matters that warrant immersion. Perhaps he could do without the ritual bath for one day?

"What do you mean?" Reb Avraham replied. "As long as one is alive, one must live!"

Imagine. A man is ninety-five years old. He knows that in order to live, he must go to the *mikve*. He can barely walk. He's crawling. Every step is agony. But he goes in order to live.

The purpose of Ḥai Elul is to infuse Elul with vitality, with life. The objective is not to just pass the time, and certainly not to waste time, but to *live* time. A person may pound his chest in repentance throughout the month of Elul, but the critical question posed by Ḥai Elul still remains: Is there life here? Did one actually *live* the days of the month of Elul? If a person wants to emerge from Ḥai Elul with a purpose, it doesn't have to be a specific action he must take. Rather, Ḥai Elul must bring the following question to the forefront: How do I make each one of my days alive and not dead? How do I live my days?

It is written that one of the ways to cleave to God is to model oneself after Him. There are many possibilities for emulating God. One can seek to be like Him through adhering to truth, for example, which, according to Rambam, exists in its pristine form only in God. But there is also another way that is associated with God: through living. By remembering that God is "the living God and the eternal King."[1] He is the living God, who gives life to the living, and by living a life of substance, of purpose, one cleaves to God who is the living God.

LIVING WITH PURPOSE ON AN ORDINARY DAY

People think that the real moments in life are comprised of exciting experiences, adventures, and celebrations, but these exceptional times are not the core of life, of living. On the contrary, the question of how to truly live is most critical during routine times, when nothing special is happening.

Hasidim say that the most significant day of the year is the one that follows Yom Kippur, the day that Ashkenazim call "*Gott's Nomen*" – the day of God's name – in Yiddish. The official reason for this title is that on that day one stops saying "*haMelekh hakadosh*" (the holy King) in the *Amida* prayer and resumes saying "*haKel hakadosh*" (the holy God), once again uttering God's name. But the day is also the day of God's name for another reason: During the course of the preceding High Holy

1. Jeremiah 10:10.

Days, one gradually scaled the heights to become purified and cleansed on Yom Kippur. Now that one has reached the summit, now that one is pure, he must ask himself: Have I truly reached a "day of God's name"? Have I reached a place where I can say that I am living with God?

This is a day when there are no celebrations, no special rites, not even special foods. Yet it is on this very ordinary day that one must attempt to live with God.

How does a person live with God?

This is, in fact, the undertaking that a person must attempt to achieve throughout the month of Elul – whether the nineteenth of Elul, the twentieth of Elul, the twenty-third of Elul, and every other day as well – working toward another day during which he will truly live. If a period of thirty complete consecutive days is hard to handle, it's possible to aim to do so for a period shorter than a full day – for three hours, perhaps, or even twenty-four minutes – and attempt to infuse those minutes or hours with life, and by doing so, give them purpose.

The month of Elul is an appropriate time for this endeavor. On the one hand, Elul is a time of revelation of God. In hasidic literature, it is written that during Elul it is as if "the King is in the field." God is more accessible to everyone. On the other hand, unlike the days that follow – Rosh HaShana, Yom Kippur, and Sukkot – there is nothing festive about Elul, and no special prayers are added. The question, then, of how to infuse the month of Elul with life reflects the real problem at hand: It's not a question of how to observe a major or minor celebration, but how to wake up on an unremarkable Wednesday morning, a Wednesday morning with nothing special about it, and infuse that day with life and purpose. The work of Elul, then, can carry over into the rest of one's days, if one succeeds in achieving it.

It turns out that in order to infuse the day with life, one need not do anything special. A person can study a page of Talmud or recite a chapter of Psalms and be alive. One can also sit in the garden and play with the grass and be alive.

It is said about the slaves in America, whose lives were truly agonizing, without respite or dignity, that when a slave wanted to experience pleasure, he would pinch his nose and hold his breath for as long as he could until he felt like he was about to suffocate. Then he would unblock his nose and take a deep breath. With that breath, he felt the pleasure of being alive.

In a certain sense, attempting to live is an attempt to experience the delight of being alive. And, as written in the holy books, this is a delight greater than any other.

WHO ARE YOU?

There are people who, for all intents and purposes, do not live, even if they travel all over the world. It's possible to live for ninety years and still be dead during every one of those years. People spend their days involved in all sorts of pursuits – eating, drinking, sleeping, and all kinds of other things – but how many of those days were they actually alive?

One way to calculate the days of a person's life is to ascertain how many of them were actually lived. For example, it is said that Harun al-Rashid, an Arab sultan of the Abbasid dynasty when it was a powerful and wealthy caliphate, had everything a person could possibly want, materially and spiritually. He related, at the end of his life, "I sought to calculate how many days of happiness I experienced in my life. I counted all the days of happiness and did not even reach seven days."

One can attempt to calculate for himself: How many days of living have there been in my life? But the question isn't how many seconds of the clock have ticked by, or even how one filled each hour of his life, but rather: For how much of that time did I live a life of substance?

When a person arrives in the supernal world, he is asked two big questions. The first is, "What did you do during your lifetime?" Some have a good answer to this question because their life was filled with accomplishments, and they can deliver a detailed report on everything they achieved. The second question is entirely different: "Who were you?"

This question is much more difficult to answer than the first. Many people work hard and accomplish quite a bit, but are still nobodies. There are nobodies who play football, nobodies who write books, nobodies who act in Broadway plays. One can ask each one of them these two questions. First: What did you do during your lifetime? And second: Who were you? The latter pertains to whether or not he lived a life of substance.

This is the question that defines the work of Elul: Who are you? What defines your days?

The Crown of a Good Name

IT SURPASSES THEM ALL

Several "*baalei shem*" (masters of the name) lived before the Baal Shem Tov was born. This was an appellation given to folk healers who employed amulets, incantations, and holy names. But the description "*baal shem tov*" has a different meaning, and it's tied to a statement in the Mishna: "There are three crowns: the crown of Torah, the crown of priesthood, and the crown of kingship. But the crown of a good name surpasses them all."[2] The three crowns – Torah, priesthood, and kingship – are great, significant, and well known. What is the "crown of a good name that surpasses them all"?

The crown of a good name represents a virtue that is impossible to quantify or define. It's a virtue that relates neither to Torah, priesthood, nor kingship, nor to money or renown. It relates to the question: Who are you? What is the essence of the person? And that's something that is impossible to pinpoint.

The commentaries on the Mishna ask, "Why does the mishna begin with the statement 'There are three crowns' when it enumerates four?" Three crowns are listed, but then the "crown of a good name that surpasses them all" is added.

It appears that the answer to this question is that there actually are just three crowns, because the crown of a good name exists on a different plane from the other three. The three crowns represent a manifestation of greatness that is accompanied by prominence and honor. By contrast, the crown of a good name defines the inherent virtue of a person, the person's essential quality, and such virtue does not bring with it prominence or honor. In that sense, it is not a crown at all and therefore is not enumerated with the others.

On the other hand, if the crown of a good name doesn't exist with the other crowns – that is, when a person is learned, a High Priest, or a king but lacks the crown of a good name – those three crowns become somewhat hollow. A good name is the crown that defines the person

---

2. *Avot* 4:13.

himself. Though not observable – one can neither see it nor hear it – it's the crown that imbues the others with life.

I've had the opportunity to meet many famous people, and quite often they reminded me of a certain creature I once saw at the zoo: a featherless peacock. The peacock is one of the most beautiful creatures in existence, and one of the most exquisite phenomena in nature can be observed when the peacock displays its magnificent tail. A featherless peacock, on the other hand, looks like nothing more than a scrawny chicken. When I saw the featherless peacock, it reminded me of famous people who had beautiful peacocks' tails, but without their tails they were, like the featherless peacock, thoroughly unimpressive creatures.

The prominent people I've met each had a quality that made them distinct: wealth, Torah scholarship, academic achievement. All of them had large, beautiful tails or magnificent horns to accompany their basic personalities. These wonderful tails and horns were real, not merely glued on, and their beauty was genuine, just like the peacock's tail. And yet, if one were to attempt to ascertain who the person really was, it became clear that the person himself was an insignificant creature. Even if I held him in high regard in terms of the area in which he achieved distinction, he was still, essentially, a nobody.

There are famous people who accomplish quite a bit in their lifetime, but when one assesses how much good there is in them, one discovers that there is very little – and perhaps there is no good in them at all.

By contrast, one occasionally encounters a person who isn't as brilliant as others, but there's something in him of true value, something greater than that seen in other people. There are heads of state and authors. There are people with the talent to speak or to sing. And then there is the person who possesses no special, beautiful tail, but who has the crown of a good name – the crown that is invisible, the crown that is unquantifiable, the crown of the personality itself.

SELF-SEARCHING AS ESTABLISHED BY THE BAAL SHEM TOV

This is also the meaning of the name Baal Shem Tov, literally, "one who possesses a good name." Just as some people are known by their status as priests, Torah scholars, or leaders, a person can become distinguished as someone with a good name. The Baal Shem Tov expected his followers to contemplate the concept of the crown of a good name and to seek it within themselves. He said to them, "Some of you are wealthy, and some are poor. Some are upright and some are sinners. Let's peel away the layers that are unrelated to your true self and see what remains of you as a person."

The Baal Shem Tov made such self-searching a defining element of the hasidic movement. His followers were encouraged to look deep within themselves to discover their own crown of a good name. This self-searching is the essence of the Hasidism of the Baal Shem Tov. Other approaches to becoming a hasid, a pious person, as described in the Gemara and other sources, were defined by specific characteristics or particular behaviors, such as meticulous observance of the *mitzvot* or love of the Creator. But the Baal Shem Tov's definition of a hasid involved a search for some innate quality that couldn't be defined.

The essence of this search involved striving to achieve one's own good name, an effort that didn't negate external achievements, nor did it compete with other efforts to elevate and improve oneself. Someone who had achieved a good name could also acquire other virtues and qualities. But the essential task of a follower of the Baal Shem Tov was to try to distinguish oneself by one's good name. They did not need to learn anything specific in order to be a true hasid.

One who succeeds in finding the crown of a good name has made a real and significant discovery. Even when a group of hasidim sought a new Rebbe, the choice hinged on the candidate's good name rather than on his external accomplishments, including scholarship. A Rebbe does not have to attain a certain achievement or form a specific following. A Rebbe is a Rebbe because of who he is, not because of what he has accomplished. As a Lubavitcher hasid once said to me, "A Rebbe does not have to be learned. Scholarship is not a required part of his identity. But when our Rebbe meets an opponent and points out that the other person does not know what is written in the Jerusalem Talmud, that is merely an extra pleasure to be enjoyed this world."

IGNORING THE NONSENSE

One of the places where they spoke about this point was in Kotzk, where a story is told about Reb Leibele Eiger, grandson of Rabbi Akiva Eiger, who was a very great man. His son, Rabbi Shlomo Eiger, was also a great rabbi, as well as a fervent opponent of Hasidism. Yet the grandson decided to become a hasid of the Kotzker Rebbe, and in taking that step, he distanced himself as far as possible from his family.

Reb Leibele fled to Kotzk as a young yeshiva student with a *shtreimel*. When he entered the study hall and the hasidim saw his beautiful *shtreimel*, one of them snatched it from his head and sold it to buy whiskey. Meanwhile, Reb Leibele's father sent an emissary to find him. When the emissary arrived in Kotzk, he encountered some hasidim and asked them, "Where here can I find Rabbi Leibele Eiger?"

The hasidim responded that they knew no one by that name. The emissary gave them some identifying characteristics, until they finally said, "You must be referring to Akiva's Shlomo's Leibel!" – Leibel, son of Shlomo, son of Akiva. They didn't call him "Rabbi" as befitting a prominent Torah scholar, but rather by his first name, as they would refer to an ordinary person.

Later, when the emissary found Reb Leibele, he looked at him longingly and said, "What happened to the young man who was once 'the glory of Israel'?" When Leibel had left home to pursue Hasidism, he wasn't a young boy. He was an adult whom everyone was certain would fill a prominent rabbinical position like his forbearers.

One of the things that the emissary discovered about the Kotzker hasidim was that they had no set rules. Famous people, great rabbis, and wealthy philanthropists sat together with ordinary people in absolute equality. Everyone addressed each other with familiarity, in the second person, as one would address a good friend.

The emissary decided that he had found himself in a place where there was no etiquette, no formally accepted hierarchy of importance. Suddenly he heard someone proclaim, "Hershele is coming!" When the emissary saw that even in a place like Kotzk, there was someone whom everyone ran out to greet, he ran along as well to see who it was. What he saw was a diminutive Jew dressed in tattered garments. He asked the hasidim, "Who is this man and why is everyone treating him with such deference? Is he a great Torah scholar?"

They said to him, "He might be able to recite a chapter of Mishna, nothing more."

"Is he of distinguished lineage?"

"He is the son of a baker."

"Is he wealthy?"

"You see how he is dressed."

"Then why is everyone treating him with so much deference?"

"Because he is humble."

It is said that when the emissary returned to the Eiger family and related the story, someone said, "If he is not wealthy, not a scholar, and not of distinguished lineage – is it any wonder that he's humble? Why wouldn't he be humble?" But in Kotzk it was clear that the opposite was true: A person with outstanding qualities can be humble without great effort. But it's particularly difficult for a person who is not wealthy, not a scholar, and not of distinguished lineage to be humble, because humility leaves him without anything else to feel proud of. What alternative does he have to feeling that he is great?

What was going through the minds of the hasidim in Kotzk when they spoke to the emissary that way? It was certainly not to be dismissive of Torah scholars. Not only were there Torah scholars in Kotzk, but there were hundreds of rabbis, some of them great and prominent rabbis. But in Kotzk, it was matters related to a person's essence, rather than external trappings, that were emphasized and valued. They didn't stress the importance of accomplishments that could be acquired through studious effort, like Torah scholarship, as much as something that was much more difficult to acquire – the crown of a good name.

The search for the crown of a good name helps a person, among other things, ignore the nonsense and assess a person's value in a different way. With the Kotzk perspective, someone who knows that he is respected and renowned begins to think, *What do I gain from all this? What is its value?* But if he is searching for the crown of a good name, he then asks himself, *What am I really worth? What is my true value?*

A person doesn't need a title, even that of *tzaddik*, to have value. Instead, he must be whole, a person of essence. Those who value essence over external accomplishments are the ones who can become *baalei shem tov* – masters of a good name.

WHERE DOES ONE FIND *BAALEI SHEM TOV*?

It's worthwhile to seek out a person who is a *baal shem tov,* about whom it is said, "One man out of one thousand I have found."[3] It's hard to find the *baal shem tov,* but once you do, you have found a person who has intrinsic value. Even if he does nothing that benefits you, and you do nothing that benefits him, it's worthwhile to attach yourself to him; it's worthwhile to be in his company.

Whenever I meet my acquaintances, my students, or anyone else, I try to assess whether I see this attribute in them. As I said, a *baal shem tov* isn't identified by titles. The search for him is tied to the question, what is his inner identity? Even if a person has a degree of *shem tov,* one must, time and again, strip away all the shells and coverings in order to find it, to attempt to ascertain what remains after all the external veneers are removed. If the person is, indeed, a *baal shem tov,* what can ultimately be found inside is the crown of a good name.

Clams aren't particularly attractive creatures, and one doesn't notice anything special about their shells, but inside the shell one may find a pearl. So it is with people. Sometimes nothing special can be seen about a person, but when all the shells and coverings are stripped away, something inside shines and sparkles – the aspect of the person that is related to the crown of a good name.

In the Gemara,[4] there is an interesting list of four individuals who died because of "the serpent," unlike everyone else in the world, who die because of their sins. The people on this list died, not because of their own sins, but because of the deed of the primordial serpent, upon which it was decreed that people will die. Four names appear on the list: Benjamin son of Jacob; Amram, the father of Moses; Yishai, the father of David; and Kilav son of David.

In truth, it's surprising that these particular individuals are singled out, because there aren't any impressive stories one might relate about

3. Ecclesiastes 7:28.

4. *Shabbat* 55b; *Bava Batra* 17a.

any one of these personalities. What can be said about Benjamin other that the fact that he had ten children? In contrast to his brothers, Josef, Judah, or even Simeon, each of whom had a certain uniqueness, Benjamin was nothing more than a good boy.

What can be said about Amram, other than the fact that he was privileged to beget three children who grew up to become the glory of Israel? Regarding Yishai, David's father, nothing is known other than the fact that he "came among men."[5] And regarding Kilav, David's son, we know nothing at all other than his name. The *Tanakh* is replete with people who were the elite of the elite – prophets, sages, righteous men, wealthy men, kings – and none of them appear on this list. It is specifically four people of whom we know virtually nothing who merited to appear on it. The question is, can we possibly find a fifth person?

One day someone who had been a Chabad emissary came to see me and said that he was going to spend some time in Jerusalem. He asked me what he should do during that period of time. I said to him, "If you'd like to do something useful, walk around Jerusalem and meet people – not the ones sitting in yeshivot, but the merchants in Maḥaneh Yehuda, the cobblers, the policemen, the ordinary people who populate the city, and speak to them."

"About what?"

"About anything at all. Ask them questions and listen to their answers."

Perhaps the suggestion sounded like very strange advice to him, but he did as I suggested. Two years later he came to me and said, "I compiled a book of insights and pieces of wisdom that I heard from the common people of Jerusalem."

Every so often I have the opportunity to ride with taxi drivers, some Jewish, some Arab, and we converse. Quite often, I'm astonished by what they have to say. How do taxi drivers know the statements of the Sages or quote passages from the Gemara that they never learned? I once got a ride with an Arab taxi driver. It was raining outside, and he said to me, "In my opinion, rain falls, not for the people, but for the fields and the cows." That statement appears in the Gemara, and this taxi driver certainly never learned that Gemara. The question of why

5. I Samuel 17:12.

rain falls and for whom it falls entered the mind of a common person, who apparently came to the conclusion on his own, that rain falls for the trees and the animals.

Years ago, I used to deliver two weekly lectures on the topic of Hasidism. One of them took place on Thursdays and was attended by respected adults, all scholarly and refined. It was an interesting experience for me as a young man, sitting and teaching the elite of society. Among the attendees was the rector of the nearby university, who was at least three times my age. Nevertheless, he sat and transcribed every word I said. The country's foremost expert on real estate law, who was well versed in Turkish law, and to whom people would come for consultation from all over the country, also attended.

The other lecture took place on Shabbat afternoons and was a completely different experience from the first. Here there was no place for philosophy, new Torah insights, or any other novel ideas. I don't know how much of what I taught was understood by those who participated. I sat with them, and we would talk. Each related what he did for a living. One said he was a carpenter, another a cobbler, yet another a storekeeper. One man used to sit there in silence. Sometime later I met him on the street, and it turned out that he was a junk peddler. He and I often had chance encounters on that street, where I often walked and where he pursued his livelihood. Every time we met he had a question for me, usually relating to *Tanakh*. I discovered that this man knew *Tanakh* thoroughly and that he always asked intelligent questions.

This man, I thought, *a junk peddler, who clearly hadn't been planning to meet me since these were chance encounters, always has a question for me.* Evidently he would walk along, all the while thinking about matters of Torah. How many people like that do you know? I'm certain that this man had no interest in my calling him "sir" or "rabbi," but he was certainly thinking about matters of Torah more than I was.

I said to myself, *What do I know about people? What do I know of their greatness?*

It turns out that sometimes it's worthwhile to search for the crown of a good name among the common people. It's possible to find it among rabbis or the wealthy, but that requires greater effort because of all the shells that must be stripped away in order to reveal their inner essence.

To ascertain a person's essence, one must see him as he truly is. When one succeeds in revealing what the person himself is, sometimes it becomes clear that he is has the crown of a good name. An encounter with such a person, who could be described as a "candelabrum entirely of gold,"[6] who is beautiful, clean, and pure in his entirety, is an unadulterated joy and pleasure.

All in all, I've tried to speak with you about matters that are perhaps not written in hasidic works but nevertheless touch the soul. I didn't speak to you about the fact that a person must delve into the depths of his heart to examine whether or not he has sinned. Instead, I spoke about something that is worthy of seeing, worthy of clinging to.

The crown of a good name is beautiful in the sense that it represents "beauty and eternity for the One who lives forever,"[7] according to the explanation of the Kotzker Rebbe. Typically, when a person sees a beautiful object again and again, its beauty fades with time. Only something that "lives forever," like the crown of a good name, can maintain its beauty and splendor forever.

Leḥayim!

---

6. See Zechariah 4:2.
7. *Sefer Hekhalot* 22:12.

4

Every Person's Crown of a Good Name

THE DIFFERENCE BETWEEN A *YARTZEIT* AND A BIRTHDAY

On Ḥai Elul we celebrate two birthdays: that of Rabbi Yisrael Baal Shem Tov and that of Rabbi Shneur Zalman of Liadi, also known as the Baal HaTanya. The very fact that we remember and celebrate their birthdays rather than their *yartzeits* (dates of death) is an anomaly. Usually we celebrate the *yartzeits* of the many reputable men who have lived throughout our great history. As a rule, we don't even know their birthdays. There are only a few exceptional individuals throughout Jewish history whose dates of birth are known. Why do we commemorate so many death days and so few birthdays?

What is a *yartzeit*? Why do we mark the date of a death?

A *yartzeit* represents the end of a person's life, or, more specifically, a summary of his life's accomplishments. If we attempt to summarize Rashi's life, for example, the summary wouldn't include anecdotes or stories because his primary accomplishment was his commentary on the Torah and Talmud. In that sense, Rashi lives on in every book of *Ḥumash* and in every volume of the Talmud. That is his legacy. There are people whose lives can be summarized by their written works, and others whose lives can be summed up by good deeds. There are some who won a war, built a town, or achieved other similar accomplishments.

That is what a *yartzeit* is about: It is a day summarizing a person's achievements during his lifetime.

A birthday is totally different. Why should I care that a person was born on a certain date? A birthday is important for people whose lives can't be summed up by any special achievement or specific accomplishment. It's merely an acknowledgment of their existence as a human being. In contrast to a person's accomplishments, which can be summarized at life's end, there is no particular time for summarizing a person's essence, his very existence. The question of who a certain person was at his essence is therefore not addressed on a *yartzeit*; it is relevant specifically to a birthday.

It is for this reason that the Gemara discusses the months in which the Patriarchs were born.[1] The birth date of the Patriarchs is significant because their primary essence was not a summary of the deeds they performed in their lifetimes. In all likelihood, Abraham and Isaac did not write books, and Jacob left no legacy of compositions. He didn't compose music, nor did he write books, and even his progeny, from whom the Jewish nation was formed, doesn't represent a summary of his life. What did the Patriarchs do? They lived. That they merely existed, that they lived in this world, has meaning far beyond their deeds or accomplishments. This is exemplified by the way Noah is described in the first verse of *Parashat Noaḥ*: "This is the legacy of Noah: Noah...."[2] The legacy of Noah is "Noah." His essence, his very existence. What was Noah's legacy? What did he create? He created Noah, and Noah himself was significant enough.

THE RIGHTEOUS ARE CALLED LIVING EVEN IN DEATH

The saying "The righteous are called living even in their death, and the wicked are called dead even in their lifetime"[3] is not meant as an insult to the wicked. It is merely stating a fact of life, one that is related to the subject we are discussing: There are people whose essence is alive, and those whose essence is dead. There are people who circulate in the world

1. *Rosh HaShana* 10b–11a.
2. Genesis 6:9.
3. Jerusalem Talmud, *Berakhot* 15:2.

for eighty years, and perhaps along the way they accomplish all sorts of things. In that sense, when the time comes, perhaps it will be possible to make a *yartzeit* for them, to build a monument to them. Yet they were never really alive. Even though no coroner pronounced them dead, they were, for all intents and purposes, not actually living.

By contrast, there are people whose lives are so filled with substance and meaning that they can't be summed up merely by this accomplishment or that achievement. Regarding people like that, one can say what is written about Benayahu ben Yehoyada: that he was *ben ish ḥai,* "the son of a living man."[4] Even if they are physically dead, they continue to live on.

This explains an interesting phenomenon: Neither the month in which Miriam died nor the date that Aaron died is written in the Torah. The date that their brother, Moses, died is also not written explicitly. It was only the Sages who calculated that he died on the seventh of Adar. Why didn't the Torah itself delineate the date that Moses died? It is because, in truth, Moses did not die. When Rambam describes Moses's death, he states that what befell Moses was "what is called death regarding other people."[5] Rambam employs this description because it's impossible to say that Moses died. Moses forever remains Moses. He continues to live, even though medically what befell him is considered death.

This is also the reason that we celebrate the birthday of the Baal Shem Tov on Ḥai Elul. The Baal Shem Tov passed away and was buried. I can attest to that; I have stood by his grave. But in truth, the Baal Shem Tov is still walking in the streets. Every so often he smiles at someone. Every so often he taps someone with his pipe the way he would during his lifetime. He continues to live on even though he is dead.

There is a reason we are not absolutely certain about the date of the Baal Shem Tov's *yartzeit* – whether he died on the sixth or the seventh of Sivan – but we are certain about the date of his birth. It is because the Baal Shem Tov was a living man. A living man need not write books – even if, sometimes, he does write books. His essence is of greater significance than anything he may have written.

---

4. II Samuel 23:20.
5. Rambam's introduction to *Peirush HaMishnayot.*

This is also true regarding the Baal HaTanya, Rabbi Shneur Zalman of Liadi. Although he is known as the author of the *Tanya,* and he wrote significant works of *halakha* and other topics, he also created a world. He built people, gave them a lifeline through his teachings and his example, and that is more significant than the books that he wrote.

THE CROWN OF A GOOD NAME

That we celebrate these birthdays on Ḥai Elul represents a certain view of those whose birthdays we are celebrating. Moreover, it reflects a fundamentally different world outlook, one that is in a sense the foundation on which Hasidism is based. The questions of whether or not a person wrote books or whether or not he fathered children are not the important questions. The important question that needs to be asked, regarding each and every person is, who was this person?

This point also relates to the name Baal Shem Tov. This name is based on the mishna where it is written that there are three crowns.[6] The first crown is the crown of Torah, this is a great and significant crown and can be given to anyone, even though not everyone achieves it in practice. The second crown is the crown of priesthood, which is passed on through inheritance. The third crown is the crown of kingship. In principle, this crown belongs to all of Israel. According to the *halakha,* any Jewish person is fit to be king, even though the supreme ruler must always be a king from the house of David. But there is an additional crown that is accessible to every Jew: the crown of a good name. This crown isn't determined by the Torah, and it is unrelated to the priesthood and kingship. It is the crown of the person himself, of his character. That's why Rabbi Shimon says, "The crown of a good name surpasses them all" – meaning all the other crowns.

The Baal Shem Tov transformed the standard appellation *baal shem,* "man of renown," into Baal Shem Tov because he based his whole approach on this aspect of the crown of a good name. Even if a person doesn't know how to study Torah, even if he isn't really diligent and even if he isn't particularly righteous, he can still attain the crown of a good name, because that crown relates to who he could be. A good name

6. *Avot* 4:13.

could surpass them all – Torah, priesthood, and kingship. Any Jew could be a *baal shem tov.*

This is a quality that I attempt to develop in my students. Perhaps one or two of them have the potential to become prominent Torah scholars; perhaps several of them could become *tzaddikim*. But what I really hope is that they will all become people who are masters of the crown of a good name.

The crown of a good name is connected to the unique essence and virtue of each individual, the special gift that every person receives from God. Likewise, Hasidism doesn't address the question of whether a person created something in his lifetime; it addresses the experience of life itself. Perhaps the person didn't create anything significant, but as he navigated the world, he spread small points of light wherever he went. Anyone who encountered him departed with a little more light. This is not an achievement that can be extolled at his *yartzeit*, because it can't be measured in the way that a person's accomplishments are summarized at his life's end. But it is significant when examining the essence of the person's life.

This is why it is written regarding Sarah our Matriarch, "The lifetime of Sarah was one hundred and twenty-seven years, the years of the life of Sarah"[7] – all those years were "years of life."

"HE BEGOT... HE DIED"

There are all sorts of people circulating in the world whose lives are meaningless. There are those whose greatest accomplishment in life was to father children. Although having children is a great and important thing, I would prefer that it not be the most significant thing that a person accomplish in life.

A young man once spoke to me of racehorses. Some racehorses win numerous races, producing profits for their owners. These horses are very expensive and renowned, and sometimes have a much larger family tree than their owners have. But when a racehorse injures its leg, what is its worth? It can no longer run, and using it just to fertilize the grass makes no sense financially. Typically a horse like that is used for

7. Genesis 23:1.

breeding. In that way it can transmit its racing potential to its offspring. Perhaps it will sire progeny from which something will develop.

I said to this young man, "Your career as a racehorse ended a long time ago. Now all that's left for you to do is to have children and send them to a good yeshiva. Perhaps they will amount to something."

That's what I'm talking about: This is a person whose life has become meaningless, whose only ambition is to father good children.

At the beginning of Genesis, there are entire lists of people like this, where all that could be said of them is that so-and-so begot so-and-so and then he died, as we find, "He begot sons and daughters... and he died."[8] It is written there, for example, "Irad begot Meḥuyael, and Meḥuyael begot Metushael."[9] No one knows who Meḥuyael was. All we know about him is that he was born to Irad, begot Metushael, perhaps begot additional sons and daughters, and then he died. That's it. This was his life.

Teraḥ, too, who is our ancestor on both sides, is an example of this. All that is written about him in the Torah is that he was born to Naḥor and had three sons, one of whom was not a typical son, and that we seek to continue the legacy of that atypical son. In other words, Teraḥ begot Abraham, and from that perspective, his life wasn't pointless. Aside from that, his existence was meaningless.

Sometimes, what happens in the best of families also happens among the Jewish people. A child who is genetically a son of Abraham is born, but in terms of his character, he is not a mini Abraham. Instead, he inherited the character traits of his grandfather; he became a mini Teraḥ – a person who can aspire to nothing more than producing offspring. Regarding such a person, nothing more can be said than "He was born, he married, he begot sons and daughters, and he died." For a person like that, there's no reason to remember his birthday or even his *yartzeit*. One remembers only his accomplishments in the area of procreation.

8. See Genesis, chap. 5.
9. Genesis 4:18.

NOT TO BE MEDIOCRE

There is another type of person who seems to be determined to remain mediocre. It's as if he made a commitment that he will never, God forbid, be more than average. This person fulfills the verse "Do not be overly righteous, and do not be exceedingly wise"[10] in its plain sense. As people would say when I was a child, "Who is mediocre? One who neither turns away from evil nor does good." Alternatively, a mediocre person is someone who is neither very wise nor very stupid.[11]

There are people who, when their knowledge of Gemara is assessed, are found to be neither total ignoramuses nor Torah scholars. One wouldn't say that they are total ignoramuses, because they know *alef-beit* and a few other things. And one wouldn't say that they are Torah scholars, because the moment they sense that the Torah is beginning to touch them, they run away from it. These are people who want to be mediocre.

By contrast, there are those who don't choose to be mediocre, but find themselves in the middle because God gave them a brain with average potential. Just as not every person is born with the potential to grow to the height of six foot three or to weigh four hundred and forty pounds, not everyone is blessed with an IQ of 150, with the ability to function successfully in the real world, or with an inner passion that makes it impossible for him to be complacent.

But according to Hasidism, every Jew was born to be more than mediocre, even if his potential for greatness is in an unexpected area. Greatness isn't always measured using conventional criteria. There are, for example, people who mediocre at best as Torah scholars, businessmen, or public figures, but when they touch greenery, it blossoms. If they plant tomatoes in the same flower pot as other people, theirs will bear fruit while those of others will hardly grow. I've heard of astonishing talents in areas that were hard to believe, but they have been observed and proven with meticulous tests. People can truly have unique abilities in surprising areas.

---

10. Ecclesiastes 7:16.
11. This is a phrase that appears often in *halakha* to indicate an average person.

GOD'S GIFT

The Baal Shem Tov believed that when a person is blessed with a unique characteristic, it is significant, because that quality is a gift from God. Every individual should seek to identify the gift that God has given him and attempt to discern his unique nature. This is actually the essence of Hasidism, and this is what we are meant to internalize on Ḥai Elul: How can we uncover our special qualities and ensure that we don't live a life of mediocrity?

There is, for example, the person who has the "crown of a smile." When he smiles at someone, the person begins to glow. This is a crown that many rabbis, priests, and kings weren't privileged to receive. Then there is the person who possesses the crown of extending a hand to another and making that person feel that he has received genuine assistance and support. These are characteristics that can't be measured with the tools people typically use to measure greatness.

There are people who have received the gift of healing, and others who have received the gift of war. Then there are those who have received an entirely different gift: Though they themselves understand very little, they can spur others to think and question. These are people one should consult, not in order to get answers, but in order to know the right questions. This person is not a mere ignoramus who asks questions, but someone who always asks the questions that need to be asked. Knowing how to ask is a virtue in and of itself, a talent in and of itself.

In essence, a person should ponder: Why did God put me in this world? There are those whom God sent to the world to extend a helping hand to others; others were put here to say a good word. Some people are capable of spurring others to action, and others know how to give good advice, not necessarily because they are particularly wise, but because they are proficient at finding the optimal path.

And so there are the well-known crowns, and there are also all sorts of other crowns, ranging from the ability to tend a garden to the ability to cook an omelet. And if a person's unique talent is in cooking an omelet, that omelet should be an omelet for a "good name." It should be channeled toward a good purpose. Only then is it meaningful.

There was once a chef who wanted to teach cooking. He signed a contract with a person that committed him to teach a thousand recipes for preparing eggs. The chef managed to teach him only eight hundred recipes. The student sued the chef, demanding that he come before a certain rabbi for judgment. That rabbi, who happened to be very wealthy, remarked, "I had no idea that there could be even eight hundred recipes for making eggs. If it's true, perhaps it's possible for someone to become a '*baal ḥavitot*' – a master of omelets."

Some people have a talent for raising money. There was a great rabbi who was extraordinarily talented in that area. The story is told that a prominent Jewish philanthropist once insisted that his portrait be hung in any institution to which he contributed money. The problem was that this Jew had no beard, no sidelocks, and no hat, and most rabbis didn't want to hang a picture like that in their yeshivot so they didn't accept his contributions. But the talented rabbi took his money for the sake of his yeshiva.

When the philanthropist visited the yeshiva and asked to see where the picture was hanging, the rabbi said to him, "Do you think that I would hang such an important picture in a place where just anyone can see it? Your picture is hanging in my office in front of my desk, right where I can see it." The rabbi showed him the photo was hanging there, exactly where he said it would be. The philanthropist was happy about the great honor accorded him, and the rabbi's yeshiva was well endowed.

There are people who – what can I say? – have a talent for politics. That, too, is a talent. The problem is that people often don't utilize it for good. The moment a person with a talent for politics utilizes that talent for the sake of Heaven – that is his crown of a good name.

Others have a talent for words, a talent for music, a talent for art, or a talent for cleaning and organization. There are people whose gift from God is that they know how to be good parents. Some who are excellent high school teachers and others superlative preschool teachers. Every person has a role, a way to achieve things in the world. If a person develops his talent, he will be able to perform that ability flawlessly. And when he does, he will have achieved purpose; he will have found meaning.

There are hundreds, thousands, of abilities, and anyone who cultivates his particular ability will not remain insignificant. That's why I say that there is no justification for anyone to be mediocre.

WHAT IS MY CROWN OF A GOOD NAME?

The problem is that very often people don't know where their ability lies, and they end up seeking to grow in an area that is not theirs. This is a common human failure. There are, for example, a certain number of people who sit and study Torah all day. Among them there may be one or two with a retentive memory, who forget nothing. The rest of them, not blessed with that kind of memory, forget more than they remember. Perhaps it's better that they follow a different path in life.

Another example is a person whom God granted the ability to be an expert in grammar. Instead of attempting to be the world's greatest editor, he seeks to become a poet or a writer. Ultimately, he will become neither a poet nor a writer. The problem is that he also doesn't become an editor.

God grants every person a different area of interest, but when one seeks to find his interest only among well-known areas, it's likely that he won't find it. A person must be able to say, "The crown of Torah belongs to so-and-so, but I can't achieve that level. The crown of priesthood belongs to so-and-so, but not to me. I'm unable to attain it. I wasn't born into the right family. Likewise the crown of kingship – that belongs to another, not to me. Not everyone can be a leader. But there are people who have the talent to know who should lead, which is a totally different talent. Maybe that's my talent."

Someone once said to me, "I'm not capable of being the Rebbe, but I understand who is capable of being the Rebbe." In the same way, there are people who are able to say, "I'm not able to be king, but I know who will be or who should be king." It's important for a person who has that capability to be aware of it.

Some are born with the innate knowledge of what their crown of a good name is, but many others waste their lives attempting to compete for a crown that is not theirs. That's why it's worthwhile for a person, if he can, to consult with others in this regard.

HOW A PERSON BECOMES A HASID

As I said, Hasidism ascribes great significance to the crown of a good name, the special ability that each person possesses, the thing that a person is capable of performing faultlessly. Hasidism asks each person: What can *you* do? Therefore, one who seeks to be a hasid must look inside himself and consider: What is the crown of a good name that God gave *me*?

Contrary to what people think, a person doesn't become a hasid by donning a *gartel*, just as a cat doesn't become a zebra if you were to paint it with black and white stripes. Someone who wants to become a hasid need not grow sidelocks, begin to pray loudly, or speak Yiddish. He need not even begin praying in *nusaḥ Sefard*. These are merely external indicators to remind him of his communal affiliation – or which community he would like to be affiliated with. The primary element of Hasidism is the change a person undergoes internally, the work he does in relation to his own essence and his own crown. This is not a question of achievement measured by the criteria of wealth, honor, or a prestigious job. This is about who the person is at his essence and whether he is able to channel his own qualities and nature toward a meaningful life.

Hasidism also doesn't focus on the obligation to fulfill *mitzvot*, because it's clear that a person must fulfill the *mitzvot*. To be a hasid, it's not sufficient to fulfill *mitzvot*, because the fulfillment of *mitzvot* is merely the framework of a person's life. The point of a person's life is tied to the question, what can *you* do?

TO BLOSSOM AND GROW

It's no small matter for a person to become a hasid. It means that this person, who has a crown of a good name, has grown to the proportions that he should be. God provides each person with the resources to grow and blossom in a certain area. Anyone who makes the most of those resources can achieve the highest heights in his area.

I might, for example, ask a person who is studying education, "What class do you want to teach?" and he says to me, "I want to teach the first grade." Being a first-grade teacher is not a demotion because it's possible to do the job with great courage and creativity. There are people who are incapable of being first-grade teachers because they are too intellectual and scholarly. They are simply incapable of speaking to children in the first grade. When a first-grade teacher does his job well, it gives him joy and meaning. I'm certain that there are any number of teachers who deserve accolades because they imparted many good lessons to their students.

This is no less true of shoemakers. It is written regarding Ḥanokh that he sewed shoes, and with each and every stitch he would recite, "Blessed be the name of His glorious kingdom for ever and ever." It is for this reason that God took him up to Heaven alive. He sits above the angels and the righteous, serving as God's interior minister. He is the angel whose name is like that of his Master, and he is the only one of all the angels who is privileged to sit on the divine throne.[12]

Who was this angel when he was living in this world? He was a shoemaker. It turns out that one can be a shoemaker who attains the loftiest heights, who now sews shoes for God in Heaven. By contrast, there are people who sit in the world and write books filled with novel Torah teachings, yet they don't reach such heights either in this world or in the World to Come.

God creates angels in bunches, on an assembly line, as it is written, "Thousands upon thousands served Him, and myriads upon myriads stood before Him."[13] He has as many angels as He wants, and they are arrayed in companies and platoons. Although He sees to it that there will be myriad angels, He does not see to it that each will have its own unique character.

By contrast, "the Holy One, blessed be He, stamped all people with the seal of Adam, and not one of them is similar to another."[14] The gift that God gives to each of us is the unique seal with which He stamps us, through which I'm me and no one else. In this way, God says to each person, "What do I want from you? I don't want you to be identical to everyone else. Otherwise you wouldn't have received a unique stamp. I also don't want you to be mediocre. I wanted you to develop and grow in the area that is unique to you. Maybe you can't achieve heights in the area of Torah, the priesthood, or kingship, but you can achieve a good name, which is the crown that surpasses them all."

The crown of a good name is the crown that God Himself bestows. When His children come to Him after their time in this world, where

---

12. See *Ḥagiga* 15a; Rabbi Menaḥem Azarya de Fano, *Asara Maamarot, Maamar Em Kol Ḥai* 3:22.
13. Daniel 7:10.
14. Mishna *Sanhedrin* 4:5.

they did whatever they did, He says to each and every one of them, "I sent you to tend your garden. What did you accomplish? Where are the things you created? Perhaps due to exigencies, you became a soldier or a writer. But beyond that, you had a certain quality, a role that you could have filled, and you should have developed it."

THE UPRIGHT OF HEART

On Ḥai Elul, we don't celebrate a day of redemption, a day of Torah study, or a *yartzeit*, but rather the birth of certain people. Although in both the book *Keter Shem Tov*, which contains the teachings of the Baal Shem Tov, and in the writings of Rabbi Shneur Zalman of Liadi, this concept isn't written in so many words, it remains the essence of Ḥai Elul. There are prominent leaders of their generations who, by the very fact of their birth – the very fact that they exist – are fulfilling God's will with everything they do and everywhere they go. As Rabbi Tzadok of Lublin states, "There are righteous men who perform the will of God. And there are even greater righteous men whose every action is the will of God."[15]

Allow me to expound on the verse "Light is sown for the righteous and joy for the upright of heart."[16] A righteous man is someone who does his job; he serves God as one should. But who are the "upright of heart"? The upright of heart are those who obey God's command that states, "You shall do the upright and the good in the eyes of the Lord."[17] This is an indeterminate decree, but it means: You were placed in this world. Do something to perfect it.

The upright of heart don't necessarily attempt to be righteous, but they naturally seek to do the right thing. They do what they do because they are upright of heart, not necessarily because the things they are doing are required or must be done. Although it doesn't say specifically that the upright of heart are righteous, what is written regarding the upright of heart is superior to what is written about the righteous. And

---

15. See *Pri Tzaddik, Lekh Lekha* 3 and *Beshalaḥ* 12.
16. Psalms 97:11.
17. Deuteronomy 6:18.

God bestows on one who "does the upright and the good" everything that He bestows on the righteous, and more.

In this sense, the level of a hasid surpasses that of the righteous. Even if he doesn't do anything remarkable – he doesn't build houses, doesn't write books, doesn't create great works – he is alive and is engaged in this world. For people like that, we celebrate birthdays.

When we celebrate the birthday of a great man, we're basically saying that from the time of his birth, he has contributed to this world by his very existence, by his very life. He may not have written any great works or composed brilliant symphonies, but he is a person who could be called living. We remember his birthday because, like Abraham, "*ba bayamim*" – he "comes" to God and brings with him all the "days" of his life, days filled with meaning and purpose. Others bring with them half their time, one-quarter of their time, one-tenth of their time, having wasted the rest of it. By contrast, when he comes before God, he brings all of his days with him.

People like that are often born with the clear sense of where they are supposed to be and what they are supposed to do. Those of us who weren't born with that knowledge must search for their own crown of a good name. This is the essential point we want to internalize, and as Hillel said, "As for the rest... go and study."[18] Discovering what we need to do in life requires a lot of work. It's not a simple task. Now that we know what we have to do, it's all up to us.

Leḥayim!

18. *Shabbat* 31a.

Yod Tet Kislev
The Festival of the Redemption of the Baal HaTanya

On Yod Tet Kislev, the nineteenth of Kislev, Lubavitch hasidim mark the release of Rabbi Shneur Zalman of Liadi, the Baal HaTanya, from a Russian prison. Rabbi Shneur Zalman had been incarcerated in 1798 in the wake of a false accusation that he was aiding the Ottoman Empire, an enemy of Russia. With this accusation, opposition to the fast-growing hasidic movement reached its pinnacle. His exoneration on Yod Tet Kislev represented the victory of the hasidic approach toward divine service over the approach of its opponents.

It is for this reason that Lubavitch hasidim call Yod Tet Kislev the "Rosh HaShana of Hasidism": because it's the day when the divine seal of approval was given to the path of Hasidism. That is also why, on this day, they inspire and are inspired to follow its path with greater commitment. On Yod Tet Kislev, it is customary for Lubavitch hasidim to conclude the year-long study of the book of *Tanya*. It's also customary to divide the tractates of the Talmud among the participants at the farbrengen, so that as a group they can complete the study of the entire Talmud by the following year on Yod Tet Kislev.

Yod Tet Kislev is also the day of the passing of the Maggid of Mezeritch, who died in 1772. He succeeded the Baal Shem Tov as leader of the hasidic movement and was the Baal HaTanya's mentor. The Maggid of Mezeritch became acquainted with the Baal Shem Tov when he was already a well-known kabbalist and Torah scholar. Despite this, the Maggid of Mezeritch deferred to the authority of the Baal Shem Tov until his passing, when the Maggid assumed leadership of the movement.

The Maggid's leadership was a period of consolidation and expansion of the hasidic movement in terms of its philosophical system and the method of meditation that he developed and taught to his disciples. Moreover, under his leadership dozens of disciples disseminated the path of Hasidism throughout Eastern Europe and became leaders of congregations and heads of hasidic courts, many of which exist even today. The Maggid himself was the great-grandfather of Rabbi Yisrael of Ruzhin, whose descendants in succeeding generations led, and still lead, many hasidic courts.

Yod Tet Kislev, the date on which these two events transpired, connects the rabbi who consolidated Hasidism with his disciple, who devoted himself to its existence and perpetuity. Yod Tet Kislev celebrates Hasidism, not only as a historical phenomenon, but also its intrinsic essence – as a new-old way of devotion to God and divine service.

A farbrengen with Rabbi Steinsaltz on Yod Tet Kislev was typically an evening of great inspiration. It was an opportunity to address matters of consequence: How do we move forward, how do we elevate ourselves, how do we fulfill the demands required of one who seeks to be a hasid?

5

The Salvation of Yod Tet Kislev

THE SALVATION OF THE BAAL HATANYA

On Yod Tet Kislev, the Baal HaTanya, Rabbi Shneur Zalman of Liadi, was released from his first incarceration. His trial was held before the supreme government of Russia – an earthly court and, actually, a second-rate one. In addition to the petty false charges brought against him, such as the accusation that he had aided the Turks, Russia's enemy, based on the fact that he had sent money to the Land of Israel, the primary matter that the Russia authorities had to resolve was whether or not Hasidism was a new religious sect, something prohibited in Russia. A bizarre situation ensued: The court of the czar of Russia and his people needed to deliberate on the nature and essence of Hasidism.

Under no circumstances would the Russian government allow the formation of sects, and any new faction was forcibly suppressed. This edict wasn't directed specifically against Jews. The local Jews had only just recently become subjects of the Russian Empire, and the Russians didn't care about Jewish worship. The Jews were insignificant. The legislation against the formation of sects was primarily intended to suppress the proliferation of sects among Russians, and anyone who was a member of such sects incurred extremely harsh punishments, among them a twenty-five-year prison sentence in Siberia or a direct trip to the World to Come.

In any case, this was the basis of the indictment against the Baal HaTanya. The Russian government now needed to determine whether Hasidism was a new sect, and they sat and deliberated over the matter as far as their intellect allowed. Ultimately, they decided that the accusation was false and that Hasidism was not a new sect. Once the central accusation was rejected, the other petty accusations that had come along with it were also dismissed.

On Yod Tet Kislev, the Baal HaTanya was released. He was overjoyed because that was also the day of the passing of his primary teacher, the Maggid of Mezeritch. Afterward, his followers did some research and found another reference to this date in a fascinating book called *She'eilot U'Teshuvot min HaShamayim* (Responsa from Heaven) in which one of the tosafists would ask a question in a dream and receive a response from Heaven. In that small volume, which we still have today, there are many interesting responsa, some as brief as a word or two and some longer. In one of the responsa to a question asked and answered on the nineteenth of Kislev, that day was referred to as a "day of good tidings."[1] The hasidim clung to this phrase as an apt description of Yod Tet Kislev.

The song that hasidim sing on this day, which begins with the words "He redeemed me unharmed,"[2] relates directly to this aspect of the salvation. Moreover, the Baal HaTanya related that he recited that verse precisely at the moment that he was freed.

From this perspective, the celebration of Yod Tet Kislev also has a basis in *halakha*. Just as a person is obligated to recite a blessing when he sees a place where a miracle was performed for his ancestors, so one is obligated to recite a blessing when he sees a place where a miracle was performed for his primary teacher, since a person's disciples and successors benefit from that miracle.[3] This also explains the custom in many communities to establish holidays commemorating miracles that transpired in their midst, as well as the custom in many families to establish a holiday commemorating miracles that transpired to the head of the household. The most famous day of that kind is the "Purim" celebrated

1. *She'eilot U'Teshuvot min HaShamayim, siman* 5.
2. Psalms 55:19.
3. *Shulḥan Arukh, Oraḥ Ḥayim* 218:6.

by the descendants of the author of *Tosefot Yom Tov*. To this day, they celebrate the day on which the patriarch of their family was redeemed.

On Yod Tet Kislev, hasidim celebrate and express thanks for the miracle that was performed for the Baal HaTanya. But that's not the only reason the day is significant.

THE ESSENTIAL PERSON IN PRISON

Someone once asked, "What would have happened if the Russian court had sentenced the Baal HaTanya to life in prison?" There are those who, if incarcerated, would lose their humanity in one day. That's what is liable to happen to most people. For them, their existence is conditional. Although they are alive, breathe, act, most of their actions are dependent on other people. If they were completely isolated and removed from the environment on which they depend, they become lesser people. Most people need the constant feedback provided by life that exists outside of them – whether it's a friend, neighbor, or family member.

By contrast, the Baal HaTanya was an "essential man." He didn't need input from the outside world because all he needed was within him. Even in prison, he could have lived in his own world, in his own reality, just as he did outside of prison. From his perspective, whether he was outside or inside prison made no difference. And this is a question that any person can ask of himself: How much of my world is internal and how much is external? Sometimes a person will discover that all he has inside are small, disjointed fragments of a world that can't be connected.

When seen in that light, the significance of the outcome of the Baal HaTanya's trial was not about the liberation of a private individual, even if he was a great man and a rabbi. The Baal HaTanya himself didn't really need this liberation. The significance of his exoneration stemmed from the fact that the salvation was more than just his personal salvation. The scope of redemption that occurred on that day was much greater and much more comprehensive. That is why it is said that Yod Tet Kislev is "the day of our salvation and the redemption of our souls."

WHO ISSUES THE RULING?

One could claim that the one who issued the ruling in this trial was the Russian czar Pavel, who was known to be quite insane. If he was the man who determined the ruling, what is the significance of this? Of course, his ruling had a practical outcome, but what is its significance from a broader perspective, over time?

This parallels the Purim miracle. The scroll of Esther is meant to be understood on at least two levels. Each time "the king" is written in the scroll, one understands that it refers to the earthly king, Aḥashverosh, who was a drunk, a ne'er-do-well, and a fool to a greater or lesser extent. It also must be understood to refer to the heavenly King.

This dual reading is tied to a broader insight: Events that transpire on earth at specific times and places are components of events of a much greater scope that extend to the highest heavens. Therefore, every ruling has two facets: the ruling that is issued in the earthly kingdom and the ruling that is issued in the heavenly kingdom. If a fundamental matter, as opposed to a private accusation, is raised in an earthly court for deliberation, even though the court is an earthly one, and even a second-rate one, this court reflects that which is occurring in Heaven. The trial that is adjudicated on earth reflects another trial that is being conducted in another realm, on another level. In that sense, the earthly court adjudicates the heavenly judgment.

In the days of Aḥashverosh, an allegation was raised against the Jewish people: "There is a certain people that is scattered and dispersed among the peoples … and they do not follow the king's laws; it is not worthwhile for the king to tolerate them."[4] This accusation was raised not only in this world, but the heavenly court also found it necessary to deliberate whether the Jewish nation was, in fact, "scattered and dispersed among the peoples." This is an accusation directed against the Jewish people: Why is it scattered and dispersed? "And they do not follow the king's laws" is another accusation. Haman and Aḥashverosh were referring to Aḥashverosh himself, to his earthly laws, but in the heavenly court, the reference was to a different King. The overriding question in the heavenly trial was whether it is "worthwhile … to tolerate them." Is there really any need for them? What purpose do they serve?

4. Esther 3:8.

AN EVENT FOR THE GENERATIONS

The momentous context in which these events transpired lends significance to them for generations to come. The difference between an event that is restricted to its time and an event that is relevant for future generations isn't dependent on its duration but on the duration of its significance. There are events that shook the entire world at the time, but with passing years their impact waned. Five or ten years after they transpired, the significance of these events totally dissipated. By contrast, there are some events whose significance endures fifty years, a hundred years, and sometimes a thousand years.

Although we mention the miracles that transpired for Daniel in the lion's den or miracles performed on behalf of Ḥananya, Mishael, and Azarya in the fiery furnace, we don't commemorate them with a holiday. Why? Because these are miracles that were performed for specific people, but they didn't change the face of a historical reality. What remains for the generations from Ḥananya, Mishael, and Azarya isn't the miracle they survived, but the fact that they entered the fiery furnace. From Daniel, Ḥananya, Mishael, and Azarya, as well as from the miracle of Abraham when he was thrown into the fiery furnace in Ur, no promise remains. After the incident involving Ḥananya, Mishael, and Azarya or after Abraham's entry into the fiery furnace, God didn't promise us that any Jew will be able to enter a bonfire and emerge unscathed. What remains of these miraculous events are examples of self-sacrifice and strength to enter all sorts of furnaces for the sanctification of God's name. But our history is filled with martyrs who died for the sanctification of God's name – people who were actually burned in fiery furnaces and didn't emerge alive. Because the miracle doesn't endure, we don't commemorate these events as a holiday.

By contrast, there are events that have endured and haven't diminished over time, that are commemorated on the day that the event took place. We continue to rejoice and celebrate the event that transpired on that day. We don't observe Purim because we were in distress and emerged from it, but because Haman's accusations were general accusations against the Jewish people. Likewise, the fact that the Jews were exonerated goes far beyond the personal decision of a certain earthly king, but had significance the reverberated for generations to come. We celebrate Purim because the exoneration of the Jews is a decision that had ramifications for generations. It is for this reason that Purim, and likewise Hanukkah, will never be nullified.

THE HEAVENLY TRIAL ON YOD TET KISLEV

The earthly trial in the Russian court may be understood in the same way. The issue that was adjudicated was a substantive problem on earth but also a heavenly issue. The question was to what extent was the hasidic approach even permitted, given that Hasidism did not distinguish between learned, righteous men and Jews who might be ignoramuses.

There was great concern that disseminating the approach of Hasidism to the public, even to those who were not prominent Torah scholars, to Jews who lacked the capacity to properly grasp the ideas and teachings, would cause more harm than good. Perhaps the philosophy of Hasidism, which included the concept of the revelation of God in everything and the virtue of every Jew, would lead to chaos. Perhaps it would result in a decrease in Torah study and a denigration of God's majesty.

The question was whether the generation was capable of grasping the teachings of Hasidism in a way that would lead to ascent and elevation. If the generation was unfit, exposing them to the hasidic approach could cause more harm than good.

This was the deliberation that took place with regard to Hasidism, and it was to this criticism that it needed to respond.

When the earthly court determined that it was appropriate and permitted to leave the hasidim alone to worship as they pleased in the world below, a much greater and more comprehensive ruling was also issued on high.

According to this understanding, the celebration of Yod Tet Kislev is much more than a commemoration of a miracle that transpired for our ancestors or rabbis. The salvation that took place was also an acceptance of the validity of hasidic worship. And even though there was opposition to this divine ruling from time to time, ultimately it has remained in effect until today.

INTERNALIZING THE FESTIVALS

What is the essence of Yod Tet Kislev? In fact, what is the point of rejoicing and celebration on holidays in general?

In essence, exceptional days in the course of the year are special in and of themselves, even if we wouldn't mark them. It's almost as though they are already sanctified, independent of whether or not we take note of it, just as it is written that Shabbat "stands sanctified"[5]. Passover is Passover and Purim is Purim, whether or not a person celebrates them. At their very essence, these days are special.

Why, then, are we obligated to hold a feast, to rejoice and perform the other actions done in honor of a certain day or festival? We do it, not in order to institute the day, but rather to internalize the day. The day exists, and we celebrate and do everything associated with that day in order to transfer something from its reality into our own existence. A person must arrive at the festival with that state of mind: to come to an awareness of the unique elements of that particular festival. He need not facilitate the institution of these elements, but rather feel and absorb them.

Likewise, when one participates in a farbrengen on Yod Tet Kislev, he doesn't do so in order to celebrate the day. If it's an inherently festive day, it will celebrate itself. Rather, the farbrengen allows him to incorporate the festival within him. In this way, he draws something of the objective experience into himself so that it will take effect within his reality – not only from without, but also within.

A QUESTION OF RELEVANCE

It isn't possible to absorb the deeper meaning behind the day by external means. It's possible only from within. Nothing external, no amount of food and drink, can change anything in that regard. If a person decides that it won't affect him, then it won't affect him.

This is true with regard to every festival and celebration. A person can decide the holiday is someone else's holiday: Passover is someone else's Passover; Purim is someone else's Purim, and so forth. And no

5. *Beitza* 17a.

one can compel him to render the festival his festival. The question of the extent to which the festival will affect a person depends on the steps he himself takes in order to internalize it.

This is the fundamental point: The teachings of Torah and Hasidism have real significance only if they are relevant to him. It's a matter of intent, of the decision that they are relevant to him and touch him.

The difference between an act that has relevance to a person and an act that does not have relevance hinges on the circumstances. For example, I came here today from a wedding in which I had some involvement, and then I stopped in at another wedding. The two weddings were very similar, but in terms of my feelings about them, they were very different. The difference between them was that one wedding was mine because I was involved in it, while the second wedding was someone else's wedding.

Likewise, when a person attends the funeral of a person he doesn't know, perhaps in the interest of etiquette he won't smile, he will even sigh a bit, but he won't do anything beyond that, because it doesn't touch him and it's not relevant to him.

A great tragedy could transpire, the entire world could be upended, but it still might not touch a person. Someone could read an article in the newspaper about an earthquake in which tens of thousands of people were killed. Even if he is mildly upset about it, it's still nothing more than an article in the newspaper. Why? It's because he doesn't care. And because he doesn't care, the enormity of the event is irrelevant. But when the tragedy relates directly to him, he reacts very differently.

One time I read an account in a book about two friends who were standing by a riverbank and saw another friend stumble and his jacket fell into the river. Both of them stood there laughing when one of them suddenly realized that it hadn't been the friend's jacket that had been lost. It turned out that the friend had mistakenly taken his jacket, and it was really his own jacket that fell into the river. His mood changed in an instant from amusement to anger. What happened? The event didn't change at all: A jacket was still floating in the river. The change was that it was no longer his friend's jacket but his jacket. When it was the friend's jacket, it was funny. Now that it was his jacket, it was upsetting.

When a person attends a farbrengen, he must, first and foremost, decide that he is participating, that it has relevance to him, that he will not listen to what is said as an uninvolved bystander but as someone to whom the matters addressed are personal. After that decision, the entire experience, his entire attitude, can change in an instant.

THE BOOKS SPEAK ONLY TO ME

Actually, this does not apply only to a farbrengen. In certain respects, the whole essence of Hasidism is based on the person relating to matters as being relevant to him.

There are many things about which a person, especially if he is a Torah scholar, can say, "It is written in the holy books," and still feel that they don't relate to him. Just as a person can trade in merchandise without necessarily partaking of it, so can a person trade in the fear of Heaven without partaking of it. He knows what's written in the holy books and he sells the merchandise wholesale or retail, according to its worth, and he earns what he earns. But none of it affects him profoundly.

One of the initial stages of a person's entry into Hasidism is the moment he realizes that hasidic books and teachings aren't someone else's business. They are not merchandise that one trades, but rather they relate to him as an individual. When that moment comes, the picture changes completely.

Imagine someone entering a room in the middle of a conversation, and he overhears people disparaging someone: So-and-so, without mentioning his name, is a thief and a swindler, a liar and a hypocrite, and more. The newcomer sits and listens, and if the conversation is particularly interesting to him, he'll listen attentively, but if there's nothing new there, he won't pay much attention. He may even doze off. But imagine that after sitting there for half an hour, suddenly someone mentions the name of the person about whom they were speaking, and it turns out that the entire conversation was about him. At that moment, his entire attitude will change dramatically.

Rabbi Simḥa Bunim of Peshisḥa was seen one day looking pallid. When asked what happened, he answered that someone had insulted him terribly. Rabbi Simḥa Bunim tended to be sharp and incisive. When asked, "What did you do?" he answered, "I kissed him."

"But what happened?"

"I opened a *mussar* book," he related, "and saw that it was speaking about me, vilifying me. It was awful. I still feel downcast even now. When I closed the book, I kissed it."

Everyone is familiar with various ideas that are written in books. Being a hasid means that these books weren't written for some great rabbi but they were written for me, speaking about me. That is the essence of Hasidism: the ability to relate to matters as if they have relevance to me personally. Sometimes it's a decision a person must make. Either way, from the moment a person is able to make that decision, he hears everything in a totally different manner.

Leḥayim!

6

How to Attend a Farbrengen

GETTING TOGETHER AND HAVING A GOOD TIME

What are farbrengens? Why are they held? Since "farbrengen" is an unusual word, people ascribe some sort of divine meaning to it. The truth is that "farbrengen" is a neutral word that in Yiddish just means getting together and having a good time. At a farbrengen, people meet and come together.

When I was a boy, I went to study in a Lubavitch yeshiva. I didn't know much about Chabad Hasidism, and I was certainly unfamiliar with their colloquial phrases. When one of the other boys invited me to come to a farbrengen, I said to him, "I came here to study, not to have a good time." Eventually, it became clear to me that his intention wasn't exactly to have a good time.

So why don't they give this event a different name? Why call it by a name that implies something so superficial? When one invites a person to come and listen to the rabbi's sermon, a very interesting phenomenon ensues, which is tied to the physiology related to hearing. Many species of aquatic mammals – seals, sea lions, elephant seals – have a muscle in their ears that functions like an eyelid and can seal off the ears so water won't enter. People also have a similar "muscle": Whenever anyone invites them to come and listen to a discourse, it immediately seals off their ears. The rabbi can say whatever he pleases, speak of the heavens and the earth, but the ears remain blocked. (Incidentally, a similar phenomenon exists in children. When their father or mother reprimands them, they lower their heads, close their ears with these ear guards, and don't hear a thing.)

If such a person were to mark Yod Tet Kislev by listening to a Torah discourse, he would absorb nothing. Because we want to prevent the evil inclination from sealing off a person's ears, we call the gathering a farbrengen rather than a sermon. It's not a lecture or speech, but merely a get-together. When people come to a farbrengen to have a good time, as they would to a get-together, their ears remain open.

WHAT YOU REMEMBER

There's another meaning to the term "farbrengen." At a farbrengen, one doesn't attempt to convey a message or to deliver a planned speech. Sometimes a person hears words of wisdom at a farbrengen, and sometimes he doesn't. There are people who are seen with pen and paper in hand, writing down every Torah insight they hear. That's not the purpose of the teachings at a farbrengen. The question isn't about the quality of the discourse – whether there were novel Torah insights or whether nothing new was revealed. A farbrengen succeeds if those present were affected. The only objective of a farbrengen is to change people's lives. The farbrengen must provide some new perspective, or at least cause them to feel a little twinge. That is the essence of the farbrengen.

That's why the farbrengen is not an occasion where one person speaks and everyone listens. At a farbrengen, when one person speaks and another listens, the listening isn't supposed to be passive. It's supposed to be active, dynamic listening – listening where a person not only seeks to hear what is being said so that he'll be able to repeat it, but also the kind of listening where one seeks to internalize the content and consider whether it might be possible to do anything with it, to build upon it. If that element doesn't exist, nothing else matters.

A great hasidic rabbi once said to me, "At a farbrengen, what matters isn't what you hear. All that really matters is what you remember." Sometimes a person remembers only a single sentence or even two words. In that case, those two words are significant and all the rest is insignificant.

At first, there was significant opposition to writing about Hasidism. Some of the early hasidim claimed that when an idea is written down, it lose its vitality, and only practices that are transmitted orally will survive intact. Only teachings that are heard, especially those said by one person to another, can be truly absorbed. A hasidic leader once saw a page that contained writings about Hasidism in the garbage. He was angry and upset that something like this had been allowed to happen. The Baal HaTanya, in whose honor this celebration is being held, responded to his outrage with a parable:

One day the king's only son fell ill. They sought remedies for the prince's illness, to no avail, until a prominent doctor came and said that there was only one remedy: They must pulverize the diamond in the king's crown, place the powdered diamond in water, and attempt to pour it down the child's throat.

The king said, "If I don't have a son, why do I need a diamond? Why do I need a crown? The crown is dependent on my son's existence. If there is no son, what happens to the crown isn't important."

He handed over the diamond. By the time they had pulverized the diamond and prepared the elixir, the boy's condition had deteriorated to the extent that he was no longer able to open his mouth and swallow. They decided to pour the elixir on top of him in the hope that perhaps one drop would be absorbed into his body and he would be cured.

This parable that the Baal HaTanya offered to justify writing down the teachings of Hasidism is also true regarding the words spoken at a farbrengen. The question isn't what percentage of the expensive elixir was spilled but whether a drop was absorbed. If one drop was absorbed, the process of healing is initiated. If it wasn't absorbed, the quality of the substance or its exorbitant price is irrelevant. That's not what interests us. At the farbrengen, what was spilled isn't important; what matters is what was absorbed.

Everything I've said is intended to explain how one should approach what he hears at a farbrengen. A person's attitude toward the ideas he is offered will determine how much he will hear, what he will hear, how he will hear it, and what he will get out of it.

That's your job. I can't do it for you.

Ultimately, the purpose of the farbrengen is to generate resonance. If there is resonance – the farbrengen was successful. If there is none – all the words that were spoken essentially had no effect. In order for a farbrengen to have that kind of effect, a person must fine-tune himself until he is on the same wavelength as the matters being discussed. The objective of the farbrengen is for something to resonate with the one who hears it. The resonance is the essence of the matter, and in order to achieve it, fine-tuning is required.

The Day of Our Salvation and the Redemption of Our Soul

WHAT IS REDEMPTION OF THE SOUL?

In Chabad literature, Yod Tet Kislev is called "the day of our salvation and the redemption of our soul." This name even contains a halakhic element. According to *halakha*, when a person arrives at a place where a miracle transpired to his parents or his teacher, he is obligated to recite a blessing because the miracle didn't transpire only to his parents or his teacher, but its effects continue to reverberate through the generations. A person can and must express thanks for the miracle because, as a physical or spiritual descendant of the person for whom the miracle was performed, he benefits from the consequences of the miracle.

If I were interested in expounding on the miracle that is commemorated on Yod Tet Kislev, I could relate its history to you – what slander was told about the Baal HaTanya, how he was incarcerated, how he sat in prison, and how he emerged from there. Essentially, this was a political event in relation to world Jewry. At the time the Baal HaTanya was considered the most important representative of the hasidic movement. His trial and salvation were not that of a private individual, but of the entire hasidic movement. When he was set free, it spurred social and political changes.

Anyone who is interested can read about it in history books, where a more or less impartial account of the events can be found. Although it's an interesting and important subject, it's not what I want to discuss.

Instead, I want to talk about the name: "the day of our salvation and the redemption of our soul."

What is the "redemption of our soul"? This expression states something simple: We believe that every person has a soul. Moreover, we believe that every Jew has not only an animal soul, which infuses him with life on a basic level, but he also possesses a divine soul, which defines the part of him that is associated with holiness.

The problem is that on most days, the divine soul is imprisoned, even if not in a very harsh imprisonment. For this reason, it doesn't manifest itself. It's like a person who is sitting in prison. He is existing, but has no opportunity to express or develop himself.

This is, to a certain extent, reminiscent of the Kanovich law, which prohibits the emission of fumes from automobiles in the State of Israel, which would contribute to air pollution. The law was legislated more than thirty years ago, and it's well known as a law that no one ever bothered to implement. It appears in the book of laws, completely dormant.

The divine soul is often found in a similar condition: It exists, but it's completely dormant.

In that sense, Yod Tet Kislev is the day of the salvation and redemption of the divine soul from its imprisonment. When the soul is redeemed, it can finally express itself and be heard.

THE IMPRISONMENT OF THE SOUL

Theoretically, a person has a holy soul, and, theoretically, a person has sacred obligations. In reality, a person can dress like a hasid, and even act like a hasid, but his soul is not at all involved in the things he does.

The divine soul may find itself in all kinds of imprisonments. One of them relates to one of the most profound problems experienced by religious Jews. Since they learn to pray from the prayer book and recite blessings from childhood, they come to recite the words by rote, whether they understand them or not. In the meantime, their soul remains constricted and insignificant. One can sit and study Torah, fulfill *mitzvot*, and try not to violate too many prohibitions, but his soul isn't involved. Where is it? Apparently, it can be found somewhere in the seventh chamber of the sixth firmament, where it is dozing restfully.

A person can study in Torah institutions – a religious elementary school, a high-school yeshiva, and a post-high-school yeshiva – and he can attend Gemara lectures and be completely surrounded by Torah, but none of it touches his soul. All in all, the endeavor has no significance for him.

There are people who are punctilious about arriving at the prayer service precisely on time, because they are decent and organized by nature. Their prayers are also efficient, precise, and sophisticated. If only their cars ran so efficiently! These people are removed from the true meaning of prayer. They cover themselves with a Teflon coating about three millimeters thick so that the prayer itself will not, God forbid, have any effect on them.

The Midrash relates how Abraham would bring people closer to Torah when telling them to recite Grace after Meals. One can learn from this the extent to which one can become elevated by reciting Grace after Meals. But Abraham had one advantage over us: In his day, there were no booklets with the text of Grace after Meals. When he would say to someone, "Come and recite a blessing over the food," the person needed to think about what to say in order to recite that blessing. Perhaps, then, there was a moment of inspiration. Today, when we have booklets from which to recite the blessings, a person doesn't need to have even half a moment of inspiration. He takes out the booklet, recites what is written, and fulfills his obligation.

Several years ago, I went on an official visit to a Buddhist Lamaist monastery in a remote area on the Mongolian border. There I saw prayer wheels, a feature to be found in every Lamaist monastery. These are wheels on which prayers are written, and each person who passes spins the wheel – and it is as though he had prayed. (Now there's an innovation: Attach wings to the prayer wheels that can be moved by the wind or even by a small motor, and the wheel spins and prays on its own.…)

I mentioned this to the head of the monastery, a very intelligent young man. I said to him, half-jokingly, "Do you think you're the only ones who has a prayer wheel? We have something similar, but ours is in the form of a book. The difference is that your wheel makes a complete revolution, while our books make only half a revolution, front to back. One moves from one page to the next, and he thinks he's praying."

The reality is that often what people do in prayer and Torah study is merely turning pages.

Years ago, I was visiting England and met with several people. We conversed, moving from topic to topic, until we came to the subject of prayer. One of the men there, a pillar of the Jewish community who had served as *shamash* of the synagogue for sixty years, said to me, "You know, I've never prayed in my life."

I looked at him and said, "You've been going to the synagogue three times a day for sixty years and you've never prayed?"

"Oh, you mean davening!" he responded. In other words: You mean turning the pages and reciting a certain number of words. "I do a lot of davening. But praying? I haven't yet had occasion to do so."

The question is whether a person is inspired as a result of prayer. The question is about the state of his soul.

There are souls, even holy souls, that are in captivity in the depths of the *kelippot*, the forces of impurity that serve as barriers between man and God. Some people obscure their souls their entire lives, by escaping into drugs or other vices, but it's also possible to obscure one's soul by wrapping it in the pages of the *Kitzur Shulḥan Arukh*. Then, too, the soul doesn't emerge. Even if they sit all day in yeshiva, their soul remains a theoretical entity that doesn't manifest.

Sometimes I hear kindergarten children speaking about God and sense that their souls are speaking. When I encounter them ten years later, they know all the reverential names, but nothing touches their souls. When they were five, they had a soul. By the time they turned fifteen, they lost it, and by the age of twenty-five, it had already passed from the world.

The person remains alive, his body is still functioning, but he's dead inside. Such people are walking around like zombies – dead bodies without souls. They look like people, eat and drink like people, sometimes even procreate, but their soul is missing from the picture.

There is a verse written regarding Sennacherib's army. "They arose in the morning, and behold, they were all dead corpses."[1] I suggest reading it with a new interpretation: People wake up in the morning, open

1. II Kings 19:35.

their eyes, and discover that "behold, they were all dead corpses." All these dead corpses then get out of bed, and go and do all kinds of things, but without a soul.

All this is to tell you that it's essential to save the soul. That is "our salvation and the redemption of our soul."

THE DIFFICULTY IN WAKING UP

Beyond what was described above, religious Jews have an additional problem that exacerbates the situation. A non-religious person has a chance, even if it's not a good chance, to wake up. It happens that something suddenly affects him, sometimes a calamity, sometimes unrequited love, sometimes even great success – some event that liberates his soul and sets him on a search for the right path. Sometimes people like that achieve an awakening of the soul; sometimes they also find their way to a life of Torah and *mitzvot.*

By contrast, someone who was born religious and lives as a religious person can't achieve such an awakening because when an event of that kind befalls him, he will simply say, "*Barukh Hashem*" (blessed is God) and continue on his way. "*Barukh Hashem*" is the Hebrew equivalent of "no comment." It says nothing, neither yes nor no. These expressions – "*barukh Hashem,*" "*im yirtzeh Hashem*" (if God wills it), "*be'ezrat Hashem*" (with the help of God) – are all empty shells that serve to conceal the emptiness within.

But someone who wasn't born religious could have occasion to read a *siddur* and suddenly notice the beautiful content it contains, and his soul will be inspired. That never happens to the religious. At most, they debate whether they should pronounce the phrase for "long life" in the prayers for Rosh Ḥodesh as *ḥayim arukim* or *ḥayim arukhim,* or whether the emphasis should be placed on the first or last syllable of a certain word.

Moreover, when the soul of a religious person awakens, he may do nothing more than shake more vigorously while praying. For a *lulav,* that's effective; for a soul, it certainly isn't. It's not my intent to disparage religious people or say that this is true of everyone. I'm merely speaking about what happens to the soul, about the awakening of the soul.

PAY ATTENTION TO THE SPIRIT

"Our salvation and the redemption of our soul" is tied to the essence of Hasidism. It's for this reason that on Yod Tet Kislev, which is called the New Year of Hasidism, we attempt to redeem our souls, to save the spirit. Hasidism does not hinge on appearances or mode of dress. A goat has a beard, but clearly it's not a hasid.

What transforms a person into a hasid? They say that the difference between a hasid and one who opposes Hasidism is that the word for "opponent," *mitnaged,* begins with the letters that spell death, *met,* and the word *hasid* contains the letters the mean life, *ḥai.* The soul of a hasid is more alive. Regarding the verse "Man became a living soul,"[2] Rashi states, "Are there souls that are not living? It means, rather, that Adam's soul was the most alive of them all." A hasid is someone who, at least on occasion, experiences an awakening and shouts, "What happened to my soul? Where did my soul go? Maybe when I was five, it experienced an awakening of sorts, but what has happened since then?"

Hasidism is tied to the salvation and redemption of the soul. It inspires a person to wake up and to ask himself, "What happened to my soul? Maybe on Yom Kippur, during *Ne'ila* prayer, my soul had an awakening of sorts, and I remembered that I had a soul. But what has happened since then?"

There is a liturgical poem that begins with the words "Pay attention to the soul." The call to pay attention to the soul is the essence of Hasidism. It inspires a person to ask whether he ever encountered his soul, whether he ever greeted it. It inspires a person to ask his soul, "Are you still in this world or are you already dead?"

How does one awaken the soul from slumber, from unconsciousness, from a coma, from clinical death? To begin to awaken the soul and save it, we hold a farbrengen, sing melodies, drink whiskey. When a part of the body is covered with dead flesh, one must cut away the dead flesh in order to reach the living flesh. Likewise, it's necessary to cut and dig deep in order to reach the place where words of prayer or words of the farbrengen will touch him. At the farbrengen, we loosen up a little with

2. Genesis 2:7.

whiskey so that something will penetrate. Then we sing a melody in order to process what entered. In that way, perhaps a word will be able to get through and have an effect.

Sometimes a person despairs and says, "What can I do? I was born religious. That led to my inability to genuinely manifest the fear of Heaven. What else can I do?"

No matter how difficult it is, he must pay attention to his soul and continue to search. The first thing that can be done, even if the person is not on that level, is to pray for it. A person can wake up every morning and implore, "Master of the universe, the soul that You placed within me – can You perhaps return it to me? Not only the soul that controls digestion, the *nefesh ha'ochelet,* 'the eating soul' – that soul, the *nefesh,* has existed and functioned for a long time. I'm seeking the divine soul. What is happening to that soul?"

What Remains from the Awakening

THE REMNANTS OF SONG

When one has times of awakening of the soul, of inspiration, the bottom line is, what remains from this awakening?

That's the way many people interpret the words of the *Yishtabaḥ* blessing: "He who chooses songs of praise [*shirei zimra*]." *Shirei zimra* can also connote *sheyarim,* "remnants." This implies that God "chooses the remnants of song." He doesn't so much care whether a person prays in this manner or in that manner. The question is what remnants linger after the song has ended. The experience itself isn't always the most important criterion. It doesn't matter whether I swayed during prayers for half an hour or for one and a half hours. What's important is what happens afterward.

What does one do when the soul is awakened? Often a person will make resolutions. Sometimes people leave a farbrengen with a firm decision to change. But a resolution of that sort is typically not very effective.

On Rosh HaShana and Yom Kippur as well, people make resolutions from which very little remains. If you want to know what really happens on Yom Kippur, after people fasted all day and then came to the *Ne'ila* prayer and were ostensibly elevated to a lofty level, after shouting seven times, "The Lord, He is God," take a look and see whether they pounce on food after the fast concludes. It often turns out that even if a person starved his wretched body, inside he didn't change at all.

One of the reasons for this is that people take on abstract resolutions on Yom Kippur. A person resolves that from now on he will be better. But abstract resolutions aren't enough. One of the things one learns in the study of exact sciences is that an approximate answer isn't a good answer. Whether one is solving an equation or constructing a machine, one must calibrate and quantify, define and reduce. One can't depend on "approximately."

This is especially true regarding complex apparatuses. The more complex the apparatus, the less it can be based on inexact calculations. A person himself, his soul and being, is exceedingly complex, and so inexact resolutions have little meaning and substance.

When a person's soul is stirred by any kind of awakening, he must, first and foremost, attempt to focus his efforts on a one specific point because it's impossible to move forward when one is spread all over the place. When a military unit seeks to breach a barrier, it concentrates as great a force as possible at a contact point that is as narrow as possible. When attempting to solve a mathematical problem as well, one must focus on a specific point in the problem. The same is true in mechanics and in many other areas.

For the awakening and inspiration to be substantive, one must channel them to a specific address and not be satisfied with generalities. One must translate the general suggestions, the wide-ranging statements, and the internal and external declarations into specific actions. Things move forward, are accomplished, and succeed in this world only through concrete action. Even if the action is exceedingly minor, it's a breakthrough. One need not begin with a great tempest or sea change. When a person is able to focus on a particular point, he begins to take action.

NO OTHER BESIDES HIM

The bottom line is substantively tied to the attention paid to the soul. A person could ask: "What do they want from me? I wake up in the morning, wash my hands, and recite the morning prayers. I say blessings before and after eating breakfast. I do everything I'm supposed to do. What else do they want from me?" Even if a person fulfills all the *mitzvot*, avoids all the prohibitions, and gets through the day unscathed, it's still appropriate to ask: What value am I left with from this day?

In the *Tanya* and other works, it is written that a person should conduct a reckoning at the end of every day. When a person thinks before he goes to sleep, *So what happened today? What am I left with from today?* sometimes he finds that he is left with something major, sometimes something minor, and sometimes nothing at all. But even if a person discovers that he's left with nothing at all, at least he goes to sleep with the knowledge that he is left with nothing, and he feels like someone who goes to sleep hungry.

This is the test of life in general. Imagine conducting an objective summary of a person's life: So-and-so, son of so-and-so, was born on such-and-such day. In the course of his life, he ate several tons of bread, several pounds of meat, drank this many gallons of water, left behind this many tons of excrement and urine. After all that, what else remains? Does anything of value remain?

That is the test of the remnants of a life.

Sometimes a person says, "I'm already a lost cause. My children are my hope." The problem is that his children do the same: They live a life without value and hope that their children will do what needs to be done. One *tzaddik* said that he is waiting to see the ultimate child for whom all these generations worked....

A person must apply this test to his own life: "I ate, drank, rested, prayed, studied. What am I left with after all that? Does anything of value remain?"

A question like that – which is not a broad question about morality, but rather a very focused question – a question like that should make a person feel like he's had an electric shock of sorts, like the electroconvulsive treatment used to treat people suffering from mental illness.

Let me tell you a hasidic tale about reckonings:

In a certain village, there lived a wealthy hasid who was a jewel merchant. One night, he was sitting in his room and calculating the daily totals of his accounts. As would happen in those days, someone peered through the window and saw him sitting and writing a list: "I bought such and such. I sold such and such. These are the expenditures, and this is the income." At the end, he wrote, "Bottom line." But then, instead of summing it up, he remained motionless. He sat and thought for several moments and then wrote under the tally of numbers, "Bottom line: There is no other besides Him."

What happens to a person who, when he comes to write something banal like "bottom line," begins contemplating, *Really, what is the bottom line? Is the bottom line that I earned five hundred and twenty rubles and sixteen kopeks?* When a person thinks seriously about the bottom line, those reckonings are no longer important. "Bottom line: There is no other besides Him."

I'm not saying that one should emulate that merchant. Still, when a person sits at the end of the day and contemplates the bottom line, sometimes the bottom line is that he did one thing of value, that he had one moment of inspiration, that he at least felt the desire to further elevate himself, even if he didn't actualize that desire. These are the things that remain, the remnants he is left with. These are the things that are important in life.

THE MEASURE OF TRUTH

In hasidic literature, there are no words of *mussar*, no words of chastisement, no discussion of this sin or that one. Rather, it addresses the question, What are the real, substantive elements in life? The truth is that I think that a person's list of sins doesn't interest even the heavenly host, because there, too, they deal with the question of whether there was anything of substance in his actions.

This explains the two contradictory approaches that can be found in hasidic literature. On one hand, there is harsh criticism of people's actions in terms of Torah and *mitzvot*. In one work, for example, there is a description of a person who lost consciousness and was dying. He saw in a dream that his Torah study and service of God were being judged. They brought all the letters of the Torah he had studied and the words he had prayed – thousands upon thousands of letters – and then the prosecuting angel came and said, "Is this Torah? Is this prayer?" All the letters flew aside, and from all the words of Torah studied and prayers prayed, perhaps only one letter remained intact.

In contrast to this harsh criticism, some prominent hasidic leaders specifically advocated in favor of the Jewish people regarding insignificant matters. The shows the greatness of a deed performed by even the most unworthy.

These two aspects aren't contradictory. This is not hypercriticism on the one hand and mercy on the other, but rather a different method of evaluation and assessment. One could come to conclusions about a person's merits based on the title he holds – *HaRav HaGaon, HaRav HeḤakham, HaRav HaTzaddik.* But though these titles make an impression, they aren't serious determinants of worth. By contrast, a person might seem inconsequential, yet still perform actions of great significance. That is the common denominator between the two approaches.

It is related that Rabbi Levi Yitzḥak of Berditchev saw a simple Jew adorned with *tallit* and *tefillin* tarring the wheels of his wagon while praying. Others saw this Jew praying while working and criticized him harshly. Rabbi Levi Yitzḥak said, "Master of the universe, what an upright Jew! Even when tarring the wheels of his wagon, he prays and dons *tefillin*."

That's one method of assessing reality: seeing prayer as a great accomplishment for a person whose mind, heart, and life revolve around his horse and wagon. By contrast, when a man who is wise, learned, and God-fearing does other things while praying, it's possible that by doing so he nullifies and devalues his prayers.

Both approaches are correct. Both measure truth according to the particular person, his internal world, and his circumstances, and both take into consideration the question, To what extent are matters of sanctity a part of his world?

THE CRITICAL STAGE

When a person seeks to adopt resolutions and effect change in his life, he shouldn't expect significant changes to happen in a single moment. On the contrary, anyone who thinks he can reach Heaven in a single bound isn't a serious person. Even racing cars don't go from zero to two hundred miles an hour in an instant.

Instead, a person should try to progress in increments, to resolve to do something that is minuscule, provided that it is genuine. That's true progress. False prayer, false Torah, and the false world are recognized as false when held up against divine truth.

Rabbi Avraham Dov of Avritch was the rabbi and the leader of the Ashkenazic community of Tzefat, and he rebuilt it after it was destroyed in the great earthquake of 1837. I heard that he said this: "When I was young and lived in the Diaspora, I would ask God to grant me the merit of praying one *Amida* prayer properly. After I grew older and became wiser, I decided that I would ask for the merit of reciting even one blessing properly. Then I moved to the Land of Israel. Since the atmosphere of the land renders one wise, I asked for the privilege of reciting even one word properly."

If a person were to recite just one word properly, that word would ignite a spark of truth. Sometimes a single "woe" that a person utters is equivalent to the entire Torah.

This leap is actually the essence of redemption. Redemption is a type of leap – sometimes from one end of the earth to the other, but sometimes an infinitesimal jump of one electron from one place to another – but always a leap. It need not be a great leap from the edge of the heavens to the ends of the earth. In order to ensure that one isn't entrenched all his life in the same route, striding along the same course in which there is no spiritual advancement, sometimes even a small change is sufficient, provided there is at least some movement.

Redemption is the willingness to leap. That very willingness to go beyond the familiar routine and leap to a different stage – that's what generates the change.

For Yod Tet Kislev to be a festival of redemption, it is necessary to leap – to take a risk and lose one's equilibrium in order to move to another medium. Only in this way it is it possible to achieve real change. A person could read ten books about swimming, but he still wouldn't know how to swim. The only way to learn how to swim is to enter the water and let the feet to disengage from dry land.

This is true regarding virtually all areas of science. There is always a critical stage. Jets, for example, have a critical speed. If a jet doesn't reach that speed, it will remain grounded; it will never be able to take off and fly. There are chemical reactions that require critical heat and physical reactions that require a critical mass. Less than that and the action won't happen at all, no matter how long one waits.

Similarly, the objective of all the talk of salvation is to create a critical mass that will cause the situation to change. If until now a person walked at a certain speed and performed certain actions that led nowhere, he must make a change. It need not be a drastic change. It could be minor, but it must be significant. When one moves things to the point of critical change, the jet will take off; the person will begin to move. This is a continuous process until it reaches the critical point. Then, in a single moment of minor change – redemption happens.

DID I MOVE?

As I said, when a farbrengen ends, the important question is not how the whiskey was, how the speeches were, whether it was a nice farbrengen. The important question is whether I remember anything. If I do, the farbrengen had value. If something touched me, it had great value. If something penetrated, its value was even greater. If I moved even slightly as a result of the farbrengen, that movement justifies the convening of the entire farbrengen. The main thing is, as I said, that one succeeds in making a change, in growing and achieving, not merely when making abstract resolutions, but when a resolution, however minuscule, is actualized. Instead of thinking about the ideas, they think the ideas themselves. Instead of speaking about them – they speak them. Instead of walking around in circles – they make a change, a movement forward, in practice. That's the main thing, and everything else is insignificant.

Inertia, which keeps objects in place, is a terrible thing. It keeps the trivialities in place and keeps the person, too, in his place. Because of it, a person can remain in the same place for five or ten years, perhaps even for seventy years. It could be that in the end, at the last moment, he has thoughts that tell him that it's worthwhile to make a change, but then he takes his last breath and the inertia ceases forever.

In order to generate change during his lifetime, a person must drag himself, his past, his present, his business, everything he owns, and move them all. This is hard work, but it must be done, because only if he breaks the inertia will change take place. After that, who knows how matters will develop?

At that moment, at that point in time, any change that a person is able to effect – even if it's incomplete, even if it's minuscule – is critical and has tremendous value.

Leḥayim!

24 Tevet
The Hilula of the Baal HaTanya

On the twenty-fourth of Tevet, the founder of Lubavitch Hasidism, Rabbi Shneur Zalman of Liadi, also known as the Baal HaTanya, passed away.

Rabbi Shneur Zalman was born in the village of Liozno in Belarus on the eighteenth of Elul, in the year 1745. In his youth, he was recognized as a genius of exceptional ability. A few years after he married, he went to Mezeritch to study Torah with the Maggid, Rabbi Dov Ber, who was the Baal Shem Tov's successor. In Mezeritch, Rabbi Shneur Zalman, the youngest of the disciples, joined a group that would eventually disseminate Hasidism throughout Eastern Europe.

Rabbi Shneur Zalman became renowned for his erudition in both revealed and esoteric aspects of the Torah. The Maggid of Mezeritch charged him with writing the great halakhic work that became known as *Shulḥan Arukh HaRav*. His other masterwork, *Likkutei Amarim*, or the *Tanya* as it is famously known, is one of the fundamental works on the philosophy of Hasidism.

Rabbi Shneur Zalman was active in the leadership of the hasidic movement, in addition to serving as Rebbe to his adherents and others who sought his spiritual guidance. He was also involved in politics when he saw it was necessary. He helped organize financial support for a group of hasidim, disciples of the Maggid, who had emigrated to the Land of Israel under the leadership of Rabbi Menaḥem Mendel of Vitebsk in 1777. He was also a central figure in the dispute between the hasidim and their opponents, beginning with his attempts at reconciliation and dialogue with the Vilna Gaon in 1774. His political activism was also exhibited when he represented Hasidism in public debates, for example, in Minsk in 1783, and it culminated in his incarceration by Russian authorities, based on information provided by one of his rivals from the camp of the opponents, in 1799.

In his later years, Rabbi Shneur Zalman stood at the center of a vehement intra-hasidic dispute, which was directed primarily against the intellectual aspects of the Lubavitcher approach to Jewish life. Rabbi Shneur Zalman was openly opposed to Napoleon's invasion of Russia because of the potential negative influence that the emancipation – promised to the Jews by the French – would have on their spiritual outlook. As the French army advanced and the Russian army retreated, he was forced to flee to Russia's interior. He fell ill on the way and died on the twenty-fourth of Tevet, in 1813. He was buried in the village of Haditch.

Rabbi Shneur Zalman left behind a legacy that has had an impact to his day. He was the founder of the Lubavitch branch of Hasidism, also known as Chabad, an acronym in Hebrew for *ḥokhma,* wisdom, *bina,* understanding, and *daat,* knowledge, a reflection of the Lubavitch approach to hasidic philosophy, of which he was the creator and consolidator. He was the first in a dynasty of Rebbes who have led Lubavitch hasidim for seven generations.

His work on hasidic thought, the *Tanya,* delineates the theological philosophy of Lubavitch Hasidism in a systematic and fundamental way. It also includes a detailed plan of action for those who seek to advance in their service of God. As those who study the *Tanya* can attest, Rabbi Shneur Zalman's hasidic doctrine is both thorough and broad in scope.

In addition to the *Tanya,* dozens of volumes of his hasidic discourses have been published. After his release from prison, he felt that the time was right to expand the ranks of Lubavitch Hasidism and disseminate its Torah among the public. The discourses he delivered during that period became more explicit and also more expansive. This becomes particularly evident when comparing his writing style to that of others in his generation.

Rabbi Shneur Zalman, the Baal HaTanya, remains a mentor not only to those who follow the path of Lubavitch Hasidism, but to others as well. On the anniversary of his passing, we remember his personality and his approach.

Rabbi Steinsaltz taught the Torah of the Baal HaTanya extensively, and in many ways, he chose to live his life following a path that was illuminated by the light of Rabbi Shneur Zalman.

In the farbrengens held on 24 Tevet, Rabbi Steinsaltz would delve into the world of the Baal HaTanya and elaborate on his understanding of his teachings and works. Rabbi Steinsaltz didn't discuss the Torah of the Baal HaTanya as a theoretical subject. For him, the Baal HaTanya's teachings constituted a practical, insistent demand for every Jew to follow the path that Rabbi Shneur Zalman paved for us.

7

The Essence of a *Hilula*

MOURNING AND LOSS

To celebrate a *yartzeit* in most communities today, a little whiskey and a little cake brought to the synagogue will suffice. But for many generations in the past, the *yartzeit* was marked by fasting.

But even when one treats a *yartzeit* as a day of mourning, the sadness is for the mourners rather than for the deceased, as we find in an ancient eulogy from talmudic times: "Cry for the mourners and not for the lost, as he has gone to his rest, while we are left with sighs."[1] On a *yartzeit*, a sense of loss is aroused in the mourners, whether they have lost an elderly father or a young child, whether those grieving got over their pain and distress quickly or the absence of the loved was still felt acutely over the course of many years. This is the meaning of "cry for the mourners" – the mourner is the one who feels the loss.

As for the deceased, we believe that the soul of the deceased is at rest. But at rest how? There are people who think their deceased ancestors are sitting on high, eating, drinking, and enjoying themselves. They also take comfort in the thought that the day will come when they will be reunited with their loved ones. But these imaginings are erroneous; the world on high is different from our world. This whole way of

1. *Mo'ed Katan* 25b.

thinking – as well as questions like how their deceased parents feel, how they look, whether they seem to be in good health, and so on – are all fantastic imaginings that are in no way descriptive of the World to Come. If one delves into the subject, it becomes clear that something very different happens to the deceased.

DISENGAGEMENT FROM THIS WORLD

What befalls the soul of the deceased? First of all, when the soul passes from this world, it undergoes a period of disengagement from the matters of this world. When the soul was in this world, it wasn't isolated from the person's affairs. The soul isn't like a ray of light that enters a house and leaves as it entered, unchanged. The soul was involved in this world and in the life of the person with whom it had been associated. Each soul is involved in a person's life to a degree that is based on that person's own particular circumstances. In order for a soul to be able to enter the Garden of Eden, it must undergo a process of disengagement from this material world.

This does not only involve disengagement from sin, which is a relatively quick process: It is written that the souls of the wicked are judged in Gehenna for a total of twelve months. Rather, it is a disengagement from the affairs of this world. When a soul reaches the heavenly world, it remembers all the events that befell it in this world, and these events are much more colorful than life in the World to Come. It's impossible for the soul to be introduced into a heavenly world in such a state. The soul must undergo a period of clarification so that it can begin to forget what the *Zohar* calls the "sights of this world."

Imagine a person who was a grocer in this world. All his days revolved around his grocery store. Imagine that when he reaches the heavenly world, he is immediately seated on a golden chair and is told to sit and learn Gemara. How long will he be able to endure, knowing that this will be his sole occupation day after day? It's not a person's sins that prevent him from entering the Garden of Eden. The issue is what will happen to him once he enters the Garden of Eden. What will he do there? For a person whose entire life centered around making money or losing money or building a house, his soul must undergo a process of purification and refinement before he can appreciate the heavenly world, where all materiality is meaningless.

THE SOUL IN THE WORLD OF THE IMAGINATION

In the books in which this process of refinement is described, it doesn't say how long the duration of the process lasts. It's conceivable that certain souls may undergo refinement over the course of twenty years. Throughout that time, it finds itself in the world of the imagination. This world is neither a reward nor a punishment. A person sometimes resides there without knowing that he's already dead.

Ultimately, what we know of the world stems from within ourselves, not from what is external to us. External matters enter our soul within, and it's there that they speak to us. Because of this, when a person passes on from this world, where throughout his life his soul was filled exclusively with matters of this world, it continues to experience the same experiences to which it was accustomed in life. A person who engaged in business during his lifetime can continue to engage in business in the heavenly world as well. Angels will circulate around him and provide him with business opportunities that will generate a fine profit. He will come to his imaginary house and tell his imaginary wife how much he earned today, and so on. Some souls exist in this sort of limbo for many, many years. They have no recourse because they live in a world that is familiar to them – a world that leads to neither good nor bad.

A story is told of a hasid who lived this way in the world of the imagination, but every few months he would wake up and say, "I must travel to the Rebbe." Angels of destruction would appear in the guise of people and would say to him, "You're busy now. It would make sense for you to postpone this trip."

From year to year he would postpone the trip until one day he insisted that he must travel to the Rebbe. The moment he arrived, the Rebbe delivered him from the world of imagination.

Another story is told about a wagon driver who died and reached the heavenly world. In the court on high, they decided that he deserved a great reward because he had saved people who traveled in his wagon from death. One who saves the life of a single Jew is considered to have saved an entire world; all the more so someone who saved several people. They asked him how wanted to be rewarded. He said, "I want a good smooth road, one without holes or curves, and a wagon hitched to four fine horses." They fulfilled his request, and today he's still driving his wagon down the smooth road. Perhaps he'll do so forever....

Sometimes a person requires a period of refinement even before he can enter Gehenna. Long after the death of the Talmudic sage Elisha ben Avuya (who became a heretic), the Sages needed to pray that he be allowed to enter Gehenna.[2] What did his soul do in the meanwhile? He relaxed and sang Greek songs, just as he had done during his lifetime in this world. Perhaps he even had new Torah insights, an activity in which he engaged until his final day. He continued to exist in that imaginary limbo until he entered Gehenna.

Similarly, in Rabbi Naḥman's story titled "An Incident with a Wise Man and a Simpleton," the wise man died and was taken to Gehenna but remained convinced that he was still in this world and that he could sue the demons for abducting and torturing him. Gehenna was of no avail to him.

WHAT IS A SON?

At a certain point, the soul begins to forget this world and the experiences related to it. The things that filled the person's life in this world are no longer of interest to him.

This happens in life as well as in the afterlife: We can become detached from material things that define us.

I once met a Jew who sold soda and sweets in a small kiosk next to the Russian Compound in Jerusalem. I had heard that he had been a millionaire in Romania before World War II. The Germans took everything he had, and eventually he emigrated to Israel. Since it isn't possible to earn a living in Jerusalem from having once been a millionaire in Romania, he sold items in a kiosk. I never spoke with him about his past, but it seems to me that he didn't spend all of his time thinking about the days when he had been on top of the world. Maybe he thought about

2. *Ḥagiga* 15b.

his previous life as a memory recorded in a diary. In the present, he was living a totally different life.

Every person undergoes similar transformations. Everyone goes through childhood, but after several years, what occurred during childhood fades. The memories remain, but the person moves on. This is what happens through the various milestones that a person passes in life: He tends to forget not only the bad, which we have a tendency to forget more readily, but he even forgets the good. As a person's circumstances evolve, so does his reality, and he forgets what came before. This is even more true when a person passes on to the heavenly world.

As the soul gradually disengages from the stimuli of this world, it slowly forgets everything he had there, even family. The story is told of Rabbi Mordekhai, one of the renowned *tzaddikim* of Chernobyl, who sought to ask his deceased father, Rabbi Naḥum, a great *tzaddik* in his own right, to intercede on high to help reverse an edict decreed against the Jewish people. Rabbi Mordekhai found a person who was dying, appointed him as his messenger, and sent him to tell his father about the problems facing the nation. Rabbi Mordekhai asked him to intercede on high, since he couldn't do so down below.

When the emissary reached the chamber where Rabbi Naḥum of Chernobyl dwelled on high and passed on the message, Rabbi Naḥum asked him, "Who sent you?"

"Your son," the emissary replied.

"What is a son?" was Rabbi Naḥum's response.

After spending time in the heavenly world, Rabbi Naḥum had forgotten what a son is.

Another story is told about a certain hasid who had grown old. His children were all married, and his wife had passed away. Alone, he decided to stay at the home of his Rebbe, where he was provided with room and board, and spend the rest of his days studying Torah and serving God. Several years passed when his daughter realized that she hadn't been in contact with her father for a very long time. When she discovered that he was still alive, she set out and traveled to the place where he was staying.

The hasid's daughter requested that he be called outside so that she could speak with him. When he came out, she asked him various questions. He courteously answered all her questions, and she quickly realized that he didn't recognize her. So many years had passed since their last meeting that he had completely forgotten who she was in the interim.

She wept and said to him, "Father, have you forgotten me?"

"Do not weep. Had I died, you would certainly have forgotten me. Does it make any difference that I'm alive?"

The prophet Isaiah asks, "Can a woman forget her baby? To be merciful to the child of her womb?"[3] But the verse continues: "These, too, may forget." Perhaps it will take a long time, but after one hundred years in the Garden of Eden, even a mother forgets her child.

This happens to everyone. A person accrues a certain amount of knowledge in this world, but when he arrives in the next word, he forgets all of it. Not just inconsequential things, like the memory of a stomachache or that of eating in a fine restaurant. Even very consequential matters also cease to be significant. Matters that relate to this world have no importance in the world in which a person finds himself after death. When a person is in the heavenly realm, engaged in other matters one way or another, his past, including people who were a part of his life in this world, are forgotten.

THE SOULS OF THE SHEPHERDS OF ISRAEL

This description is true regarding ordinary upright Jews. After a certain amount of time, the souls of these people are elevated, and they disengage from this world. The process is different for the souls of certain *tzaddikim*. These are souls that arrive in this world in a new incarnation but not as a punishment or to atone for sins, as would be the case for an ordinary person.

In a past life, these souls performed what they needed to do in this world. When they arrived in the heavenly world, God then requested or decreed that they descend to this world again. He said to the soul, "You did well, but the world needs you now. As uncomfortable as it may be for you, please descend again to the world below and do what needs to be done there."

3. Isaiah 49:15.

Souls of that sort descend to the world as true leaders of Israel. The connection between such a person and this world is odd. On one hand, he lives in the world like other people; he has a body and all the other elements that ordinary people have. On the other hand, he doesn't really belong in this world. He volunteered to reside here and tend to others, to listen as they relate their troubles to him. One person tells him that he has problems with his wife or with his children. Another tells him that he has problems making a living. Such a *tzaddik* is like a person who volunteers in a children's orphanage. The children aren't his, but they need help, and he helps them. He devotes himself to them and what befalls them.

Unlike others whose ties with this world are severed at death, and whose connections to this world wane with time, such a soul maintains ongoing ties with the living. This is because even after death, his soul has a responsibility and commitment toward the people in this world, just as it did throughout life.

This concept is expressed in a letter of condolence written by Rabbi Shneur Zalman of Liadi after the death of Rabbi Mendel of Vitebsk, his mentor and his teacher.[4] In the letter, Rabbi Shneur Zalman explains the *Zohar*'s statement "A *tzaddik* who passes from the world is found in all the worlds more than during his lifetime."

When the *tzaddik* was alive, his place was restricted to his body. After his passing, when no longer confined to a body, he is found everywhere – in more worlds than he could exist in during his lifetime.

The Baal HaTanya explains that a *tzaddik* of that kind fulfilled his task in life by using his elevated soul to benefit the Jewish people in general and individuals in particular. Just as there are people whose primary service in this world is prayer, so there are people whose primary service is communicating to the people – and not only with those with whom it is a pleasure to speak. This *tzaddik* was their doctor in the sense that he tended to them all. This divine service doesn't end even when the *tzaddik* passes from the world. Regarding a *tzaddik* of this kind – a *tzaddik* who did not isolate himself but illuminated the world – the aspect of his soul that illuminated the world remains connected to this world and continues to exist in it.

---

4. *Tanya, Iggeret HaKodesh,* epistle 27.

It is said that Elijah attends every circumcision as the "angel of the covenant." He is the prophet who cried out to God, saying, "The children of Israel have forsaken Your covenant."[5] Every time Elijah attends a circumcision, he sees Jews continuing to commit to the covenant, even if it transcends their reason or understanding. They still circumcise their sons because they feel the obligation of the covenant.

Why must Elijah attend every circumcision? For Elijah the prophet, who certainly could have reached the Garden of Eden, there's no personal need to revisit this world. Yet he returns because as the angel of the covenant, Elijah remains connected to us even now, both with respect to circumcision and other matters in whose context we mention his name. It is for this reason that he will return before the coming of the Messiah, as the verse states, "He will restore the heart of the fathers to the children and the heart of the children to their fathers."[6]

This was the mission that God imposed on Elijah the prophet, and he returns to this world in order to fulfill it. The scope of his service in the context of the world order is greater than that of his personal soul. There is the realm of the personal soul, and there is the realm of what each soul does in the context of the world order. When a certain soul functions in the context of the world order, its actions are more significant than its function in the realm of the personal.

Tzaddikim don't retire. It is actually written that they have no rest in this world or in the World to Come. Their work is never done, even when they pass on to the next world. Some *tzaddikim* continue their personal divine service, that which is individual to them, while others – the shepherds, the leaders of the people – continue to perform their tasks for the Jewish people.

THE CONNECTION TO THE *TZADDIKIM*

This is justification for requesting in our prayers that God remember Abraham, Isaac, and Jacob. Why are they mentioned in our prayers? What do they have to do with us?

5. I Kings 19:10.
6. Malachi 3:24.

The answer is that they remain our Patriarchs, not only because we are their descendants, but also because their light and legacy continue to illuminate the world. That is why we mention their names and pray that their merit stand on our behalf. The shepherds of Israel continue to come to our *sukkot* as guests, not because of their past virtues, but because what they accomplished in this world has ongoing significance for their descendants.

This also explains the custom of prostrating oneself at the graves of *tzaddikim*. Going to the cemetery is merely a technical matter; the soul isn't located in the grave. But since we don't have an address for the soul, we go to the place that marks the body of the *tzaddik*.

When we visit a *tzaddik*'s grave, we are, for all intents and purposes, seeking to connect with his soul. There is a long supplication recited at the graves of *tzaddikim* called *Maaneh Lashon*. It partially describes the ways in which souls are connected to one another and how they seek assistance from one another. In it, we are saying to the *tzaddik*, "You were a leader of Israel. You were our shepherd, and because of this, part of you will always remain tied to us. That's why we are here. That's why we are requesting that you arouse compassion for us."

(Incidentally, the connection between a father and son is also eternal, even though we don't understand the nature of that relationship. As stated above, the father may have forgotten what a son is, yet his soul remains connected to that of his son.)

This is why we celebrate a *hilula* for *tzaddikim*. The focus is not on the absence of the *tzaddik* or the question of what our world would be like if he were still alive. At a *hilula*, we focus on our ongoing connection to the *tzaddik*. It's as if we are saying to him, "You concerned yourself with us a hundred, a thousand, or three thousand years ago, and you still have a connection to us. Please continue to act in our favor."

At a *hilula* for a *tzaddik*, we don't think of the mourners, but rather of the one who perished. And we don't express sorrow over the loss; we speak instead about the *tzaddik*, his greatness, and our connection with him, which remains an integral part of his role. May it be God's will that our words will be acceptable.

Leḥayim!

The Character of the Baal HaTanya

A MULTIFACETED PERSONALITY

There have been people in the world who were prominent Torah scholars or renowned leaders in other areas, and nothing is known about their abilities in any other area. There are experts in Talmud, in Mishna, in *aggada,* and in Kabbala. Among the Sages in the Talmud, there were those who taught and studied both *halakha* and *aggada.* There are some whose halakhic and aggadic statements are minimal, and there are some in whose name virtually nothing is written. Although Rabbi Ḥanina ben Dosa was an exceedingly great man and a miracle worker who had dominion over the heavens and the earth, I know of no *halakha* cited in his name, though we are familiar with aggadic statements he made. Apparently, his halakhic statements weren't noteworthy. It's possible that we don't know of his prominence in *halakha* because he was circumspect. In any case, we're aware of his greatness only in other areas.

The distinction between the experts in *halakha,* experts in *aggada,* and miracle workers is an ancient one. In *Tanakh,* there are prophets whose prophecies we study, and then there are prophets like Elijah and Elisha, who performed great miracles, but we are not familiar with many of their Torah insights or prophecies.

Here is another example: A certain person, whose name I won't mention, was exceedingly accomplished in Kabbala. The significance of his work in the world of Kabbala can't be overstated. Several years ago, manuscripts of his were found and published, and they included comments that he had written on Gemara. When I encountered a Torah scholar and we discussed it, we both agreed that it would have been preferable not to print those insights – not because they were nonsense, but because there was nothing remarkable about them. Publishing them besmirched that great man, who it turns out was great in Kabbala, but less so in Gemara.

The Baal HaTanya, Rabbi Shneur Zalman of Liadi, was a multifaceted man whose abilities were also multidimensional. He excelled in Torah as well as in many other areas. One example can be found in his masterwork of *halakha, Shulḥan Arukh HaRav,* when discussing a halakhic question that sought to determine the direction that faces Jerusalem in connection with building synagogues. The Baal HaTanya wrote that in order to determine a specific direction, complex mathematical calculations are required. "This calculation," he states, "is simple to those familiar with the mathematical methods of calculating a spherical triangle"[7] – what is known today as spherical trigonometry.

When the Russian authorities confiscated the Baal HaTanya's library, they made a list of all of the books it contained. We have access to this list, which included a text, in Hebrew, of the most advanced mathematics known at that time. It turns out that the Baal HaTanya was interested enough in mathematics to find that extremely rare book. This gives us a sense of the breadth of his interests.

HIS CLASSICAL WRITINGS

The Baal HaTanya's writing style is somewhat detached, whether he is writing rulings of *halakha*, hasidic thought, or matters related to the soul. This is less evident in books that others wrote in his name, either from memory in transcribing his teachings or in translations of his books from Yiddish.

By contrast, the writings of Breslov hasidim are much more gentle, the language much warmer and friendlier. (This is not necessarily true of the writings of Rabbi Naḥman himself, such as *Likkutei Moharan* or *Sippurei Maasiyot*, which are written in a different style.) To generalize, the writings of Breslov are romantic, while the writings of the Baal HaTanya are classical. The difference between them is similar to the difference between romantic and classical works in other areas, such as music, art, and architecture. The Baal HaTanya's writing is classical in the sense that it is clear and organized and not emotional and free-flowing.

Breslov works have become popular in our generation because, among other reasons, we're not a generation motivated by the intellect. We are people of emotions; we speak of matters of the heart with respect to faith, love and fear of God, and other spiritual matters. Breslov teachings speak to us because they are written with great warmth. The *Tanya*, on the other hand, must be read several times, with great effort, for one

7. *Shulḥan Arukh HaRav, Oraḥ Ḥayim* 94:2.

to connect to the content. This is not because the *Tanya* is written unclearly. On the contrary, the *Tanya* is so clear it can be blinding. At times, a person needs a little vagueness, a bit more romanticism. This is not the *Tanya*'s style.

Character differences such as this can also be discerned in other generations. Although both Rashi and Rambam write with immense clarity and precision, there is a noticeable difference between them. Rashi writes with warmth even when addressing halakhic matters, and one can relate to his beautiful writing. In one of the letters in his responsa, Rashi addresses his correspondent as "my brother, my friend." Rambam, on the other hand, never addresses a correspondent as "my brother, my friend." This is not because he was disassociated from other people, but rather because he wasn't the kind of person who hugged everyone he met. Their different writing styles stems from their different personalities rather than being a reflection of their contents' profundity.

The writing of Baal HaTanya is organized and detached, not because his words are uninspiring, but because he doesn't express them emotionally, with pathos or exclamations. And to absorb his content, one must become familiar with that manner of expression.

AN ARDENT PERSONALITY

A lesser-known aspect of the Baal HaTanya's personality was that he was very enthusiastic about spiritual matters. Unlike Rambam, the Baal HaTanya was capable of reaching a degree of fervent devotion that led to an unrestrained shedding of the corporeal. Sometimes he would become so enthused when delivering Torah discourses that he would fall off his chair and roll under the table, all while continuing to deliver his Torah discourse. There was one hasid who would roll under the table with him so as not to miss a word.

There are many stories about the ardent nature of the Baal HaTanya. For those familiar with his detached, deliberate writing style, it's difficult to identify him as the same person described in these stories.

Another unexpected aspect of the Baal HaTanya was that he was a serious musician who composed various types of music in addition to *niggunim*.

Another indication of the personality behind the *Tanya* can be seen in who he chose to endorse it. It would have been easy to find someone to write an endorsement for the *Tanya,* because it is an ordered and organized book, unlike most hasidic works, which are filled with extraneous ideas. The Baal HaTanya could have, for example, sought an endorsement from Rabbi Pinḥas HaLevi Horowitz, the author of *Sefer HaHafla'a,* who was his friend and would certainly have accorded him the appropriate respect. But the Baal HaTanya sought an endorsement from Reb Zusha of Anipoli, who was well known for his volatile temperament. Reb Zusha isn't depicted in any of the stories about him as someone whose opinion about an intellectual work like the *Tanya* would be considered appropriate.

Incidentally, among the books written by the Maggid's students, the one whose style is most similar to works of Chabad Hasidism is *Kedushat Levi* by Rabbi Levi Yitzḥak of Berditchev, a good friend of the Baal HaTanya and whose grandson married the Baal HaTanya's granddaughter. Given Rabbi Levi Yitzḥak's fiery personality, one would have expected his writing to be emotional and spontaneous, but, in fact, his style was very clear, though not quite as profound as Chabad teachings. To reinforce the point, it's clear that the Baal HaTanya was a complex person, and his detached style of writing isn't reflective of other aspects of his personality.

What Did the Baal HaTanya Want?

ACHIEVING AWARENESS

As I said, the Baal HaTanya, who is the subject of this *hilula,* certainly didn't oppose the expression of feelings. He was actually an ardent person with strong feelings, such as love and fear of God. But he didn't want Judaism or Hasidism to be solely based on feelings because he thought that anything based on feelings will quickly dissipate. He sought to build something more stable and durable.

This entailed more than just applying the intellect to the service of God. After all, everyone employs his intellect in the service of God. Unlike other hasidic Rebbes, the Baal HaTanya was of the opinion that the intellect must be employed in matters of faith as well as active service, but that's not the point. He wanted people to achieve awareness.

When a person questions himself about the degree of his awareness, he's asking himself, in all seriousness, what honestly exists within him. A person must mean what he thinks and what he says and not deceive anyone, especially not himself.

People can get excited when praying, gesticulating with their hands and feet, crying out and shouting, clapping their hands – but if they're not serious, it's all meaningless.

Someone was once standing in a synagogue in Kotzk, crying out, "*Tatte! Tatte!*" Father! Father! A Kotzker hasid passing by heard him. Kotzker hasidim, it's well known, weren't particularly nice. He said, quoting the Gemara, "And perhaps He is not his Father?"[8]

This quote passed from person to person until it reached the Kotzker Rebbe, who said, "'*She'al avikha*'[9] – if you don't have a father, borrow one [*kaḥ oto behashala*] and turn him into your father."

This wasn't only a sensitive answer but also a resolute demand. If you want to turn the Father in Heaven into *your* Father, crying "*Tatte, Tatte*," isn't enough. You need to work at it. It doesn't matter if a person is speaking or crying out. What matters is whether he means what he's saying.

SENSING THAT GOD IS REAL

There's a difference between feeling and being aware. A feeling is vague and nonspecific. Awareness, even when it's simple and crude, is incisive. Anyone who sees a table knows that it's real. One can put food on it, and it hurts to bump into it. By contrast, when a person believes in or senses the existence of a spiritual table, he can't place food on it and it doesn't hurt to bump into it. Items formed from clouds or a haze of purity can seem very beautiful, but they are outside a person's awareness. Awareness includes everything a person can say with certainty.

For this reason, it's much more difficult to cheat on the matriculation exams in mathematics than in literature. On a literature exam, a student can ramble on a bit hoping to touch on the right answer, and

8. *Ḥullin* 11b.

9. Deuteronomy 32:7.

the unfortunate teacher grading the test may still give him a passing grade. In mathematics, if the student writes an incorrect answer, it's obviously an error to the teacher grading the test and the student receives no credit. In a field like mathematics, it's easy to determine who understands the material and who doesn't.

The aspiration to be aware of God does not imply the possibility of touching Him with one's hands. It is the aspiration to know and sense that God is no less real than the table. (In reality, He is much more real than the table.) If God isn't real to a person, if a person feels that he is praying in front of a wall and not in front of God, this is a problem of awareness, even if the person is going through the motions of prayer. There is a well-known saying: "The entire world is a very narrow bridge." Our world, in its entirety, is merely a passageway to the next world. The problem is that a bridge can be shaky; one must constantly test its sturdiness.

WHEN THERE IS NO AWARENESS

An example of lack of awareness is described in *Ein Yaakov*. It says, "A thief, at the entrance to the tunnel, cries out to the All Merciful." This describes a person who recites a prayer before he goes out to steal: "Master of the universe, help me, support me, send angels before me to open the door for me, so that the hinge will not squeak," and so on. That the thief prays indicates that he believes. But if he believes, why does he steal?

The answer is that his belief is nebulous; he thinks that he can be both a man of faith and a thief. A person with true awareness understands that one can't be both. If he's determined to steal, at least he shouldn't pray at that moment, and if he prays – he shouldn't proceed to steal after praying.

The question of awareness exists regarding other matters as well. A person can be aware that the Earth is round and still wonder how it's possible. Do people in Australia, on the other side of the globe, walk around upside down? The thought probably wouldn't prevent him from traveling to Australia, because he believes that there must be a reasonable answer to his question. But in order to understand the matter more clearly, he requires a greater awareness of how the world works.

This awareness doesn't stem from divine wisdom but from simple understanding of a matter. Often people say things without really understanding what they're saying. They just assume that somehow what they're saying will become clear. But in matters of faith, at least, a person must have a clear awareness. Lacking that, words become meaningless, no matter what is being said.

A certain *tzaddik* interpreted the verse "For I know the Lord is great"[10] in this way: I'm not only declaring that God is great. Anyone can say those words. I'm saying that I know and understand His greatness.

CONTEMPLATION

The works of the Baal HaTanya address the question of how to achieve awareness. This isn't an easy thing to achieve. Becoming aware requires experience along with a concerted effort at contemplation. The contemplator considers a certain matter and delves into it, seeking to understand its meaning. Only when a person truly understands a matter can he deal with it and relate to it.

For example, one who studies the tractate of *Yevamot* encounters the concept of the levirate bond. Even a three-year-old child can utter those words, but in order to understand what they really mean, one must contemplate them and attempt to clarify what one understands and what one doesn't. To understand their meaning, one must ponder them again and again.

When a person seeks to resolve practical problems that he is confronted with, he engages in contemplation rather than feelings. A person standing before a locked door must find a way to open it. He could, of course, stand there, extend his hands heavenward, and say, "Master of the universe, please send the angel Gabriel to bring me the key," or "Send the angel Rephael to open the door from the other side." But ultimately, in order to arrive at a solution, he must think for himself and contemplate how to solve the problem.

Similar experiments have been performed with monkeys. A banana is suspended from the ceiling and the monkey must find a way to reach it. Sometimes the unfortunate monkey sits for three hours, engaged in

10. Psalms 135:5.

contemplation. It attempts to figure out how to get the banana. On a vastly different note, isn't it worthwhile to invest the effort in contemplation in order to try to comprehend the living God? Isn't worth at least as much as a banana to a monkey?

Though the Baal HaTanya instructs his adherents to study a substantial amount of material, the study is only a basis for allowing person to perform divine service. Aside from the material that a person studies, the Baal HaTanya instructs him to also contemplate, to take a certain point, consider it, and delve deeply into it, until it hatches and becomes clear to him. Then the person will say, "Now I grasp what it's about."

LYING OVER THE COURSE OF SEVENTY YEARS

One who wishes to pray seriously, and not merely go through the motions as if he is praying seriously, confronts many problems that he must resolve and clarify. Faith alone isn't enough, because faith doesn't clarify anything. Only awareness can do that.

People who study and pray but never contemplate the words they are saying have heads filled with words and nothing more. When they speak these words and consider them, they are like people playing Monopoly – buying and selling properties, earning and losing money, but the money isn't real money and the property isn't real property. Often people who pray are doing nothing more than saying words. Were they to actually see and sense what they're saying, they would be shocked, and would, perhaps, even stop praying.

People pray and pray, but do these prayers have any substance? In the early days of Hasidism, when a hasid was asked, "Did you recite the morning prayer?" he would answer, "I'm permitted to eat." In other words, he couldn't say that he had actually prayed, but in strictly halakhic terms, he was no longer at the stage prior to prayer and was therefore permitted to eat.

The question has been asked: Who can a person deceive? Not others, since people don't allow themselves to be fooled by others. And it is, of course, impossible to deceive God. So who can a person deceive? The answer is himself, and it's no great accomplishment to deceive a fool.

When a person sits and prays without knowing what he's actually saying, he's deceiving himself. His neighbors generally don't assume that he's praying seriously. God knows that he's not praying seriously. And if there are ministering angels present, they also don't believe that he's praying seriously. If he alone thinks that he's actually praying, who is he fooling?

On arrival in the Land of Israel, one of the Zionist leaders, a contemporary of Theodore Herzl, saw Tel Aviv for the first time and remarked, "Look, what a miracle! It turns out that all the things I've been lying about for over thirty years have all turned out to be true!"

I fear that when some good Jews ascend to the world on high, they will have precisely the same reaction. That the things they had been lying about for seventy years have all turned out, remarkably, to be true. It's shocking that a person can lie over the course of an entire lifetime, but that is what people do.

EXERTION OF THE SOUL AND EXERTION OF THE FLESH

One must be willing to devote much time and effort in order to achieve awareness. Prayer with song and dance doesn't require much effort. Prayer of this kind often functions like a pub. A person can enter a nightclub and dance, and even sing, but what does he get out of it? Not love, not even necessarily excitement.

Moreover, one must also raise the question, How much of that prayer is actually internalized? What's the result of this prayer other than the fact that, after praying, those who prayed can eat their breakfast with a heartier appetite? For most people, there is complete awareness of breakfast but no awareness at all of the morning prayer. People eat the meal after Yom Kippur with great gusto, but as for the fast that precedes it, it is by no means certain that they observed it with the same degree of seriousness.

Contemplation demands effort, and in that sense, it's very different from seclusion. In seclusion, a person pours out his heart – this can be done by anyone at any time. After pouring one's heart out to God, hiding nothing, speaking even of matters that would be kept from a spouse, he feels good. He is unburdened, freed from a heavy and troublesome load.

Contemplation is different. It's hard work. In the *Tanya*, Rabbi Shneur Zalman of Liadi states that service of prayer demands "exertion of the soul and exertion of the flesh."[11] "Exertion of the flesh" isn't referring to the effort expended in standing in prayer. Rather, it refers to the effort required to understand the interpretation and the meaning of the words recited in prayer. Exertion is required, demanded actually, not only to understand the entire prayer, but to try to truly understand one sentence or even just one word of the prayer.

A certain *tzaddik* was three hours late for the morning prayer service, holding it up for the rest of the congregation. When he finally arrived and was asked why he was so late, he answered, "I opened my eyes in the morning and recited *Modeh Ani*, and then I began to think, *What is ani and what is lefanekha?* Three hours passed until I arrived at some understanding of these words."

This is an example of the most basic level of an attempt to understand prayer. Understanding the absolute truth, divine truth, are higher levels. A penitent once came to a *tzaddik* to confess his sins. The *tzaddik* said to him, "If you really wish to repent, confess more profoundly."

The man considered his sins, delved deeply into them, and confessed again. He returned to the Rebbe, and the Rebbe said to him, "More profoundly. You must feel the sin itself, and not merely feel that you violated specific paragraphs in the *Shulḥan Arukh*."

He delved deeply into his sins, again and again over the course of several hours, until he fainted. The *tzaddik* said, "You have now, apparently, repented."

Repentance involves more than just striking one's heart. That's easy to do. One could teach a monkey to beat on his breast and recite, "*Ashamnu, bagadnu....*" We have been guilty. We have acted treacherously.... True repentance occurs when the heart strikes the person, and that's much more complicated. It has been said that sometimes when a person strikes his heart while reciting "*Ashamnu, bagadnu...*," the heart believes it is being caressed for each sin. If the person's heart was actually hurting, he wouldn't reach the end of the confession so easily.

11. *Tanya, Likkutei Amarim*, chap. 30.

"TO PERFORM IT"

Of the numerous matters it is possible to speak about at the *hilula* of the Baal HaTanya and his teachings, I have chosen to speak about one point: the Baal HaTanya's demand that we achieve awareness, whether substantially or minimally.

The Baal HaTanya defines this task with a verse that is the motto of his work: "Rather, the matter is very near to you, in your mouth and in your heart to perform it."[12] Every word in this verse is significant. First, "the matter is very near to you" – meaning, this is not an impossible demand, though it might require a person to move. In order to reach another place, whether it's America, Australia, or Ramat Gan, a person must move. If he fails to move, he can't even reach a place that is nearby.

Second, the verse points out that the matter should be "in your mouth and in your heart to perform it." "In your mouth" – it's important to speak of the fear of God. When people speak of fearing God, the speech itself is beneficial. "And in your heart" – clearly, a person must worship God in his heart. But the word *laasoso*, "to perform it," is perhaps the key word in this verse. The emphasis is that this is something that must be performed. It's not sufficient to say, "Master of the universe, I love You," because God could say, "I've heard that nonsense from people older and greater than you." Sometimes it's only when a person says, "Master of the universe, give me ten thousand dollars," that He says, "This time your words have some truth to them."

In light of this, the meaning of "to perform them" is that a person must work on himself. The entire *Tanya* addresses the question of how a person can act on his love of God and not merely speak of it.

In the book of Esther there is a verse that states, "These days are remembered and observed,"[13] meaning that it's important that these events be remembered – that people read the *megilla* – but they must also be observed. How are they observed? In my father's family, the custom to this day is to assemble on Purim, recite confession with great seriousness, and weep. Why on Purim? Because after a person has drunk a bit, he can no longer deceive God as he does on Yom Kippur. That's

12. Deuteronomy 30:14.

13. Esther 9:28.

why it has been said that Yom Kippur, or Yom HaKippurim, is a "day like Purim" – *yom kePurim.*

Talk is cheap; a person can say whatever he wants. But how can a person reach a point where he really means what he is saying? In order to attain that level of honesty, he must sit and think about what is being said.

Leḥayim!

8

The Path of the Baal HaTanya

This farbrengen celebrates the day that the Baal HaTanya passed away – the twenty-fourth of Tevet – but the matters I'd like to speak about are relevant every day of the year. Having said that, when discussed in the context of the Baal HaTanya's *yartzeit,* the subject deserves special emphasis.

ACHIEVING SPIRITUAL ELEVATION WITH THE *TZADDIK*

It is written in the holy books, which include the *Tanya,* that on the day of his *hilula,* a *tzaddik* ascends one level in the World to Come. What's the connection between this ascent and the *hilula* held in its honor?

It is written that the righteous have no respite in this world nor in the World to Come. What can this mean, that the righteous have no respite in the World to Come? One would think that after a righteous person has died and entered the Garden of Eden, he would find a room in which to stay, a book from which to study, and a chair in which to sit as he enjoys the radiance of the Divine Presence with a crown on his head. But it is written that if he is a genuinely righteous man, he will never stay put. He will be cast into another Garden of Eden, where he will again need to find himself a room, book, and chair, and he will continue to ascend from one Garden of Eden to another for all of eternity.

The wicked, by contrast, are placed where they are placed and remain there. That is the indication that they are wicked.

This distinction is tied to the way the righteous and the wicked are depicted in the book of Proverbs. On one hand, it is written, "For the righteous man falls seven times and rises,"[1] and the Sages juxtaposed to that verse the words "But the wicked man falls with one."[2] The wicked man falls once and stays down. By contrast, though the righteous man may also fall, even seven times, seventy-seven times, or seven hundred seventy-seven times, he rises Because of this, he continues to ascend, level after level, even when he reaches the world on high.

The righteous man ascends each and every day, but on the anniversary of his passing, his ascent is special. This ascent is tied to the Sages' homiletic interpretation of the verse "For man shall not see Me and live."[3] They comment, "In their lifetime, they do not see, but after their death, they see."[4] According to this interpretation, the moment the soul departs from this world, it is elevated and merits seeing God. And that is the special ascent that the righteous man's soul merits each year on the anniversary of his passing: It is privileged to see God again and again. But with every year after its passing, the righteous man's soul merits a greater and more profound sighting than it did the previous year. In that way, the righteous person continues to ascend.

When the *tzaddik* ascends, he doesn't ascend alone. He draws with him everyone who cleaved to him and even everyone who sought to cleave to him. That is why we celebrate the *hilula* of the *tzaddik*. The literal meaning of *hilula* is "wedding." A *hilula* is like a wedding, where the rejoicing is primarily that of the groom. The circles of people singing and dancing with the groom are swept up in the joy and ascend to his level of rejoicing. So it is at the *hilula* of a *tzaddik*; the people who have ties to him gather together and join the ascent that the *tzaddik* merits on his *yartzeit*, and they are elevated together with him.

---

1. Proverbs 24:16.
2. Based on Proverbs 28:18; see *Sanhedrin* 7a.
3. Exodus 33:20.
4. *Sifra Nedava* 2:12.

It's possible to speak at great length about the guest of honor of this *hilula*, the *yartzeit* of the Baal HaTanya. His personality and character merit immense praise. But singing praises of the *tzaddik* does little more than warm the heart; it is not a particularly effective way to get a soul to cleave to the *tzaddik*. The most significant objective of this *hilula* is not to describe the greatness of the Baal HaTanya, but rather to form a connection with him and to achieve practical results from that connection. To that end, I would like to speak about one of the Baal HaTanya's greatest innovations in Torah. It's not a single specific point, but rather a general, comprehensive innovation related to the path he paved.

BECOMING A HASID

In the path of Hasidism that preceded the Baal HaTanya, the assumption was that in order to become a hasid, a person had to effect a drastic change in his soul. To reach a higher level, he had to leap into a new reality.

There is a certain hubris involved in the aspiration to make that leap. According to the natural order of the world, if someone aspires to be a hasid, the first stage toward becoming a hasid is simply to fulfill one's obligations as an ordinary Jew. When a simple Jew has perfected his character as well as deeds, he can become a *tzaddik*. Above that is the level of hasid, as described by the Sages and works of *mussar*, but it is a level that only an isolated few can attain. When the Gemara states, "There was an incident involving a certain hasid," it is referring to only one of two people: Rabbi Yehuda ben Bava or Rabbi Yehuda bar Ilai.[5] And yet today anyone can decide to be a hasid.

If being a hasid is such an unattainable level, how is it possible for a person to simply declare that he is one? This declaration must be understood in the same way one understands the declaration "I am going to Jerusalem." In order to reach Jerusalem, a person must first travel to one stop, and from there to another stop, and so on. Even though he makes several stops along the way, and even though he might get a flat tire at some point, he ultimately reaches his final destination.

5. *Bava Kamma* 103b; *Temura* 15b.

By the same token, when a person declares, "I am a hasid," he's not referring to his current location; he's referring to a point that he aspires to reach. It's as if he said, "I want to become a hasid."

The path is a long one. It might take seventy years – but that's the desired destination.

Being at the level of a hasid entails transcending the mere fulfillment of obligations that are incumbent on others. Of course, a hasid is obligated to perform mitzvot according to *halakha* and does everything that is required of him. But a hasid aims to reach higher and higher. Hasidism presents each and every Jew with the opportunity to say, "I don't merely wish to fulfill my obligations – I want to attain higher and higher levels. I want to be more, to do more than is required of me. I want to be a person who serves God 'with all my might.'"

"WITH ALL YOUR MIGHT"

"With all your might" is the highest of the three levels described in *Shema*. At the most basic level, a person is commanded to love God "with all your heart" – that is, "with your two inclinations, the good inclination and the evil one."[6] This means devoting your entire heart to Him. The next level is "with all your soul" – that is, "even if God takes your soul."[7] Only when a person is willing to die for the sake of God can he proceed to the next and highest level of "with all your might." When a person is commanded to love God with all his might, he is being told, "Give even a bit more." This "a bit more" that a person is commanded to give includes a willingness to experience something worse than death, even the torments of Gehenna, for the love of God.

In books of homilies and hasidic literature, a question is raised: Why does the first passage of *Shema* state, "You shall love the Lord your God with all your heart, with all your soul, and with all your might,"[8] while the second passage only says "with all your heart and with all your soul"[9] but not "with all your might"?

---

6. Mishna *Berakhot* 9:5.
7. Mishna *Berakhot* 9:5.
8. Deuteronomy 6:5.
9. Deuteronomy 11:13.

The answer is that the first passage is directed to the individual, while the second passage is required of the entire Jewish people. It's possible to tell an individual, "You must go above and beyond to the point that you transcend all boundaries," but it's impossible to demand that of the masses. One can demand that they love and worship God with all their souls – to reach the level of self-sacrifice. The Jewish community throughout the ages has, indeed, sacrificed itself in sanctification of God's name. But it's difficult to demand that an entire population do so "with all its might."

In any case, only when an individual seeks to transcend all levels can he begin to be a hasid. A hasid isn't necessarily someone who has attained a given level. Even someone on the lowest level, even someone who is far below the level of "with all your heart," can aim to reach that of hasid and say to himself, "If only I could serve God with my good inclination. I haven't even begun to serve with my evil inclination!" If he knows that each level is only a station along the way and wishes to keep reaching for the next level and beyond – he is a hasid.

MAKING A DECISION

Don't think that I'm speaking to the air; I'm speaking to you. Where you come from or who your parents are doesn't matter. I'm speaking to each one of you, whether you're old or young, wise and knowledgeable or replete with good deeds. I'm speaking to you and saying that this is possible. All you have to do is make a decision. It's not contingent on the *nusaḥ* of your prayers or other external matters, but rather on what you are willing to take on. Being a hasid demands that a person say just one thing to himself: I will not rest and I will not be silent until I reach that level. Whether I'm a carpenter, a computer programmer, a PhD in physics, a mathematics professor, or a rabbi, I will not give up on my desire to worship God with all my might.

One could be sixty, seventy, or ninety years old; all desires may have dissipated except for the desire to devote himself to God "with all his might." A person can say, "I still haven't achieved this status still now. Maybe ninety years aren't enough time. If God grants me another year, perhaps I can achieve it, and if not in this incarnation, maybe I can achieve it in the next. But I know what I want."

When a person resolves not to rest or be complacent, neither in this world nor in the World to Come, God grants him another opportunity to achieve his goal.

This is one interpretation of the verse "If I ascend to Heaven, You are there; if I lie down in the netherworld, You are here."[10] It doesn't matter whether I'm in Heaven or in the netherworld. What's important is that I know where I want to be: I want to be with God. A person needs to make the decision not to sit on his laurels, that He will love God whether he's in Heaven or the netherworld.

Why does God need people to love Him from Gehenna? What satisfaction does He receive from them? Even if a person shouts from the lowest tier of the netherworld that he wants to be a hasid, no allowances are made and no privileges given. The contrary may be true: He is flogged more extensively because of his pretentiousness. He wants to be a hasid? Wasn't it enough for him to be an upright person who fulfilled his obligations?

But perhaps it is specifically those who seek God from the netherworld that God wants to hear from. He doesn't need to hear from the righteous in the Garden of Eden that they love Him. He wants to hear from those in Gehenna, those who are being whipped and beaten, yet still say, "Only to the Lord alone."[11]

The hasid says to God, "Watch over me, for I am a hasid."[12] He says, "You know all my sins, but You also know that I want You. Even while I walk 'in the valley of the shadow of death' – even though I find myself in the deepest netherworld by choice, because of my own foolishness – I want You to be with me. I may have fallen into a pit, broken my hands, feet, and head, but I still want to be with You. I've always wanted to be with You."

THE LONG YET SHORT PATH

This was the essence of Hasidism before the Baal HaTanya came along. It required a leap, a personality change, in order for a person to attain

10. Psalms 139:8.
11. Exodus 22:19.
12. Psalms 86:2.

the lofty level of hasid. The Baal HaTanya realized that this path wouldn't work because practically that degree of change never takes place, and if it does, it's only in the person's imagination. In other circumstances, such a leap would be considered a kind of insanity if it results in a drastic personality transformation to a degree that a person will not be anything like he had been before. More, when a person doesn't belong at the level to which he aspires yet still leaps in an attempt to get there, he's liable to fall, catch fire, and get incinerated. And even when this path is appropriate for the person, he won't be able to prepare and plan ahead for it when it would entail saying to himself, "I will now, at this moment, take the plunge and cease being the person I've been until now."

That's why the Baal HaTanya constructed an alternative path of Hasidism, which he characterized as a "long yet short path." In contrast to other *tzaddikim* who established the path of a great leap, achieved by traversing reality all at once, the Baal HaTanya paved a path on which it's possible to progress step by step, a path with clearly defined challenges and goals.

This long path is not as exciting as a giant leap from earth to Heaven, but it's much more stable. It demands perseverance and exceedingly hard work, yet by following this path it's actually possible to reach the world on high. It is a very long path, but at the same time, it's shorter than the other one, because it involves much less self-deception.

The Baal HaTanya claimed that it's not possible to base one's path on leaps. Instead, one's path must be based on the fact that a person first stands and only then begins to walk. A person who wishes to ascend the mountain of God can say, "Would that I had wings like a dove; I would fly away and come to rest."[13] Would that I could sprout wings and fly up to the mountain of God, like a bird that can fly and reach greater heights. The problem is that a person doesn't always merit wings, and a person can't always leap from earth to Heaven. To a person like that, the Baal HaTanya says, "With all due respect, lift one foot and then place it down, then lift the second foot and place it down. Then continue to move forward, taking one step at a time."

13. Psalms 55:7.

THE PATH THAT THE BAAL HATANYA PAVED

The Baal HaTanya opened up to people a path that has virtually no epiphanies or special transcendent experiences. In general, the realm of spiritual experience varies from person to person. Some merit a special experience while others don't. Some experience it in this world, and others will merit it only in the World to Come.

To someone who takes the path laid out by the Baal HaTanya, spiritual "experiences" are irrelevant because the path is mainly about rolling up one's sleeves and getting to work. The person may sweat and curse, but he perseveres. *Deveikut*, cleaving to God, is not a matter of experience or a moment of inspiration. The cleaving is found within the path and within the work. The persistence as one marches on, the falling and subsequent rising on the way, and the insistence on moving forward – that is *deveikut*.

The path paved by the Baal HaTanya was a significant innovation. On the one hand, it basically represented the desire to reach the highest levels; on the other hand, it consisted of taking small steps in order to get there. The Baal HaTanya revealed that it's possible to ascend not only by life-altering leaps and decisions, but also by prolonged, exhausting walking.

Today, the day of his *yartzeit*, we are thankful to him for this.

On the path paved by the Baal HaTanya, a person can take a specific action while having in mind that it is "for the sake of the unification of the Holy One, blessed be He, and His Divine Presence." By doing so, he takes one step. Then he performs another action, again with the intent that it is "for the sake of the unification of the Holy One, blessed be He, and His Divine Presence," and in so doing takes another step. He knows that regardless of the length of the path, he will continue to traverse it, one step at a time. From a certain perspective, this is the root, the secret, and essence of Hasidism.

It seems to me that the Baal HaTanya himself didn't need this path. I believe he was a child prodigy. I'm not sure whether he ever needed to toil in his studies or overcome his evil inclination, or even to ascend to the world on high. But he knew that not everyone was made like him. Not everyone were members of the elite, capable of igniting, in one instant, a spark that could burn and turn into a conflagration. There are people who feel that they don't possess any spark at all. He paved the way for people who believe they have a soul, but since they can't see it or feel it, they must work and sweat in order to make progress.

At this farbrengen, we attempt to attach ourselves to a person who invested time and energy to enable people to climb upward, step by step. One who seeks to cleave to the Baal HaTanya and ascend with him must traverse the path that he laid out, without deviating from it or withdrawing from it. One who cleaves to the Baal HaTanya and to his path will receive from him the strength to continue on and reach a much higher level than the one he started from.

Leḥayim.

9

A New Soul

It's possible to speak about the Baal HaTanya, the subject of this *hilula*, from many different perspectives because he was so accomplished and so multifaceted. This is obvious from the many ways in which he is known – as the Baal HaTanya, the Alter Rebbe, the author of *Shulḥan Arukh HaRav*. I would like to explain one of the more unusual ways in which he can be praised, and that is that he had a new soul.

EACH PERSON'S PLOT

A great many obligations and missions are imposed on Jews who live in this world. In addition to all these expectations, God imposes a unique and specific task to each soul that He dispatches to this world. Each soul is given a plot that it is obligated to cultivate during its lifetime, and as stated in the holy books, each soul receives a plot appropriate to its stature. There are souls that receive a plot that measures four-by-four cubits, and there are those that receive a plot of several acres.

One of the problems preventing us from performing our unique tasks in this world is that we don't always know what they are. Sometimes a person is mistaken regarding the plot of his life and he does things he's not supposed to do. This doesn't mean that he chooses evil instead of good; his actions aren't necessarily evil. It's about a person who performs deeds that aren't his to perform; he is doing someone else's task.

There are people who are certain that they are doing what they are supposed to be doing, but in most instances a person has no clear idea about what he should be doing. People can spend years in a particular vocation, even successfully, but it's not what they are supposed to be doing. The plot that a person is meant to cultivate over the course of his lifetime is given without any instructions from Heaven. Since no one tells him, "You must plant pecan trees in your plot," he's liable to plant the wrong trees.

"What is my unique task?" is a great and significant question, and a person doesn't always find the answer. It should trouble everyone. There was a time when, given the opportunity to meet a great man, a person would ask him, "What is the root of my soul? What is my role in the world?" Today many people don't even consider this question. A person can reach middle age before he begins to think that perhaps he should be doing something completely different from what has been occupying his time.

In one interpretation of the verse "They placed me as guard of the vineyards; my own vineyard I did not guard,"[1] it is the soul speaking to God. The soul is saying, "I did what they told me to do. I guarded other vineyards, but I didn't guard my own." What about my own vineyard? Sometimes people reach the conclusion that they haven't guarded their own vineyards. My vineyard may not be as magnificent as others, and I might have actually done good work in other vineyards, but I didn't fulfill the mission unique to my soul.

PROBLEMS AND OBSTACLES

This problem is tied to several human characteristics.

First, it relates to our freedom of choice. We have the ability to choose to go in different directions: up or down, forward or back, by air, by ground, or by sea. Only God on high and people below have this ability. Angels have no freedom of choice, beasts have no freedom of choice, and cars certainly have no freedom of choice. In my opinion, freedom of choice is the image of God that is within a person, the living soul that

1. Song of Songs 1:6.

God breathed into us. But freedom of choice is also what enables us to go in directions that are wrong for us.

The problem is also tied to the wide range of human abilities. Occasionally there are people who have talent in a certain area – music, writing, or chess, for example – that is so conspicuous and outstanding that engaging in anything else would be an unthinkable waste of time. In most instances, though, human abilities are multifaceted and undeveloped. Most of us are capable of doing many different things. A person can wonder whether he should be an official for the IRS, an author, or a military man. The fact that animals don't have this freedom of choice can also work to their advantage. Clearly, a lion isn't made to plow fields or care for babies. Aquatic creatures don't have to decide where to live. The roles of animals are specific and obvious. People, on the other hand, have neither physical nor spiritual specificity. That's why they are able to go in different directions.

Third, there is the evil inclination, which can manifest itself in many different forms. There is an entire spectrum of manifestations of the evil inclination ranging from an absolutely despicable evil inclination to a refined one, from an evil inclination that is a wild monkey of sorts to an intelligent one with academic honors. But these differences are superficial and not substantive. The evil inclination is essentially the same: It misleads people and is able to prevent them from performing what is incumbent on them to do.

REINCARNATION

Because of these problems – freedom of choice, a person's many and varied abilities, and the evil inclination – a person often doesn't find his plot. When a person who hasn't fulfilled his mission arrives in the heavenly court, he is told, "Whether or not you made mistakes in your lifetime, you must return to the world again. You didn't pass through it successfully and you cannot move forward. You need to start all over again."

It's like being left back in school.

This is the reason souls undergo reincarnation, not only once, but several times. Were a man to live his life in his second incarnation as if it were a makeup test, when he more or less knows what the questions will be, perhaps he would have more success. In general, that's not the way it plays out, as described in Ecclesiastes: "He put the world, too, in their heart, notwithstanding that man will not discover from beginning to end the accomplishment that God has accomplished."[2] Man doesn't know what plot God expects him to cultivate and repair.

There are stories of people who underwent several incarnations in order to complete their mission and repair that which they had distorted. For example, a story is told about a decent, righteous man who had a tendency to be envious of others. He underwent one incarnation after another in order to rectify that sin. Ultimately, he was brought back into the world wise, wealthy, and successful so that there would be no reason for him to be jealous. On a certain winter's day, wet and cold after being caught in the rain, he walked into an inn where a gentile was warming himself by the hot furnace and drinking. His envy was immediately aroused, and it again became necessary for him to undergo yet another incarnation.

Most people don't complete their mission in the first incarnation and must undergo several incarnations until they fulfill it in the world. They aren't necessarily defective, evil, or sinful. They merely didn't complete their mission for one reason or another.

Other people have exalted souls and are sent back to this world for a second or third time in order to fulfill an additional task. They had already completed their mission and for all intents and purposes could rest in peace. But when God asks, "Who wants to come to the aid of the Jewish people?" this soul volunteers to return to the world to fulfill this new task.

USED SOULS

Despite the uniqueness of each and every soul in this world, most are incarnations. Some need repair in more than one area; sometimes the needed repairs are subtle. Some are required to perform their task from the beginning, and some especially exalted souls descend again to this world to perform additional tasks.

---

2. Ecclesiastes 3:11.

Generally we don't remember previous incarnations. This leads to phenomena that we can neither understand nor explain. There are books that describe that, on occasion, something befalls a person that is connected to his previous incarnation. Although the person himself is unaware of it, his souls knows. It's conceivable, for example, for a person's soul to be extraordinarily excited about a certain passage in prayer. He feels a special connection to this passage without knowing why.

The story is told of a certain Jew who would recite *Pesukei DeZimra* with great concentration and at great length. It turned out that in his previous incarnation, although he recited *Shema*, the accompanying blessings, and the *Amida* prayer appropriately, he never considered *Pesukei DeZimra* very important. He needed to be reincarnated so that he would be brought back into this world in order to make up for this.

The Arizal once said to two people: "You love each other because you were father and son in an earlier incarnation, and the love between you endures."

Two people can meet and feel a profound connection that's not based on reason, a connection that neither understands. It's very possible that it is related to the memory of a deep relationship in a previous incarnation. On the other hand, there are people one would expect to be very close and friendly but don't connect at all. There may even be unexplainable enmity between them. This can happen because of unresolved issues from a previous incarnation.

In any event, virtually all of the souls found in this world are old, used souls. Almost all of us have previously been here in one form or another.

WHAT IS A NEW SOUL?

On rare occasions – and with time this has become even more rare – a new soul is born into the world. God releases a brand-new soul. A new soul isn't necessarily a great soul; it's merely a soul that has never existed before.

How can one identify a new soul? What does it do? Since it has no past and no memories, it can sometimes perform interesting or significant actions. The memories from previous incarnations influence the way older souls behave. This phenomenon is not unlike situations that psychologists deal with. There are certain things a person isn't able to do because of past experiences and associations, and these past events are usually discoverable and can be addressed. When it comes to reincarnated souls, however, matters are different. A person has no knowledge of his soul's memories, yet its past incarnations can, for better or for worse, have an impact on the way he navigates this world. As a result, there are actions he performs that are dictated by the manner in which his soul performed them in the past, because it's easier to follow a familiar path than to change.

A new soul is uninfluenced by past incarnations and therefore has more freedom to be original. Even if it doesn't invent the wheel, the way it behaves is unique. A person whose soul is new approaches matters from a new perspective, and because of this, he may act in a way that is different, though not necessarily better, than others.

This phenomenon also exists in relation to matters of this world. When a stranger arrives in a new place, he encounters things that are new to him, and he sees them differently from the way everyone always has. Because of this, he has the ability to resolve problems that have not yet been resolved.

Many years ago, light bulb manufacturers conducted calculations and computations and reached the conclusion that if they were to coat the entire bulb with a white coating from the inside, the efficiency of the illumination would be greater, and the intensity of the bulb's light would increase. But since the bulb was made of glass, figuring out how to coat it from the inside wasn't simple. For years, attempts to do so failed.

In one factory, this undertaking became a secret joke among the workers. When a new engineer was hired, they would give him the task of coating the bulb from the inside. He sat and put his mind to it, experimenting and making calculations, until he finally gave up, whereupon he was let in on the joke – that the task was impossible. They did this over the course of many years, until they tasked a certain new engineer with the undertaking. He, too, began working on it, and not knowing that it was "impossible," he succeeded. Only someone who didn't know that the problem was considered unsolvable was actually able to solve it.

In the same way, a new soul doesn't necessarily create everything anew, but it discovers new facets to issues and problems that other people have already faced. The new soul does things differently from others because it never experienced them before.

When people praised the Baal HaTanya by saying that he had a new soul, they didn't mean to underscore that he was unencumbered by transgressions from a previous incarnation. They meant to say that the things he did were novel.

New doesn't mean something that is in opposition to the way things have always been done. It also doesn't have to refer to a great invention, or even an improvement on an older one. But sometimes a new soul comes along and solves a problem that has existed forever in a substantially different manner. Whether the innovation relates to one specific point or to many, it's still an unprecedented finding.

As a person who every so often reads all kinds of books, including books of Torah teachings, I have occasion to see beautiful ideas, even on the weekly *parasha*, an area that has already engaged many scholars over the course of many generations. But I don't often encounter ideas that are genuinely new. New ideas that are introduced in books are actually refurbished old ideas that have been written about before.

In view of this, when one compares the treatises of the Baal HaTanya to those of his descendants and disciples – some of whom were men of great stature – it becomes evident that many of the Baal HaTanya's ideas were truly new. Others took his material, developed it, revamped it, and presented it in a different form or construct, but they didn't have many new insights.

THE INNOVATION OF THE *BEINONI*

I will conclude this section with one example from the *Tanya*, a work that is written in a classical style. In a variety of art forms, classical works tend to be much simpler than works in the rococo or baroque styles, which are characterized by ornamentation and opulence. People who don't really understand art tend to be drawn to the opulent, ornamented works. They look at them, are impressed by them, and purchase them. But those who have an understanding of the world of art are impressed by classical works. In that sense, the *Tanya* is a classic.

On the other hand, the *Tanya* contains quite a few elements that are truly novel. I will focus on one idea that is new, not only in the realm of

Jewish ethics, but in all literature that deals with ethics. Works of ethics tend to depict a dichotomy between the wicked and the righteous; every person has the potential to be one or the other. By contrast, the Baal HaTanya called his work *Sefer shel Beinonim*, the Book of the Intermediate, because he introduced a new, third element to the picture, and that is the *beinoni*, the intermediate-level person – someone who is neither righteous nor wicked.

In past generations, a *beinoni*, as described in the *Tanya*, has been subsequently understood to be righteous by some and wicked by others. The Baal HaTanya, on the other hand, wrote that both the level of *beinoni* and that of the *tzaddik* are ideals, but being a *beinoni* is more complex. The levels of the righteous and wicked are more clearly defined than that of the *beinoni*.

A *beinoni* occupies two different worlds. Even when he reaches the peak of his potential, he doesn't win the war, doesn't win the grand prize. He never has a moment of respite. If he isn't striving for good, he is falling to the other side.

The Baal HaTanya wrote that the *beinoni*, who spends his life in a never-ending struggle, is just as important as someone who emerges from the battle victorious. The *Tanya* not only establishes the *beinoni* as a new type of personality, which does not appear in earlier *mussar* works such as *Reshit Ḥokhma* or *Mesillat Yesharim*, but he also considers it to be an ideal to strive for. The *beinoni* is an ideal *because* of the ongoing struggle. He is glorious in that he continues to engage in this battle for his entire life. It is a different type of glory than victory; it is defined by restlessness, disquiet, and the willingness to engage in an endless struggle.

The *Tanya* interprets our Patriarch Yitzḥak's words to Esav, "Prepare delicacies that I like for me,"[3] in the following way: The word *matamim*, "delicacies," in the plural, alludes to two types of delicacies: sweet ones, perfect in and of themselves, and spicy, sharp ones. One can't compare the taste of chocolate to the taste of hot sauce. They are totally different flavors, and neither is better or worse than the other.

3. Genesis 27:4; see *Tanya, Likkutei Amarim*, chap. 27.

According to the Baal Tanya, the Divine Presence asks its children, the entire Jewish people, to prepare delicacies "that I like" – delicacies of two kinds, sweet and sour. It says, "Give me those who have succeeded in sweetening all the evil within them (the righteous), as well as those who remain entangled with it until the end of their lives (the *beinonim*). Give Me them, too, because they each have different advantages."

Being a *beinoni* as an ideal to strive for is a novel concept. There is an ideal that it is incumbent upon a person to strive to complete his unique task in life. The new ideal of striving as a *beinoni* is based on Rabbi Tarfon's statement "It is not incumbent upon you to complete the task, nor are you free to be idle from it."[4] Although you haven't completed the task, it's conceivable that you have done your share of what needed to be done, and perhaps someone else will complete it.

This represents a certain perspective on how people act in this world. As individuals, as a people, or as humanity in general, we repeatedly work on tasks that we don't complete. We don't resolve all the problems, but we try to bring about a situation that will make it easier for the world to cope with them. One could say that man's objective is to perform incomplete actions. God Himself expresses it with the words "that God created to make."[5] He created things for us to act on but not necessarily for us to complete. We know that whatever we do, others will continue our work.

There are many books on ethics containing many beautiful ideas. One can study them, better himself through them, and ascend to loftier levels. But these books are all based on only one paradigm, even if they may allude to others. Then a new soul descended to the world, the soul of Baal HaTanya, who created a paradigm that represented a completely new way of thinking about the topic.

This is the meaning of a new soul: It is a person who deals with matters that others already dealt with, and he doesn't invalidate them or erase them, but comes up with a direction or nuance that makes people view them differently than before.

Leḥayim!

4. Mishna *Avot* 2:16.
5. Genesis 2:3.

The Baal HaTanya and Rambam

THE SIMILARITIES BETWEEN THEM

We don't know the exact day of Rambam's death, but there is a consensus that he passed away on the twentieth of Tevet or shortly afterward. I imagine that Rambam, like the Baal HaTanya, had a new soul. Rambam's originality is manifest both in wide-ranging ideas and in small details. His *Mishne Torah,* for example, sought to include the entire Oral Law, not only laws about practical matters that applied to his day, but also portions of the law that couldn't be carried out at the time. Although there had been great men who addressed these matters before Rambam's time, nothing like it had ever been undertaken before. His very idea – to include the entire Oral Torah in a halakhic work – was new.

Rambam's approach to halakhic rulings was also a novel one. More than half of *Mishne Torah* addresses matters that no previous book on *halakha* covered. For example, Rambam gave the same attention to the mishnaic order of *Teharot* as he did to orders that had been previously addressed by the Rif and other halakhic authorities, even though much of the *halakhot* and topics of *Teharot* do not have practical application today.

There is also a remarkable similarity between the writing style of Rambam and that of the Baal HaTanya. They differ in some aspects, but their writing styles are so similar in places that it's hard to distinguish between them. At a certain juncture in the *Tanya,*[6] the Baal HaTanya quotes Rambam, then transitions to his own words, and it's hard to discern when Rambam's words end and the Baal HaTanya's words begin. The transitions are simply undetectable. This is not because the Baal HaTanya sought to imitate Rambam; it's simply that their styles are so similar. That is why the words of Rambam can be incorporated quite elegantly into the words of the Baal HaTanya.

Another similarity between them is that both Rambam and the Baal HaTanya had more than a bit of the daring of a *gaon* – not in the conventional meaning of the word as "genius," but rather in the sense of *ge'ut,* confidence. Both were secure in their abilities. When Rambam

6. See *Shaar HaYiḥud VeHa'emuna,* chap. 7.

wrote his commentary on the Mishna, he was a young man in his twenties. He was still young when he wrote the *Mishne Torah* over a ten-year period. The Baal HaTanya also began writing his first book, *Shulḥan Arukh HaRav*, when he was only around twenty years old. He did this work at the behest of his Rebbe, but still, imagine taking a young man and saying to him, "Write a new *Shulḥan Arukh*." Anyone would be intimidated by the prospect. But just as Rambam wasn't intimidated by the magnitude of his challenge, neither was the Baal HaTanya intimidated by his.

ORDERLY WRITING

In addition to their originality, their courage, and the similarity of their writing styles, there is another significant characteristic that Rambam and the Baal HaTanya shared: Both had a similar sense of order.

In general, Jewish books don't start at the beginning. Typically, they begin slightly after the beginning or in the middle, then return a bit later to the beginning, then jump to the end. Something along those lines. Neither the Mishna nor the Gemara start at the beginning and conclude at the end. Even the Torah doesn't start at the beginning. How should the Torah have begun? One would have thought that the Torah might start the way Rambam began his book: "In the beginning there was God." Books that deal with the beginnings of the world – none of them comparable in any way to the Torah – tend to start from some original point in time.

But the book of Genesis does not start that way. The *Tanakh* contains many kinds of beginnings, such as that which conveys that God, the Creator of the world, exists for eternity, for example: "I am first and I am last, and besides Me there is no God."[7] But that is not how the book of Genesis begins. It starts in the middle of the story. The Torah is also not ordered chronologically, and that is true of almost all Jewish books.

I once tried to defend the lack of order in Jewish literature, explaining that their disorder reflected the disorder that is inherent in nature. When a child enters this world, he doesn't encounter it in an orderly fashion. He always enters it in the middle and takes it from there. He

7. Isaiah 44:6.

must somehow learn to navigate his way and uncover what came before and what comes after. And these revelations continue for the rest of his life. This is a natural and authentic way to learn. A person is cast into an existing reality, and within it he seeks to find the beginning and the end. The same is true for Torah study. True learning is organized in the natural order; it doesn't begin at the beginning.

But Rambam was an orderly man. His book is the first and perhaps only Jewish book written in order. Rambam had the ability to compile ideas and topics into one place and build a construct from them. This ability was critical in the writing of the *Mishne Torah* because sometimes a single *halakha* is derived from many sources found in different places. Aside from that, the *Mishne Torah* has a comprehensive structure that is intentional and orderly. Whatever questions we may have about it, they are not the result of an error in the Rambam's organization but are tied to other problems. For example, the placement of *Hilkhot Evel,* the laws of the mourner, in *Sefer Shofetim,* the Book of Judges, in the *Mishne Torah* is a bit strange. This placement stems from the fact that if those *halakhot* weren't placed in a separate book, there would be no other appropriate place to put them. (Incidentally, the *Tur,* too, does not have an appropriate place for those laws and cites them in the *Yoreh De'a* section of the *Shulḥan Arukh* which is its omnibus section.)

Until Rambam's time, all written commentary or rulings on the Oral Law were built on the existing order. The Rif's comments, for example, followed the order of the tractates of the Talmud. But Rambam created a whole new order. His book didn't begin and end like the Mishna. His writing is completely different, starting from generalizations and moving on to specific details. In truth, the *Tur* is also like that. It's not constructed according to the order of the Mishna, the order of the Gemara, or the order of Rambam. Instead, he created his own completely new order. In any event, the initiator of the idea was Rambam.

A brand-new order of this kind also exists in *Shulḥan Arukh HaRav* as well as in *Tanya.* The structure of *Shulḥan Arukh HaRav* is in the style of Rambam: concise, classic, and perfectly organized. When the Baal HaTanya began writing the *halakhot* on a certain topic, he first wrote an appropriate introduction in which he presented the basis of the *halakhot* and then went on to build the construct on that basis.

The same is true of the *Tanya*. It, too, is similar in style to Rambam's works in terms of order. This is in contrast to many of the thousands of books of hasidic teachings, which were written by people who took notes rather than by the authors themselves. Many Rebbes didn't write down their own Torah insights; their attendants did. The fact that many books were written in this manner led to an enormous number of publications, many of which contain invaluable insights. On the other hand, it created a problem, since most of the literature is disorganized. I say this as someone whose life has been nurtured by these books. One will read beautiful ideas, but it's difficult to find them because they can't be found in any predictable context. By contrast, the works of the Baal HaTanya and his disciples are organized and systematically written. By comparison, in the writings of Kabbala, Rabbi Moshe Cordovero had a well-organized style, but the writings of the Arizal, which were written by his disciple Rabbi Ḥayim Vital, lack an internal order, even though they still can be read and understood.

That the works of Rambam and the Baal HaTanya are so orderly reflects an internal sense of order. It turns out that the tendency to be organized is often inborn. I remember a young man who, while on drugs and intoxicated, came to me to pour out his heart. I myself am not a very organized person; the mess is evident to anyone who enters my room. I noticed that this dazed young man, while sitting across from me telling me his story, couldn't stop organizing my books. He had no reason to do so; he simply needed for them to be in a straight row.

Other issues aside, the ability to take bits of reality and connect them, the ability to view them within a space, within a reality, or within a philosophy – the ability to take certain details and form patterns from them – is tantamount to an act of creation.

On this subject, I'd like to give advice that isn't related to my personal preferences. If one wishes to study Hasidism or Kabbala, one should first study the books of Chabad. Even if his soul isn't completely drawn to them, he can receive a comprehensive overview of the topics in a way that he can absorb them. When a person studies other works first, he may not receive a clear picture. It's akin to moving from place to place without a map. Later he can't even describe where he had been. In that sense, it's crucial to study works of Chabad and understand their organized approach to the material. Others may have disputed certain details of this configuration, but they didn't argue with the organization itself.

THE UNIQUENESS OF THE BAAL HATANYA

As stated, in terms of organization, the writings of the Baal HaTanya were unquestionably in Rambam's style. At the same time, I don't think he was an incarnation of Rambam because of the significant personality differences between them.

In contrast to many great rabbis and prominent leaders, the Baal HaTanya excelled in many ways. Most people have talent in a specific area. There are philosophers, mathematicians, scientists, authors, musicians, each one excelling in his area. But the Baal HaTanya was, as stated above, multifaceted. He wrote *halakha* in a halakhic manner, teachings of Hasidism in a hasidic manner, and Kabbala in a kabbalistic manner. He also composed music, a skill that wouldn't necessarily go along with the other aspects of his personality that he exhibited.

Beyond all that, the Baal HaTanya was a Rebbe whose hasidim were bonded to him with their souls. Thousands of people came to him for guidance and counsel, and he knew how to speak to each one, how to listen to the afflictions of their hearts, to their material and spiritual problems. He may not have liked some aspects of this role, but he fulfilled it for many years.

Although Rambam was also admired during his lifetime, I don't think a simple Jew could have sat with him and asked him, "*Nu*, Reb Moshe, what do you think about my business? Should I buy or should I sell?"

Were someone to tell me that Rashi would warmly receive widows and all sorts of people, I would have agreed that this was characteristic of Rashi. But I don't think it was characteristic of Rambam. That isn't to say he was less righteous; he just had a different personality.

There was another strange and rare aspect of the Baal HaTanya's personality. He thought, wrote, and spoke very clearly, but he was also known to have ecstatic outbursts. He could be deeply enthusiastic yet remain clear and lucid. He could be sitting and teaching Torah, and then become so excited, he would roll around on the floor and end up under the table. I can't envision Rashi, Rambam, or Rabbeinu Tam, for that matter, in that scenario.

But beyond the sheer diversity of the components of the Baal HaTanya's soul, he had a special ability to integrate all these components into a single soul.

I would like to conclude with a beautiful story about the *"Arba Bavot"* (Four Gates) melody that he composed. The Baal HaTanya became a Rebbe at a relatively young age. Some of his followers were many years older than he was and had been followers of the Maggid and other Rebbes.

Moreover, he taught several classes of disciples. For a student to enter the first class, he needed to be expert in the Talmud and in the works of *halakha*. In order to enter the second class, one needed to be expert not only in the Talmud and the works of *halakha*, but also in kabbalistic literature. In order to enter the third class, he needed to be expert not only in the Talmud, in the works of *halakha*, and kabbalistic literature, but also in all the scholarly literature of the Middle Ages, works such as the *Guide of the Perplexed* and the *Kuzari*.

Since these were the kinds of students in his classes, it's possible to understand why he didn't feel the need to explain the basics when giving Torah discourses. One time, a simple hasid who was his fervent follower heart and soul, came to him and wept, saying, "Rebbe, I attempt to listen to your Torah discourses to the best of my ability, but I don't understand anything. Your Torah discourses are above my head. Is there, perhaps, something you can say that I could understand?"

The Rebbe gave it some thought. Then he said, "I'm unable to verbalize anything like that. Instead, I will sing you a melody, and that melody contains all of my Torah."

They say that the melody he sang was *"Arba Bavot."*

This story indicates that the Alter Rebbe had musical talent, but more than that, it expresses his personality. He was a person who could internalize what is found in Heaven above, as well someone who could relate – on a different plane – to the insane czar of Russia. He also had the ability to relate to an elderly Jew, someone who at best could perhaps read the *Ḥumash*, and attempt to transmit Torah to him using the internal rhythms of music that need no words. Someone who possesses all these qualities – and I'm speaking of his personality, not only of his works – is one of whom the verse states, "Can we find someone like this?"[8]

Leḥayim!

8. Genesis 41:38.

10 Shevat
The Hilula of
Rabbi Yosef Yitzḥak Schneerson

Two significant events transpired on the tenth of Shevat. On this date, in 1950, Rabbi Yosef Yitzḥak Schneerson, the sixth Lubavitcher Rebbe, passed away. Exactly one year later, on that same date, his son-in-law, Rabbi Menaḥem Mendel Schneerson, was appointed the seventh Lubavitcher Rebbe. Their tenures as Rebbe, which coincided with historic developments in the world in general and in the Jewish world in particular, are interwoven and complement one another.

Rabbi Yosef Yitzḥak Schneerson was born in Lubavitch in 1880. He grew up in the hasidic court of his father, Rabbi Shalom Dovber Schneerson, and was groomed to become Rebbe from his childhood. In his memoirs, Rabbi Yosef Yitzḥak Schneerson describes many details about his childhood, his education, and his father's household. He wrote about many traditions and memories associated with the Chabad dynasty that he learned from his father and others who were in the Rebbe's hasidic court. Much of the information available to Lubavitcher hasidim regarding the history of the households of their Rebbes is based on his books (books such as *Sefer HaZikhronot, Likkutei Dibburim*, and *Iggerot*).

In his youth, his father made him responsible for managing certain aspects of the hasidic court, including its involvement in national Jewish politics. When he was only fifteen years old, Rabbi Yosef Yitzḥak Schneerson represented Chabad at various rabbinic conventions. After his marriage, he was appointed administrator of the first Lubavitch yeshiva called Tomekhei Temimim.

In the wake of the Communist Revolution in Russia in 1917, and after the death of his father in 1920, Rabbi Yosef Yitzḥak Schneerson became one of the most important Jewish leaders in what turned out to be a critically difficult time for Russian Jewry. He assumed the yoke of preserving the embers of Jewish life under the Communist regime, establishing a Talmud Torah network as well as a network of yeshivot. He was also active in providing essential materials for religious Jewish life, at great personal danger, since this was in violation of the law. In 1927, he was incarcerated by the Soviet authorities and was sentenced to death because of these activities.

After international pressure was exerted from multiple sources, his sentence was initially commuted to exile in Siberia and later to deportation. As a result, he took up residence in Latvia and Poland for several years. Rabbi Yosef Yitzḥak Schneerson was able to escape the Nazi occupation by the skin of his teeth, and in 1940 he arrived in New York. Immediately upon his arrival in the United States, accompanied by a handful of family members and friends, Rabbi Yosef Yitzḥak Schneerson began building a new infrastructure for Chabad Hasidism and for Judaism in general. He established, among other things, a network of yeshivot, an educational center, and a publishing house.

In his struggle against the Communist repression of the practice of Judaism, Rabbi Yosef Yitzḥak delineated a path, not only for his hasidim, but for many others for generations to come. He taught how Jewish life can exist even under a hostile regime. His activities in the United States injected a spirit of vitality and optimism into the future of Judaism and generated substantive change in American Jewry. As a result of his efforts, Jewish life in the United States went from a period of decline and depression to one of growth and prominence.

Throughout his life, Rabbi Yosef Yitzḥak Schneerson acted on behalf of his hasidim, and on behalf of the entire Jewish people, with great self-sacrifice of his own body and soul. The projects he organized and the leadership paradigms he initiated laid the foundation for the work of his successor, Rabbi Menaḥem Mendel Schneerson. Rabbi Menaḥem Mendel relied on the foundations established by his father-in-law in the technical-practical sense, but even more so in the substantive sense. He asserted that it was Rabbi Yosef Yitzḥak who deserved credit for his accomplishments and aspired to perpetuate projects that his father-in-law had initiated.

10

Like a Phoenix

The tenth of Shevat is the *yartzeit* of the sixth Lubavitcher Rebbe, Rabbi Yosef Yitzḥak Schneerson, as well as the day that Rabbi Menaḥem Mendel Schneerson assumed that role one year later. Although it is the custom of Chabad hasidim to focus primarily on the fact that the Lubavitcher Rebbe assumed the leadership on this date, I'd like to speak now about his father-in-law.

Rabbi Yosef Yitzḥak Schneerson was the only son of Rabbi Shalom Dovber Schneerson and succeeded his father as the leader of Chabad. Rabbi Yosef Yitzḥak Schneerson's leadership lasted thirty years, from 1920 to 1950. Those thirty years can be divided into three periods. He lived in Russia for approximately ten years before he was deported. He lived in Eastern Europe – for a brief time in Latvia and a more extensive time in Poland – for the next decade, and he lived in the United States for his final decade.

Few people experience transitions such as these. They were not only changes of address; they involved moving from one culture to a completely different one. When reviewing the activities of Rabbi Yosef Yitzḥak Schneerson in each of these places, one can learn a great deal about the uniqueness of his personality.

RUSSIA: ORGANIZATION OF JEWISH COMMUNAL LIFE

Prior to the Communist Revolution, Jewish life in Russia was very rich and productive. Most of the large population of Jews who lived there were religious, whether hasidic or not. It was a world in which both Torah and Hasidism flourished.

That entire Jewish world was forcibly eradicated by the Soviet authorities and their collaborators. All of the awful pressure that the Communist regime was capable of exerting was exerted on the Jewish world. The problem wasn't only Soviet harassment of Jewish leaders and successful, talented, or dedicated people. The entire structure of Jewish life in the cities and villages of Russia was destroyed, crushed under the coarse boot of the authorities. Almost all of the rabbis were smuggled out of the country, not because their lives were necessarily in danger, but because it was impossible to maintain a Jewish school, yeshiva, or other Jewish institution in Russia. Rabbis could no longer exist there. Perhaps in a less totalitarian place, some semblance of Jewish life could have survived, but in Communist Russia, the practice of Judaism was completely devastated. It became impossible to organize it anew.

Rabbi Yosef Yitzḥak was one of the last rabbis with the will and ability to attempt to preserve the structure of Jewish life – not by organization from the top down, and not by reaching out to isolated, broken, and scattered individuals, but by attracting Jews who were still somehow part of a community. During those ten years, he tried to sustain some sort of Jewish communal life that would be capable of enduring. That work took place in the first decade of Rabbi Yosef Yitzḥak Schneerson's leadership.

With the passage of time, those efforts became more difficult because Jewish education was almost completely prohibited. Maintaining any Jewish education at all involved greater and greater personal danger and self-sacrifice. At a certain point, it became impossible to accomplish almost anything. Although there are survivors who managed to grow up in that terrible environment and endure – some even managed to have children who continued to practice Judaism – as a rule, Jewish life in Russia became so weak and so scattered that it collapsed entirely, leaving virtually no survivors. For all intents and purposes, Rabbi Yosef

Yitzḥak Schneerson's departure from Russia was the beginning of the end of Russian Judaism.

POLAND: THE LUBAVITCH STYLE IN NEW SURROUNDINGS

From Russia, Rabbi Yosef Yitzḥak Schneerson moved to Latvia, and from there, to Poland. During the period between the two world wars, he lived primarily in Poland. Poland at the time was a thriving center of Judaism, though with internal problems, since the majority of Poland's Jews were no longer religiously observant. Despite this, Poland still had a massive community of hundreds of thousands of observant Jews who lived, worked, and practiced Torah there, each in his own way.

In Poland, Rabbi Yosef Yitzḥak Schneerson encountered a different world from the one he knew in Russia. Most of the Jews in Poland, including the hasidim, knew nothing about the Chabad approach. Polish Jews lived in another universe; there was no common language between them and Chabad Hasidism.

With the disintegration of Jewish observance that had already begun in Poland, Rabbi Yosef Yitzḥak sought to build a new Jewish world with the Chabad approach, and he succeeded. Most of the people who were drawn to him after he left Europe and came to the United States were alumni of the yeshivot that he had established in Poland. In the old parlance, descendants of families who have been Lubavitch for generations are called "*geza*." Poland had very few *geza* hasidim. The Polish Jews who became Lubavitcher hasidim in every sense entered that world as a result of Rabbi Yosef Yitzḥak's efforts.

Here, then, is an important question: What becomes of a person who moves from one place to another, uprooted like a tree? Does he become a mere shadow of his former self or does he seek to revitalize his essence on new ground, in a totally different world? Before speaking of Rabbi Yosef Yitzḥak Schneerson's personality, I would like to address one of his talents – specifically his ability to rebuild an old world in a new form, to take new surroundings, personalities, and materials and to use them to build, more or less, a structure based on an existing framework.

SCION AND STOCK

To understand how this came about, I will employ imagery appropriate to the month of Shevat: the beginning of spring in Israel. When growing different plants, like roses or lemon and orange trees, for example, grafting is sometimes employed. This is an agricultural method in which one attaches a branch (the scion) from one plant to the branch or trunk (the stock) of another. The scion joins the stock and becomes one of the branches of the plant. In Israel, oranges are grown on stocks of the *ḥushḥash,* which is a very durable tree that produces the bitter orange. When a branch of the delicate orange tree is grafted onto a *ḥushḥash* trunk, the new branches produce sweet oranges. That is, for all intents and purposes, what Rabbi Yosef Yitzḥak Schneerson did in every place where he lived. He grafted new branches onto the local population in order to produce fruits that would be similar to the scions.

Rabbi Yosef Yitzḥak Schneerson's success was tied to his personality as well as his abilities. In other places, people tried but were unable to reconstruct a community on new ground by employing similar methods. Their old ideas couldn't thrive in a new location. There are many large hasidic sects, but most of their members are descendants and descendants of descendants of the original members of those sects, even though, on occasion, other people may join. Those hasidic sects had absolutely no interest in bringing their message to new populations. They didn't graft their scions onto other stocks. They were capable of growing only within their world. When their numbers increased, it was only because children were born to the community. They sought only to preserve their particular way of practicing Judaism.

Rabbi Yosef Yitzḥak Schneerson couldn't have done that even if he wanted to, and I don't think he wanted to. He took the essence of what he brought with him from Russia – the Chabad approach – and grafted it onto Polish stocks. This grafting was, to a large degree, successful, since one can't differentiate between Russian or Polish Lubavitch lineage and customs unless one is told.

This is what occupied Rabbi Yosef Yitzḥak Schneerson between 1928 and 1940, the year he succeeded in fleeing Poland. In 1940, he and some members of his family received permission to enter the United States, but he wasn't able to bring out his entire family; a daughter and grandchildren remained in Poland. This was the beginning of the end of East European Jewry, which was almost completely destroyed. Only remnants survived – those who either miraculously escaped slaughter or somehow managed to survive the camps. That great Jewish world was exterminated and no longer exists.

AMERICA: ESTABLISHING INSTITUTIONS IN A TAINTED LAND

In 1940, when Rabbi Yosef Yitzḥak Schneerson arrived in the United States, he was already in his sixties and quite ill, possibly due to the manner in which he had been treated in Russia. In his final years, he was hardly able to speak. This didn't prevent him from continuing his work. His power of renewal was still as strong as if he were a young man beginning a new project.

The United States was a completely different world from Eastern Europe. Although no country is completely devoid of anti-Semitism – including the State of Israel – the great tolerance of religious diversity that existed in America enabled Jews there to grow and thrive. Many Jews who immigrated to America succeeded financially as well as in bettering their social standing. But their Judaism suffered. They felt that they were the end of the line, possibly the last generation of practicing Jews. There was a time when upright Jews didn't want to go to America, despite its economic opportunities, because they felt that the atmosphere made it difficult to live a full Jewish life.

Many Jewish communities in the United States had died out. Synagogues had closed. Members of the first generation of immigrants went to synagogue and observed *mitzvot*. The second generation was Conservative, the third generation was Reform, and the fourth generation was completely ignorant of Judaism.

A story is told of a Reform temple in Dallas. On the synagogue's one hundredth anniversary, the rabbi decided to have a great celebration for which he sought to gather the descendants of the Jews who had initially established and attended the temple. It turned out that only one descendant of the initial members was Jewish; the rest were gentiles. This was the one-way direction in which American Jewry was headed. It was absolutely clear that, in terms of Jewish life in America, the situation would continue to deteriorate.

When Rabbi Yosef Yitzḥak Schneerson first arrived in the United States, there were many people who cared about Judaism, but they were usually impoverished immigrants. The Jews who were well off financially weren't particularly interested in Judaism. We have a letter of thanks that Rabbi Yosef Yitzḥak Schneerson personally wrote to someone who had sent him a contribution; it included a receipt for the sum of five dollars. During his first year or two in New York, it wasn't unusual for men to have to go outside to search for a tenth man to complete the *minyan* for the *Minḥa* prayer. What Jew had time to recite the *Minḥa* prayer? What Jew even wanted to?

Rabbi Yosef Yitzḥak Schneerson once again set out to rebuild the Jewish world. He sought to reestablish yeshivot in Jewish neighborhoods so that Jews could study Torah. He insisted that all the young men in his yeshivot grow beards; at the time, this was tantamount to asking them to grow tails. No one had beards then. The thought that anyone would consent to grow one was preposterous.

During the final decade of Rabbi Yosef Yitzḥak Schneerson's life, more and more Torah institutions were built in the US. With varying degrees of initiative, he expanded Jewish observance so that it reached beyond existing frameworks.

LIKE A PHOENIX

Rabbi Yosef Yitzḥak Schneerson's power of renewal evokes a midrash on the verse "I will multiply my days like the phoenix."[1] When the phoenix grows old, it enters its nest, catches fire, and emerges as a new bird.[2] Rabbi Yosef Yitzḥak Schneerson was like a phoenix. He was able to start anew time and again. Not only was his homeland destroyed, his entire world was destroyed. The past was demolished. And from the ashes, he built the world anew. When he saw that Jewish life in the new world was also in danger of dying out, he worked to rebuild that, too.

1. Job 29:18.
2. *Bereshit Rabba* 19:5.

After the war, many people wrote letters to Rabbi Yosef Yitzḥak Schneerson, describing what they had lost as well as what had survived of their families and their lives. In their letters, they shared past and present difficulties, as well as dark worries about the future. Rabbi Yosef Yitzḥak wept upon reading those letters. Some of his adherents tried to spare him by weeding out the more painful letters, but when Rabbi Yosef Yitzḥak learned that his letters were being filtered, he shouted at those who were trying to protect him. "My role as Rebbe is to bear everyone's suffering," he insisted. "I can't relinquish that role and leave it to others."

This ability to bear others' suffering was as much a part of Rabbi Yosef Yitzḥak's greatness as his ability to rebuild. He was certainly tormented by the suffering, but he wasn't broken by it. There were calamities, there were setbacks, but he knew that one must recover and go on. Branches may have been chopped off, the tree itself may have sustained extensive damage, but he knew it was essential to attempt to regrow it.

Rabbi Yosef Yitzḥak Schneerson retained the ability to act even when the odds were overwhelmingly against him. He was like a phoenix – able to regrow, to renew himself, and cause new life to emerge from the ashes.

THE JEWISH PEOPLE'S ABILITY TO RENEW ITSELF

The ability to renew itself is part of the essence of the Jewish people. In Isaiah's vision, they are described with the words "There will still be a tenth in it, and it shall continue to be subject to elimination, like the terebinth and like the oak whose leaves fall; their trunk remains. The holy descendants will be its trunk."[3] During the summer, the terebinth, like the oak, is an impressive tree, full of leaves. In the autumn, after all of its leaves have fallen, the remaining skeleton of branches bears no resemblance to the tree it was in summer. Isaiah's prophecy describes a time of tragedy that befell the Jewish people, when everything appeared to have fallen and collapsed. And yet "the holy descendants will be its trunk" – the descendants of those who experienced devastation will be renewed and grow even more vigorously.

3. Isaiah 6:13.

This is also the theme of *kiddush levana*, the blessings said upon the sanctification of the moon. We sanctify the moon, not only because we see it reappear from time to time, but because it's an allusion to the renewability of the Jewish people. The moon wanes, becoming smaller and smaller, then begins to wax and regrow. It represents the Jewish people's ability to renew, to grow and flourish after descent and destruction.

This special ability to renew itself was exemplified and manifest in Rabbi Yosef Yitzḥak Schneerson, who took on great missions at a time when Jewish life and communities were destroyed and diminished.

RENEWAL: THE SECRET OF LIFE

The ability to renew is part of the secret of life itself. Renewal differentiates between what's alive and what's not. Objects that are not alive gradually deteriorate and cease to be. That's the way the world is constructed. Even something as large as a mountain or iceberg gradually diminishes with time. Neither an old pencil nor an old computer can regenerate. Other than life itself, everything is subject to inevitable and irreversible attrition, erosion, and expiration. The ability to renew, then, is an indication of life.

Among living beings, part of the seed from which they are able to renew themselves endures. Adam was denied immortality, but he did live on in the human species, which continues to propagate and exist after the death of the individual. Even from a biological perspective, part of Adam survives in the chain of human existence.

It is written, "For the righteous man falls seven times and rises."[4] Our Sages juxtaposed the following words to that verse: "But the wicked man falls with one."[5] The righteous man can fall seven times, or even seventy-seven times, and still rise to continue on his path. One who lacks this ability isn't truly alive, and if one isn't alive, one cannot rise. Rabbi Yosef Yitzḥak Schneerson possessed the ability to rise after every fall.

4. Proverbs 24:16.
5. Based on Proverbs 28:18; see *Sanhedrin* 7a.

The Essential Person

THE LUBAVITCHER REBBE'S ADHERENCE TO RABBI YOSEF YITZḤAK SCHNEERSON

Rabbi Yosef Yitzḥak Schneerson was inarguably a talented person. His leadership, his enterprises, and his organizational activities were exceptional. But in many ways, his light was less radiant than that of his son-in-law, Rabbi Menaḥem Mendel Shneerson, who succeeded him as Rebbe.

Rabbi Yosef Yitzḥak Schneerson acknowledged his son-in-law's greatness and appointed him to respond, in his name, to complex letters dealing with questions in the realm of Kabbala as well as *halakha*. Rabbi Yosef Yitzḥak also sent him on various missions, primarily so that people could get to know him.

At a certain point – I don't know if this happened at the time of his wedding or a bit earlier – Rabbi Menaḥem Mendel became his father-in-law's "number one hasid." Until then, he was just one of the hasidim, but from that pivotal point, he cleaved to Rabbi Yosef Yitzḥak Schneerson with absolute adherence and, in many ways, with tremendous deference. Showing honor and respect toward a great man doesn't necessarily turn him into his hasid. A person can heed a Rebbe and receive guidance from him, but that's not the same as becoming his hasid – as becoming someone who adheres to a Rebbe absolutely. Being someone's hasid requires an essential acceptance of his leadership.

Many other hasidim, including an older son-in-law, were also attached to Rabbi Yosef Yitzḥak Schneerson. What was unique about Rabbi Menaḥem Mendel's relationship to Rabbi Yosef Yitzḥak was his own self-negation, as well as his complete and utter, heartfelt acceptance of his father-in-law as his Rebbe.

The connection between the Lubavitcher Rebbe, Rabbi Menaḥem Mendel Schneerson, and his father-in-law and predecessor, Rabbi Yosef Yitzḥak, apparently continued until the final day of the Lubavitcher Rebbe's life. At that point, of course, the attachment wasn't to Rabbi Yosef Yitzḥak in body, but to his soul. Time and again, the Lubavitcher Rebbe would converse and consult with his father-in-law.

How did Rabbi Menaḥem Mendel Schneerson come to be chosen as his father-in-law's successor? Rabbi Yosef Yitzḥak didn't leave a will and never said explicitly who he wanted to succeed him as Rebbe. Both sons-in-law were likely candidates for the position. The elder of the two was already serving as chief administrator at the time of Rabbi Yosef Yitzḥak's passing. Rabbi Menaḥem Mendel, the younger son-in-law, was an unknown to most people at the time. It was logical and presumed by all that the senior son-in-law would become the next Rebbe.

In practice, both sons-in-law served in tandem for about a year after the passing of Rabbi Yosef Yitzḥak, since it had not yet been decided who would succeed their father-in-law. Would it be the elder son-in-law, who wanted the leadership (but didn't receive it), or the younger one, who didn't want it (and received it)?

Ultimately, the elder son-in-law, of his own initiative, accepted the authority of the younger son-in-law and conceded the leadership to him.

I remember seeing the elder son-in-law at Chabad headquarters. Though he was always seated in a place of honor, it was clear that he consistently deferred to his brother-in-law the Lubavitcher Rebbe, even when it was very difficult for him. Even when there was ostensibly competition between the two, there was no apparent enmity.

One time the Lubavitcher Rebbe said to his brother-in-law, "We don't accept new ideas in such-and-such matters."

His brother-in-law responded, "But there are problems that are new to the world. If you don't want to introduce new solutions, how do you deal with new problems?"

The Lubavitcher Rebbe answered, "I go to our father-in-law, and ask him."

Rabbi Yosef Yitzḥak Schneerson, of course, had already left this world. When he heard the Lubavitcher Rebbe's answer, the elder brother-in-law said, "Of one matter I am certain: My brother-in-law isn't a liar. If he says that he goes to the father-in-law and asks him questions, that is what he does. I'm unable to do so. That's why he is the Rebbe and I am not."

THE ABILITY TO IDENTIFY A TRUE LEADER

The connection between the Lubavitcher Rebbe and Rabbi Yosef Yitzḥak Schneerson was one of absolute adherence and persisted even after

Rabbi Yosef Yitzḥak's death. Why did the Lubavitcher Rebbe attach himself to Rabbi Yosef Yitzḥak to that degree? What did he see in him?

In many ways, the ability to find a person who is worthy of leadership, who is capable of serving as a true leader, is in itself a special talent.

Rabbi Yitzḥak Meir Alter, the first Rebbe of the Gur dynasty and author of *Ḥiddushei HaRim*, was once asked why he had deferred to the Kotzker Rebbe for so many years. The Kotzker Rebbe didn't write any works of Torah insights, though he was apparently an accomplished Torah scholar. The Gerrer Rebbe was also an exceptionally accomplished Torah scholar; he was also gifted as a hasid of piety and devotion. It was because of this that the Gerrer Rebbe was able to see the Kotzker Rebbe as the leader. In answer to the question, then, he said, "Before me stood a pillar of fire, and I bowed before it."

Another example, this one from *Tanakh*, is the strange story of two other brothers-in-law: David and Jonathan. Jonathan, the son of King Saul, had many virtues; he was a great warrior and a victorious commander. He wasn't a person about whom one would say, "He is his father's son and nothing more." Yet when David was at a low point in his life, Jonathan said to him, "You will be the leader, and I will be your second-in-command. I may be capable of being a great general, but you are destined to be king."

The Sages see Jonathan's deference to David as evidence of his great humility and considers him one of the three most humble men in history.[6] But humility aside, what did Jonathan actually see in David? It had to be something more than his military accomplishments, considering that Jonathan also excelled in that sphere. After all, he had defeated the enemy, almost single-handedly, in a great war.

The answer is that Jonathan was able to envision David as God's anointed.

The prophet Samuel, on the other hand, was unable to discern precisely who would be king when he saw the sons of Yishai, perhaps because they all seemed worthy. The Midrash says the following, with

6. *Bava Metzia* 84b–85a. The other two were Benei Beteira and Rabban Shimon ben Gamliel.

an undertone of criticism of Samuel: "The Holy One, blessed be He, said to Samuel, 'You call yourself a seer? Then show us what you see.'"[7] Even the prophet Samuel lacked the ability to identify David as king. Only a person on a very high level can identify a true leader and say, "This is the one."

I'd like to return to the question of the Lubavitcher Rebbe's relationship with his father-in-law, Rabbi Yosef Yitzḥak Schneerson. The Lubavitcher Rebbe was an extremely talented and brilliant man in his own right. He had probably been a hasid of Rabbi Yosef Yitzḥak from his youth. But at some point he made a conscious decision to cling to Rabbi Yosef Yitzḥak and defer to him on all matters. What did he discern in Rabbi Yosef Yitzḥak that made him decide to adhere to him so strongly?

RABBI YOSEF YITZḤAK SCHNEERSON'S COURAGE

Rabbi Yosef Yitzḥak was a man of great courage who had the ability to confront challenges on many fronts.

There are different kinds of courage. People who have physical courage are willing to endanger themselves. They head toward danger even if they might hesitate at first. Others have spiritual courage. They are morally courageous and are able to withstand the pressure of public opinion, the pressure of "everyone says" or pressure from the authorities, for example. They are able to stand up to someone who might be greater and wiser than they are without compromising their values.

There are times when a person knows he has heard something that sounds wrong, but doesn't speak up because he feels unable to hold his own against an esteemed authority figure. I've known people who lacked nothing in terms of talent and intelligence, but who lack the courage to state their opinion or defend their position.

A person with physical courage doesn't necessarily have moral courage. Many great, courageous people – people capable of leaping into enemy fire, if need be, have buckled under in the face of spiritual pressure. The opposite is also true. A person with great moral courage can be a physical coward, for example, when merely confronted by a small barking dog.

---

7. *Sifrei, Devarim* 17.

Another form of courage is the courage to bear pain. It's astounding to see a seemingly strong, tall man, a veritable giant, unable to tolerate a slight wound. Women can sometimes be heard saying about their husbands, "He acts like a child when he has a stomachache or comes down with the flu." Some people are capable of confronting an enemy but incapable of tolerating a few bacteria. All of their power dissipates when they are in pain. Then again, there are those who are able to bear exquisite pain and continue to function despite it.

I have been privileged to see courage in the face of pain in a young friend who had cancer. As he lay ill and dying, he didn't break – not from the pain of his illness and not even from the pain of knowing that he was young and talented and about to leave this world before he was ready. He knew that he could have accomplished so much had he only been granted more time. We happened to have the same doctor. The doctor told me he spent time with this young man, not only because he was his physician, but because he could see the image of God in him.

As my friend's body deteriorated with the progression of his illness, something much more beautiful, clean, and exalted shone through. Many people in the same dire physical situation would shrivel up due to fear, terror, pain, and the approaching end. But some remain intact in the face of it all and will not submit to their pain.

Rabbi Yosef Yitzḥak Schneerson had many different kinds of courage. He had the courage to withstand temptation, the courage to face terror, and the courage to hold his own before authority. He had physical courage, too. He suffered torments and died a harsh death, but he was never broken.

Rabbi Yosef Yitzḥak's courage is evident from reports, some of which he wrote himself, of his incarceration in Soviet prison. Among other things, he wrote that the Russian gentile who took him to the interrogation room told him, "Yesterday several priests were brought here. I had to shoot them, one at a time. You can't imagine what fun it was for me to kill those people. When I saw one priest's leg twitching, I kicked him, then put a second bullet in his head."

The interrogators had the power to sentence people to death at a whim. Rabbi Yosef Yitzḥak Schneerson knew this and understood that he could be facing death at any moment. Yet he not only stood up to his interrogators – he provoked them. When brought into the interrogation room, he said, "You know, this is the first place I've been where people don't stand up when I enter."

His interrogator, who happened to be Jewish, asked him, "Do you know where you are?"

"Yes, I'm in a place where it is forbidden to affix a *mezuza*" – referring to the precept that forbids affixing a *mezuza* to the doorpost of a lavatory or a barn.

The interrogator placed his pistol on the table and said, "Do you see this toy? It has changed the minds of many people."

"That toy is effective on people who have one world and many gods," Rabbi Yosef Yitzḥak Schneerson responded. "A person like me, who has two worlds and one God, doesn't fear it."

That's an example of the courage Rabbi Yosef Yitzḥak Schneerson manifested when his life hung in the balance.

Courage in the face of death is a rare phenomenon, but there's also courage that manifests itself when a person is unafraid of life – of living people in particular. Rabbi Yosef Yitzḥak's ability to approach new problems and find innovative solutions to resolve them was never impaired by the opinions of others, no matter who they happened to be. It was only because of his circumstances, as well as the lack of financial support and manpower, that Rabbi Yosef Yitzḥak Schneerson functioned on a small scale. His son-in-law, Rabbi Menaḥem Mendel, who didn't face these limitations, was able to complete what Rabbi Yosef Yitzḥak started and expand on those innovations exponentially. Rabbi Yosef Yitzḥak's efforts were essential building blocks, the foundation, for the accomplishments that followed.

THE ESSENTIAL PERSON

Chabad characterizes a person like Rabbi Yosef Yitzḥak Schneerson as "essential." When a person is essential, external circumstances have no real impact on the path he has chosen or on his elevated status. His essence remains intact, even as he experiences ups and downs. Circumstances may change, but his essence does not. The personality of someone who is not essential, on the other hand, is pulled in different directions and unable to withstand changing circumstances. An essential person follows his path even when it's circuitous. Where he's going and what he must do remain clear to him.

Rabbi Yosef Yitzḥak Schneerson initiated several important projects that began on a small scale, but went on to grow and flourish later. Because of this, it seemed as if they were later initiated by others, but they originated with Rabbi Yosef Yitzḥak. For example, the institution of Chabad *sheliḥim,* emissaries sent out by the Lubavitcher Rebbe to foster Jewish life, which today is its own entire multifaceted world, was created by Rabbi Yosef Yitzḥak and not by his son-in-law, Rabbi Menaḥem Mendel. Rabbi Yosef Yitzḥak Schneerson sent out a total of three, or at most five, *sheliḥim.* Later, hundreds, perhaps even thousands, joined their ranks, but it was Rabbi Yosef Yitzḥak who originated *sheliḥut,* and it was Rabbi Yosef Yitzḥak who determined what they must do and how. He was the one who introduced the concept and protocols of *sheliḥut*: The Rebbe sends a young man or a young couple to the ends of the earth, to a place where the language and customs are completely foreign, and tells them to build a new world. That is how Rabbi Yosef Yitzḥak Schneerson built new worlds.

Rabbi Yosef Yitzḥak is also the one who began to describe and record Chabad customs and way of life. This project had far-reaching, practical significance. Rabbi Yosef Yitzḥak depicted Chabad life in detail – what a person is supposed to do, how a person should comport himself. These were customs and practices that had previously been considered personal matters that people tended to observe but kept to themselves, and Rabbi Yosef Yitzḥak Schneerson decided to write about them and publicize them. The reach and scope of this work increased exponentially during the tenure of the Lubavitcher Rebbe, Rabbi Menaḥem Mendel Schneerson, but it was his father-in-law, Rabbi Yosef Yitzḥak, who lent these practices a structure.

This is not merely of historical interest; it has practical significance. By constructing an organized, defined way of life, Rabbi Yosef Yitzḥak Schneerson transformed a large, dispersed body of people into a unified society. Customs that had been practiced by some individuals, but were not necessarily common knowledge, became a shared framework that effectively enabled Chabad hasidim to observe uniform practices.

Rabbi Yosef Yitzḥak Schneerson's efforts resulted in the perpetuation of a venerable dynasty and great tradition. Some of his ancestors were individuals of extraordinary intellect, talent, and wisdom. He sought a way to encapsulate their entire world so that it would be possible to transmit it to subsequent generations. Although his personality wasn't expansive, and he may not have had the sparkle or shine as some others, he possessed an eternal flame that couldn't be extinguished. It remained steady and true to its core, even when blown by the wind. It was that fire inside him, that eternal flame, that fueled his ability to perpetuate the Chabad approach and teachings for generations to come.

IDENTIFYING THE ESSENCE

As stated, Rabbi Menaḥem Mendel Schneerson's admiration for his father-in-law stemmed from his unique ability to see things that others couldn't. Most people can quickly identify certain talents – a brilliant personality, an exceptional ability to articulate, a sharp memory, vast knowledge. But the ability to identify the essence of a person is rare and indicates a particularly high level of understanding. Aside from his brilliance and positive character straits, Rabbi Menaḥem Mendel was able to see when another's essence made it fitting for that person to be a great leader. He understood that Rabbi Yosef Yitzḥak was a true rock, the nucleus that encompassed everything, and just as the nucleus contains all the information needed to produce a tree or create a human being, Rabbi Yosef Yitzḥak had the ability to sustain Jewish life and propel it forward.

This may seem otherworldly, but these nuclear concentrations of life are everywhere to be seen in nature. Life forms have the ability to contract to a point where all content is concentrated, in which life in its entirety is contained. Its outward form may not look impressive, but life itself, in its most highly distilled form, is concealed within. If you compare the apple seed to the apple tree itself, the seed has none of the outward characteristics of the tree. The apple tree is tall and has beautiful leaves and flowers; its fruits are tasty and fragrant. The seed of the apple tree contains all the characteristics of the tree – its appearance, fragrance, taste, height, leaves, and flowers – but this seed, this minuscule point of origin, is much less impressive than the tree itself. Yet someone with understanding can see that there is a whole apple, an entire tree, a whole world, within that little seed. To realize the value of the seed, one must possess the special ability to discern its essence.

A story is told of a diamond merchant who happened to be a hasid of one of the Lubavitcher Rebbes. The wealthy hasid wanted to know about certain people in the Rebbe's court, and the Rebbe mentioned that one of them was an exceptional person. The hasid replied with the impudence that some wealthy people tend to have: "I know him, and I don't think he is particularly extraordinary."

One day the Rebbe requested to see a sampling of the hasid's merchandise. He brought several diamonds to show the Rebbe and exclaimed repeatedly, "This is a first-class diamond.... This one is exceptional.... This diamond is rare.... This one is the rarest of the rare...," and so on. The Rebbe looked at the diamonds and said, "I don't know why you say this one is exceptional. In my opinion, that other one is much more impressive."

"To know the value of diamonds," the hasid responded, "you must have an understanding of diamonds."

The Rebbe replied, "And to know the value of souls, you must have an understanding of souls."

Diamonds in their natural form, covered with a layer of raw material, can look a little like potatoes. People could certainly kick it aside when encountering one, mistakenly thinking it worthless. To find diamonds, one must be able to tell that there is a real diamond beneath the outer layer. Not everything that is shiny and sparkling or able to scratch surfaces turns out to be a diamond. Only an expert on diamonds can determine if a rock is worth more than a person could earn in a lifetime.

The same is true regarding souls. To understand souls, I myself must have an elevated soul, one that is capable of identifying an essential person. One must understand that a person could be the wisest man of the generation, or extremely virtuous, and yet still he's not an essential person, while someone who possesses an essential soul could very well be outwardly unimpressive.

A wise, insightful, intellectual Lubavitcher hasid once asked me to recommend essays that I thought would be worthwhile for him to study. When I told him to study the essays of Rabbi Yosef Yitzḥak Schneerson, he grimaced. He thought them too simple and inappropriate for a person at his level of learning. In my opinion, that hasid didn't understand that it's sometimes more difficult to create something simple but perfectly constructed than to make something complicated. Sometimes what seems strikingly complex can turn out to be impressive garbage, even if some people buy it. One must have a deep understanding of a topic in order to create something simple that encompasses everything.

The Lubavitcher Rebbe, Rabbi Menaḥem Mendel Schneerson, had the ability to see clearly through all the veneers. That's why, when he met his father-in-law, Rabbi Yosef Yitzḥak Schneerson, he could see that Rabbi Yosef Yitzḥak was essential – a true Rebbe and leader.

THE KERNEL OF TRUTH

At the revelation at the crevice of the rock, God uttered the thirteen attributes of mercy. Immediately afterward, the Torah states, "Moses hastened and bowed to the ground and prostrated himself."[8] What made Moses prostrate himself? The Sages say that it was the sight of the attribute of truth that caused him to fall on his face.[9]

At times, it's possible to discern the truth by comparing two things or sometimes two people. The comparison shows one to be true and the other not to be true. Among the different personalities who lived in Rabbi Yosef Yitzḥak Schneerson's generation, there were prominent, exceptional people about whom I can say wholeheartedly and honestly that they didn't approach his level of truth. Rabbi Yosef Yitzḥak possessed a core of truth that is extremely difficult to retain.

As I said before, I didn't come to speak about history for its own sake. I'm recounting this history because it raises a moral question: How does one distinguish between students or friends and identify the true student or true friend? How can one tell if someone is the kind of ephemeral being that will be swept away by the wind – here today and gone tomorrow? Where can truth be found?

---

8. Exodus 34:8.
9. *Sanhedrin* 111a.

There are shining paths and there are pathways to victory. And there's another path that's not paved like a runway or superhighway. It may be a meandering goat path, but it takes a person to the truth. May each and every one of us be privileged to find that path to truth.

Leḥayim!

11

His Love of the Jewish People

THE REVELATION OF THE ESSENCE OF A *TZADDIK*'S LIFE

On the anniversary of a person's passing – the *yartzeit* – we hold a farbrengen and focus on the essence of the person rather than on the sadness of the loss.

It is written that on the day that a person passes, his life's accomplishments and deeds are tallied and assume great significance. Along these lines, the Sages understand the verse "Man will not see Me and live"[1] to mean that "during their lifetimes they do not see Me, but upon their death, they see."[2]

The revelation that a person merits upon death is not mysterious or remote. Each person is enlightened according to the nature and essence of his personality. His life is condensed into one single point that is a kind of pinnacle of everything he achieved, and this point is given expression on his *yartzeit*. That's why, on a *yartzeit*, we focus on an aspect of that person's life that is related to the sum total of his actions.

Occasionally, a person's life assumes a different character from the one it had before due to the revelation that transpires on that day. On

1. Exodus 33:20.
2. *Sifra Nedava* 2:12.

Lag BaOmer, for example, the entire Jewish people conducts a *hilula* for Rabbi Shimon bar Yoḥai, who commanded them to celebrate rather than mourn his passing. During his lifetime, he was seen as an austere, punctilious person, but he possessed an inner joy. On his final day in this world, his inner joyousness was revealed.

The *yartzeit* of a *tzaddik* assumes a special character that is related to his essence. Of course, on each and every *yartzeit*, several *tzaddikim* passed away. Today, for example, is the day of the passing of Rashash, Rabbi Shalom Sharabi, who was one of the greatest kabbalists in recent times. But I would like to speak today of Rabbi Yosef Yitzḥak Schneerson's *yartzeit*, which commemorates his passing today, on 10 Shevat, in 1950, which was more recent and is, perhaps, more relevant.

The essence of Rabbi Yosef Yitzḥak Schneerson's wasn't characterized by mysticism, though he engaged in it. It wasn't related to the revealed Torah, though he engaged in that as well. It wasn't characterized by many other matters in which he was engaged. The starting point and origin of his life, the point of entry and exit of his life – the point around which his life revolved – was his love of the Jewish people.

SELF-SACRIFICE ON BEHALF OF EVERY JEW

Love for the Jewish people has many forms and is expressed in many nuanced ways. Rabbi Yosef Yitzḥak Schneerson's love of the Jewish people reached such an exalted level that he was willing to die for it. He wasn't satisfied with speaking in praise of the Jewish people, nor with banners expressing love of the Jewish people. He actually devoted his life to the Jewish people, wherever he was and in every situation.

Although Rabbi Yosef Yitzḥak Schneerson was a hasidic Rebbe, the main focus of his life wasn't as the leader of a specific group. His life revolved around his concern for every individual Jew, whoever and wherever he was. Rabbi Yosef Yitzḥak's love of the Jewish people included everyone about whom it may be said, "He will be called [*yekhaneh*] by the name of Israel."[3] If we are precise in defining the term *kinui*, it's a label ascribed to a person rather than a specific name. There are people whom we would call Jewish even though they have neither

3. Isaiah 44:5.

the character nor the essence of a Jew. God still loves the person – protects him, relates to him, and saves him. And just as God on high cares about every Jew, whoever he may be, so Rabbi Yosef Yitzḥak Schneerson cared about every Jew with genuine, unlimited self-sacrifice, even when facing death.

In general, love of the Jewish people is not about speaking of the virtue of that love. Rather, it is love based on action that can lead to self-sacrifice on behalf of the Jewish people.

There are two types of self-sacrifice: the kind where a person devotes his life to something and the kind where a person is even willing to give his soul. A person can devote his life to something even while ensconced in a warm, pleasant place, as many have done and continue to do. By contrast, giving of one's soul involves venturing outside one's comfort zone, as the prophet Isaiah described his own experience: "I did not hide my face from humiliation and spittle."[4] One who ventures outside is basically telling those on the outside that they are still Jews. That was how Rabbi Yosef Yitzḥak Schneerson loved the Jewish people.

I recounted the following story earlier when speaking of Rabbi Yosef Yitzḥak's courage, but it bears repeating here, since it also illustrates his love of the Jewish people. His Communist interrogators were known to shoot and kill people even prior to judgment. When he first entered the interrogation room, he said, "You know, this is the first place I've entered where people don't stand in my honor."

The interrogators, who were Jewish, were also the authorities in power, the ones with the pistols. Rabbi Yosef Yitzḥak wanted them to know what he thought of them. They looked at him in disbelief. Here was a prisoner about to be interrogated and likely to be executed criticizing them for not standing before him! Their response was "Do you know where you are?"

Rabbi Yosef Yitzḥak answered, "Yes, I'm in a place that is exempt from the obligation to affix a *mezuza*" – referring to the *halakha* that states that it's forbidden to affix a *mezuza* to a barn.[5]

4. Isaiah 50:6.
5. *Shulḥan Arukh, Yoreh De'a* 286:2.

This story is about an encounter with people, members of the Jewish people, about whom it is written, "For, Lord, do I not hate Your enemies and contend with those who rise against You? I hate them with utter hatred; they have become my enemies."[6] But in the *Tanya* it is written that just as it is a *mitzva* to hate people of that kind, who oppose God, it is also a *mitzva* to love them.[7] Loving such people is far from simple, and it constitutes a kind of self-sacrifice of the soul. In such a situation, a person isn't required to agree with the other, nor is concession or approval of their actions expected. One is required to confront them and say things that are liable to be harsh and possibly distressing, but one must do so with love. Love of the Jewish people doesn't entail merely pouring saccharine on another person. Sometimes one must actively oppose him, yet still continue to love him. That is love of the Jewish people.

To express it in the words of another lover of the Jewish people, Moses, "Let Moses and one thousand like him be eliminated, and let not one person of Israel be eliminated."[8] Moses said this when he pleaded with God not to destroy those who worshipped the golden calf. Even if a person thinks of himself as important as Moses, he must be aware that Moses said to God, "Erase me please from Your book that You have written."[9] Moses pleaded that he himself be eliminated, while those who had danced around the golden calf be spared, because each and every one of them is a member of the Jewish people.

This is love for the Jewish people.

SHARING IN THE TROUBLES OF ISRAEL

The generation that preceded ours experienced three major tribulations, which were, in a sense, a microcosm of all manifestations of pain experienced by the Jewish people over centuries. Since Rabbi Yosef Yitzḥak Schneerson's essence was love of the Jewish people, he witnessed each of these three troubles and suffered in their midst. The first trouble was

6. Psalms 139:21–22.
7. *Tanya, Likkutei Amarim,* chap. 32.
8. *Midrash Tanḥuma, Va'etḥanan* 6.
9. Exodus 32:32.

the torment of the Jewish people under the Communist regime, a regime that totally eradicated anything that contained an element of Judaism. After his expulsion from Russia, he witnessed the beginning of the second trouble: the physical extermination of the Jewish people in Poland. He literally left there at the last moment. In America, he witnessed the third travail of the Jewish people: the dissolution of the Jewish soul.

Rabbi Yosef Yitzḥak Schneerson saw how the Jewish nation was being dissolved by oppressive, wicked regimes that were forcibly destroying Jews, body and soul. He also saw the Jewish soul disintegrating though it was in an environment that was ostensibly welcoming. Just as it's possible to dissolve something in acid or fire, so, apparently, it's possible to dissolve something in sweet Coca-Cola. Cola doesn't kill as quickly, but its effect is no less lethal.

Rabbi Yosef Yitzḥak lived in all the places where these troubles transpired. He also acted with overt self-sacrifice to meet the Jewish people's particular needs in each place. Every location required a different type of sacrifice. In one place it was necessary to fight, in another, it was necessary to speak, while in the third it was necessary to be resolute. In each of these places, Rabbi Yosef Yitzḥak Schneerson took appropriate action to preserve the remnants of Israel.

In *Megillat Esther* it is written about Purim, "These days are remembered and observed."[10] This is also true of a farbrengen. We don't seek merely to commemorate a certain date, event, person, or history. Matters that are remembered must also be observed. What a person ate or drank at a farbrengen isn't important; whether or not he paid attention is also not critical. What matters most is whether anything of the essence of the farbrengen will be retained. Since Rabbi Yosef Yitzḥak Schneerson devoted his life to love of the Jewish people and to concern for those near and far, his *yartzeit* is an especially propitious time for promoting love of the Jewish people.

Love of the Jewish people requires action, not just words, even if action must reach a level of self-sacrifice.

10. Esther 9:28.

On Love for the Jewish People

A SIGNIFICANT PRINCIPLE IN THE TORAH

The *mitzva* to love the Jewish people is derived from the verse "Love your neighbor as yourself; I am the Lord."[11] This *mitzva* is only one of 613; thank God, we also have additional commandments relating to every aspect of life, including the *mitzva* of Torah study, the *mitzva* to honor one's father and mother, the *mitzva* of Shabbat, and the mitzva to honor Torah scholars. But a person can fulfill a whole world of *mitzvot*, adorning himself with *mitzvot* on all sides, and it turns out that the commandment to love the Jewish people is more central and significant than any of the others.

The Gemara tells of a proselyte who asked Hillel to teach him the entire Torah on one foot. Hillel responded, "That which is hateful to you, do not do to another."[12] Similarly, Rabbi Akiva said, "Love your neighbor as yourself. This is a significant principle in the Torah."[13] According to both Hillel and Rabbi Akiva, the entire Torah is based on the command to "love your neighbor as yourself."

With so many significant *mitzvot*, why is it so important to care about what happens to the neighbors? What makes love of the Jewish people such an important *mitzva*? Why is it considered a principle upon which the entire Torah is based?

THE CLUB OF THE RELIGIOUS

Before I answer this question, I'd like to discuss common misperceptions about love of the Jewish people, and about Judaism in general.

A person often thinks to himself, *I have to first take care of myself. When I have the time, I'll think about others – or maybe not. The mitzva to love the Jewish people begins with the first-person singular: me. I also happen to be a Jew who needs to eat, drink, be clothed, taught Torah, and even indulged every so often. What? Is it a problem to give a Jew a little piece of chocolate every so often?*

---

11. Leviticus 19:18.
12. *Shabbat* 31a.
13. *Bereshit Rabba* 24:7.

Another attitude one might hear from so-called enlightened religious people is, *Let each person live as he chooses. I choose to be religious and fulfill mitzvot. Another Jew may choose not to do so. The main thing is to be nice to each other. We need to be tolerant of each other and not cast stones. Then everything will be fine.*

"Tolerance" is a highly valued word these days. Everyone, including respected, decent, enlightened heads of yeshivot, speak in praise of tolerance. The gist of what they are saying is, "I won't bother you, you don't bother me, and we will all be good friends."

In truth, this attitude isn't limited exclusively to liberal observant Jews. There is a kind of consensus across the entire spectrum – from the most liberal Jews to the most extreme religious zealots – that may be phrased differently in different places, but the concept is the same: There is a club of the religious, and we are dues-paying members of that club. We wake up in the morning, turn pages in the prayer book, and put *tefillin* on our heads. Before we go to sleep, we turn more pages, and so on. People who are not dues-paying members don't belong in our club. They can sit in their own clubs, and as long as they don't throw stones at us, we can ignore them.

NEGATING JUDAISM IN ITS ENTIRETY

This approach is wrong, not only because it shows no love of the Jewish people, but also because, for all intents and purposes, it essentially negates Judaism. Judaism is not a club. A person who landed in a nonobservant home is considered just as Jewish as the person who is observant because he was randomly born into a religious home. Anyone who is fine with the widely accepted view that all is well as long as a religious person and nonreligious person don't steal from each other or kill each other undermines the root, the foundation, and meaning of what it means to be of the Jewish people. I decided to be a Jew of faith, to fulfill *mitzvot,* and my counterpart chose not to. So what? Both choices are legitimate. Both of us are upright people, and each of us can live as he chooses....

But no. This viewpoint negates the entire essence of Judaism.

If the fact that you are religious is equivalent to being a member of a voluntary club like a book club or a karate club, which you can join or not – where it is a fine choice either way – then your religiousness is meaningless. No decent person should practice that kind of religious observance. Who needs this nonsense if it's so trivial?

This attitude toward religious observance is analogous to the way fans of different football teams feel. One fan is an ardent supporter of the Dallas Cowboys, while another supports the Pittsburgh Steelers. But there is really no difference between the two. A person is thrilled when his team wins and he gets to light firecrackers, but it has no real meaning in his life. This is also true of those who see religion as a club – they are in the club of believers. They may not know how to play football, but they play with other things. Some of them, for example, play with *tefillin* of Rabbeinu Tam. This approach strips faith of any seriousness.

Sometimes a person's parents are the ones who decide that he will observe *mitzvot*. They cover his head with a *kippa* and dress him in *tzitzit*, and he's too good a boy to defy his parents' wishes. If the only reason he is observant is because he doesn't have the strength to rebel, then his observance is meaningless from beginning to end.

The essence of the Jewish people is serving God. If I'm a true servant of God, it's not in the sense of belonging to a club. It's something to which I am tied and which I will fight for until the final shovelful, until the end of my life, because the extent of my commitment isn't dependent on whether or not I feel like it, but on the fact that it's the truth, that this is the way it must be. I can't diverge from it, and I can't digress from it. If, from my perspective, another individual is also a servant of God, I can't ignore him, even if paying attention to him isn't exactly comfortable for me. Even if I'd rather be sitting in my *shtiebel* enjoying the company of a thousand like-minded people. A person who says that each person can choose to go his own way – to the Garden of Eden or to Gehenna – believes in neither. Someone who doesn't care about non-religious Jews doesn't care about religious Jews either. He's essentially saying that he doesn't care about God.

A person who views being Jewish as a substantial truth rather than as belonging to a club understands that there is either the way of truth or a way that is not. There is no middle ground.

THE FOUNDATION ON WHICH EVERYTHING STANDS

Love of the Jewish people means that we're a single collective, one totality. This totality isn't dependent on whether or not someone feels like being part of it. If I believe that there is a way to serve God, then that way isn't just a personal matter for me. It's not determined by my mood or instincts. It's related to the Jewish people as a whole – regardless of who they are, who is the majority and who is the minority.

The entire Jewish people, by its very existence, is obligated to be connected to God. Since each individual Jew has the same obligation regarding this connection, love of the Jewish people isn't a peripheral matter; it is central to Judaism. If a person doesn't accept the obligation that is incumbent on every Jew to be connected to God, and so does not value love of the Jewish people, then religious observance is merely a game, and a pretty foolish one at that.

Jews who see a return to religious observance as a form of insanity on the part of other Jews aren't merely rejecting an aspect of what it means to be Jewish or some subparagraph of which they aren't particularly fond. Rather, there is a fundamental flaw in their entire perception of the essence of Judaism.

It's been said that everything in the world can be quantified. If so, how does one measure the love of God? The volume of one's cries in prayer doesn't indicate how much a person loves God. The answer found in the holy books is that love of God can be measured by the degree of love one shows to the Jewish people. When a person's love of the Jewish people is approximately at the level of minus three, his love of God is also at that level, perhaps even below that. That is why "love your neighbor as yourself" isn't merely a particular *mitzva* that happens to appear in chapter 19 of Leviticus. It's actually the foundation on which everything stands.

PROCLAIMING THAT GOD IS TRUTH

Love of the Jewish people is actually rooted in a person's commitment to himself, not just to his fellow Jew. The declaration that "God is truth and His Torah is truth" means that we remain committed to being Jewish, not because we randomly fell upon it, but because it is truth. And if it is, indeed, truth, then the obligation to be committed to it is equally incumbent on every Jew, whether or not he is aware of it, whether or not he cares about it, whether or not he agrees with it.

Everyone, regardless of the size of his head or the size of his *kippa*, can understand that if a matter is true, it is true everywhere, and must apply to everyone. If it is false, it is false everywhere and has no value anywhere. Let's say a child who is asked for the sum of two plus two concludes that the sum is three, then sees that the teacher doesn't like the answer. The child then says the sum is three and a quarter. He sees that the teacher still doesn't like the answer, and proceeds to add another eighth.

People scold the teacher: "Have mercy on this child. He's close to the right answer. Compromise with him – you concede half and he will concede half."

What can the teacher do? He can't concede to the child, because he isn't arguing with him about the question of how large a slice of cake he will receive. The answer to two plus two is either correct or it's not. A math teacher who would say, "In truth, the correct answer is four, but since you're a good child, I'm willing to concede to you and let the answer be three," isn't a teacher. That isn't arithmetic; it's merely nonsense.

I can never say – about anything – that it's true for me and false for someone else. That's why, when a person goes out and concerns himself with the souls of others, he is actually worrying about himself, confirming his very own existence as a person.

The root of the love of the Jewish people is tied, not only to love of God, but also to the fact that God is truth.[14] That's why this truth resonates everywhere and belongs to everyone – to my neighbor no less than to me. When I concern myself with other Jews and take action on their behalf, I proclaim, not with words, but with my very being, that God is truth.

If I truly believe what is written in the Torah, I'm obligated to see myself as part of a larger picture. My specific role as part of this larger

---

14. See Jeremiah 10:10.

totality requires me to see that others are as important as I am and to relate to them accordingly.

If this is the way I understand how to serve God, and I see a person who isn't following the path of God, I'm compelled to try to save him, just as I would try to stop a person from drinking bleach instead of water or from placing his head in a gas oven. When resuscitating someone who almost drowned, does the rescuer consider his own appearance? When I act on behalf of another Jew, should I first consider what people will say about me? Should I care about whether or not others, including my parents, approve of my actions?

DIVERGING FROM THE WAYS OF THE COMMUNITY

Love of the Jewish people is based on the assumption that there is one body of the Jewish people comprised of all of its individuals and their concerns, and included within it is my own essence. This is the essence that belongs to God, and I am therefore unable to relinquish any part of this body. If I don't care about another, if I'm willing to give up on another Jew, I'm essentially saying the same thing about myself.

Imagine a person looking at his own body and saying, "This finger is a little crooked. I'll just amputate it. My nose, too, could be a bit more attractive. I'll amputate it as well."

A person doesn't act that way.

Although this isn't included in any of the thirteen principles of faith, a person who disassociates himself from the essence and collective of Israel isn't merely denying a specific detail. He's denying the entire essence of the Torah. He's denying his commitment to it, to its truth, to its very existence. He transforms it into a mere instrument, a violin played by jesters – with or without *kippot*.

Rambam compiled a list of those who are denied a share in the World to Come because of specific transgressions. It includes people who diverge from the ways of the community.[15] Rambam explains that even if a person fulfills the entire Torah but he doesn't care about other Jews, doesn't share their troubles, and doesn't rejoice in their celebrations, he has no share in the World to Come. It doesn't matter how profound his

15. *Mishne Torah, Hilkhot Teshuva* 3:11.

mitzva observance – he can don six pairs of *tefillin*, cry during prayers, even pray with the liturgy of the Arizal. He still has no share in the World to Come.

Rambam is very clear about the finality of that fate: "Annihilation after which there is no annihilation, punishment after which there is no punishment, destruction after which there is no destruction."[16] People who disassociate themselves from the Jewish collective share this irreversible fate with others who performed certain severe transgressions.

The problem is not only that the person distances himself from others; it's also about the manner in which he chooses to live. A person who diverges from the ways of the community, who separates from the essence of the Jewish people and says, "Allow me to live as I please, and you can live as you please – just don't drive on my street on Shabbat because it interrupts my nap," that person is actually saying that Shabbat is an environmental issue. The fact that he wears a *shtreimel* makes no difference. A person must feel pain when someone else drives on Shabbat. One whose only issue with other Jews driving down his street on Shabbat is that the noise disturbs his afternoon nap is not only disconnected from Shabbat, but he is essentially disconnected from God.

THE FEELING THAT SOMEONE IS CUTTING INTO MY FLESH

Someone who understands the meaning of love of the Jewish people feels that the problem of any Jew is his own problem, even if the Jew lives in a remote place. If one's foot is pierced by a nail, he can't say, "There's a huge distance between my foot and my head, so I can ignore the nail." When a person walks with a nail in his foot, he knows that there's something painful stuck in his body, something that's affecting his well-being.

If you don't believe me, try the following experiment: Take off your shoes and kick the wall, hard. You will quickly realize that even though your toenail isn't a major limb and not even living tissue, and even though it's in your foot and not your head, every part of you will scream, "Ouch!" Similarly, even a Jew whose distance from me is greater than the distance

16. *Mishne Tora, Hilkhot Teshuva* 8:1, 5.

between the head and the foot, and even if his personality, soul, and life may seem as insignificant as a toenail, his situation can cause me pain because I care about him.

Years ago I had a friend who had recently become religious. The friend showed me something he had written in his diary:

"I was walking home from the synagogue on Shabbat, feeling the tranquil atmosphere of the day all around me. Suddenly, a car passed me, its radio blasting. I felt like bending down, picking up a stone, and throwing it at the car."

This is clearly not a manifestation of love of the Jewish people, but it's an example of how deeply the atmosphere of Shabbat had permeated him. Several months earlier, he himself could have been driving that car on Shabbat. He's not the kind of person who throws stones, and he also knew that from a liberal and democratic perspective, it's appropriate to allow people to drive cars on Shabbat. But once he had truly experienced Shabbat, he felt its desecration as painfully as a cut into his own flesh.

The kind of pain illustrated by this story can also be felt regarding the love of the Jewish people. It's the pain a person feels when the actions of another wound him personally. When I feel hurt in this way, it's not necessarily because he is doing something shocking, but because I consider it to be terribly wrong. The ability to feel this kind of pain is the pinnacle of loving one's fellow Jew.

THE NEURAL NETWORKS OF THE JEWISH PEOPLE

There are people who are unable to feel pain because of damaged nerve endings. This may occur due to illness or a spinal cord injury. Sometimes a child is born that way. The child is in danger because nothing hurts him; he bumps into objects or walls, feels nothing, and incurs bodily harm.

A story is told of a man with this disorder who arrived home one rainy day and noticed that his shoes were wet. He placed his shoes and his feet before the fire to dry and sat down to read the newspaper. Suddenly he smelled the odor of scorched flesh. He looked down and saw that his shoes were burning and his feet were on fire. Since his nerves didn't transmit pain signals, he didn't know that his flesh was burning until he smelled the odor.

This can also happen to the body of the Jewish people. A Jew can see that flesh is burning and smell the odor of roasted flesh, but he still needs to be told that these are his feet that are on fire, not the feet of someone else.

The inability to feel pain indicates that a person is ill. If he says he doesn't care, it indicates that he's seriously ill. And if the matter is completely irrelevant to him, it indicates that he is already dead. It's as if he has departed from the world and is exempt from all obligations.[17] By contrast, when a person feels that, as someone famously said, "your foot hurts me," it indicates that a connection exists.

There are wax museums that display models that look exactly like real people, sometimes even with lifelike human smiles. How can one tell if the model is made of wax or is really a person? Jab it with a pin. If it cries "ouch," it's a person. If it doesn't cry "ouch," it's a mannequin. If we don't feel the pain of another, if we don't live as a single body but rather as disparate groups, then the entire Jewish people is a kind of wax model, a mechanical construct, a house of cards.

In the twentieth century, the Jewish people were almost annihilated, our neural networks cut and sliced. First and foremost, our response had to be to reattach the nerves and repair them. If a person's hand is severed, and he is brought to the hospital quickly enough, it's possible for the hand and blood vessels to be reattached. It's not a simple task, and the results aren't immediate. But if the vessels and nerves can be successfully reconnected, there is hope. Initially the person might not recognize his own hand; it may feel as if he is dragging it along with him. But if, suddenly, he is able to move his pinky, he is overjoyed because it becomes clear to him that the hand that was attached to him is, in fact, his own. If he feels pain in the finger, it's another indication that the hand indeed belongs to him.

The question remains: How does one reattach the neural network of the Jewish people so that a person will feel their pain and know that it is his own finger and his own hand that has been damaged? What can be done so that a person will feel not only the pain caused by his personal problems – such as if he forgets to recite *Shema* before bed one

17. See Psalms 88:6.

night – but so that he feels the pain of another Jew who may not have recited *Shema* before bed for thirty years?

WHAT TO DO WHEN IT HURTS

Attempt to get through one day when your stomach hurts. A person with a stomachache acts differently than he does when feeling well. He has a different smile, a different gaze, and a different outlook on life. A person who receives a powerful kick in the rear reacts differently than he does when his good neighbor receives a kick. When the neighbor is kicked, the most he will say is, "I'm very sorry for your pain." But when it happens to him, his entire approach is different.

How does a person react to his own pain? One person screams, another weeps, and a third will try to treat it or consult a doctor. If he doesn't find an answer with one doctor, he will consult another.

What does one do with pain felt for another? I have no real answer of what to do or how to do it. I have never told anyone, "Go, assemble multitudes of people, and shout in public, to all of your neighbors, that they need to serve God." (Even though, in my opinion, if a person truly speaks from the heart, those words will be heard and taken to heart. If a person's words are not heard, he must ask himself, "Am I truly speaking from the heart, or will my words have as much influence as a hiccup?") What I'm trying to say is that a person must see his fellow Jews as if they are a part of his own body – his own stomach, his own legs, his own arms and teeth.

A person whose teeth hurt does what he can to feel better. If he's unable to do anything, he runs around the room screaming, "Ouch!" If he doesn't scream, the teeth in question are probably not his own.

When a person feels that the Jewish people are a part of one body and one essence – that other Jews are a bone from his bones and flesh from his flesh, when the pain of another is his pain, his life and his essence – he will do what he can to relieve it. One who is in pain does something about it, whether or not that turns out to be effective.

Love of the Jewish People in Practice

SPEAKING ABOUT LOVE FOR THE JEW

I'd like to move on and discuss this subject in a more practical way.

People often invoke love of the Jewish people with an ulterior motive in mind. To receive another fifty-thousand-dollar donation for one's institution, a person will talk about his love of the Jewish people. The thinking is that it can't hurt, that it causes no harm.

Our ancestor, Lavan the Aramean, was very good at this. He went to Jacob and said, "You are my bone and my flesh."[18] What expression of love is more powerful than that? But then: "Work for me seven years, then work seven more years" while I seek to deceive you in every way I can. That was Lavan's "love." He was like a modern-day politician who says, "I really love you. You are my bone and my flesh." And yet, if a clash of interests arise, he won't hesitate to deceive you.

Do you think that Lavan the Aramean didn't know how to make speeches? Do you think he would be unable to deliver an excellent lecture at a podium? Think about it. He knew precisely what to say to Jacob: "What you're saying is correct, but we do things differently in this community. Work for me another seven years before you marry Rachel. Between you and me, what's another seven years?"

On the day before Yom Kippur, it's customary to ask the forgiveness of those we have wronged. Typically, a person goes to another and asks perfunctorily, "Do you forgive me?" The other responds, also perfunctorily, "I forgive you." Now he can go home and continue hating the other person on Yom Kippur itself and certainly afterward. But I'm not speaking of words; I'm speaking of feelings of the heart and what one does with those feelings.

Some prayer books instruct a person to recite the following statement before beginning to pray: "I hereby accept upon myself the positive commandment of 'Love your neighbor as yourself.'" A wise Jew once admitted to me, "I recite what I'm obligated to recite. If I must say, 'I hereby accept upon myself the positive commandment to 'love your neighbor as yourself,' then that is what I say."

In truth, a person can fulfill his duty when reciting this declaration, but that is analogous to placing a bumper sticker on one's car that says.

18. Genesis 29:14.

"I am in favor of love of the Jewish people." I would like to address what it really means to love the Jewish people. Loving the Jewish people isn't only a fundamental principle; it has practical ramifications as well.

THE FEELING OF CONNECTION

Love of the Jewish people is not a matter of reciprocity or contracts. It's also not about human or social interactions. Love of the Jewish people is the knowledge and the sense that the other is tied to me simply because he is a Jew. That's why I must do everything I can to show love for him. If he is a person I don't like and with whom I don't agree, and I'm still prepared to expend the effort to relate to him as if I truly care about him, then I'm working on refining my love for the Jewish people.

Love of the Jewish people doesn't mean that I forgive them of all their wrongdoings. It also doesn't mean that I must see others as perfect and myself as flawed. It doesn't mean that I must approve of someone who slaps my face. It doesn't mean that I must agree with all people. Moreover, the question of whether someone likes me or not, or how he reacts to me, is irrelevant. He can frown at me or say outright that he can't stand my face. The only real question is, how do I feel and act toward him?

Love of the Jewish people means that as a Jew I feel connected to other Jews and feel hurt if that connection is lacking. I feel the connection of unity – that the blood flowing in me is the same as the blood flowing in the other. We are tied to one another, not only because of the past, but because of present, because I feel that we are together, not only in the same land or in the same plain, but because we share some kind of internal existence.

Sometimes a six- or seven-year-old boy looks at his baby brother and feels like picking up the dirty, screaming little kid, and throwing him outside. A couple years later, the older brother begins thinking, "He may soil his bottom and scream his head off, he's still my little brother and I love him."

A person can evolve in his feelings. An initial feeling of distance can become one of caring until a person understands that his fellow Jew is actually part of his family.

THREE FRIENDS

The Gemara asks, "Why is a stork called a *ḥasida*?" And the Gemara answers, "Because it performs charity [*ḥasidut*] for its friends."[19] The author of *Ḥiddushei HaRim* goes on to ask, "If so, why is the *ḥasida* considered to be ritually impure?" And he answers, "Because she is kind only to her friends and not to others."

There is a person who is kind to his associates, loves those beloved to him, and is close to his friends. He says, "I am filled with love for the Jewish people – when it comes to my own two and a half friends," or "I love all Jews, except for the three, four, or five million whom I can't stand, another million whom I can't abide being near, another few hundred thousand with whom I can't be in the same room, and a few more of whom I'm just not fond. As for the rest, I'm completely filled with love for them. You can't say that I don't love the Jewish people!"

This phenomenon is rampant. There are people a person simply doesn't like. What can he do? They didn't grow up together, they went to different schools, may not speak the same language or share the same worldview. Perhaps they even do things that are prohibited, and that's why the person doesn't feel deep love toward them. He sees them as exceptions to the collective body of the Jewish people and says whatever he pleases about them. Who then remains part of the Jewish collective? Just him and his three friends.

There are many different levels of love of the Jewish people. One of the great lovers of the Jewish people, Rabbi Moshe Leib of Sassov, said, "Anyone incapable of sucking infected pus from the wound of a Jewish child has not yet reached half of the appropriate level of love of the Jewish people." He himself lived on that elevated level. But I'm not speaking here of aiming for that extreme expression of love.

I'm speaking of another level whose demands are much simpler. How should a person act toward those who are not like him, those who don't think like him and don't conduct themselves like him? He might say, "When I tell so-and-so that I love him, he responds that he can't stand me. What am I supposed to do?" But this is not about feelings or mere social interaction, but one of identity: Is the other person a "bone from

19. *Ḥullin* 63a.

my bones"? If so, he is a part of me, part of my bones, my flesh, and my body. Even if I don't feel that I love him, I still need to do everything in my power to relate to him.

It is written, "As water reflects a face to the face, so does the heart of a person to a person."[20] If I look into the water, make a face, and stick out my tongue, I shouldn't be surprised when the face in the water makes a face back at me and sticks out its tongue. It's extremely difficult to remain hostile when someone says to you, "I know that you are flawed, but I still care about you. No matter what, we belong to each other."

THE DISTANT AND THE NEAR

I'm not only speaking about how religious Jews should relate to nonreligious Jews or to Jews who belong to a different political party. I'm also speaking about those who consider themselves religious and yet are capable of hating other religious people in theory as well as practice. I'm speaking about people who are not diametrically opposed to my spiritual world and don't say that the things I believe are false, but whose view of reality is different from mine.

When we're speaking of love of the Jewish people, whose view is correct has no relevance. If a part my left hand was injured, I wouldn't cut it off. Even if claims against other Jews are justified, I must not cut them off. If they are really my bones and my flesh, I must take practical steps to build a relationship with them.

When a person says, "I can't even stand being in the same room with those Jews," it indicates that something is wrong within him. The challenge is to ask oneself: How can I relate to them? How can I make the effort to connect with them? Practical expression of love of the Jewish people isn't just about taking to the streets and engaging those who deny Torah, God, and Moses. Sometimes a person must ask himself how he can love Jews who also believe in God, Jews who also fulfill *mitzvot*.

We've spoken of the requirement to love Jewish people who have distanced themselves from Judaism to the extent that they eat pork with butter in order to demonstrate their personal freedom. I'm commanded to remain connected to them, to love them, to show them abundant

20. Proverbs 27:19.

mercy, and to see them as a part of the Jewish people. We've also spoken of the obligation to love Jewish people who are less distant from religious observance, but with whom it is still challenging to connect.

I would now like to tell some of you that even if it is exceedingly difficult, you are also permitted – obligated – to love your brothers, sisters, and parents. At times, it's relatively easier to love a person whom you don't know well, someone you meet once or twice and may never see again, than to love a relative. The stranger will be courteous, you will be courteous, and no real connection is needed. It's much more difficult to love someone you live with and does things that you can't tolerate.

SELF-REMEDY

All the evil and corruption in the world began with the question "Am I my brother's keeper?"[21] This was Cain's response when asked about Abel, the brother he had murdered. Everything would have been different had he cared about his brother. But someone who has that attitude must address it, because it's a shortcoming in himself, not in his brother.

There is nothing easier than hating or disliking another Jew because he is different. Instead of thinking about how to cast out someone who is "different," think of lack of love of the Jewish people as one's own personal illness. Even if one fulfills the entire Torah, lack of love of the Jewish people is a shortcoming indicative of sickness. A person must begin to think about what he must do in order to heal himself so that he can begin to feel connected to his fellow Jew.

If a person is able to say, "These are my brothers, my relatives, flesh of my flesh," and really feel that this is true regarding all of the Jewish people, be they distant, near, far, or close family, he can be certain that at least his part has not been corrupted.

LOVE YOUR NEIGHBOR – AS YOURSELF

Why is one obligated to "love your neighbor as yourself"?[22] What does the term "as yourself" add? What would have been lacking if we were just commanded to "Love your neighbor"?

---

21. Genesis 4:9.
22. See Leviticus 19:18.

The emphasis on the term "as yourself" expresses a simple idea. In general, a person tolerates himself despite his shortcomings – his own crooked smile, bloodshot eyes, two left hands. He knows there are people who are more handsome, better, and smarter, but he still gets along well with himself and even likes himself. "Love your neighbor as yourself" simply means that just as you are able to put up with yourself despite your own shortcomings, so must you put up with another, despite his shortcomings, blemishes, and deficiencies.

After all, I know much more about myself than I do about others, and certainly much more about myself than others know about me. Others don't know about my wrongdoings. Even if they do, no one can know my thoughts, some of which are prohibited and some of which are just filth that crossed my mind. Yet, wonder of wonders, I still don't hate myself even though I know that I have many faults in need of repair.

Regarding my fellow Jew, I must struggle to find a delicate balance between "You shall not hate your brother in your heart" and "You shall rebuke your counterpart."[23] It's much easier to rebuke a person one hates or to rebuke him and then hate him. The challenge is how to say something harsh to another without hating him.

"AND I WILL HEAL HIM"

Not long ago there was an article in the news about Siamese twins, one of whom drank and the other who smoked. Since they shared a bloodstream, when one drank, the other would also get drunk; when one smoked, the other would also suffer from the effects of nicotine. To remedy this, both needed to change their ways. This is our situation. If one Jew drinks poison, a second drinks urine, and a third drinks cola, it all gets intermingled in a single bloodstream. I can't say, "Why should I care about what someone else does?" I need to feel that he is my Siamese twin and that what he does has a direct impact on me, that we are essentially connected.

When it comes to love of the Jewish people, one must begin with the words of the prophet "Peace, peace for the far and for the near."[24]

---

23. Leviticus 19:17.
24. Isaiah 57:19.

One must greet a distant Jew first. Often it's easier to reach out to him because he is distant. Next, one must greet those who are near. That's much more difficult because we know each other, and there are issues between us that can lead to confrontation. After a person greets the distant and the near, he can begin to think about what comes next.

That is addressed in the continuation of the prophet's words: "And I will heal him." Where does the healing come from? When there is one body, one flesh, one bloodstream, the healing process can begin. Is it possible to heal scattered limbs, bones, or skulls rolling around in the cemetery? Of course not. The first stage in the prophecy of redemption is "The bones drew near, each bone to its bone."[25] Bone draws near to bone, and they begin to join together and become one body. It's still a skeleton, but it's unified. From this point, it can grow flesh, skin, and tendons, and ultimately, perhaps, the breath of life will be breathed into it. The first step, though, is to bring bone close to bone.

As with other matters, it's not incumbent on me to complete the task; it's incumbent on me to want to, to try. Even if it's not possible to achieve everything I want to achieve, I must still attempt to realize the dream and to know that it's based on one unifying principle: that we, the Jewish people, are one flesh – one body that cleaves to God. When we acknowledge this, we realize that it's impossible to sever our connection to each other, and it's impossible to sever the connection between us and God. If we're aware of this connection, and we attempt to work at it, to repair it, or at least to feel it, then we will have brought about the remedy and healing.

Leḥayim!

---

25. Ezekiel 37:7.

22 Shevat

The Hilula of the Rebbe of Kotzk

The twenty-second of Shevat is the *yartzeit* of Rabbi Menaḥem Mendel Morgenstern, the Kotzker Rebbe. Rabbi Menaḥem Mendel of Kotzk was born in 1787 in the village of Goraj in eastern Poland and passed away in 1859 in the village of Kotzk. In his youth, he traveled to Rabbi Yaakov Yitzḥak Horowitz, the Ḥozeh of Lublin, and then to the Ḥozeh's disciple, Rabbi Yaakov Yitzḥak Rabinowitz of Peshisḥa, also known as the Yid HaKadosh, the Holy Jew. After the passing of the Yid HaKadosh, Rabbi Menaḥem Mendel of Kotzk became a prominent disciple of his successor, Rabbi Simḥa Bunim of Peshisḥa. The great, well-known hasidic courts – of Gur, Alexander, Vurka, Izhbitza, and others – all developed and branched out from the Yid HaKadosh and Rabbi Simḥa Bunim.

Rabbi Menaḥem Mendel of Kotzk had a powerful influence on the development of Polish Hasidism. His acuity, sharpness of thought and expression, his striving for truth in general and for the internal point of truth specifically, as well as his lack of patience for compromise and self-deception, were characteristic of him and the path that he forged.

The Kotzker Rebbe's character, the path he followed, and the hasidim of Peshisḥa and Kotzk in general were a real part of Rabbi Steinsaltz's world both in terms of family connections and ideology. Many aphorisms of the Kotzker Rebbe are included in Rabbi Steinsaltz's writings and lectures.

Over the years, at the request of his students, Rabbi Steinsaltz began holding a farbrengen on the day of the Kotzker Rebbe's passing. These farbrengens deviated somewhat from the standard structure of the Lubavitch-style farbrengen in that they provided an opportunity for discussion about topics at the heart of the hasidic experience, topics that were near and dear to him.

12

Lubavitch, Breslov, and Kotzk

THREE CENTRAL BRANCHES

Within the multifaceted and nuanced world of Hasidism, there are, in my opinion, three branches that represent its essence – though Hasidism as a whole is comprised of much more than these branches, both quantitatively and qualitatively. One branch is Lubavitch, the second is Breslov, and the third, Kotzk. Each of these branches is more than just an offshoot; it is a foundation and path that is correct in both theory and practice.

Lubavitch Hasidism places a huge focus on theoretical, abstract material about God and about man. The world of Breslov Hasidism – and here I'm referring primarily to the source, Rabbi Naḥman, as well as his disciple, Reb Noson – is much more spontaneous than the ordered, structured world of Lubavitch. The path of Lubavitch is directed more toward systematic thought, while Rabbi Naḥman's is directed more toward the heart.

The difference isn't manifest only in how the soul is expressed – that with one approach one weeps more, and with another, one weeps less, for example. Rather, Rabbi Naḥman opens possible paths that are different from the path of the intellect. Much thought is contained in *Likkutei Moharan* and *Sippurei Maasiyot,* but it's not formulated in an intellectual manner, with ideas structured in an orderly way. Conceivably,

Rabbi Naḥman was capable of writing in an orderly fashion. He was, after all, a Torah scholar as well as creative. But he didn't choose to do so.

It is possible, more or less, to define the way of Lubavitch and the way of Breslov Hasidism – but what about Kotzk? The Kotzker Rebbe didn't write down his Torah insights, even though he was accomplished in both the revealed and the esoteric parts of the Torah. There are no Kotzk works of homiletic literature or theory, and there are relatively few stories and tales. We are left with a variety of statements and aphorisms. Any attempt to read all the sayings and ideas stated in the name of the Kotzker Rebbe is not a particularly useful plan of action, because, among other reasons, it isn't possible to rely on everything people say in the name of the Kotzker Rebbe. What, then, is the way of Kotzk?

The Kotzker Rebbe once said. "There were seven generations. There was the Baal Shem Tov, after him the Maggid, then Reb Elimelekh, and so on. And I'm the essence of them all."

If in Lubavitch the emphasis is on understanding and elaboration, and in Breslov on "the understanding of the heart through which the heart understands,"[1] Kotzk represents essence.

This essence is that which is close to the point of truth. This idea can certainly be found elsewhere. People know that truth is God's seal, but they also know that people are ordinarily unable to exist solely on truth. Life based on truth is risky, because truth is intolerant. The intellect is tolerant; the heart is tolerant. The truth is not.

Regarding the verses "Kindness and truth have met; justice and peace have touched. Truth will spring up from the earth as righteousness looks down from Heaven,"[2] the Sages comment, "When the Holy One, blessed be He, created Adam, the ministering angels divided into various factions. Some said, 'Let him not be created,' and some said, 'Let him be created.' Truth said, 'Let him not be created, because he is full of lies.' Peace said, 'Let him not be created, because he is full of discord.' Righteousness said, 'Let him be created, because he performs acts of righteousness.' Kindness said, 'Let him be created, because he performs

1. *Tikkunei Zohar* 17a.
2. Psalms 85:11–12.

acts of kindness.' What did God do? He dismissed truth, and the majority then favored the creation of man."[3]

Why did God cast aside truth rather than peace?

The Kotzker Rebbe provided two excellent answers: Once truth is cast away – peace has no say; it becomes meaningless. This is worthy of consideration, because we witness the actualization of this wise statement on a regular basis. The second answer is also excellent: There can be a majority opposed to righteousness and to peace. But a majority opposed to truth is meaningless.

BETWEEN THE VERTICES OF THE TRIANGLE

The Kotzker Rebbe's emphasis on the attribute of truth isn't my original insight. It has been noted by many others before me. I would like to address a different point, and that is that these three hasidic branches were not necessarily at odds with each other. There were points of interface between the three vertices of the triangle – between the three heads and to a certain extent between their successors as well. Though apparently distinct, they actually found common ground, specifically at a time when others dismissed some branches of Hasidism as inauthentic:

"The Breslovers are not real hasidim."

"The Lubavitchers are really *mitnagdim*, opponents of Hasidism, to a certain extent; the structure of their prayers is different."

"The Kotzkers are complete savages."

One might expect that Kotzker hasidim – sharp, scholarly, and acerbic – would ignore Breslov hasidim, who were called nothing more than "little sheep." But it turns out that there was great respect for Rabbi Naḥman in Kotzk. Astonishingly, Kotzk was perhaps the only place outside of Breslov where Rabbi Naḥman's writings were studied. This is documented in a book written by Aharon Marcus, a German Jew who wasn't fond of either group.

Marcus became a hasid of the Radomsker Rebbe, an exceedingly great man who vigorously opposed and fought the Kotzker hasidim to the best of his ability. In Marcus's book about the hasidic movement, he

---

3. *Bereshit Rabba* 8:5.

showered his Rebbe with extreme praise, as a hasid should, but he wrote defamatory words about the Kotzker hasidim. He called them wild and inhuman and noted that they were the only ones who studied Breslov teachings.

Another example of the Kotzkers' esteem for Rabbi Naḥman can be found in a book by one of the early Gerrer hasidim called *Shem HaGedolim HeḤadash,* which was an effort to update the book *Shem HaGedolim* by the Ḥida with more recent personalities and works. Rabbi Naḥman of Breslov is described in that book as an extremely great man whose own hasidim did not understand fully.

My *sandak,* who was a member of a very well-known Chabad family, once told me that his father – a distinguished leader of Chabad hasidim, David Tzvi Ḥen – spent two hours at the conclusion of every Shabbat studying Rabbi Nahman's *Likkutei Moharan.* This was unusual in the world of Chabad, but it wasn't unheard of. I'm not sure that Breslov hasidim ever studied Chabad writings.

Relations between Kotzk and Chabad were ambivalent and unstable. There was a connection of sorts between the Kotzker Rebbe and the Tzemaḥ Tzedek, the third Lubavitcher Rebbe, Rabbi Menaḥem Mendel Schneerson (not to be confused with the seventh Lubavitcher Rebbe). I can't vouch for the credibility of the report, but it is told that the Kotzker Rebbe once said, "What is the difference between my approach and the Chabad approach? Chabad goes from the brain to heart, and things therefore become increasingly better for them. I go from heart to brain; things therefore become increasingly worse for me."

I've never heard of a Breslover hasid becoming a Kotzker hasid; it's not simple for these two approaches to coexist harmoniously. I also haven't heard of many Lubavitchers becoming Breslover hasidim. This is not because of fundamental differences; it is rather due to a disparity in lifestyle and approach. But there were Kotzker hasidim who became Lubavitcher hasidim or Breslover hasidim.

A certain Polish Jew named Moshe Meshel Gelbstein, who was a bona fide hasid of the Kotzker Rebbe, went to Lubavitch on festivals and became a hasid of the Tzemaḥ Tzedek as well. The Kotzker Rebbe reportedly said, "Mendele is analogous to Mendele," referring to the name he shared with the Tzemaḥ Tzedek. It appears that the Kotzker Rebbe thought that they had more in common than just a name.

A story is told that one year, on the day before Passover, Moshe Meshel sat by himself as a guest in Lubavitch, wondering where he would have the Seder. Since he had become close to the Tzemaḥ Tzedek, he approached the Rebbe's attendant and gently asked if he could be hosted by the Rebbe. The attendant answered, "Our Rebbe conducts his Seder only with his family. Even the *gadol hador* (the leader of the generation) wouldn't be allowed to join him."

Moshe Meshel returned to his lodgings and asked his host to arrange a place for him to have the Seder. Later that same day, an emissary of the Tzemaḥ Tzedek arrived at his door and relayed the Rebbe's message: "What impudence! Here you are, in my city, and you're not coming to my Seder tonight?!"

Moshe Meshel apologized and said he had been told that even the *gadol hador* wouldn't be welcome at the Rebbe's Seder.

The emissary replied, "The *gadol hador*, no, but you – yes."

Later in his life, Moshe Meshel emigrated to the Land of Israel. Wondrous stories are told about him. He conducted himself like a Kotzker hasid and was recognized widely as a genuine giant of Torah. When he prayed at length, continuing until very late, others knew that lofty truth was behind this conduct.

Moshe Mesel sometimes spent the summer months in Hebron. One year, on the day he intended to return to Jerusalem, the author of *Sedei Ḥemed* came to bid him farewell. Moshe Meshel remained immersed in prayer as the Sedei Ḥemed, accompanied by his grandson, waited at the synagogue entrance for two hours. When Moshe Meshel finally emerged, they parted in peace.

As they left, the Sedei Ḥemed's grandson asked him, "Did you have to wait two hours for this little Jew?"

The Sedei Ḥemed answered, "For this little Jew, one needs to wait even two days."

I bring up Moshe Meshel here as an example of a real Kotzker hasid, one who remained a Kotzker hasid even though he also traveled to Lubavitch.

He wasn't the only one. There were other hasidim who found an intrinsic connection between these vertices.

Though they disagreed on some matters, those who formed the sides of this hasidic triangle understood one another and were able to distinguish between style and content on one hand and essence on the other. They had much more in common regarding essence than they did regarding external factors. The expression "This sage said one thing and that sage said another thing, but they don't disagree" applies here. In order to see things this way, one must delve deeply into the matter rather than look at it superficially.

The Kotzker branch of Hasidism was self-contained, but it still maintained ties with Chabad and Breslov, as well as with other branches. They may not have celebrated together, but there was an inherent connection between them.

Truth and Essence

A PATH THAT IS TRUE AND CORRECT

I've heard that the melody we just sang in this farbrengen, "*Pelia Daat Mimeni*," may be from Kotzk. I don't know if this is true. Even if we do have melodies from Kotzk, they are very few. Kotzk had some, but melody and song didn't play a significant role in their observance.

There is a famous story about the renowned prayer leader of Kotzk, who came to tell the Rebbe that his house had burned down. The Rebbe said to him, "Do you know why your house burned down? It is because you prolonged the phrase 'who by fire' in the Rosh HaShana prayers." (In Gur, even today, that phrase in the *U'Netaneh Tokef* liturgy is recited very quickly, the same way that the names of the ten sons of Haman are recited during the reading of the *megilla*.)

This is not a peripheral point. That melody wasn't central in Kotzk is related to the very essence of Kotzk. Kotzk Hasidism was actually the third generation in a process that began with the Yid HaKadosh of Peshisḥa and continued with Rabbi Simḥa Bunim of Peshisḥa. The Yid HaKadosh and his successors looked at Hasidism with all of its branches and blossoms, its forms and nuances, and sought to prune away everything that wasn't essential. They did away with a variety of customs and patterns of prayer that were seen as adornments and flourishes and weren't deemed to be the essence.

Legitimate grievances and disputes arose because the Yid HaKadosh, a disciple of the Ḥozeh of Lublin, had turned to a path that was different from that of his mentor. It wasn't necessarily a more intellectual path, even though many studied Torah exclusively in his study hall, and a large percentage of the most prominent rabbis in Poland emerged from there. The Yid HaKadosh and his followers felt that, first and foremost, one must engage in the fundamentals and essence of Hasidism; only afterward could one add flourishes. With regard to the essence, the question they felt they needed to address was, Is what we are doing correct and true?

One hasid explained: "The adherents of the Enlightenment succeed where hasidim don't because the enlightened engage in their falsehood truthfully, while we hasidim engage in our truth untruthfully."

The Kotzkers sought to ensure that their path of Hasidism would be both true and engaged in correctly.

DO WHAT YOU DO – PROVIDED IT IS TRUTHFUL

The absolute focus on truth attracted – perhaps strangely – people of different types to Kotzk. Some were learned Torah scholars who were considered outstanding leaders of their generation, several of them rabbis of the greatest communities in Poland. Some were from distinguished families, some wealthy, while others were not. The common denominator was their desire to approach matters truthfully. If something is true, there is no need to be concerned about what others think, no need to take their opinion into consideration.

Kotzker hasidim were known for the way they prepared to pray. They would stand for two, three, even four hours, just in preparation. The author of *Ḥiddushei HaRim* had a son who was a devout Kotzker hasid. He attested that this son would walk through the study hall with his prayer shawl on his shoulders for hours before he would begin to pray. "You could say that my son is a Kotzker," the Ḥiddushei HaRim reportedly commented.

But in Kotzk there were also Jews like Rabbi Yeḥiel Meir of Gustinin, who was known as the "*Tehillim Yid*" (the Psalms Jew). He would always pray on time, in accordance with the *halakha*, and was well known for routinely advising people to recite Psalms. Even after he became a Rebbe with hasidim of his own, the recitation of Psalms remained his standard prescription.

He once said, "When I speak to simple Jews and tell them to recite ten chapters of Psalms, they do so immediately. When I tell the same thing to a hasid, he invariably begins to philosophize: 'I don't know how. I need to know from what perspective to recite Psalms.' What can be done with a person like that?"

He, too, was treated with great respect in Kotzk, because neither the duration of one's prayers nor the presence of melody or song during prayer mattered. The one thing that did matter was intent. Does the person have genuine intent for what he is saying and doing? If so, he is one of us. Without true intent, nothing has value.

There were people in Kotzk who were absolutely meticulous in their performance of *mitzvot*, and others who didn't attribute importance to the details. Some were courteous and got along well with people; others were well known for their lack of manners. None of these things were important. What mattered was whether or not a person followed the path of truth. Anything other than that wasn't taken into consideration. In Kotzk, truth was of primary importance in everything a person did, be it great or trivial. Whether praying, reciting *Shema*, sounding the *shofar*, giving charity, speaking, working, or thinking – one needed to determine if these behaviors were genuine or just done to keep up appearances.

A person who wasn't genuine in his behavior wasn't wanted in Kotzk. He would be asked to leave before being forcibly expelled. If one acted truthfully, the way he behaved was irrelevant, and he would be graciously accepted in Kotzk.

The Kotzker Rebbe's son-in-law, who later became the Sochatchover Rebbe, was a child prodigy. He could have been a prominent rabbi even before he was old enough to marry. He wrote that when he was young and had just become the Rebbe's son-in-law, the Kotzker Rebbe taught him what true learning is all about: how to rid oneself of vain and vacuous reasoning and how to cast aside all extraneous and imprecise matters. In Kotzk, hasidim strove for absolute truth in prayer, in Torah, in work – in all that they did.

THE TRUTH OF KOTZK

Rambam, who was similar and dissimilar to the Kotzker Rebbe, also wrote about truth. At the beginning of *Mishne Torah*, Rambam seeks to define who God is. He writes that He is the first to exist and that "His truth is unlike the truth of any other."[4] In other words, God's truth is unlike the truth of any of His creations, because everything relating to them is false, and He Himself is the only truth.

Though it differs somewhat, the Kotzker understanding of truth is no less extreme and no less demanding. It seeks to reach to the roots of the fact that God is truth and there is no other truth. This is the meaning of the verse "But the Lord God is truth."[5] Truth isn't merely an attribute of the Creator, the Generator, the Sustainer, and the Merciful. God is truly the only point that exists, the absolute point that is found in this disjointed world that is full of contrasts and contradictions. In this world, there is only one Being that exists in all circumstances, that is true through all transformations.

There are different ways to define truth, and philosophers have addressed the issue at length. For Rambam, truth stands as an unshakable stake in the ground. Another definition, found in the book of Psalms is "Truth and righteous together"[6] – there is truth when different shades of meaning and understandings are harmoniously integrated.

I heard another definition of truth from a certain philosopher, who said, "Truth is what is acknowledged when someone sees something and says, 'Aha!'" He came to that conclusion after quite a few years of deliberation.

The hasidim of Kotzk wanted to know how to say even one word of prayer or perform one deed in an absolutely true way. If not truly expressed, it would be a lie, and how could a person possibly stand before God and lie? That would be an extremely shameful, unparalleled disgrace.

The books of the Maharal of Prague were studied in Kotzk. The Kotzker Rebbe once said that the Maharal's writings were lengthy in

4. *Mishne Torah, Hilkhot Yesodei HaTorah* 1:3.
5. Jeremiah 10:10.
6. Psalms 19:10.

order to make it difficult for people to study them. He explained that the Maharal didn't write just one unwieldy version of his commentary; he wrote several unwieldy versions. The same idea was expressed in five or six different ways in his attempt to reach the truth. His thought processes weren't convoluted; his writings were repetitive because he sought to express the concepts as precisely and as truthfully as possible.

WHETTING THE AX

Stating even a single matter truthfully requires a person to engage in extremely rigorous internal work, an effort that differs from other kinds of work. The Bershader Rebbe's hasidim, for example, were extremely careful to avoid untruths. Falsehood occupied their thoughts extensively in order to eliminate it. By contrast, the hasidim of Kotzk focused on how to achieve truth.

One who seeks truth in everything – whether in the performance of *mitzvot* or even the commission of transgressions – expends a great deal of effort in an almost desperate attempt not to falsify or misrepresent. It's possible that the effort to arrive at this correct and precise point will take an extremely long time. These mindful preparations are not undertaken to gain insight or understanding; the effort is made in order to reach a moment when one is able to say, "This is it! This is correct! This is the real thing!" It can take hours, even days and months, to reach the moment of truth.

When Reb Leibel Eiger, the grandson of Rabbi Akiva Eiger, went to join the followers of the Kotzker Rebbe, a genuine scandal ensued since Reb Leibel's father was a resolute opponent of Hasidism. It wasn't unheard of for the son of an opponent to become a hasid. But a Kotzker hasid? That was going too far!

Someone tried to comfort the father by saying, "You know your son. He's been unconventional from childhood. There are three things he could have done. He could have gone insane, become a priest, or become a hasid. Take comfort in the fact that he became a hasid."

Reb Leibel once asked his Rebbe, the Kotzker, "What will I say to my grandfather when he asks me why we pray so late?"

The Rebbe answered that he should tell his grandfather that the Kotzkers follow the ruling of Rambam: "When one hires a laborer to chop wood, and he spends half the day whetting his ax, he must be paid a full day's wages. This is what we do: We whet the ax until it is able to chop properly."

The search for the essence of truth isn't simple. The criteria aren't clear; they require repeat polishing – like the whetting of the ax. On the other hand, after sitting for four hours preparing for prayer, the actual prayer can be very brief as well as very precise. It is said that the Kotzker Rebbe would pray with relative brevity, though he kept pace, more or less, with the rest of the congregation. His prayer was still and silent, and for a long while afterward he had to make an effort to identify the people around him. During prayer, he would truly be transported to a different world. By contrast, the prayer of his great disciple, the Ḥiddushei HaRim, was tempestuous, ecstatic, and lengthy. Both sought, in different ways, to achieve truth in their prayers.

The Mishna states that the early generations of hasidim would wait for an hour before beginning to pray.[7] That's understandable – they were preparing. But a *baraita* states that they would wait an hour after prayer as well.[8] Why would a person wait for an hour after praying?

When a person prays correctly, he needs time before he can return to this world. One doesn't achieve that kind of mindful prayer by shouting and weeping. Prayer of that kind results when the person who is praying becomes aware that he stands, not only before the lectern, but before God. For someone who genuinely stands before God, even an hour might not suffice before being able to return to matters of this world.

A story is told of a famous Zen master who participated in an artistic competition that was staged by the emperor of Japan. Artists competed to determine who could draw the best possible rooster. The artists sat, toiled, drew, and spent time modifying and perfecting their drawings. When the Zen master arrived, he spent just two minutes drawing a rooster that everyone agreed was the best.

7. *Berakhot* 5:1.

8. *Berakhot* 32b.

The emperor asked, "Why didn't you spend more time on your drawing? If that's what you could do after two minutes, you could have produced an even more perfect drawing had you spent more time on it."

The Zen master responded, "I've been drawing this rooster in my thoughts for two years, enhancing it again and again. Now I only drew in actuality what I had been preparing for all that time."

This is the crux of Kotzker Hasidism.

HASIDISM ACCORDING TO KOTZK

Behind all the beautiful, even romantic, descriptions of the hasidic movement was the underlying search for truth – whether in Torah or in prayer. This is why Hasidism was willing to accept a simple person's cry of "*Oy vey!*" in prayer or the sound of a child crowing like a rooster, because those cries were true. In that sense, the Kotzk hasidim strove to achieve the same thing that Hasidism in general desired from the very beginning, which was a path to the truth. Emmanuel Kant called it "seeking the thing itself."

I will share another story to illustrate this point, this time about the Karliner Rebbe. During the early days of Hasidism, its opponents would occasionally attack hasidim physically. One time they seized the Karliner Rebbe, who was no pushover and no weakling. It is said that people were afraid of him and no one would dare to say no to him. He would arrive at a community and instruct the Jews, "Change the ordinances of this community in the following manner," and then proceed to dictate the new ordinances, word for word.

These are not just hasidic tales. Stories about the Karliner Rebbe are also found in the memoirs of Shlomo Maimon, who was affiliated neither with the world of hasidim nor that of its opponents. Presumably, if Maimon related such a story about hasidim, it's entirely true. He wrote that someone once began to argue with the Karliner Rebbe, who just glared at him and scared him to death. In any event, after these opponents seized the Karliner Rebbe and gave him a beating, he said, "All the blows they gave me weren't serious – they didn't really mean it. But there was one person who pinched me, and I felt that he really meant it."

The Kotzker Rebbe established his branch of Hasidism so there would be absolutely no room for even a trace of falsehood. Adhering to this principle didn't preclude behaving like hasidim in practice. Kotzker hasidim would still eat from the Rebbe's table, sing and to dance, and do all the things that other hasidim did – provided that it be done in truth, which is very hard to do. That is a heavy burden to bear.

A PILLAR OF FIRE

The Kotzker Rebbe was considered a great scholar, and several of his Torah insights remain in our possession. Even his opponents would say that he "steeps himself in matters of *halakha*." He would stand with a heavy volume of Gemara in his hand, and remain in that position for ten or twelve hours, doing nothing but studying. His insights were often profound, despite their brevity and succinctness. He asked, for example, "When an impure person touches a pure person, why does the pure person become impure, but the impure person doesn't become pure?" This is a truly great halakhic question. He answered, "The reason is because the pure person didn't touch the impure person." This is not a homily for *seuda shelishit*. An entire world of thought is encapsulated in that one answer. It is necessary to sit and think for a day or two, or three, to understand it fully.

This brevity wasn't intended to "confuse the enemy," so that others wouldn't understand him. The objective was to refine and enhance the text so that it need not be written as a book consisting of fifteen folios. Stating something clearly in one sentence requires much more thought and time than filling a notebook. This writing style was fundamental to Kotzk. Extreme economy of words reached its peak with the Kotzker Rebbe, but continued with his successors, as well as some of his descendants.

The Kotzker demand for clarity and brevity stemmed from, among other things, the personality of the Rebbe himself. When Rabbi Simḥa Bunim of Peshisḥa passed away, three potential successors were considered for the position: his son, the Kotzker Rebbe, and the Ḥiddushei HaRim (who became the first Gerrer Rebbe, succeeding the Kotzker Rebbe at a later date). The Ḥiddushei HaRim excelled in Torah, wisdom, fear of God, and divine service, as did the Kotzker Rebbe. It was customary to name brilliant young scholars after the city they were from: the prodigy of Rogatchov, the prodigy of Lublin, and so on. The

Ḥiddushei HaRim was called the prodigy of Poland because at an extremely young age, he was the most outstanding scholar in the entire region.

After extensive deliberations about who would succeed Rabbi Simḥa Bunim, it finally came down to two: the Ḥiddushei HaRim and the Kotzker Rebbe. The Ḥiddushei HaRim related that the Kotzker Rebbe said to him, "It falls to the two of us, me and you," and the Ḥiddushei HaRim responded, "It's you."

The two men were very close, but the Ḥiddushei HaRim always deferred to the Kotzker Rebbe, humbling himself before him. Later, when students of the Ḥiddushei HaRim asked him, "Why was it so clear to you that the Kotzker Rebbe should assume leadership? You were already esteemed and honored as one of the most outstanding figures of your generation, in Torah as well as fear of God. Besides, as leader you wouldn't have incited all the controversies that Rabbi Menaḥem Mendel of Kotzk did!"

The Ḥiddushei HaRim answered, "I saw a pillar of fire blazing in front of me, and I bowed before it."

The Kotzker Rebbe was a pillar of fire, and the Ḥiddushei HaRim conducted himself as Moses did. When the thirteen attributes of mercy were revealed to him, and he saw the attribute of "truth," Moses fell on his face and prostrated himself.[9] The Ḥiddushei HaRim simply saw the element of pure truth in the Kotzker Rebbe and said, "Before this, no person can stand." Imagine facing a small pillar of unadulterated truth, a small pillar of electricity with the voltage of a million volts. I know that in the face of that, I for one, wouldn't be able to stand before it.

EXTREMISM FOR THE SAKE OF TRUTH

The Kotzker Rebbe was known for taking extreme positions, but his extremism was neither simple nor simplistic. First of all, he was well versed in worldly manners, and regarding certain questions he was much more lenient than *tzaddikim* who were considered less rigid than he. When the Russian government issued an edict that the Jews must dress in the European style instead of the old Jewish mode of dress,

9. See *Sanhedrin* 111a.

prominent leaders of the generation assembled, among them the Ḥiddushei HaRim, to decide how to respond. They came to the conclusion that this edict fell into the category of "let him be killed and not transgress"[10] and publicized their opinion.

When the decision was relayed to the Kotzker Rebbe, he said, "I, too, know how to read the subparagraphs in books of halakhic rulings. Where did they get the idea that this is 'let him be killed and not transgress'? It is unfortunate. Instead of exerting pressure on Jews and bringing about the arrival of the Messiah, they issue an edict of 'let him be killed and not transgress'!"

One time people appeared before one of the Kotzker Rebbe's hasidim, who was the rabbi of a town, in order to test him. They posed a fabricated halakhic question to him, and when he didn't answer properly, they sought to dismiss him from his position. The Kotzker Rebbe summoned several dozen rabbis, all of them community rabbis who were subordinate to him, and asked them, "Do you know absolutely everything that a halakhic arbiter needs to know?" He formulated a long list, along with numerous citations from the Talmud and various halakhic rulings.

"You can't know all of this," he said, "so how do you issue halakhic rulings? When a person comes to ask a question, the merit of the one asking and the merit of the one being asked together comprise a true ruling. In this case, since the question was fabricated, there was no merit in the one asking. That is why the rabbi was unable to give an answer."

The Kotzker Rebbe's widespread reputation for always being extreme and never being considerate of people, their concerns, or their suffering is false. The Kotzker Rebbe's rulings weren't extreme in principle. When he was extreme, it was because he thought that was the way to arrive at the truth. When a person is concerned about truth, he doesn't focus on his own popularity. He doesn't behave in a certain way because he wants to be unpopular or because he wants people to talk about him in the street, but because he wants to be honest. All the rest – whether or not others support him, whether or not they stand with him – is of no consequence to him. The Kotzker Rebbe went to places where he

10. See *Sanhedrin* 74a.

thought it was incumbent on him to go for the sake of truth. If he had to go all the way, he would go all the way, and even beyond it.

This characteristic also explains a frightening aspect of the Kotzker Rebbe's personality: People were terrified of being in his presence. A story is told of a night when the Rebbe emerged from the room where he had secluded himself and asked one of his hasidim a benign question. "Did so-and-so frequently travel to Kotzk?" The hasid answered yes. The Rebbe said thank you, went back into his room, and closed the door while the hasid fainted.

Sometimes people would sit in the study hall for weeks, waiting to see him. One time, on the day before Pesach, he suddenly went into the study hall and shouted, "Get out of here, you detestable things!" Everyone there jumped out of the windows in terror. Later, when he asked where everyone was, he was told that they all fled after he screamed at them. He replied, "I wasn't referring to them. I was referring to other things."

This conduct and his leadership in general both resulted from his stubborn pursuit of truth and how far he would go to achieve it. How far was that?

The furthest possible.

THE MEASURING STICK

This was who he was. What remains of him?

Some stories remain. I've told you some of the great stories about him, but all in all there aren't many. He had contempt for tales of wonders. He saw wonders and other similar phenomena as mere adornments. A story is told of a Jew who exclaimed excitedly that he'd had the merit of seeing the table of the Baal Shem Tov. A Kotzker hasid asked him, "Why are you so excited? You know when the Baal Shem Tov lived. His table is no more than a hundred years old. At the Kotzker Rebbe's table, we learn about how and on what basis the world exists, and the world has been here for much longer than just one hundred years."

Incidentally, all three branches of Hasidism that I described – Lubavitch, Breslov, and Kotzk – placed little emphasis on wondrous events and sightings. They all have stories telling of miracles, but supernatural events were not the basis of these hasidic worlds.

As for homilies and Torah discourses, several insights of the Kotzker Rebbe remain in our possession. A fascinating book called *Emet Ve'Emuna,* written by a venerable Gerrer hasid, contains several pages of sayings and lessons from the Kotzker Rebbe. To the best of his ability, the author attempted to present the Rebbe's ideas clearly, but it wasn't possible to construct a cohesive structure from them.

The Kotzker Rebbe may not have left us a complete edifice, but he did leave us a criterion for building one – a measuring stick for truth. This measuring stick was used to search for the absolute truth and was always in the background. Whether you were a Kotzker hasid or a Lubavitcher, a Breslover or an opponent of Hasidism, or anything else, the question would always remain: How much of what you are thinking, saying, and doing is true?

One doesn't satisfy the criteria by donning hasidic garb. The Ḥiddushei HaRim, who was a disciple of the Kotzker Rebbe, said, "When the Satan robs a person of his point of truth, his *gartel* and *shtreimel* make no difference." This harsh expression may be insulting, but it's a statement of truth.

The question of truth is relevant in all contexts – in the realm of action and thought, in the realm of business, and in all other areas. The question that always remains is, where is the point of truth? A person may determine that he hasn't reached that point, but he must not stop seeking it in every possible way.

THE EDGE OF TRUTH

The message of the Kotzker Rebbe has endured over time, though his statements are brief and some of them are vague and difficult to understand. Even so, the expectations and demands inherent in his words still resonate. The Kotzker Rebbe doesn't instruct a person to pray for a specific period of time or to study specific texts in detail. He makes one demand: Strive to reach a point of truth in all matters. When a person delivers a homily, writes a book, speaks with people, or does anything else, he should seek to find its true substance.

When the *shofar* is blown on Rosh HaShana, many different types of sounds are produced in order to confuse the Satan. What can this mean? Is the Satan so easily misled? Is he a fool? The Satan has been around for a very long time and is exceedingly experienced in what he does. How can we possibly confuse him?

I think the following scenario can help us understand what confusing the Satan really means:

The great Day of Judgment has arrived, and the fate of the entire world hangs in the balance. Suddenly, the sounds of the *shofar* are heard, and in each of the many different sounds it makes, there is one tiny kernel of absolute truth – maybe just one fraction, one thread, one hairbreadth, one seed, one iota that represents absolute truth. This little seed of truth is what terrifies the Satan, because his expertise is in falsehood. He knows that in the midst of all the sounds and the noises and thoughts, the person blowing the *shofar* identifies a point of truth. This is what frightens and confuses the Satan. And it is this minuscule point that we seek.

This is what we say in *Vehi She'amda* on Seder night: "And it is that which stood for us...."[11] "That" represents the pure element of truth that stood for our ancestors and for us. In every serious and not so serious matter, in every important and unimportant matter, in every internal and external matter, what we're seeking is the "edge of truth," which "will be established forever."[12] We seek at first to reach the edge of truth – not even its core. We can get there later. We attempt to speak of it, hoping that somehow it will cleave to us. If it doesn't cleave to us, we can at least hope that it will niggle at us. Where we awaken one morning, exhausted and bleary-eyed, thinking, "What am I in truth?" Such thinking is the beginning of the redemption and makes everything that led up to it worthwhile.

All the things that the Kotzker Rebbe said can be understood as "the seed of truth."[13] One must think about this seed again and again until it develops and produces fruit, which goes on to produce more fruit.

11. Passover Haggada.
12. Proverbs 12:19.
13. Jeremiah 2:21.

The Kotzker Rebbe sowed small seeds that were capable of producing entire trees, and he did this wherever he could. A person must absorb what he can of these seeds of truth, until he is certain that wherever he may be, something will grow out of them.

Leḥayim!

13

The Path of Individuals

THE STATUS OF A *MET MITZVA*

It is written in *Sefer Ḥasidim* that it is appropriate to study a tractate of Gemara that is learned infrequently because it has the status of a *met mitzva*.[1] Something similar can be said about observing the *yartzeit* of a person like the Kotzker Rebbe, whose path in life wasn't perpetuated. In that case, it is especially appropriate to ensure that his *yartzeit* is observed. Like a *met mitzva* or a neglected tractate of Gemara, this kind of *yartzeit* in particular should be commemorated

The Kotzker Rebbe was maligned throughout his life, and though his early hasidim were also attacked from all sides, they remained an elite group. Despite their reputation for impudence, many of them were great men – great in Torah, great in wisdom, and even great in wealth. As a result, people were afraid to harm them, and any attacks against them weren't serious. Breslover hasidim, on the other hand, were aggressively vilified to the extent that they were often beaten physically. They lacked the resources or power to prevent it, since they were almost always from the lower classes. Because of persecution, they remained few in number for many years.

1. This is a person who has died with no one to bury him. In that case, there is a *mitzva* incumbent upon everyone to bury him.

It didn't take long for Kotzker Hasidism to not only become mainstream, but to grow to be the most influential hasidic group in greater Poland. Gerrer hasidim, today a large and influential hasidic sect, are, for all intents and purposes, a legacy of Kotzker Hasidism. Alexander hasidim, too, though not students of the Kotzker Rebbe, were products of the study hall of Peshisḥa, which was also affiliated with Kotzk. And many more Rebbes in Poland emerged from that movement.

So although the Kotzker Rebbe was ostensibly marginalized during his lifetime, he ultimately became a foundation and focal point for all of Polish Hasidism. Some of his sons and grandsons, authoritative figures in their own right and also possessed of sharp tongues, became leaders of Polish Hasidism. Despite all this, the style and the path of the Kotzker Rebbe wasn't perpetuated. That's why it is particularly important and appropriate to commemorate his *yartzeit*.

THE BOOK THAT IS WITH THE DEMON

Why was the path of the Kotzker Rebbe not perpetuated?

For one thing, the Kotzker Rebbe didn't leave behind any books.

In truth, the essence of Hasidism wasn't to be found in books. Someone once said, "The *mitnagedim* produced books; the hasidim produced people."

Once, when I had a little time, I researched the matter numerically, empirically. I created a list, albeit an incomplete one, of all hasidic books. My list included thousands of books, though many of the great personalities from the world of Hasidism didn't write any. Even books attributed to those personalities didn't necessarily do them justice or reflect the greatness of their personalities. Sometimes a book about a genuinely great man wasn't even considered to be an important book.

This phenomenon stems, first and foremost, from the fact that virtually none of the hasidic Rebbes wrote their own books. Instead, their teachings were written down by their followers or students, a method that relied on luck. Some prominent Rebbes were privileged to have wise, insightful students who transcribed their significant teachings clearly; others weren't. For example, I'm certain that had Rabbi Naḥman of Breslov not found the appropriate person, Reb Noson, to be his scribe, nothing more than a few booklets would have remained of his teachings.

Rabbi Naḥman himself valued Reb Noson as a person who could successfully transcribe his Torah, both preserving his language and communicating the essence of his primary message.

By contrast, only a few insights remain from the teachings Rabbi Yehuda Leib of Shpola, also known as the Shpoler Zeide. He was a learned Torah scholar and a great personality, as well as Rabbi Naḥman's first serious opponent, but he wasn't privileged to have a student who could evoke and disseminate his Torah.

Sometimes a hasid's transcription of his Rebbe's teachings are like the strainer described in *Pirkei Avot*: It lets out the wine and retains the sediment.[2] There were great men whose scribes didn't really comprehend their teachings or else were just incapable of transmitting them properly. This is true of the author of *Shivḥei HaBesht*, who didn't know the Baal Shem Tov personally, though he did have contact with his direct disciples. Also, his father-in-law was very close to the Baal Shem Tov and served as his scribe and ritual slaughterer for a time.

Though *Shivḥei HaBesht*, as the title suggests, is a book in praise of the Baal Shem Tov's wonders and deeds, it doesn't give a sense of his essence. The book mentions that the Baal Shem Tov spoke about the phenomenon of Shabbetai Tzvi. Sabbateanism began shortly before the Baal Shem Tov's time and remained a controversial issue in his day. At the peak of Shabbetai Tzvi's prominence, a significant portion of the Jewish people – possibly a majority that included prominent leaders – were drawn to him. The Baal Shem Tov himself had a confrontation with the Frankists, who represented the last of the Sabbatean movement. In *Shivḥei HaBesht*, one can find many interesting statements about this matter that don't appear in other books. The author, citing the Baal Shem Tov, wrote that Shabbetai Tzvi initially had a spark of sanctity, but because of his arrogance and crude nature, he became what he became. The author then stated that there was a great deal more that the Baal Shem Tov had to say about the matter that was not included in the book. By contrast, an exchange between the Baal Shem Tov and a certain priest is related in detail, even though the topic they discussed was totally inconsequential.

2. *Avot* 5:15.

The perfect illustration of the way a student's recordings of a Rebbe's teachings don't necessarily reflect the Rebbe's approach and character is related in *Shivḥei HaBesht* itself. It tells about a dream the Baal Shem Tov had of a demon walking with a large book under his arm as he went along his way.

The Baal Shem Tov asked, "What is that book you are carrying?"

The demon answered, "It is your book."

The Baal Shem Tov was alarmed. He summoned all of his hasidim and asked them: "Who among you wrote a book of my words of Torah?" One of them confessed to have written it. The Baal Shem Tov asked to see his notes, and then remarked: "There is not one word in there that I have said."

THE MOST SUCCESSFUL INTERPRETATION

In any event, the reason the Kotzker Rebbe didn't write a book of his teachings was because he didn't want to. He reportedly said, "If I did write a book, who would read it? Only our hasidim and followers. When would they have time to study that book? Only on Shabbat afternoon. The Jew would finish his meal and head for his bed, tired and sluggish. He'd lie down with the book in his hands and fall asleep. I don't want to be in that bed."

Another reason the Kotzkers didn't write books can be understood from the following story, which is actually Chabad in origin.

Once, a hasid returned from a visit with his Rebbe with a new melody for the words "Lift your eyes on high."[3] His good friend, who happened to be a prominent opponent of Hasidism, heard the melody and said, "I've heard thirty or forty interpretations of that verse, but none as powerful as the interpretation evoked by that melody. Why didn't your Rebbe write it down?"

The hasid answered, "Had the Rebbe written it down, it would have been no different from forty other interpretations."

There are things that can be expressed in song that can't be expressed orally or in writing. They lose their intrinsic quality when written down, and what remains is lifeless – just another interpretation, another

3. Isaiah 40:26.

comment on a phrase of Torah, and nothing more. Along the same lines, the Kotzker Rebbe didn't write, because he thought that if he did, his teachings would turn into just another book.

In my opinion, this is related to the essence of Hasidism. The Mishna states, "There are three crowns: the crown of Torah, the crown of priesthood, and the crown of kingship, but the crown of a good name [*keter shem tov*] surpasses them all."[4] In Hasidism, emphasis is placed on the crown of a good name. The crown of a good name is tied to the development of one's personality, so that the person himself will aspire to become great. In my opinion, that is the why the Baal Shem Tov changed the laudatory description of a worthy person from *baal shem* to *baal shem tov*.

Some hasidic works are important, invaluable sources for us, even though the person himself, the personality of the great Rebbe and *tzaddik* that stands on its own, can't be encountered in those books. Often a person becomes known by the title of his book, and this makes sense, because it's difficult to discern the person behind the work that he wrote, behind the Torah that he taught. The hasidic movement sought to remedy this by attempting to portray the personalities of Rebbes, as well as their teachings, as clearly as possible, so that even if little is written of those teachings, there will still be a certain amount of clarity, a certain clear definition of who they were.

Until this point, we have offered explanations for why the Kotzker Rebbe left us no books so that his legacy wasn't perpetuated. Another reason the path of Kotzk did not continue as a hasidic dynasty is tied to the very essence of Kotzk.

THREE HIGHWAYS

Of the many paths in the greater world of Hasidism, three branches are preeminent: Chabad, Breslov, and Kotzk.

I myself am a descendant on both maternal and paternal sides of other esteemed hasidic branches. It's possible that most hasidic leaders as well as their followers were on different paths from the three main branches. But a portion of those alternative hasidic paths thrived only

4. *Avot* 4:13.

briefly. Even those that still exist today don't comprise a unique path. One example is the branch of Hasidism that began with the Maggid of Turisk. In his time, the Maggid was a great Rebbe; many people cleaved to him and to his descendants. I'm certain that there was much more to that branch than just the custom that he instituted – to recite in *Kaddish* the words "*v'karev ketz Meshiḥei.*" Yet it's not clear that this branch had its own unique path that differentiated it from other sects.

As I mentioned, even though some of these hasidic Rebbes were exceptional leaders and personalities, they didn't pave the way for the majority. For example, the Piaseczner Rebbe, who was a very great man and one of the last members of the Koznitz dynasty, left behind books that are more than notes and insights on the Torah; his books also contain guidance and a path to follow. The Berditchever Rebbe also left behind stories, Torah, traditions, melodies, and books, among them the significant book called *Kedushat Levi.* Yet even though there are people who feel connected to these paths from the depths of their souls, the paths remain narrow; they are not highways. As stated, I have identified three main highways – even though they differ in size.

One path is Chabad. This is a great and broad path that Rebbes, *tzaddikim,* and thousands of hasidim and upright men have followed for generations. In a very general sense, Chabad directs a person to approach the service of God through one's intellect. A significant part of this service is undertaken with intellectual awareness and is based on an attempt to define matters clearly.

The second path was developed by Breslov, which is the diametric opposite of Chabad, both in terms of size as well as direction. Breslov was a small and persecuted branch of Hasidism, and yet its path was great. This is the path of the service of the heart, involving a conscious distancing from intellectualism.

Kotzk was completely different from these two paths. Kotzker Hasidism sought to hone every matter to its most extreme and precise point. Kotzk approached matters like a laser beam, like a beam of isolated electrons. Its path was the thinnest of the thin, the most precise of the precise. A powerful laser of that kind is capable of cutting any material in the world – a wall of steel or even a diamond. This was precisely the inclination of the Kotzker Rebbe. He sought a path that would dissect and hone matters to the *n*th degree.

A HIGHWAY FOR INDIVIDUALS

The first two paths were accessible to the multitudes in both principle and practice; the path the Kotzker Rebbe paved was not. The relevance of the path is independent of the number of followers, so when I say he paved a path, I'm speaking in principle and not from a practical perspective. Kotzker Hasidism is similar to that of Chabad and Breslov in that each has its own unique identity and customs. The difference is that the two great leaders of these branches of Hasidism – Rabbi Shneur Zalman of Liadi and Rabbi Naḥman of Breslov – paved highways on which many people could stride. The Kotzker Rebbe paved a route that, although equally great, could be followed only with tremendous difficulty.

With all its various and strange elements, Breslov remains capable of attracting and sustaining a community of hasidim. Breslovers raise children who study in the Breslover Talmud Torah and continue to follow that path as they grow. In a similar fashion, Chabad sustains its continuity starting with a Lubavitch Talmud Torah. A Jew can be an enthusiastic, serious, and genuine Lubavitcher hasid yet also have an ordinary family life. Throughout the years, many – possibly hundreds of thousands of Jews – have lived simple lives as Chabad hasidim. This is also true of Breslov. As long as a Jew can study Breslov literature and find time to isolate himself to engage in dialogue with his Maker, he can be a Breslover hasid. He can do this while living an unexceptional life with his wife and children. I personally know a good number of both simple and elite Breslover hasidim. The unsophisticated Breslov path of innocence and simplicity is one that many different kinds of people can follow.

Kotzk stands in contrast to Chabad and Breslov. It's impossible to build a Kotzker community. It's impossible to build a study hall in which Kotzker hasidim will sit and study, because Kotzk by definition, by its very essence, lacks patience for ordinary Jews. Few individuals would be able to attend a synagogue of Kotzker hasidim because of the difficulty of living up to the substantial demands of the great path of Kotzk.

According to the Chabad model, which calls for intellectual service, the course one should follow is clear and unambiguous even when problems arise. The Breslov model also defines a path that instructs a person on what he needs to do with his life. The Kotzk model doesn't establish any course of that kind.

The Kotzker Rebbe once said that he would have liked to have three hundred hasidim, each of whom would wear a straw *gartel,* cover his head with a cabbage leaf, and walk in the forest shouting, "The Lord is God." It's impossible to build a community with that formula. It's impossible to reproduce or imitate it, even if there did happen to be a store selling cabbage hats and straw belts at a dollar apiece next to the ritual bath.

According to Kotzk, whether a person is intellectual or emotional has no relevance. What matters is whether he is capable of living up to its exacting and far-reaching demands, by living a life that is absolute truth, perfect in every sense. You can cry tears of emotion all day, but not one tear can be false. You can be the most brilliant intellectual, but not one of the thoughts in your head can be groundless.

Among the Kotzker hasidim, there were sharp, astute individuals whose ability to show contempt for people reached unparalleled heights. There were also great Torah scholars. The Kotzker Rebbe was outstanding in revealed as well as esoteric matters. The first Gerrer Rebbe, who was known as the most outstanding prodigy in Poland, told of a time when he struggled with a particular version of a *mishna,* thinking it to be faulty. He approached the Kotzker Rebbe, who clarified the matter and apprised him of his error. In his work *Ḥiddushei HaRim,* the Gerrer Rebbe comments, "What could I say? Something that I sat and pondered for twenty-four hours, he understood in a moment."

In that same hasidic court, which contained many brilliant minds with a scholarly approach, there were also Jews with a diametrically opposite approach. The goodhearted Rabbi Yeḥiel Meir of Gustinin, the "*Tehillim Yid*" had a reputation as a great Torah scholar, but all he instructed others to do was recite Psalms.

I'll tell you another story. The son of Rabbi Shlomo Eiger, Reb Leibele, began traveling to Kotzk. From Rabbi Shlomo's perspective, the fact that his son was becoming a hasid was reason enough to rend his garments – but a Kotzker hasid! As far as he was concerned, that was the lowest level in Gehenna. He sent an emissary to search for his son and bring him home.

The emissary arrived in Kotzk and began to search for "Rabbi Leib Eiger," to no avail. Suddenly, someone said, "Ah, you mean Leibel, son of Shlomo, son of Akiva. He is sitting there in the corner."

It turned out that the Kotzker hasidim had taken almost all of his belongings, even his *shtreimel*, and used it as collateral. The emissary was appalled by the way they treated this young man, who was of distinguished pedigree, as well as the son-in-law of a very wealthy man. He was also appalled that they referred to two of the great rabbis of the generation as Shlomo and Akiva. Apparently, the attributes of greatness and wealth weren't very important to the Kotzker hasidim. Then someone came up to them and said, "Reb Hershele is entering the *shtiebel*."

When he saw that everyone was running to see Reb Hershele, the emissary said to himself, *If there is a person whom the Kotzker hasidim respect, it's certainly worthwhile to see who he is.*

He went over to see Reb Hershele, a diminutive Jew dressed in rags. The emissary asked, "Who is this man? Is he a Torah scholar?"

"No" was the answer. "He hardly knows a chapter of Mishna."

"Is he a man of pedigree?"

"No, he is the son of a laborer."

"Is he wealthy?"

"Do you see how he is dressed?!"

The emissary asked, "If so, what is his virtue?"

"He is humble."

The emissary laughed and said, "Given that he is neither wealthy, nor a scholar, nor a man of pedigree – why is his humility considered to be a great virtue?"

This story went on to be told again and again. It was the Radziner Rebbe who I believe provided the answer: "If he is neither wealthy, nor a scholar, nor a man of pedigree, and he still is humble despite all that he lacks – *that* is a great accomplishment."

There were hasidim in Kotzk who had no regard for rabbis, saw Torah scholarship as vanity and nothingness, but had esteem for a Jew about whom all that could be said was that he was humble. The really important question in their eyes was, "Is he truly humble?" Only if he was truly humble was it appropriate for him to be in Kotzk. On the other hand, a person could be wealthy, a scholar, and a man of pedigree and still belong in Kotzk, as long as his integrity to truth was as close to perfection as humanly possible.

ON THE RAZOR'S EDGE

This fundamental requirement, by definition, isn't intended for the masses. If we were to examine almost any person, we could immediately discern that his intelligence, his scholarship, and his righteousness aren't complete. The Kotzker Rebbe didn't say that one should take an imperfect person and drown him in the nearest swamp. On the contrary, encourage him to travel to another Rebbe with whom he'll thrive. He simply doesn't belong in Kotzk. Kotzk is a path for individuals.

The Kotzker Rebbe once looked out on a large assembly of hasidim and said to someone close to him, "When I was young and still had the strength, I never would have allowed a mob like this in my court."

One must understand that even though this "mob" included distinguished rabbis and great Torah scholars, this was the Kotzker Rebbe's fundamental perspective. The Kotzker Rebbe viewed Kotzk, not only as an elite unit, but as an exclusive one. Even if he had no particular interest in keeping it specifically small, its self-classification dictated that it would be appropriate only for the few.

The Rebbe worried about the arrival of masses of followers. Among other reasons, he knew that a great many people would come because they had heard that Kotzk was interesting and unusual; extremism, by definition, attracts interest. The Rebbe didn't want those kind of followers, and it wasn't because he hated the average Jews. It was fine for a Jew to have deficiencies – thirty percent wise or sixteen percent righteous – but in his view there was no place for someone like that in Kotzk.

There is a species of plant called gingko, which originated in China and was brought from there to the four corners of the world. It looks like a tree, but, botanically speaking, it doesn't belong to any known classification in the plant kingdom. Perhaps it belongs to a plant category from distant prehistory, but nothing living in modern times is similar to it. Botanically and taxonomically, gingko is a unique division in and of itself, one that includes two species at most, alongside divisions like grasses and vegetation.

There are two creatures in Australia, the platypus and the short-beaked echidna, that also can't be clearly categorized. They lay eggs but are also warm-blooded mammals – a unique combination that isn't found in any other living being. Even the Gemara states that a creature that lays eggs isn't a mammal.[5] Scientists nearly tore each other's hair out over the question of how to categorize the platypus and echidna. They seem to constitute a division in and of themselves. From a zoological perspective, they are different from all the thousands of other species, even though there are only two species of their kind in the entire world. They are a category that stands alone.

The same can be said about Kotzk. Fundamentally, it is a world in and of itself. It doesn't have the potential to reach the masses, as other central hasidic sects have done. The Kotzker formula as a way of life will necessarily self-destruct. A community of that sort isn't sustainable; it's impossible to educate children in a school that follows the way of Kotzk.

The Kotzker way is to sharpen the razor to the point that only one atom will remain on its edge, to hone matters to the farthest extremity. In other hasidic paths, one can explain to people precisely what the ideal is and point out where they are along the way. But one can't expect throngs of people to aim for an ideal life on the edge of a razor. It's possible to place something on one side of a razor and it's possible to place something on the other side of the razor, but it's virtually impossible to place anything on the edge of the razor. It's too narrow. By its very definition, it leaves room for almost no one.

CRITERIA

If it's impossible to follow the path of Kotzk, and impossible to live on the edge, why are we having a farbrengen on this topic? Why is it worthy of our attention?

The answer is that some things are highly significant even though they may be impractical.

---

5. *Bekhorot* 7b.

One can see a similarity between the opinions of Beit Shammai and the path of Kotzk. Beit Shammai tended toward stringency, but their opinions were articulated comprehensively, and their precision about the underlying principle was taken to the ultimate extreme. It is written that in future times, halakhic rulings will follow the opinions of Beit Shammai. What this means is that although it's impractical to try to live according to Beit Shammai in this world, in a future perfect world we'll be able to live with rulings that have been established correctly.

Why do we study the words of Beit Shammai even though the *halakha* is almost never in accordance with their opinion? Wouldn't it be preferable to skip directly to the rulings of Beit Hillel, since the *halakha* is almost always based on their opinions?

The words of Beit Shammai are recorded not only to clarify matters, but also because it's crucial to be aware of the path of justice each time an alternate path is taken. The world we live in can't exist exclusively according to the attribute of justice. As Abraham said to God, "If You want justice, there will be no world; if You want the world, there is no justice. It is impossible to ride two horses at the same time."[6] So we say in prayer, "If You exhaust justice with us, who can be justified before You in judgment?" At the same time, a person must know that there is a standard of truth, even if it's impossible to live up to.

Following the path of truth and justice to the point of absolute truth may be impossible, yet knowledge of the point of truth is crucial. Its significance is related to the mathematical concept of a boundary point. Clearly, it's impossible to reach the boundary point, but the point is necessary, if only to define and delineate the path. This point, no matter how distant, helps determine the way and the direction.

The Gemara states that in the effort to produce just a half-dinar of pure gold for the menora in the Tabernacle, artisans placed it in a crucible a thousand times.[7] Actually, it's impossible to produce gold that is 100 percent pure. When one tries to purify something from dross, it can be relatively easy to get it to be 90 percent pure. It's much more

6. *Midrash Rabba, Bereshit* 49:9.

7. *Menaḥot* 29a.

difficult to reach a purity of 95 percent or 96 percent. Every attempt to progress another fraction of a percentage point to reach 99 or 99.9 percent purity requires tremendous effort. The closer one gets to the limit, the more unrealistic actually reaching it becomes.

In physics, there is a value called absolute zero, which is a bit less than 273 degrees below zero Celsius. It's the lowest temperature possible; there is nothing colder. Relative to absolute zero, liquid oxygen – at approximately 180 degrees below zero – is considered to be pretty warm. There are actually materials that boil in liquid oxygen. Scientists have invested massive amounts of money in attempts to reach absolute zero. They've managed to get very close, but reaching it has proven impossible. Each time they succeed in lowering the temperature a little bit more – another tenth, thousandth, or millionth of a degree – it's considered a tremendous accomplishment, written up with excitement in scientific journals. At absolute zero, everything changes; it's the extreme boundary. Absolute zero has no practical use as yet, but it remains important to identify and study it. Things are measured relative to boundaries in terms of how close they are to the absolute.

Much more than relentless effort is required to get to aboslute truth. In a certain sense, absolute truth can be found on the border of our world but not within it. Yet it's important to consider this in order to provide our reality with a frame of reference. A person needs to know that the way he judges and assesses matters is far from perfect.

That's why, despite everything, we commemorate the *yartzeit* of the Kotzker Rebbe, a man who was a flaming fire. What characterizes Kotzk? Insulting the entire world is not Kotzk. Lack of consideration for the whole world is also not Kotzk. The determination and wild enthusiasm of a person's effort to break through walls even if that effort causes damage to himself or others are also not the essence of Kotzk. There is only one thing that actually represents Kotzk: It is the search that a person conducts, typically within himself, to find the point of absolute truth, a truth that can't be expressed or put into words. The crux can be understood by asking this simple question: Where can one find absolute truth? The question has no answer, but it leaves an impression on the person.

UNTIL EXHAUSTION OF THE SOUL

The essence of the path of Kotzk is the attempt to reach an absolute boundary, to whatever degree this is possible. By its very nature, this path is relevant only to a select few. It is written that after death, all that remains of the body is a small indestructible bone called the *luz*. The entire body is destined to be reincarnated from that little bone. The search for the *luz* – for the core that can't be destroyed and can't die – is of critical importance because it's the standard against which every other path is measured.

A person can follow other paths and live the kind of good Jewish life described by the prophet Jeremiah to King Yoshiyahu: "Did your father not eat and drink and perform justice and righteousness? Then it was good for him."[8] A person can study Torah in the morning and evening, treat the members of his household reasonably well, not deceive people, and perform his work honestly. Nothing can be said against that kind of life. That Jew is entitled to his share in the World to Come. Accommodations are prepared and waiting for him, though not necessarily exclusive ones. He has a place that is appropriate for a good Jew who is satisfied with being righteous "in his generations"[9] – that is, a decent, upright, God-fearing person who emerges righteous from the heavenly court because his *mitzvot* outweigh his transgressions. Based on that majority, he is able to enter a special Garden of Eden for upright people.

Good for him. But it's possible to demand more from one's soul – to demand nothing less than the total utilization of the soul. Even if a person can't achieve it from a practical perspective, the demand persists. That's why the formula of Kotzk is crucial even for a Lubavitcher hasid, even for a Breslover, and for anyone who chooses to follow any other path.

There is a path of divine service, a path of betterment of attributes, a path of Torah study, a path of fulfillment of many *mitzvot*, a path of

8. Jeremiah 22:15.
9. See *Rashi* on Genesis 6:9, which states that Noah was considered righteous in his generation, but he may not have been considered righteous in the generation of Abraham.

education of students. All of these paths are suitable and worthwhile choices. Yet every so often, a ray of truth must enter. It's a ray that on the one hand causes everything to collapse, because the moment I contrast anything with the magnitude of absolute truth, everything else disappears: "To whom would you liken Me that I would be equal?"[10] On the other hand, this flash of truth restores perspective and puts everything in order.

Anyone who had dealings with the Kotzker Rebbe or who has written about him came to know that he was a pillar of truth. He honed this aspect of his character with greater vigor and greater force than any of his teachers. He knew that the more he continued to refine his path, the more narrow and dangerous it would become. It would also become more and more difficult to follow. Despite this, he continued to adhere to the path of truth, for "the Lord God is truth."

This is why it's appropriate for us to mention him and remember him. On every road and path that we follow, in all areas and all contexts, in matters of the intellect and matters of the heart, in Torah and *mitzvot*, in noncompulsory matters and even sinful matters, the same question arises: It's true that I experienced, understood, lived, and acted – but where was the actual point of truth?

TOUCHING THE EDGE OF TRUTH

Rambam begins his book with the words "The Lord God is truth." He existed first, and all who exist were created only from the truth of His existence; there is no creation that is truth like Him. The truth, in its absolute sense, in its ultimate extreme sense, is God alone, and it is one. It cannot be otherwise. "There is none besides Him"[11] – everything else is relative: relatively small, relatively large, close to the truth or far from it. A person, then, must ask himself: Where is the point of truth? We must seek to draw a bit nearer to it, to touch it, or to at least touch the edge of it.

Someone brought a commentary he had written on a certain book to a rabbi. The rabbi read it and said, "*Nu,* it is close to the truth." He

10. Isaiah 40:25.
11. Deuteronomy 4:35.

immediately explained, "Do you know what I mean? I mean that your commentary printed on the page is physically close to the actual work on which you commented. In that sense, it is adjacent to the truth."

Having said that, there can be real value in finding things that are close to the truth. This is what the Baal HaTanya wrote about the verse "The language of truth will be established forever."[12] The word for "language," *safah*, also means "edge." Not only the absolute truth, but even the edge of truth, that which touches it, is tied to eternity.[13]

I once sat with the previous Slonimer Rebbe when he was well advanced in years. He spoke to me about his many experiences in life. He didn't do this in my honor, but in honor of my grandfather's father, whom he knew. He recalled that when he was young, the Beit Shmuel, who was then the Slonimer Rebbe, sent him to all of the greatest Rebbes in an attempt to form an organization. Describing his own joy at seeing the Slonimer Rebbe's emissary, one of the Rebbes said, "Happy are the eyes that saw the eyes that saw the eyes."

Something similar can be said about the edge of truth. Even if you don't completely internalize truth, even if you just touch it, even if you cleave to someone who once cleaved to something like it – this indirect contact makes an impression that will leave its mark on you.

A story is told of an elderly man who was dying slowly, getting closer and closer to the end. He wanted to die, but death wouldn't come. In the attempt to determine why, someone discovered that he had once visited Reb Elimelekh of Lizhensk, who told him that no one who stepped over the threshold of his house would die before repenting. As long as this old man didn't repent, he couldn't die. So it was that a person could be in contact with something, however briefly, that could interfere with his death, even if the experience didn't interfere with his life.

THE BOOK OF THE RIGHTEOUS

We're speaking of Kotzk to remind ourselves that an extreme path like this exists and that it's not inferior to any other path. It is great in its scope, in its demands, and in its ability to change the person who adheres to it.

12. Proverbs 12:19.
13. *Likkutei Torah*, Behar.

God keeps a book of the completely righteous, a book of the completely wicked, and a book of those who fall in between. In hasidic literature, as in other works, there are many different answers to the question of who is deemed to be righteous, who is considered to be a *tzaddik*.

Rava is quoted in the Gemara as saying that there are eighteen thousand rows of *tzaddikim* standing before God. Rabbi Shimon bar Yoḥai, on the other hand, said there are but a few: "If there are one thousand *tzaddikim*, my son and I are among them. If there are two, they are my son and I. If there is only one – it is I."[14] According to another definition, there are myriads upon myriads of thousands of *tzaddikim*. And yet another may state that the book of the righteous contains more empty pages than those with names. Either way, we must remember and mention, time and again, that a book of the full-fledged righteous is possible and actually exists.

A person can say, "Kotzk has never been the path for me – neither in my youth nor my old age. I'm not worthy of it." This may be true, but still he should remember that there is actually a Kotzker hasid who wants, from the depths of his soul, to attempt to reach the extreme edge of truth, the unadulterated truth. What is the truth of a stone? What is the truth of a flower? How can I reach the root of roots, the essence, that which is closest to God who is truth?

This point is a particularly frightening one, much more frightening than the terror anyone may have felt when meeting the Kotzker Rebbe in person. This sense of truth is one of the most frightening things a person can experience.

A pillar of truth, though likely to be exceedingly powerful, is also made of the finest of materials. It stands alone and doesn't need to lean on anything, but everything else depends on it and leans on it. The point of truth is found at the root of everything and provides vitality to everything. At least once a year, it behooves us to hold a farbrengen to remember this.

Leḥayim, leḥayim!

---

14. *Sukka* 45a; *Bereshit Rabba* 35:2.

11 Nisan
The Birthday of the Lubavitcher Rebbe

The eleventh of Nisan is the birthday of the Lubavitcher Rebbe, Rabbi Menaḥem Mendel Schneerson. He was one of the most prominent leaders of our generation and the Rebbe of Rabbi Steinsaltz, who was bound to him heart and soul.

The Lubavitcher Rebbe was born in 1902 and passed away in 1994. His lifetime spanned almost the entire twentieth century, and his activities and accomplishments as Rebbe can be seen in light of the cataclysmic events that befell mankind in general and the Jews in particular during that time. The Rebbe experienced all of these events – the Bolshevik Revolution, the rise of the Nazis and the Holocaust, the Jewish migration to the United States and Israel, and more – on a personal level yet responded to all of them as the leader of the generation.

The Lubavitcher Rebbe was a descendant of the Tzemaḥ Tzedek, the third Lubavitcher Rebbe. He married the daughter of the sixth Lubavitcher Rebbe, Rabbi Yosef Yitzḥak Schneerson, who was his distant relative. As Rabbi Yosef Yitzḥak's son-in-law, he was heir apparent to fill the position of Rebbe. In practice, it wasn't at all easy for him. Rabbi Steinsaltz often said that one of the most noteworthy characteristics of the Rebbe's tenure was that he assumed the onus of leadership despite his extreme reluctance to take it on in the first place.

The Rebbe's leadership brought the Lubavitch movement to a new phase. He was the driving force behind the massive emissary enterprise that blanketed the globe with Chabad houses, which operate on behalf of Jews wherever they might be.

The Rebbe also initiated a *baal teshuva* movement, which encouraged and enabled Jews to return to the traditions of their ancestors. In a world characterized by assimilation, and withdrawal from religious practice, especially among American Jewry, the ongoing Jewish existence was his top priority. The underlying philosophy motivating all of his activities and accomplishments was that our generation is the generation of the final redemption. Everything he did stemmed from that basic belief.

Rabbi Steinsaltz considered the Lubavitcher Rebbe to be the ultimate paradigm of a great man, one who radiated greatness evident in every aspect of his existence. The birthday of such a person is a fitting time for hasidim to convene and have a farbrengen in order to engage in a reckoning of the world and to take responsibility for it.

14

The Essence of the Lubavitcher Rebbe

A PERSON'S EXISTENCE VERSUS HIS ACTIONS

The acknowledgment and commemoration of a person's birthday is a rare occurrence in Jewish tradition. It's even more unusual to mark a birthday when that person is no longer with us. The Jewish calendar is filled with special dates that have been celebrated by generations, year after year. But days of remembrance of specific individuals are almost always commemorated on the date the person passed from this world, on his *yartzeit,* rather than on his birthday. The reason for this lies in the essential difference between a person's birthday and his *yartzeit.*

A person's life achievements are commemorated on his *yartzeit,* when his life is seen from the perspective of his actions. That's why these accomplishments are noted and addressed on the anniversary of his death. Marking a person's *yartzeit,* though, is more than just a summation of past achievements, since the summation can change with time. Just as the righteous go from strength to strength in the supernal world, as described in the holy books, something similar transpires in the earthly world, since it's possible for a person to continue to function after death.

Unlike those whose memory diminishes with time, there are people whose memory and the impact of their actions continue to grow stronger with every passing year. This going from strength to strength happens in actual reality, in this world. Sometimes the memory of a person grows to such an extent after his passing that it changes into a different kind of memory altogether. It's like a tree that continues to grow well after the person who planted it has passed from this world. The tree grows and grows, and after five years or fifty years it bears little resemblance to the original sapling. Because of this, the *yartzeit* of a righteous personality is devoted to noting accomplishments that include those that took place after his death as well as those that took place in his lifetime.

By contrast, the celebration of a person's birthday is related to his very existence rather than his accomplishments. When assessing a person's life, one can ask what he did with it. Actions are quantifiable; they can be evaluated and defined. One can even say that his essence is less significant than his actions, that the achievements he left behind are his true legacy. In that sense, his existence is merely the instrument through which he achieved and accomplished the enterprises that remain after he left this world.

By contrast, when we celebrate a person's birthday, whether during his lifetime or after his death, we relate to his existence regardless of his actions. His accomplishments are not part of the consideration. This perspective, that a person's existence or personality has left a significant impression on the world, is something most people don't merit during their lifetime, let alone after the conclusion of their lives. That's why, in contrast to the celebration of a *yartzeit*, marking the significance of birthdays is a practice that occurs very rarely in the Jewish world.

THE SIGNIFICANCE OF A PERSON'S EXISTENCE

If one delves deeply into the matter, one can ask whether a person's essence, or very existence, can have significance on its own, and if so, to what extent? How is it possible to speak of a person's existence without addressing his actions?

To explain this, I will relate something I heard from an acquaintance. He told me that throughout his life he has felt haunted by the persistent presence of another person. It turned out that his parents had a child who died before he was born at the age of ten. Though he never met this older brother, he was constantly aware of his existence. This awareness apparently stemmed from the fact that his parents related to him as a kind of substitute for their deceased son or, at least, as the second chapter of their family saga.

He told me that among other things, the shadow of his legendary brother hovered over him constantly and impelled him to accomplish things that were far greater than his parents dreamed. I imagine that his accomplishments also exceeded what his brother could have achieved. In any case, what haunted him was his brother's existence, not his brother's legacy of deeds. After all, what could a ten-year-old have accomplished in the world? The essence of the deceased brother was substantial and extant to the point that his living younger brother found it relentlessly haunting.

It turns out that sometimes, even if nothing practical remains of it, a soul that existed briefly in this world remains alive and significant to the extent that it has an ongoing effect on the world.

Distinguishing between a person's achievements and his essence isn't simple, because we tend to measure matters externally and not internally. If one wishes to distinguish between these aspects, it's necessary to consider what would have remained of the person had he not succeeded in accomplishing any of the things he achieved. For some people, nothing would remain had they not succeeded in life for some reason – for example, if all of their writings had been lost or all their investments depleted. By contrast, there is a certain person whose existence endures, whose presence continues to be felt, even after his passing. This is the sort of person who attempted to accomplish things but failed, yet his personality, and even his determination, were powerful enough to inspire others to follow in their footsteps. In other words, the image itself, the unadulterated personality, with no specific, actual action associated with it, continues to make itself heard, speak, and motivate others to act.

I once heard this idea expressed differently: "So and so is a person whose presence is felt just as strongly as his absence." There are people whose absence is noted by everyone, but it's much more rare to find someone whose presence s noticed and remembered by all.

To put it simply, when people sit together and one person gets up and leaves, people usually notice his departure, but his presence made little difference to others. By contrast, there are people who, when present, are truly present, and their existence is sensed and has an effect on others. This is not an existence defined by absence, but rather an existence defined by substance.

UNQUANTIFIABLE GREATNESS

It's unusual to find this kind of substance in the world, but it is recognizable as genuine when one does encounter it. Even if it's not precisely understood, it leaves an impression.

There is a verse in the book of Malachi that is usually read as part of the *haftara* of *Shabbat HaGadol*: "For the lips of the priest will safeguard knowledge, and they will seek Torah from his mouth, as he is a messenger [*malakh*] of the Lord of hosts."[1] The Sages expound on this verse: "If a teacher is similar to an angel [*malakh*] of the Lord, seek Torah from his mouth. If not, do not seek Torah from his mouth."[2]

How can I know if the teacher is like an angel if I've never seen an angel?

I once heard an answer to this question that rings true, though it's not the plain understanding of this statement of the Gemara: Even if I don't know what an angel looks like, when I see one, I'll know, without a doubt, that I'm in the presence of an angel. Similarly, when I see a person about whom I can say with certainty, "This is my teacher," I can receive Torah from his mouth.

This is not based on specific qualifications. You don't need to check to see if he has wings or how big they are. Rather, you must identify authenticity – whether the person's greatness is immediately apparent, genuine, and outstanding. The essence of the man is far greater than the things he accomplishes in the world. That is what one should seek when searching for a rabbi.

Take, for example, the Kotzker Rebbe. His Torah teachings can be found in several different anthologies, but even the relatively large ones don't contain enough of his teachings to fill an actual book. He left no well-organized philosophy, no guide on how a person should conduct his life from the time he wakes up in the morning until the time he

1. Malachi 2:7.
2. *Mo'ed Katan* 17a.

recites *Shema* in bed at night. And although these anthologies do contain important and interesting ideas, they don't convey who the Kotzker Rebbe was, and they are not his most memorable legacy. The legacy of the Kotzker Rebbe was his essence – his very existence.

There's an interesting anecdote that encompasses this point in a different way. One of the Kotzker Rebbe's closest disciples was Rabbi Yitzḥak Meir Alter, the first Gerrer rebbe, also known as the Ḥiddushei HaRim. The Ḥiddushei HaRim was a brilliant personality. In addition to his outstanding abilities, his sharp mind, and his immense intellect, he was God-fearing from childhood to old age. This unusual combination of attributes can't be taken for granted.

The Ḥiddushei HaRim was also a friend of the Kotzker Rebbe, and after the Kotzker Rebbe's second marriage, he became his brother-in-law as well. But at a certain point, the Ḥiddushei HaRim decided to become the Kotzker Rebbe's follower and disciple. This transpired after the passing of Rabbi Simḥa Bunim of Peshisḥa, when the question of who would succeed Rabbi Simḥa Bunim arose. Would it be the Kotzker Rebbe or the Ḥiddushei HaRim?

It is said that the two friends were overheard conversing at the time, and one said to the other, "The future of the leadership is now between us. Either you or I will succeed the Rebbe of Peshisḥa."

This was actually true because each of them was qualified and capable of assuming leadership. This private conversation ended with the Ḥiddushei HaRim deferring to the Kotzker Rebbe. He became his disciple and hasid, and the Kotzker, his Rebbe. This outcome was by no means obvious because the Ḥiddushei HaRim was renowned throughout the Jewish world as the prodigy of Poland, and his status and influence were greater than the status and influence of the Kotzker Rebbe. Besides, had he become Rebbe, the *mitnagedim* wouldn't have been able to attack and disparage him the way they attacked the Kotzker Rebbe. Despite all this, the Ḥiddushei HaRim remained subordinate to the Kotzker Rebbe for many years.

The Ḥiddushei HaRim himself explained the reasons for his decision. "Why did Moses prostrate himself," he asked, "when God appeared to him in the crevice of the rock and revealed the thirteen attributes of mercy? What did he see that caused him to prostrate himself?

"Moses saw the attribute of truth, and when one sees the truth – one bows before it."

The Ḥiddushei HaRim is also quoted as having said, "I saw before me a pillar of fire and I bowed."

The decision in this case wasn't based on who was the greater Torah scholar. The Kotzker Rebbe happened to be a rare genius and a very great Torah scholar, but his Torah scholarship wasn't the main factor in this context. It was his personality that made him the natural choice. The Kotzker Rebbe was a pillar of fire before whom it was impossible to remain indifferent.

A story is told about the beginning of a meal at a certain Rebbe's table. Bread was broken, and since neither of the two halves of the loaf was bigger than the other, a halakhic question arose: On which half should the blessing be recited? The Rebbe heard the question and said, "If it has to be measured in order to determine its size, then it's already not considered so big."

That is the heart of the matter. When I see a huge mountain, I need not measure it in centimeters to ascertain its magnificence. The same is true when encountering beauty, wisdom, or greatness. The sense that "this is it" is evoked. It transcends quantification and definition.

On many occasions, an individual's personal greatness is shrouded from others. People may go to a rabbi or a *tzaddik* expecting to hear insightful interpretations of the Torah or new ideas and are disappointed when they don't. They sit in the lecture or farbrengen and don't hear ingenious comments or Torah insights that can be repeated at home or written in a notebook. They don't understand that the point isn't whether something deep or novel was said, but whether something authentic was communicated. When encountering something authentic, there is no need for adornments or wrappings. The idea itself stands alone as something great, even when what was said is nothing new.

The search for leaders who could be described as both great and authentic is exhausting and complex, but it's important, especially in the world in which we live. In general, our world is one of falsehood upon falsehood, because even the lies can't be relied on to be consistent. In a world like this, the question is even more critical: How can I discern authenticity – authenticity that I don't have to question or ponder or deliberate about?

WHAT THE REBBE DID AND WHAT HE DIDN'T DO

Rabbi Menaḥem Mendel Schneerson, the Lubavitcher Rebbe, whose birthday we have gathered to celebrate today, most certainly had intrinsic, existential greatness – greatness of his very essence. This remains true even though it's also possible to define his greatness by his actions, accomplishments, and the influence he had in various areas.

Rabbi Menaḥem Mendel brought about a historic change in trends that had long been entrenched in Jewish communities. Until his time, there was a clear generational flow in Jewish observance. In my youth, it was clear to everyone that this flow was similar to that of the four sons in the Passover Haggada: The grandfather is wise and righteous, his son is wicked and leaves Judaism, his grandson is simple, and the great-grandson is one who "does not know to ask."

I remember reading something at the time that was intended to shock people about the possible future of Israeli society. Jews were depicted going to a museum, seeing a Torah scroll, and saying to their children, "This was a scroll that was very significant to our grandparents." The concern about the future of Jewish observance wasn't an exaggerated fear. The trend of continued abandonment of the practice of Judaism was perceived by everyone as the natural course of events, a one-way street with no going back.

The Lubavitcher Rebbe initiated a shift in that historical trend. It wasn't a complete revolution; even in the post-Rebbe world, people continue to alienate themselves from the Jewish collective. But this phenomenon stopped being inevitable. It stopped being one of the inexorable laws of nature. Among all the households of Israel, can you find a person who can say with certainty that his children will never return to Judaism? I heard, for example, that one of the great-grandchildren of Leon Trotsky is an ultra-Orthodox Jew with a beard and *peyot*. Today the direction of observance from one generation to the next can be one where progeny move toward rather than away from Jewish practice. This is just one of the things that the Lubavitcher Rebbe changed in this world.

Several generations ago, it seemed as if the end was near for the Jewish world. In many ways, the Lubavitcher Rebbe can be likened to a person standing before a train that is hurtling with great speed toward a canyon, attempting to stop it from falling into the abyss. He knows very well where the train is headed and he tries to halt its movement so that it can be turned in the other direction. The Lubavitcher Rebbe was somewhat successful in braking the movement of millions of Jews turning away from Judaism and in generating movement back toward Judaism. The power of this directional change, which continues to this day, is amazing in and of itself. It is undoubtedly one of the Lubavitcher Rebbe's greatest achievements, but at the same time, when we speak of him, the deeds he performed are not the crux of the matter.

The Lubavitcher Rebbe's essence is tied specifically to what he was *not* able to accomplish. It's clear to me that had he been asked if he had managed to accomplish his life's mission, he would have said that he didn't achieve even half of it. He wouldn't be saying this out of modesty. He believed it to be true. As far as he was concerned, he didn't accomplish even half of what he wanted to achieve.

The Rebbe really wanted to bring the Messiah, and he wasn't able to achieve that. Everything else he did, he did because it had to be done, not because it was the expression of his innermost will. Had he been asked, "What did you do?" he might have said, "I accomplished various projects, for which I deserve a reward, but I didn't accomplish the most important thing."

The Rebbe wasn't successful in realizing what he considered to be his mission and destiny in this world.

A PROPHET WHO DIDN'T COMPLETE HIS MISSION

There has already been someone like the Lubavitcher Rebbe in the sense that he, too, didn't complete his task in the world. We know almost nothing about the background of this man – where he came from, who his parents were, the environment in which he grew up, who taught him, and how he learned. Yet he was, in his day, the leader of his generation, and since he was last depicted in *Tanakh* as ascending heavenward in a tempest, all kinds of stories are told about him.

Elijah was one of the greatest Jewish prophets. In many senses, he is comparable only to Moses himself. The book of Kings tells us that Elijah merited a revelation in the crevice in the rock, like the one Moses experienced, apparently in the same place. Rarely do we have stories like that in *Tanakh*, even about prophets. Even the revelation of Isaiah, who "saw the Lord sitting on a throne, high and exalted,"[3] was not considered to be at the same level as the revelation experienced by Elijah.

Elijah performed wonders in the heavens and on earth even before he ascended and was transformed into an angel. There are more stories about him than about any other personality in Jewish history. In all sects of Israel, from his own lifetime until today, tales and anecdotes about Elijah continue to be told.

One of the unique features of Elijah's life was his ascent to Heaven in a tempest. In Jewish history, there aren't many people who are described as having ascended to Heaven in a tempest. Abraham didn't, and neither did Moses. They were exalted enough, and they, too, could conceivably have ascended heavenward in a tempest, but they didn't, because they wanted to fulfill the decree "For you are dust, and to dust you shall return."[4] A person must return specifically to the dust, the material from which he was made. In contrast to Abraham and Moses, Elijah the prophet didn't return to dust – he ascended heavenward.

This ascent to Heaven is an essential part of Elijah's image and activities in this world. It is related to the fact that, despite his unique greatness, Elijah didn't complete his essential mission. In a certain sense, he didn't fulfill his potential. Although God granted him abilities on par with those granted to Moses, Elijah didn't succeed in accomplishing the great undertaking of his life.

What was it that Elijah sought to accomplish?

He wanted to transform the kingdom of Israel, bringing it from the extreme of idol worship to the other extreme of pure devotion to God. Elijah didn't accept the presence of golden calves in the world. All of his efforts and all of the wonders that he performed were intended for

3. Isaiah 6:1.
4. Genesis 3:19.

the sole purpose of making the citizens of the kingdom of Israel finally acknowledge that "the Lord is God."[5]

On Mount Carmel, they did shout, "The Lord is God." Immediately afterward, no man, not even adherents and followers of the prophets of Baal, lifted a finger in protest when Elijah began to slaughter their prophets. The tragedy was that when night fell, they all went home to eat dinner. When they awoke in the morning, they were precisely the same people they had been the day before. Nothing had changed.

Elijah left his mission unfinished in many ways. He lived half of his life span and completed half of his undertaking. He began something in this world, but it would only attain meaning when completed. This didn't occur at that time. Rather, the kingdom of Israel gradually declined until it ceased to exist.

After the event on Mount Carmel, Elijah was forced to flee and hide. He was ostracized from society and from the world. He turned to God and said, "I sought to accomplish something in this world. I stood on Mount Carmel before all of Israel and demonstrated to them in the most dramatic way possible that You are God. It turns out that I accomplished nothing. The place remains the same place, the king remains the same king, the queen remains the same queen, and their ne'er-do-well children haven't changed. I alone remain a prophet of God. I wasn't successful in completing my mission in the world."

God's answer, as relayed in the book of Kings, is as follows: "There remain many missions to complete: A new king must be crowned in Aram, but you will not be the one to do it. A new royal house must be established in Israel that will oust the present one, but you will not be the one to do it."

In essence, God was saying something wondrous and awesome: "It is true that you did not complete your mission. I will take you to Me for a period of time, but ultimately you *will* complete your unique mission and affirm your declaration that 'I have been zealous' – your determination to turn all of Israel toward God."

---

5. I Kings 18:39.

"I HAVE BEEN ZEALOUS"

How will Elijah complete his mission? To answer this question, one must delve into the essence of Elijah the prophet, as well as the deeds he performed in the world.

In the revelation that Elijah experienced at Ḥorev, he expressed a grievance to God: "I have been zealous [*kano kineti*] on behalf of the Lord."[6] Elijah is also described as the "man who was zealous [*kineh*] in the name of the Lord."[7]

There are two diametrically opposite meanings of the word *kina*. There is *kina* of someone and *kina* on behalf of someone. *Kina* of someone is envy – the desire to be like him or to have what he has. *Kina* on behalf of someone is zealotry – an impassioned demand for exclusivity in the relationship. Elijah was zealous on behalf of God or, in other words, passionate on His behalf.

This is precisely the same kind of *kina* that Joshua had for Moses. He was devoted to Moses with all his heart and all his soul. When he saw Eldad and Meidad prophesying in the camp, his immediate response was to say, "My lord Moses, arrest them."[8]

Moses understood this reaction as zealotry and asked Joshua, "Are you zealous on my behalf?"[9] Joshua loved Moses to the extent that he wasn't able to tolerate any other prophet.

When Elijah or any other person is described as being zealous on behalf of God, it means that his only consideration is God. A person who is zealous on behalf of God can't compromise; he can't be partially committed. He can't agree to people "hopping between two opinions."[10] He must rise and shout, "I am zealous with my whole heart and with my entire personality!"

This is the meaning of the verse "Love is as intense as death; *kina* is as cruel as the grave."[11] Zealotry begins with love that is far greater and

---

6. I Kings 19:10.
7. This description appears in the song recited at the conclusion of Shabbat, "*Eliyahu HaNavi Eliyahu HaTishbi*."
8. Numbers 11:28.
9. Numbers 11:29.
10. See I Kings 18:21.
11. Song of Songs 8:6.

more intense than standard love. It is a love that leaves no room for anything else.

The intensity of zealous love can be seen in Psalms 104. No other psalm addresses the beauty and harmony of the world to the same extent, yet the psalm concludes with the words "May sinners be removed from the earth, and may the wicked be no more." How does this verse relate to the beauty and harmony depicted in the rest of the psalm?

It can be understood in this way: If, when steeped in harmony and beauty, someone suddenly comes and throws manure into the picture, it is intolerable. It's not a matter of the manure itself, but rather the context in which it is placed. In this particular depiction of the world, it can't be tolerated. In the same manner, zealotry that is as cruel as the grave is a love that is as intense as death. It leaves no room for compromise, and I can't tolerate anything that runs counter to that love.

This understanding of zealotry also addresses a significant question about Elijah's personality. In the book of Kings, Elijah is depicted as someone who is capable of killing people with a single glance and who spews damaging curses: "There will be neither dew nor rain during these years, except by my word."[12] He was not only a flaming fire of passion – he actually burned people. After demonstrating to the Jewish people that the Lord is God, he slaughtered hundreds of prophets of Baal, then cast them into the Kishon Stream.

By contrast, none of the tales about Elijah that appear in rabbinic literature, or in thousands of stories told about him throughout the generations, evoke the harsh image from the book of Kings. Elijah the prophet appears in stories and tales as the epitome of kindness, fulfilling *mitzvot* here and there, assisting a person who lost his way, coming to the aid of a person in trouble.

Actually, the depiction of Elijah as a loving, kind person is first noted in *Tanakh*, in the book of Malachi, rather than in rabbinic literature or tales of the righteous. A verse at the end of Malachi states, "Behold, I am sending Elijah the prophet to you before the coming of the great and awesome day of the Lord."[13] And what is it that Elijah will do "before

12. I Kings 17:1.
13. Malachi 3:23.

the coming of the great and awesome day of the Lord"? "He will reconcile parents with children and children with their parents."[14] This is the work that Elijah the prophet will do after his ascent to Heaven.

How does this depiction of Elijah fit with the Elijah we know from the book of Kings?

The essence of Elijah is not hatred. The zealousness of Elijah is driven from a love that knows no boundary.

THE OTHER HALF

The anticipation of Elijah's arrival on Seder night is also related to this idea. When we recite the liturgical poem *Vayhi BaḤatzi HaLaila* from the Passover *Haggada,* we recount a long list of miracles that transpired at midnight throughout history. And yet we ask of God: When will He address what comes after midnight? What about the second half of the night? We say to God: We have performed the rite of Passover Seder. We have remembered and discussed how You redeemed us and took us on as Your people. Now please complete the job for us.

Master of the universe, Your work is not done. True, You took us out of Egypt, performed many acts of kindness on our behalf, and yes, *dayenu* – it is enough for us, it is enough for us, it is enough for us. But have You completed Your mission? After performing all the miracles and wonders with spectacles in the heavens and on earth that caused the entire world to quake and rage, we settled our land, and we became petit bourgeois and then became minor idol worshippers as well. Does that really suffice for You?

On Seder night, we eagerly anticipate the arrival of Elijah because until now we have been engaged in the first half of the story and now we want the other half. We want Elijah to come and finish his work.

The tragedy of Elijah is the tragedy of anyone who doesn't attain the second half, who doesn't see things through to completion. He was a person who performed spectacles in the heavens and on the earth, who halted the rain, and who caused fire to descend from the heavens, but he wasn't successful in completing his life mission. The tragedy is not in his ascent heavenward in a chariot of fire. It was that when he was

14. Malachi 3:24.

taken heavenward in fire, he was sent into forced retirement. As far as he was concerned, after standing in the crevice in the rock and proclaiming, "I have been zealous," he might have wanted God to grant him the ability to finish his mission in this world. He wasn't granted this ability at that time. When will he receive it? "Before the coming of the great and awesome day of the Lord." The day will come when all reckonings have been done, and then Elijah will be granted the second half and be able to complete his task.

That is the essence of Elijah the prophet, and that is what we remember of him. We remember him, not because of the Torah he taught, though the books of Isaiah, Jeremiah, and even Obadiah, have more citations of Torah than we can cite in Elijah's name. The essence of Elijah is not what he said and did, but what he was. He was a fire that descended from above and burned here below. It was impossible to ignore Elijah's fire during his lifetime, and it's impossible to do so after he departed in a chariot of fire. It doesn't matter whether he is alive or dead, because in the most important sense, Elijah remains present. I need not proclaim that he is alive and endures, because it's still possible to encounter him on any given day. We remember Elijah as the angel of the covenant because we continue to seek the angel who will renew the covenant between us and God.

THE LONGING REMAINS

All of this discourse about Elijah the prophet can be seen as a parable for the Lubavitcher Rebbe and what he sought to accomplish. As stated earlier, the Rebbe sought to accomplish only one thing: to bring the Messiah. The Lubavitcher Rebbe's tragedy is similar to that of Elijah the prophet.

There have been great people who succeeded in completing their missions. The holy Ari is an example. He may not have revealed all the secrets he wanted to relay, and it's likely that he hoped he would have more time to do so. Who knows what else he could have revealed had he had the opportunity? Everything we have of the Ari's Torah is the product of only two years. Yet he constructed an edifice that still stands to this day. In that sense, his task was completed.

The Baal Shem Tov also constructed an edifice that has remained standing. Both the Ari and the Baal Shem Tov sought to build something in this world, and each of them succeeded in building something magnificent. And they departed from the world because they had completed their tasks.

By contrast, Elijah's task wasn't completed, and because of this, he didn't really depart from the world. When we sing about Elijah the prophet, Elijah the Tishbite, Elijah the Giladite, we sing with a longing for him. The miracles he performed and the matters he spoke about are not important; the fact of his very existence is. It's important that a person like him existed and that we can rely on the actual truth of the promise he embodied. That's why we attempt to remember the man he was through stories.

The Lubavitcher Rebbe, too, didn't complete his work. It's clear that he did manage to accomplish a great deal. He did great and important things that changed the face of Judaism, but they weren't what he felt was his unique task in this world. He didn't construct the building that he dreamt of building. His longing for the expression of his essence remained unfinished.

THE MESSAGE OF THE REBBE

In the Gemara, Rabbi Yehuda HaNasi states that he merited his considerable wisdom only because he was able to see the back of Rabbi Meir.[15] Many hasidim merited seeing the back of the Lubavitcher Rebbe through his books and photographs of him, but that wasn't the Rebbe's essence. How many hasidim he had is irrelevant. It's possible that he has more hasidim today than he had during his lifetime. The real or alleged wonders attributed to him are also beside the point. The wonders and stories told about the Lubavitcher Rebbe are like the wonders and stories told about Elijah the prophet. What's important is the existential presence of the Lubavitcher Rebbe. Like Elijah, the Lubavitcher Rebbe is significant because of the message intrinsic to his personality.

Who was the Lubavitcher Rebbe? He was a person who began to dream of the coming of the Messiah when he was still a young child, imagining what it would be like when the messianic king arrives. And

15. *Eiruvin* 13b.

he continued to dream about it more than eighty years later. Anticipating the arrival of the Messiah was the essence of his existence.

As Jews, we all know that awaiting the coming of the Messiah is an essential part of our belief system. After all, it is written that one of the questions that a person will be asked on high is, "Did you await salvation?"[16] But for the Lubavitcher Rebbe, all of his strength, his entire essence, was invested in awaiting the salvation. From his perspective, all other matters may have been good, important, and even magnificent, but the paramount, motivating, and persistent question of his life was, where is the Messiah? He is standing behind our wall, peering, seeing, looking, but where is he? Where are the signs of the Messiah's arrival?

It was said, in the early days of Hasidism, that after the destruction of the Temple, the first generations were still nourished by its light. A period of darkness followed when everything was pitch black. Now *tzaddikim* say that we are beginning to reach the end of the tunnel. We are beginning to see a point of light, even though it's merely an obscure fragment. As long as we can see this point of light, we can hold on to it, knowing that it's there, that "the sound of my beloved, behold he approaches."[17] We may not know where or when it will be revealed fully, we may not even have an idea, but we are paying attention.

The Lubavitcher Rebbe left us a legacy of longing for the arrival of the Messiah. All the wisdom, talent, energy, and resources he had were focused on this overriding single vision, which he sought to realize his entire life. This was his legacy: If I look to one side and see darkness, an abyss of pitch-black melancholy, he turns my head, directs my vision to the other side, and says, "Do you see a twinkle of light? That is the light of the Messiah coming closer."

We celebrate this day because the person we saw with our own eyes told us that there is light and that we must seek and desire to see the light – a portent to the realization of the second half of our story as a people.

Leḥayim!

---

16. *Shabbat* 31a.
17. Song of Songs 2:8.

15

The Essence of a Birthday

A PERSON'S ACTIONS AND HIS EXISTENCE

We are now holding a birthday celebration for the Lubavitcher Rebbe, Rabbi Menaḥem Mendel Schneerson. I have said more than once that for most *tzaddikim* and prominent leaders of a generation, we commemorate the date of their *yartzeit*, not the date of their birthday.

As I've said before, a birthday's significance is related to the essence of the person, which is what we remember and stress on that day, rather than what they accomplished, which is stressed on the *yartzeit*. There are people whose accomplishments can be calculated and summarized after their death, and there are people whose essential nature is considered to be more significant than the sum of their achievements.

Through the distinction between a person's essence and his deeds, it's possible to delineate different types of people. There are people who attained impressive achievements, but whose influence is short-lived; nothing remains of them that will be remembered for generations. By contrast, there are people we remember for generations because of who they were. They may have also accomplished great things, but the very fact of their existence in the world is the more important and significant point.

One example of a person whose impressive achievements are not remembered is Yorovam son of Yo'ash, or Yorovam II. He was a great ruler, and during his reign he expanded the borders of Israel to reach from Levo Ḥamat to the Arava Sea, even beyond the borders that were in place during the reigns of David and Solomon. Despite this, he is mentioned only briefly in Prophets. We hardly even remember his name. The key fact that we remember about Yorovam II is that during his reign, Jonah's prophecy about the expansion of Israel's borders was fulfilled. But, as opposed to Jonah, whom we remember thousands of years after he died – though he was not a king and wasn't victorious in wars – we hardly remember Yorovam at all. It turns out that Yorovam's achievements, including those that are worthy to have been recorded in the annals of history and politics, weren't significant in the long run. The territories he conquered and the borders he expanded returned to their original dimensions, and little remains of his memory.

It is told that the king of Persia once assembled the greatest scholars in his land and asked them to collaborate on a book that would tell the entire history of the world, the entirety of human history. The scholars convened and began working. After intensive labor over the course of twenty years, they completed the project and submitted a large compendium of volumes that summarized world history.

The king looked at the volumes and said, "When I asked you to write these books, I was thirty years old. Now I'm busier and older. Condense the work so I will be able to read it."

The scholars reconvened and toiled for several more years, until they produced a condensed twelve-volume set. They brought the volumes to the king, but meanwhile twelve years had passed, and the king said, "It's hard for me to read these volumes. Condense them into one volume that will include everything that was in the twelve volumes."

The scholars reconvened, and again worked for years until they produced the final volume. The chief historian, who was responsible for the book, was old by then and could hardly walk. He came to the king with the book in his hand and submitted the finished product.

The king himself, who was now on his deathbed, said to the scholar, "I'm about to die and can't read this book. Can you perhaps tell me with absolute brevity, 'What is the history of the world?'"

The elderly scholar answered, "People are born; they suffer, then die."

A nice story that imparts a truth. In a certain sense, the entire history of the world in general and of each individual in particular can, indeed, be summed up with the words "They were born; they suffered, then died."

On the other hand, there are people who live lives of substance that leave an impression long after they are gone. This is rare. Not every person, alive or not, is worthy of having his birthday celebrated. It's interesting that there are discussions regarding the birthdays of the Patriarchs, for example, but the dates of their *yartzeits* are unknown. This is tied to the fact that the significance of the Patriarchs was their very essence rather than their deeds. But this concept, that a person's essence and nature can leave an impression above and beyond his list of accomplishments, is not only true in relation to great *tzaddik*im. I can know if a person is unique, righteous, or pious. And then there is the kind of person about whom I can say, "Whenever I speak of him, I remember him still; therefore My innards yearn for him."[1] These feelings are tied to the person's essence, not his actions.

The third chapter of tractate *Taanit* tells of Rabbi Beroka, who went to a marketplace with Elijah the prophet and asked him if anyone there was destined to receive a share in the World to Come. Elijah responded that there was not. Just then, two men entered the marketplace and Elijah said, "There are now two men here who are destined to receive a share in the World to Come."

Rabbi Beroka asked the men, "What is your occupation?"

"We are jesters. When we see a person with a broken heart, we tell him jokes until he begins to smile."

It's conceivable that there were Torah scholars in the marketplace as well as authors of holy books and men of good deeds. But of all the people in the marketplace, only those jesters were destined to receive a share in the World to Come. They earned a place in the World to Come because of their jokes.

This anecdote describes a level of righteousness that is related to a person's essence rather than to his accomplishments. It turns out that a

---

1. Jeremiah 31:19.

person who makes the people around him smile can be doing something much more significant than one whose accomplishments make headlines.

All of this has been an introduction of sorts to the topic of people whose existence we celebrate on their birthdays. This is not to say that we consider their existence because they lack concrete accomplishments worth remembering and celebrating. On the contrary, it's conceivable that they have accomplished great things and many significant deeds. But on a birthday we focus on the matter of their existence in and of itself.

In honor of the Lubavitcher Rebbe's birthday, I would like to focus on his existence, specifically on aspects of it that comprised the essence of his life. I'm not going to address his many considerable achievements, or his Torah insights, his treatises and discourses, which were published in dozens of volumes. All of these are important, but they are not his essence. I would like to concentrate on the Lubavitcher Rebbe himself.

The Lubavitcher Rebbe's Leadership

HIS AGREEMENT TO BECOME REBBE

The Lubavitcher Rebbe's self-sacrifice was manifest most profoundly in his assent to become the Rebbe. The assumption of that responsibility was perhaps the most difficult challenge of his life because he didn't want to be the Rebbe. From various letters that remain, one can see just how much he didn't want to take on that job. From the outset, he built his life to follow a quiet and modest private track. His decision to accept the leadership as Rebbe was clearly a divergence from the life he had planned.

This step taken by the Rebbe is similar to Moses's rise to leadership. God had to convince Moses to lead the people of Israel. When God commanded Moses to take the Jewish people out of Egypt and give them the Torah, Moses replied, "I cannot – I am not suitable for the task."

God asked Moses, "What, then, do you want?"

Moses replied that he wanted to be a shepherd, to continue to herd Yitro's flocks and bring the goats home. And God punished him in many ways, including giving him leprosy, because of his refusal to accept the mission.

Moses emphatically didn't want to be the leader of the Jewish people. But that doesn't detract from the fact that he was great because he did become their leader. The Lubavitcher Rebbe, too, didn't want to lead, yet he accepted the responsibility and led.

IN THE PLACE OF HIS GREATNESS, YOU FIND HIS HUMILITY

In order to further clarify the self-sacrifice embodied in the Lubavitcher Rebbe's agreement to become a leader, I'd like to elaborate a bit about the nature of this role.

First and foremost, it required dealing with trivialities, and sometimes even the most trivial of trivialities. For this reason, Moses, every so often, resented the role that had been imposed on him. He needed to bear the brunt of an entire people. At times, he almost said, "I can't tolerate them. They drive me crazy." At one point he in effect said to God, "How much longer will I have to keep changing diapers? I don't have the strength for it." God said, "You're right. It's necessary to ease your burden a bit. I will find you assistants. But you must continue to tend to these people."

Lowering himself to deal with all of the people's trivial matters was one of the things that made Moses great. And this was the Lubavitcher Rebbe's greatness as well. He took on the burdens of the Jewish people in every sense.

Leadership that involves lowering oneself evokes what we say regarding God: "Wherever you find the greatness of the Holy One, blessed be He, you find His humility."[2] There are any number of explanations and homiletical interpretations of this statement. One insightful explanation found in hasidic literature is that when one perceives God's greatness, one is actually perceiving His humility. The very fact that God agrees to be the King of the world is a reflection of His unparalleled humility; His agreement to be King of Israel is an even greater sign of humility.

2. Liturgy recited at the conclusion of Shabbat; *Yalkut Shimoni, Yeshayahu* 489; *Pesikta Zutreta,* Ekev; see *Megilla* 31a.

Imagine children playing a game of make-believe with a king, a royal court, servants, and so on. The children ask, "Who will be king? None of us is worthy of being king."

They find an adult and ask him, "Would you like to fill the role of king for us? You can sit in the teacher's chair and be our king!"

Is the adult haughty if he agrees to participate in the children's game and be king? Of course not. We view him as humble and modest if he is willing to serve as "king" of the children.

In the same manner, describing God as "great, mighty, and awesome" attests specifically to His humility in that He agrees to fill that role. He is willing to play a game with us in which He is our king and we are His servants.

One can detect something like that in the Lubavitcher Rebbe. His greatness was his humility, and his humility was evident specifically in that he agreed to fill the role of Rebbe. To illustrate, the Rebbe's photograph is ubiquitous in the Jewish world, even though, from his personal perspective, the proliferation of his image was like a stab in his heart.

Though the Lubavitcher Rebbe neither wanted nor even dreamed of being Rebbe, he agreed to assume the yoke of leadership though it necessitated certain personal concessions. The Lubavitcher Rebbe's sacrifice wasn't merely physical, nor was it merely a sacrifice of time. It was a sacrifice of the soul, a letting go of his own personal dreams and aspirations, because there were other roles to be filled and other pressing matters to be done.

THE FATHER OF ALL OF ISRAEL

Greater than the Lubavitcher Rebbe's sacrifice involved in taking on the role of Rebbe, I would like to address the sacrifice involved in his actual leadership. In the past, there were great rabbis who would conclude their letters with the words "Servant to the servants of God in such-and-such community." The position of rabbi entailed being a servant to the servants of God in their community. Based on that coinage, one could say that the Rebbe was a servant to the servants of God in the entire Jewish world.

I will tell you a story that underscores the Rebbe's enormous devotion to the hasidim more than his holiness or greatness. There was a time when the Rebbe asked his hasidim – and he already had quite a few at that stage – to submit weekly reports about their activities. Although it is written in the holy books that a hasid must not be a fool, and that foolishness is antithetical to the essence of a hasid, accidents apparently happen in this world, and some of his hasidim could be characterized as foolish. They submitted weekly reports that included the most trivial details: "On Wednesday at four in the afternoon, I went shopping with my wife and bought black socks. Does the Rebbe think that I bought the right socks? I then bought underwear for my child. Was it the right kind?"

The Rebbe would read each of these letters because he saw himself as the father of the entire Jewish people. That was why, from his perspective, it was incumbent on him to tend to everyone. Even if the person wrote to him about ripped pants, or related a difficult conversation that he had with a third-grade teacher, from the Rebbe's perspective it was necessary to pay attention and read the words through to the end. Since he agreed to be a father, he conducted the relationship like a father and not like a commander or an inspector general.

This leadership template of the Lubavitcher Rebbe is a very old one; it was also employed by Moses. The Torah states that Yitro came and advised Moses on how to organize and manage the people of Israel. Yitro came from Midian and was apparently a prominent person there. But Moses came from Egypt, a much larger country that already had a massive and fearsome bureaucracy, and grew up in the royal court of the most powerful country in the world at that time. He undoubtedly knew how to manage a country by means of departments, subdepartments, delegation of authority, and so on. In light of all this, it's difficult to understand why Moses needed Yitro's advice. Why did he need to wait for Yitro's advice to organize the people into a graduated hierarchy?

The answer to this question is that Moses didn't know whether he was permitted to do something like this to the children of Israel, whether he was permitted to divide them up and to build a system with delegation of authority. In his role as leader of the children of Israel, he felt as though he had six hundred thousand (or three million) children of his own. Can one tell a child that he is more important than another child?

They are all his children. Because of this, Moses gave the same attention to each person who came to him, regardless of the nature of the complaint. If a woman told him that a neighbor broke her dish, Moses would have addressed the matter. That's why he needed to hear advice from Yitro. He needed another person to tell him that he was allowed to distinguish between a major matter that would remain in his purview and a minor matter that would be addressed by subordinate leaders because Moses initially perceived his role in an absolute manner: He was the father of all of Israel.

The Lubavitcher Rebbe's perception was a direct extension of Moses's perception of his leadership. The Rebbe was willing to devote the time and effort to be the father of all Jews and to attend to every silly problem and every minor matter that came to him.

A father's job includes some unpleasant aspects that, like it or not, he must do. I can't say, "I am a father, but I didn't commit to change diapers." Diapers are part of the job. It is similarly written regarding God Himself, "When the Lord will have washed the excrement of the daughters of Zion …."[3] Many people aren't moved by this verse, but I'm moved every time by these words: "The daughters of Zion were soiled, and someone must wash them. I will do it."

When God Himself says that He engages in these matters, how can I say that this pursuit is beneath me?

An Eternal Flame

NO REST

At this point I would like to discuss another characteristic that was an essential part of the Lubavitcher Rebbe's makeup – a quality of his very essence that we can cleave to and try to emulate.

The Lubavitcher Rebbe didn't acknowledge the possibility of rest. When asked why he didn't take vacations – after all, he was human – his answer was basically, "Had you been doing your job, perhaps I could have taken a vacation."

3. Isaiah 4:4.

The Lubavitcher Rebbe was motivated by a powerful sense that the work must be done, that the fire must continue to burn. He didn't need to emphasize his sense of urgency or even state it at all, because in many senses his very essence shouted it out.

If you're weak – run. If you're weary – run faster. If you don't feel like it – run even faster. After all, if a person wants to commit suicide, one must prevent him from doing so; sometimes it's even necessary to intervene physically. Similarly, when one sees a person doing nothing, one must rouse him. The Lubavitcher Rebbe didn't believe in slumber and tried awaken every person with whom he had contact.

The Kotzker Rebbe would say that there are matters that have a time, there are matters that have a place, and there are matters that have neither a time nor place. The time for eating is when a person is young, hungry, and growing physically; then it's necessary to nourish the body. The place for sleep is the grave; one can sleep there as much as one wants. For sadness there is no time and no place.

Continuing this line of thinking, when someone asks, "When is the time to rest?" I can answer, "Find a headstone, lie underneath it, and you can rest endlessly, as written explicitly in Psalms, 'Set free among the dead.'[4] After a person dies, he's free to rest; he has both the time and the place for it.

DOING MORE

A person shouldn't rest, but not because it's prohibited to do so. No one is standing over him and telling him to keep going without interruption. Restlessness should stem from a flame that burns unceasingly in his heart: "A perpetual fire shall be kept burning upon the altar; it shall not be extinguished."[5] The fire must not be extinguished; it must burn continually.

The message that the Lubavitcher Rebbe sought to convey to each and every person was more than just to negate the possibility of rest. It was to encourage people to keep doing more. The Rebbe said, "You do what you do very well, but you must do more. If you're standing

4. Psalms 88:6.
5. Leviticus 6:6.

still – begin walking. If you're walking – run. If you're running – run faster. And if you're running faster – fly and seek to ascend on high."

The Gemara states that Torah scholars have no rest, neither in this world nor in the World to Come.[6] It's as if a righteous man sitting in the Garden of Eden on a gold chair is approached by God, who says, "You are a righteous man; you must not rest. Leave the chair for someone else. You need to move on. Since you are righteous, that means you have already started to run. You must continue to do so. You cannot rest."

This is what the Lubavitcher Rebbe said: As long as you're alive, you have work to do. If you've reached a place where you feel that you have done as much as you can, that's an indication that you don't know that more needs to be done. Whatever you have done isn't enough; you must do more. There is a minimum amount of work that a person is obligated to do, and it's prohibited for a person to do less than that. But there's no limit to how much a person can add to his efforts and accomplishments.

SQUEEZING UNTIL THE ESSENCE CHANGES

The last letter I received from the Lubavitcher Rebbe specifically addressed this matter. I had written to him frequently about a matter that continued to trouble me: "I'm busy with several different things. Each one of them would justify a full day's work. This has become more and more onerous. I'm unable to decide what to forgo, what to delegate to others, and what to continue doing myself."

I had asked for his guidance about this many times, but he never responded until that last letter, when he answered, "Everything that you are doing, continue doing, and do more."

There is a famous story about a person who lived in very crowded conditions in a very small house. He went to the town rabbi, who told him to bring his goat into the house. The Jew heeded the rabbi's advice and brought in the goat.

Two weeks later he returned to the rabbi. The rabbi said to him, "*Nu*, was my advice effective?"

6. *Berakhot* 64a.

The Jew said, "What do you mean? Things are much worse! It was hard for us to breathe in the house before the goat came inside. Now he takes up all the room!"

The rabbi replied, "Now take the goat outside."

The man took the goat outside and was immensely relieved.

A similar version of this story took place with the Lubavitcher Rebbe. A person would go to the Lubavitcher Rebbe complaining that he had too much to do, and the Lubavitcher Rebbe would say to him, "Take on more work. If your house is cramped – bring in a goat."

Sometime later, when that person would cry that he already had a goat in the house, the Rebbe would tell him to bring in a cow as well. After he would bring in the cow, the Rebbe would tell him to bring in a camel or two.

The question is, what's the limit? How far can one stretch the boundaries?

It's possible to explain the answer by means of an analogy in physics: When a suitcase is overpacked and can't be closed easily, one sits on it, exerting more and more pressure until it closes. Ostensibly, the limit of the suitcase's capacity depends, more or less, on how much pressure can be exerted on it without breaking it. But if one were to place a press on the suitcase that would crush the contents with several tons of pressure, it would be possible to contract everything inside and pack in much more. One could think that there is a limit to how much pressure the press can apply before the suitcase breaks, but in truth, the analogy can be extended further.

There are stars called white dwarfs, some of which aren't much larger than Earth, but their density far exceeds that of our planet. A white dwarf can weigh as much as the sun because the structure of its atoms have broken down, and all of the available space has contracted. What remains is pure matter. It is said that one cubic centimeter of matter in a white dwarf weighs approximately one ton, because the essence of its matter has been altered. After the pressure of approximately one million atmospheres has been exerted on them, the star's very molecules have changed.

The Lubavitcher Rebbe wanted people to alter their characters so that their "molecules" would change. He believed that a person should push more and more, exert more and more pressure, until a substantive change in his nature has occurred.

CONTINUING THE PUSH

Today is the Lubavitcher Rebbe's birthday. On a birthday, the accomplishments one achieved are less important than what remains of one's essence. The essence of the Rebbe's legacy is the call to continue running. To continue accomplishing. To keep going.

The Lubavitcher Rebbe essentially believed that Jews should be motivated to be like "a perpetual fire burning upon the altar." For the fire to keep burning and not be extinguished, it's necessary to keep adding wood. There is no limit to the amount of wood – to the ongoing effort – required to keep the fire burning. That's how the Lubavitcher Rebbe himself lived and conducted himself, and that's what he told others to do to the extent he was able to reach them. This is what we must learn from the Lubavitcher Rebbe's existence.

I would like to inculcate this impulse into each and every one of you. I would be happy to convey it to others who aren't within my reach, but I can't. If every so often it happens that I push someone, I do so because I want them to keep running.

When taking the Torah scroll from the ark, we recite, "I am the servant of the Holy One, blessed be He." What does it mean to be "the servant of the Holy One, blessed be He"? When a servant is told to go, he goes. When he's told to move, he moves. When told not to sleep, he does not sleep. Until when? Until he ceases being a servant of the Holy One, blessed be He. In other words, forever.

This was the essence of the Lubavitcher Rebbe. If one wishes to receive something from him, one must absorb and embrace the strong feeling that a person works for God. There is no break and no rest. The work is like the fire on the altar, an eternal flame that must not stop burning.

Leḥayim!

3 Tammuz
The Hilula of the Lubavitcher Rebbe

The third of Tammuz is the *hilula* of one of the greatest leaders of our generation, Rabbi Menaḥem Mendel Schneerson, the Lubavitcher Rebbe. He was also the Rebbe of Rabbi Steinsaltz, who bonded with him heart and soul.

Rabbi Menaḥem Mendel Shneerson was born in Mykolaiv, a city in southern Ukraine, on the eleventh of Nisan in the year 1902, and passed away in New York on the third of Tammuz in 1994. After his marriage, he spent several years in Berlin, Poland, and France, where he studied at the Sorbonne, among other places. Rabbi Menaḥem Mendel was able to flee Europe via the south of France during World War II, and he arrived in New York before his father-in-law, Rabbi Yosef Yitzḥak Schneerson, the sixth Lubavitcher Rebbe.

In Rabbi Yosef Yitzḥak's final years, Rabbi Menaḥem Mendel was his right-hand man, helping him establish hasidic institutions in the United States. After Rabbi Yosef Yitzḥak's passing in 1950, Rabbi Menaḥem Mendel agreed, after a one-year waiting period, to take on the leadership of Chabad. From that day until his own passing, the Lubavitcher Rebbe devoted himself completely to his role as leader. He worked virtually without a break, without ever taking a vacation, in order to support, counsel, teach, establish institutions, and do everything he could on behalf of the Jewish people and for the sake of Judaism.

The Lubavitcher Rebbe departed from this world after leading the Lubavitcher hasidim for over forty years, but for all intents and purposes, he was the leader of a population of Jews and gentiles that was much greater than his hasidic followers. His leadership years were characterized by his relentless striving to bring about the messianic era. He had a powerful, unending desire for the salvation of the entire world. As the years passed, his sense of urgency intensified, as did the demands he made of himself, his hasidim, and everyone he encountered.

The period after the Lubavitcher Rebbe's passing was difficult for all of his hasidim. Rabbi Steinsaltz himself also experienced great emotional hardship during this period of time. The void left by the Lubavitcher Rebbe wasn't just a private, personal one. A leadership vacuum was created with the loss of the man who bore the onerous yoke of responsibility for the collective Jewish people and for each individual Jew. This is why the farbrengen on the third of Tammuz demands personal action by each and every individual present. A sense of responsibility, coupled with an intense awareness of the urgent need to act on behalf of Judaism, stands at the center of the farbrengen held on the third of Tammuz, the day of the Lubavitcher Rebbe's passing.

16

An Incomplete *Hilula*

REJOICING IN THE JOY OF THE *TZADDIK*

The *Shulḥan Arukh* states that on the anniversary of person's death, his children fast.[1] In our days, because the hasidic custom has prevailed, this is rarely done. Instead, on the anniversary of the passing, people gather in the synagogue after prayer for a *tikkun*. They drink a little whiskey, eat some cake, and say, "May his soul have an ascent." In terms of the ascent of the soul, it is conceivable that a *tikkun* is as effective as fasting – perhaps even more effective, because a fast isn't always taken seriously. But people are serious about their drink, so the *tikkun* does have a substantive element. In any case, on the anniversary of the passing of a *tzaddik*, one makes a *hilula*, which, as you all know, is a real celebration. I would like to explain its underlying concept.

The passing of a *tzaddik* is not the same as the departure of an ordinary person from this world. With rare exceptions, ordinary individuals want to go on living, regardless of whether they have reason to do so. By contrast, the day of a *tzaddik*'s passing is a day of great ascent for the soul. By its very essence, the soul of a *tzaddik* ascends higher and higher, level after level. Regarding the verse "As man shall not see Me and live,"[2]

1. See *Yoreh De'a* 376:4.
2. Exodus 33:20.

the Sages said, "During their lifetime they cannot see, but upon their death, they can see." Upon his death, a *tzaddik* merits the status of being able to see God.[3] For a *tzaddik* who longed to achieve this throughout his life, it is an unquestionably great day.

The word *hilula* actually refers to a wedding. In one hasidic work, the connection between a *hilula* and a wedding is explained in the following manner: The bride and groom are two souls that were already connected before they were born. It is written that before a person is born, God decrees, "The daughter of so-and-so to so-and so...."[4] Consequently, they were already familiar with one another before they were born; they just happened to be separated for twenty or thirty years, and the wedding celebrates their reunion.

With the passing of a *tzaddik*, something similar transpires. When the soul of a *tzaddik* descends into this world, he takes leave of the upper world. When he passes away, he returns to the place where he actually belongs. He rejoices, and the upper world rejoices with him. It's for this reason that we, too, rejoice at the *hilula*. The departure of a *tzaddik* certainly doesn't benefit our world, but from the *tzaddik*'s perspective, his own death is an ascent into the upper strata. At a *hilula*, we rejoice in the joy of the *tzaddik*, just as at a wedding people rejoice in the joy of the bride and groom.

THE PERSONAL LOSS

Two aspects of the Lubavitcher Rebbe's *hilula* render it a somewhat different circumstance. The first relates to the difficulty in objectively contemplating and rejoicing at the Rebbe's passing. Usually, at the *hilula* of a *tzaddik* – Rabbi Shimon bar Yoḥai, for example – we are able to contemplate the fact that his soul ascended to upper spiritual strata, and we can rejoice as we seek to benefit from his light. With the Lubavitcher Rebbe's passing, objective rejoicing is more difficult. For me, it's hard not only because I was close to the Rebbe personally, but also because of another, very substantial aspect of loss.

3. See, e.g., *Kalla Rabbati*; *Sifra* 2:12.
4. *Sota* 2a.

Those who were privileged to have a relationship with the Lubavitcher Rebbe that was of a profound, intimate nature lost a guide for their lives. During his lifetime, the Lubavitcher Rebbe was an address to which we could turn, not only to request a prayer or a blessing, but also for direction and counsel.

Often people find themselves with troubles or in conundrums, and they seek to find a way to resolve them. A person could turn to the address that is always accessible – he could turn to God Himself – and request that he be granted the wisdom, understanding, and knowledge to arrive at the proper decision. If a person wishes to turn to the original Source, he doesn't need an intermediary – neither an angel nor an emissary. He can turn to God and speak to Him, just as a son can speak with his father. This is the case whether he is an accomplished son or less accomplished, whether he is replete with good deeds or hasn't performed any good deeds at all.

The problem is that we can't always hear God's response. We don't always hear His answer. The Lubavitcher Rebbe was an address that a person could turn to for guidance. One could approach him and ask for his counsel about anything and receive a response.

Now that he has departed, the primary feeling is one of great loss. Although Torah scholars and *tzaddikim* remain in this world, the number of people from whom one can seek counsel and wisdom is diminishing. I'm not saying that the world lacks people who can provide counsel; after all, nothing is easier than giving advice. But knowing that someone serious is behind that advice is a different matter altogether. It's difficult to accept the reality that there is no one from whom one can truly seek counsel.

The resting place of the *tzaddik* is in the Garden of Eden; it's good for him there. But for those left behind, those who had a personal relationship with him, what remains is the void left by his departure. In the Gemara, this emptiness is expressed in a eulogy that still resonates today: "Weep for the mourners and not for the departed, as he has gone to his eternal rest, and we are left with our sighs."[5]

5. *Mo'ed Katan* 25b.

We don't bemoan the departed, the one who passed, because he is at rest in a good place. We bemoan his absence.

A PERSON DOES NOT ACHIEVE EVEN HALF OF HIS DESIRES

Another difference between the passing of the Lubavitcher Rebbe and the passing of other *tzaddikim* relates to his essence and his role in the world. It is written that a person doesn't die having achieved even half of his desires. If he has had one hundred desires fulfilled, he wants two hundred; if he has had two hundred fulfilled, he wants four hundred.[6] Many people, including those who have accomplished a great deal – people who wielded tremendous influence in this world – have wanted to achieve even more. We know that Rambam, for example, tried to accomplish things that he was ultimately unable to see to fruition. Had he lived to the age of ninety instead of seventy, had he been given some respite from all the responsibilities that demanded his time and attention, who knows what else he could have accomplished in this world?

The tendency to want more is true regarding all people, including *tzaddikim*. Not all the efforts of the *tzaddik* are rewarded with completion of the task; not all aspirations are realized. On the contrary, part of the essence of the *tzaddik* is related to the fact that he aspires to keep doing more and more. He isn't satisfied with what he has already done, even after having accomplished a great deal. He doesn't feel that he can go to his eternal resting place in peace and tranquility.

Even though the desire to achieve more is true of human beings in general, and *tzaddikim* in particular, the Lubavitcher Rebbe's desire to accomplish was extraordinary and, as stated above, is tied to his essence and his role in the world.

THE SELF-SACRIFICE OF THE SHEPHERD

There are people who became communal leaders because it was the path on which they began. It came naturally to them, without sacrifice. They proceeded ambitiously along that track until they became great leaders. These people aspired from the outset to scale heights. Once they reached

6. *Kohelet Rabba* 1:34.

a certain level, they aspired to attain the next one, until they reached the uppermost stratum.

The Lubavitcher Rebbe wasn't like that. For him, communal leadership involved self-sacrifice on behalf of the Jewish people throughout his life. There are people who sacrifice their bodies – sleepless nights, failure to eat – for higher purposes. This is a lofty virtue, but the Lubavitcher Rebbe sacrificed not only his body but also his soul for the Jewish people. He devoted his entire existence, his entire personality, to the role he took on as shepherd of Israel. When he accepted this position, he no longer functioned at the exalted level that he had previously. He began to engage in the shepherd's labor – tending to the sheep's tails, the sheep's filth, and all their needs. This was his calling, and that's why he did all that he did.

In that sense, we can liken the Lubavitcher Rebbe to Moses, whose acceptance of the position of shepherd also involved self-sacrifice. In fact, because of the sacrifice he knew was essential to that role, Moses didn't want to accept the mission that God imposed on him. Of course, Moses did desire the connection with God that the role would afford him, desired to be able to be in dialogue with Him. He even employed a tactic that was, perhaps, improper by indirectly asking God for His name: "They will say to me: What is His name? What shall I say to them?"[7] After he heard God's name, Moses said, "Nevertheless, I do not wish to go on Your mission."

Moses wasn't interested in fulfilling the mission of leadership because he knew what leadership of Israel meant. When Moses was alone with the sheep, he was able to sit, to commune with God, to cleave to Him and focus on his personal service of God. By contrast, as leader of the Jewish people, he was no longer able to sit alone and focus on his own growth and spiritual advancement. Instead, he occupied himself with all the needs of the people, no matter how inconsequential.

At the end of his life, Moses conveyed to Joshua his understanding of the difficulties involved in the leadership of the Jewish people. He told Joshua to take on the burden of this role with awareness that the

7. Exodus 3:13.

people could be naysayers, irritable, wicked, annoying, bothersome, and so on.[8]

This is also what the Lubavitcher Rebbe took on when he accepted the leadership. People, many of whom were great hasidim if not great intellectuals, wrote to the Rebbe about every event in their lives. They didn't write only about their work, their successes as emissaries or teachers. They would also tell him, for example, that they were planning to buy furniture and ask him what type of furniture to buy. There were people who would send him, on a weekly basis, a thick notebook filled with details and minutiae – so-and-so quarreled with his wife, and this is what he said to her, and this is what she answered him, and so on. I'm not joking; I know several people who would regularly send him letters with questions about every detail of their lives. Imagine the Rebbe, who was a genuinely great man, reading all of these stories and sometimes even responding to them.

He had to engage with all of these Jews. He couldn't say that he didn't want to be involved with them.

Knowing what the role entailed, why did the Lubavitcher Rebbe accept this position? Like Moses, he sacrificed himself on behalf of the Jewish people. This self-sacrifice wasn't manifest in one specific deed done on their behalf, but by the fact that he took on the onus of leading them. In doing so, he literally and genuinely sacrificed his soul, his life, his thoughts, and his desires for the sake of all types of Jews.

HALF *HILULA*

There have been people, among them some of the greatest *tzaddikim,* who during their lifetime succeeded in attaining outstanding spiritual achievements. When they passed on to their eternal resting place, they were able to say, "Master of the universe, I taught students. I instituted good ordinances. I wrote books. I accomplished something in my life." Regarding such *tzaddikim,* it is said that after their passing, their souls ascend heavenward and continue to rise, level by level, to greater and greater heights. With the passage of time, the souls of these *tzaddikim* lose touch with worldly matters. They achieved a great deal, but after

8. See *Shemot Rabba* 7:3; Rashi, Numbers 27:19.

ascending heavenward, they forget their prior affiliation with this world and become detached from its affairs.

There is a story about Rabbi Mordechai "Mottele" of Chernobyl, a renowned *tzaddik* in his time and his father, Rabbi Naḥum of Chernobyl, who was also a man of distinction.[9] Once, at a time when a misfortune befell the Jewish people, Reb Mottele visited one of his hasidim, who was dying. Reb Mottele had a request for the hasid: When he reached the afterlife, could he deliver a message to his father, Reb Naḥumke, who was already in the next world?

The hasid took an oath promising to do so and to report back to Reb Mottele with his father's reply. Sometime later, the hasid appeared to Reb Mottele in a dream. He told Reb Mottele that after he passed away and reached Heaven, he requested to be taken to Rabbi Naḥum of Chernobyl. Initially he was told that this was not possible, because Reb Naḥumke was in a very exalted world, a world where he himself didn't belong. The hasid was insistent, saying that he was an emissary who had made an oath to fulfill his mission.

Ultimately, the hasid was brought to Reb Naḥumke. He said, "Rebbe, I have a message for you from your son."

Reb Naḥumke replied, "What is a son?"

It turns out that Reb Nahumke's soul, in ascending to the highest worlds, forgot everything related to our world. He didn't only forget simple things, like what one does with shoes. He forgot more significant things, like the concept of a son. He lived in a world that was so abstract that the concept of son had no meaning. *Tzaddikim* of that caliber ascend to upper worlds that are so removed from ours that for all intents and purposes they forget this world and everything in it.

By contrast, there were leaders of the Jewish people – *tzaddikim* engaged in bettering this world – who never totally abandoned it when they passed away. They don't want to reside in the Garden of Eden, even

9. Rabbi Naḥum was once a guest in the home of the Baal Shem Tov, who said to his wife, "Be careful with this Jew. He is a thief." After she witnessed his behavior and his comportment, she said to her husband, "To me, Rabbi Naḥum seems to be a righteous Jew, not a thief." The Baal Shem Tov replied, "He seeks to steal the entire World to Come for himself."

though they have the option of doing so. They choose to remain here because they still have things to do. Because they devoted themselves to the Jewish people in their lifetime, they remain connected to the entirety of the Jewish people after death. They continue to sacrifice themselves on Israel's behalf.

It is said of the seven shepherds[10] that although they ascended to the highest level in the exalted heavens, they remain shepherds of Israel even today. This doesn't apply only to the seven shepherds; in truth, everyone who was a shepherd of Israel remains a shepherd of Israel after death. This is why they remain part of our world even after they have reached the upper worlds.

The Lubavitcher Rebbe was among those who devoted their lives to shepherding the Jewish people. As a shepherd of Israel, he has never really departed from this world. In a certain sense, he is still with us because he still has things to do here. As stated above, the Lubavitcher Rebbe wanted to accomplish more than he could during his lifetime, and not only because of a natural human tendency to want more time. Throughout his life, he insisted that all he desired was to bring about the redemption of the Jewish people. From that perspective, even though he performed good deeds, wrote books, delivered homilies, and accomplished a great deal for the benefit of the Jewish people, he didn't succeed in fulfilling his life's mission. Though the Mishna states, "It is not incumbent upon you to complete the labor,"[11] a person can still depart with the feeling that his life's work remains unfinished. This feeling can persist even for a person who is able to say, "Master of the universe, You have taken me from the world. The books of life and death are in Your hands, and You decree everything in accordance with Your will."

Even though at this farbrengen everyone is expressing joy at the Lubavitcher Rebbe's *hilula*, as long as his life's work remains incomplete it is not quite a *hilula*. It is a "half *hilula*," and perhaps not even that, and certainly not a joyous wedding.

---

10. Abraham, Isaac, Jacob, Moses, Aaron, Joseph, and David.

11. *Avot* 2:16.

THE MINOR ACTS THAT WE ARE ABLE TO PERFORM

On many *hilula* days, one speaks in praise of the *tzaddik* who passed away, and recounts his deeds, each *tzaddik* in accordance with his standing and his virtues. Relating the praise of the *tzaddik* is a significant part of the *hilula,* and it has an ancient source.

It is written of Elisha's servant Geiḥazi that he would tell of "the great exploits that Elisha performed."[12] Elisha was a great *tzaddik,* even though he left no written record and we know none of his Torah insights or words of prophecy. We do know that he performed wonders in the heavens and on the earth, and Geiḥazi would circulate among the people and retell the wonders of his mentor. (We don't know if he also told others that Elisha had banished him; that tale, too, is tied to a wonder…). One could say that the practice of relating stories about *tzaddikim* originated with Geiḥazi, who told of the great exploits of his mentor, Elisha.

At the *hilula* it is appropriate to eulogize and praise a *tzaddik* who has accomplished his mission. But at the Lubavitcher Rebbe's *hilula,* our objective is to accomplish one thing – and that is to discuss ways in which we can continue his work. We don't assemble to speak about miracles he performed or his acts of righteousness. Our primary focus is to speak about what he would have wanted us to speak about: What can we do to continue his work?

There was a time when the Lubavitcher Rebbe would pray, and many hasidim would gather to watch him. Often he would stand up and shout, "I don't understand these people! Instead of praying to God, they stand and watch what another person is doing!"

That quote is almost verbatim. He was saying, "Instead of looking at me, do what you're supposed to do!"

We are sitting at the Lubavitcher Rebbe's *hilula,* speaking about what each of us can do so that his essence and what he wanted to accomplish will be perpetuated. We aren't sitting here in order to speak about him or about events that occurred in his lifetime, even if on occasion we relate stories about him or about the past. We are primarily interested in speaking about the present and the future.

12. II Kings 8:4.

It is said that on the day of a *hilula,* the soul of the *tzaddik* is revealed to a greater extent. Because of this, it's possible to cleave to him to a greater degree; it's possible to draw strength and encouragement for what needs to be done. In order to cleave to the Lubavitcher Rebbe, there's no need to speak of his greatness; we must instead try to accomplish what he would have wanted to see completed.

This is the essence of the matter. We're not here to look backward and recall and speak of the great deeds that the Lubavitcher Rebbe performed. We're here to ascertain the minor deeds that we ourselves can perform, looking forward, in order to perpetuate his legacy.

Bringing About the Messianic Era

THE LUBAVITCHER REBBE'S INVOLVEMENT WITH THE MESSIAH

Later in the Lubavitcher Rebbe's life, he spoke again and again about the coming of the Messiah. Anyone paying attention would have realized that this wasn't a new development. He spoke about the Messiah and related matters in a variety of ways from the first very time he spoke in public.

Interestingly, at all the farbrengens, the Lubavitcher Rebbe always spoke in Yiddish. I expect that seventy-five percent of the large congregation who attended didn't understand Yiddish. People stood on their feet and would listen to him speak for four, five, sometimes even eight hours, without understanding a word.

He would speak in fifteen- or twenty-minute segments because he assumed, correctly, that his congregation wouldn't be able to concentrate for longer than that. Throughout the years, he would conclude each segment with the words "May we arrive at complete redemption by means of our righteous Messiah." Every time the assembled crowd would hear those words – which were the only words most of them understood of the entire address – they would shout, "Amen!" It was an impressive experience to hear four or five thousand people answer "Amen!" in unison.

In any event, the topic of Messiah wasn't introduced suddenly into the Lubavitcher Rebbe's discourses at a certain stage. He had always thought about and focused on the coming of the Messiah; that focus merely intensified over the years.

THE MESSIAH AND THE GOOD LIFE

Once, when the Alter Rebbe was asked when the Messiah would come, he replied, "I don't know why you need to know this. The Messiah that you await never was and never will be. The Messiah who will actually come is a Messiah you don't want."

Many people anticipate the coming of the Messiah, particularly during troubled times. A person often makes assumptions: I have no money now, but when the Messiah comes, I will. I have an unpleasant and wicked wife now, but when the Messiah comes, she will be beautiful and virtuous. I earn little now as a salesman in a shop, but with God's help, I'll earn three times as much when the Messiah comes, and so on.

Everyone has his own personal interests in mind when awaiting and praying for the coming of the Messiah. This is no joke. Ask people on the street what they think life will be like when the Messiah comes, and they'll tell you, "Life will be good. Everything I want will happen." Those are the expectations.

I would like to clarify matters. True, it is written that the Jewish people are all princes. As princes, they are entitled to the best of everything: good, happy lives, freedom from financial hardship, success in all of their endeavors, enjoyment from their children.

Sometimes troubles inspire a change in direction. I once knew a person who had reached the lowest point of his dark life; twenty years of imprisonment in Siberia had transformed him completely. Regretting his prior behavior, he repented and went from one extreme to the other, becoming a devout, upright Jew. Suffering, though, is not always transformative. There are those who suffer and remain evil. A person's faith in God can sometimes be awakened particularly during good and profitable times. In a football stadium, one occasionally sees a Jew whose team is winning lift up his arms and shout wholeheartedly, "There is a God!" with a fervor possibly greater than that of Jews praying in a synagogue. It seems clear that when a person has wealth, honor, and everything good, it's easier to say, "There is a God."

Of the statement in the Mishna that "anyone who fulfills the Torah when poor will ultimately fulfill the Torah when wealthy; anyone who forsakes the Torah when wealthy will ultimately forsake it when poor,"[13] one *tzaddik* expounded the following: The *tanna* stated this passage as a prayer to God for the financial well-being of all the Jewish people: "Master of the universe, make all Jews in the world wealthy, since anyone who fulfills the Torah when poor will also fulfill it when wealthy. Since that's the case, make them wealthy now. As for the wealthy who forsake the Torah – do You believe they will begin to fulfill the Torah if they become poor? Wealthy or poor, they won't fulfill it, so allow them to remain wealthy!"

In a similar vein, one can ask, "Will the Lord's hand be limited?"[14] Does He have a ledger of income and expenditures? Is His budget limited, so that if so-and-so becomes wealthy, someone else has to become poor? God can give anything and everything. It's within the realm of the possible for every Jew to be free of physical and emotional struggles.

I don't want to disparage any Jew, and I pray that all will be well with everyone in accordance with his own perception of well-being. This is as true for someone who finds pleasure and sweetness in studying tractate *Nedarim* as for someone who enjoys eating chocolate. But I must add that in spite of all my prayers and good wishes, the coming of the Messiah will not make life in this world more pleasurable for anyone.

THE END OF HISTORY

The coming of the Messiah is the phenomenon that can be characterized as the end of history. People call the messianic era, not always accurately, the "end of days" – not because there will be no more days or years, but rather because there will be no more history.

In general, history is a record of troubles: wars, plagues, earthquakes. It can also be said that happy people have no history. People about whom there are no reports in the news apparently live tranquil, uneventful lives. It's possible to write a lengthy novel about a person's adventures, troubles,

13. *Avot* 4:9.
14. Numbers 11:23.

or tribulations, but one can't write more than a few lines about someone who lives a good and happy life.

This is not to say that over the course of history there has been no change for the better. Throughout the generations, many changes have been implemented by individuals or groups, and some of those changes have brought progress or advancement. But as is evident from the last hundred years, even when great, fortuitous events transpire, sooner or later the situation deteriorates once again. Even when it seemed like a great change had transpired, it did not endure, but dissipated like a dream.

History progresses like a ball one is trying to push to the top of a mountain. When the ball is pushed ten feet up, it rolls back down fifteen feet, and the effort to keep climbing must continue. Such is the history of the world. There are two rhymes, based on the names of the Sephardic cantillation symbols, that express this realistic view of change in this world: "Miserable man, do not sigh, because after travail [*tarḥa*] comes rest [*atnaḥ*]. Lordly man, do not be haughty, because after rank [*darga*] comes the rupture [*tevir*]."

The nature of history is tied to the essential nature of this world. The moment one succeeds in creating an opening on one side, problems are created on another. Every achievement that has the positive aspects of progress and usefulness also creates new negative aspects. What resolves one problem can cause another, so that even if the world isn't set back to its previous state, circumstances don't improve much.

The end of history means an end to the rise and fall, an end to the ebb and flow, an end to a pattern of good things being followed by misfortune.

GALUT: UPS AND DOWNS

The world is, indeed, beset by troubles. May we all be spared minor and major troubles, individual and collective ones. But it isn't because of problems that we await the coming of the Messiah; his arrival is unconnected to these troubles and pains. We yearn for the coming of the Messiah because the world isn't progressing as it should. Each step forward is followed by a step back; each ascent is followed by a fall. No great movement that is directed upward remains unobstructed.

This is actually the definition of *galut,* the exilic era in which we find ourselves. In *galut,* we find ourselves trampled under the boot of history. Even during times when we remain undisturbed and manage to survive – and possibly even blossom – growth isn't sustainable. A person who awaits the coming of the Messiah is basically admitting that for all intents and purposes he's had enough: "We've spent enough time in this *galut.*" One need not be inspired by *ruaḥ hakodesh,* prophetic intuition, in order to say this.

Some believe that the State of Israel is the first flowering of our redemption. There is room for doubt regarding this belief, though many good things have been accomplished and many significant events have occurred as a result of it. But positive occurrences are a natural part of life, and as long as good things don't progress exclusively forward or upward, everything ultimately reverts to the way it was before.

I remember, for example, the words to songs that were composed right after the Sinai campaign, when all of Sinai was newly in Jewish possession. People flocked to see the mountain commonly known as Mount Sinai (even though, at least according to our Sages, it is not *the* Mount Sinai). Someone even blew a *shofar* at the site. One of those songs went like this: "It is not a legend, my friend, and not a passing dream; behold, opposite Mount Sinai, the bush, the bush is burning." Less than two months later, the IDF withdrew from Sinai, leaving no vestige of our presence behind, not even a small bush, burning or otherwise.

It turns out that certain world events can bring us joy, but they don't necessarily last. Time passes, the wheel spins and completes another revolution, and we can see that we didn't gain what we thought we had. We didn't receive what we thought we had, and what we thought had been done actually remained incomplete. We can tell where the world is headed. It becomes clear, in retrospect, that despite past efforts and accomplishments, the same problems remain. In short, we find ourselves experiencing another round of *galut.*

There is harsh *galut* and benign *galut,* and there is *galut* that is so benign that people fall asleep and remain there. Life in this type of *galut* can be compared to that of a tired person who falls asleep in the snow. Because he is deep in snow that surrounds and cocoons him, he doesn't move to save himself and simply dies there in that place. There are Jews who live in precisely that kind of *galut*. They aren't beset by too many problems. They feel very comfortable surrounded by a kind of beautiful white snow, and they remain asleep. Ultimately, when they wake up and attempt to emerge from the snow, it turns out that they are no longer Jews. In any event, as long as our world progresses as usual, with highs and lows, good times and bad times, peaceful times and less peaceful times, it remains a world of *galut*.

Once the Messiah arrives, the entire world will move in just one direction: forward and upward, without backward movement, without stumbles or falls. In this life, maintaining balance is difficult and tenuous. We yearn to achieve a stable balance; we yearn for a time when things will remain in their appropriate places, when there can be real progress. This is the entire essence of the messianic era. After the Messiah arrives, is seen, and is revealed, the world's problems will gradually be resolved, humanity will become better, and we will be able to proceed forward in a straight line toward what is called life in the World to Come.

NOT ACCEPTING *GALUT*

The Lubavitcher Rebbe's desire and efforts to bring about the messianic era were intended to express the idea that we don't want these ups and downs anymore. He tried to make people understand that we can't continue to accept this perpetual process of forward and backward. We can't accept the interminable existence of insoluble problems. We don't wish to remain in this reality.

Sometimes it seems as if we are approaching the messianic era, and if we try just a little harder, if we take just a few more steps forward, we'll reach the next stage. But in order to reach the next stage, merely yearning for the coming of the Messiah the way people usually do isn't enough. People pray for the coming of the Messiah – provided that he won't come today or tomorrow, because there is some transgression that they wish to perform today and they have business to transact tomorrow. It would be preferable if he came at a more convenient time.

Many people feel this way, even if they don't say it openly.

People should ask themselves: How can we bring our unstable reality to an end? How can we change things so that there will no longer be ups and downs? People know how to do only one thing in a complete, absolute manner, and that is to kill. In killing, one performs a final, irrevocable act. The question is, how can one perform an act that is as decisive in the opposite direction? How can we bring the world to a state of "a haven and inheritance"[15] that we aspire to? How can we finally become capable of continuing to climb without concern that any minute we'll stumble and slip back down?

The Lubavitcher Rebbe spoke about bringing about the messianic era primarily to make people aware of this concept.

PUTTING THINGS INTO PROPORTION

Awareness of the significance of the coming of the Messiah influences a person's actions as well as how he perceives them. At times, a person is satisfied with his minor accomplishments and doesn't strive to achieve anything more. He's unable to deal with matters of significance because his entire world is small and limited.

I once knew a person who was always in debt. Every time he found an opportunity to take out a new loan (with which he would repay a previous one), he was elated. But the new loan didn't solve his problem; he had merely received another loan he would need to repay. People who are satisfied with their own minor achievements are in a similar situation. Their accomplishments can be compared to loans that don't resolve problems. Nothing changes significantly. Even if a person lays a foundation, places a cornerstone, and etches an inscription in stone, it has no lasting effect if the edifice is never constructed – if the big picture remains the same.

It's important for a person to be aware of proportions if he wants to assess the significance of his attainments. This is true even if one has reason to brag about what he has already achieved. Engaging in ongoing efforts to bring about the messianic era restores a proper perspective. Accomplishments that don't fade away like a dream are the only ones that have true significance in achieving that goal.

It's true that every good deed a person performs is inscribed in Heaven, where apparently there is room for all the books chronicling

15. Deuteronomy 12:9.

all deeds, major and minor. Presumably, if a person is about to curse and at the last moment decides not to, three points are recorded in his favor in the heavenly records. But this kind of good deed is irrelevant in terms of bringing about the messianic era.

The Sages note that to date there have been only nine songs in this world – for example, the song at the sea and the song at the well – but in the era of the third Temple, a new song will be sung. The nine songs that currently have a role in our world are termed *shira,* in the feminine, since they celebrate redemption that is preceded and followed by distress. Analogous to labor pains that culminate in birth, pains and troubles are followed by redemption and the song is sung. But the cycle repeats itself again and again. There is more pain with the next pregnancy, which again ends with redemption and song.

In the messianic era to come, there won't be *shira* but a *shir,* in the masculine. It will be a new and different kind of song – one that won't be followed by renewed pain. This new song, this *shir,* will celebrate the final end of distress.

To sing a new song means being conscious of the difference between things that are ephemeral and things that last. This awareness enables a person to focus on matters that have true significance, matters that can transform and elevate the world, step by step, without recurrent backsliding.

When we speak of the messianic era, we aren't referring to a time when there will be a new Rebbe in the world, or even a time when there will be a third Temple. Even if there were no obstacles to rebuilding it, the Temple alone wouldn't necessarily mark the beginning of the messianic era. Picture the entire site of the Temple Mount vacant and available with unlimited funds on hand for construction. I'm certain that all sorts of Jews would donate money to rebuild the Temple, including those who wouldn't want their names recorded. Imagine that architectural plans are in place, a contract has been signed with the builder, and the job is undertaken and completed. I expect that people would do in the third Temple what they did in the two Temples that preceded it: Someone with a guilty conscience would bring a bull, goat, sheep, turtledove, or young pigeon to the Temple, offer it up as a sacrifice, and then feel relieved and happy.

Sacrificing an animal is much easier than genuinely repenting. In order to bring the messianic era, we need to do more than check the right boxes on a to-do list. We need to do more than just say, "We did it! We built the third Temple in Jerusalem!" To bring about the messianic era, we need to try to figure out how to bring about lasting, significant, positive change in the world. That's our real challenge.

It's important to make a distinction between matters that are significant and those that are minor. Significant matters advance the world toward positive change. Minor matters are fine and good, but they ultimately have no lasting effect. We need to put things into perspective and aspire toward achieving progress in truly significant ways. As long as the Lubavitcher Rebbe was able, he never stopped speaking about the Messiah because he wanted us to focus on matters that really count in the long run. He wanted us to realize that we tend to busy ourselves with the minor matters when we should be doing great things.

ACTIONS THAT ENDURE

How does one do great things? First of all, a person needs to ask himself what he can accomplish that won't fade or depreciate with time.

I often have the opportunity to meet with couples before their wedding. I say to the bride-to-be, "Look, undoubtedly you are a God-fearing, committed young woman who prays three times a day. But before your wedding day, the day of the heart's rejoicing, it's worthwhile for you to commit to performing at least one *mitzva* that you will continue to perform throughout your marriage, no matter how busy you get. It's important to decide on this now, because once married, many people become entangled in apron strings, overwhelmed by children and family life, and feel they aren't able to take on any other responsibilities."

I give similar advice to fourteen-year-old boys, young men on the cusp of entering the yeshiva: "Instead of making many resolutions that you won't keep, make one resolution that you'll always keep, so that it remains firmly embedded like a nail that can't be extracted."

How can a person bring the Messiah? If a person were to get up and go outside crying loudly and bitterly, "Master of the universe, bring the Messiah!" it's conceivable that his prayer would be heard on high. But if a person isn't able to bring the Messiah in that way and still wants to bring on the messianic era, he must take steps toward lasting progress. He may resolve to take at least one step, but it must be a step that will endure. He must build an actual edifice, one brick at a time. He must accomplish things that will last forever, even if they are perceived as minor. Those achievements will build the "Mount Zion that will never topple."[16]

The Kotzker Rebbe expounded on the statement "Open for Me an opening like the point of a needle, and I will create an opening for you that is like the entrance to a hall through which wagons and carriages can enter." He said, "The eye of a needle may be small, but it is open from one side to the other. A person must persevere until he succeeds in reaching the other side, while making sure that the slot remains open. Only then can he be considered to have accomplished anything. From that point on, an opening through which wagons and carriages can enter are opened for him."

King Solomon said, "I have built You an abode, a seat for Your dwelling forever."[17] Even if a person builds just a small house, the house must be "a seat for Your dwelling forever." "The great and holy Temple upon which Your name is called" is constructed with bricks whose basic characteristic is truth, and truth, as defined by Rambam, endures forever.

Ultimately, we won't be able to achieve all the great things we set out to do or that need to be done. Still, we need to do what we can; we need to keep trying to progress toward completion of significant as well as less significant goals. But even when our goal is a relatively minor one, we must ensure that it represents truth.

The coming of the Messiah will come about step by step. Progress is more like climbing stairs than skating on ice. The stairs may be small, but every irreversible step up brings us closer to the messianic era, which will last forever.

We are engaged in a continual war with the evil inclination, sometimes we lose and sometimes we win. But even when we succeed in wresting something from the evil inclination, the question remains as to whether "liberated territory will not be returned," to quote the song.

16. Psalms 125:1.
17. I Kings 8:13.

Sometimes a person knows that his victory in a battle with the baser factors of this world is a transient one, nothing more than a passing dream. The real question is what steps forward a person can take that will ensure that progress will endure – that will bring the world closer to the messianic era.

The coming of the Messiah will be a significant step for the entire world, as well as for the Jewish people. A person must ask himself, "How can I bring about the coming of the Messiah?" And answer: "By taking even one step that actually makes something in this world better." Even if he does nothing more than that, if more and more people were to take that kind of step, we could pave a path, a stairway, that leads to the messianic era.

MAJOR AND MINOR

What did the Rebbe speak about? On the one hand, when he said, "May the time of His Messiah draw near," he was speaking about great things to come. He wasn't just talking about the arrival of another *tzaddik*, one who will wear a larger *shtreimel*, have a longer beard, or perform more wondrous acts than *tzaddikim* who preceded him. Rather, the era of the coming of the Messiah represents a time when there will be significant positive change throughout the world. Systems that have been entrenched for thousands of years will change for the better. The Lubavitcher Rebbe wanted us to think about the big picture so that we would be aware of where we need to go.

On the other hand, the Rebbe didn't want us to belittle the value of minor accomplishments. He said, "Don't minimize the significance of anything, not even the small matters. Don't occupy yourselves solely with matters you see as great."

A person must be engaged in both momentous as well as less weighty tasks – things that can change the world and things that may benefit only one person.

Someone recently said to me, "I did something today that took me a really long time, and I'm still not sure I achieved anything. I think I expended too much effort for too small an outcome."

I said to him, "If you sit with someone who is troubled and manage to distract him from his worries with small talk, you've still performed a *mitzva*."

On a given day, one need not say to the first person he encounters, "Let us, the two of us together, bring about the redemption!" If that were possible, it would be huge, but sometimes a person just needs to sit and talk to someone, to pat a needy friend on the back, maybe even tell him a joke. If that succeeds in evoking a little smile, he has done something good, and I'm certain it also brings smiles to Heaven on high.

We shouldn't make light of minor matters because, first of all, one penny added to another can ultimately add up to a large sum. Another reason is because a person can't always know the outcome of the actions he performs: "In the morning sow your seed, and in the evening do not rest your hand, as you do not know which will succeed."[18] Occasionally a person thinks that he's doing something important, but with time it becomes clear that the results were "futility and herding wind."[19] By contrast, there are minor things one does that can result in true, substantive change in the world. It's not always possible to differentiate between significant and less significant matters, between a major and minor deed.

Having said that, it's still important for a person to be aware of priorities and focus on things that truly matter instead of just checking off boxes on a to-do list and ultimately rummaging through garbage hoping to find something there of value. These major efforts need not be to the exclusion of minor tasks; if there's something small one can do, he should do it. But he must work within a larger framework that clarifies what it is incumbent on him to do so that he won't end up spending all of his time on things that turn out to be trivial.

It is written of Rabbi Yoḥanan ben Zakkai that there was nothing he would neglect to study. It didn't matter whether the topic was major or minor. The Gemara expounds: A "major matter" is Ezekiel's vision of

18. Ecclesiastes 11:6.
19. Ecclesiastes 1:14.

the divine chariot; "minor matters" are disputes between Abaye and Rava.[20]

Rabbi Yoḥanan ben Zakkai was one of the few Sages who was able to see the chariot, yet he spent time debating matters disputed by Abaye and Rava. Sometimes a person must engage in less significant matters.

These two aspects are part of the dialectic of Heaven and earth. Heaven extends to infinite heights above us, and the earth is below. On it, we have the right to exist, as do even minuscule lice eggs. God tends to matters that from our perspective are as great as the heavens, but also as minor as the horns of an oryx.

Caring for the Lost and the Outcasts

THOSE WHO ARE NOT WITH US

The Lubavitcher Rebbe often spoke about another point that I'd like to address. Moses said, "Not with you alone do I make this covenant and this oath; rather, with those who are here with us, standing today before the Lord our God, and with those who are not here with us today."[21] We must all think about what we can do to care for those who are not here with us today.

We tend to notice the needs only of those in our immediate surroundings. The *halakha* does state that charity begins with relatives and expands from the center outward; whoever is closer takes precedence. With respect to charity as well as other matters, a person often stays within his own milieu, his own inner circle. That circle can consist of me alone, me and my family, me and my *shtiebel*, or me and my friends. I'd like to emphasize that it's truly important for a person to have intimate and tight circles. It's important that a person draw his relatives near, and it's important for him to have friends who are both physically and spiritually close, friends with whom he can scale heights.

A person can, indeed, rejoice in his inner circle. But at the same time, he must remember those who are "not here with us."

20. *Sukka* 28a.

21. Deuteronomy 29:13–14.

When a person enters a synagogue, he sees only those who are there. He may see many friends – the synagogue may be filled with people in his circle – but he doesn't see the people who didn't come. We must be preoccupied with the question of what happens to those who are not present, those who are "not here with us today."

The Lubavitcher Rebbe was preoccupied with that question, and said that we, too, must be concerned about the plight of those who are not participating.

THE LOST AND THE OUTCASTS

We must be aware of the one who is "not here with us" because he was unable to come, the one who is "not here with us" because he doesn't want to come, and "the one who is not here with us" because it's not relevant for him to come.

In the past, the Jewish world included two primary circles: the small circle of contacts that the Torah calls *amitekha* – those with whom you share Torah, *mitzvot*, wisdom and understanding – and the circle of *amei ha'aretz*, those who are not knowledgeable in the fulfillment of *mitzvot*. Today, sadly, the problem isn't with the *amei ha'aretz*, or even with the one or two rare and unlikely heretics. The problem is with people who exist on an even baser level.

One of the Zionist leaders who knew, idolized, and spoke well of Theodore Herzl wrote, "Herzl knew so little about Judaism that it wasn't even possible to call him an *am ha'aretz*." If it's true that Herzl couldn't even be characterized as an *am ha'aretz*, then there are some Jews alive today who are so removed from anything Jewish that they would be outside any circle we could draw. We must try to do things that will touch even "the lost in the land of Assyria and the outcasts in the land of Egypt"[22] – Jews we don't see, don't hear, and don't know. Sometimes they are located at the ends of the earth, and sometimes they're located very near to us.

I have a friend who is involved in searching for the ten lost tribes of Israel. He travels to remote countries looking for tribes that may be descendants of the lost tribes. I once asked him, "Why are you looking

22. Isaiah 27:13.

for the ten tribes in such faraway places? Why not gather the one and a half million people in New York City who are certainly the offspring of Jews?"

The truth is that there are also people like that in Jerusalem and Tel Aviv. They don't live in unreachable places on the other side of the Sambatyon. They can easily be found on the other side of the Yarkon.

A story is told of a *tzaddik* who developed an exceptionally close relationship with a very simple Jew. When asked to explain why, the *tzaddik* replied, "It is written that when the Messiah arrives, leaders of all the nations will come to honor him with gifts and show their subservience. What gift can one possibly bring to the ruler of the entire world, a ruler who doesn't need gifts, money, or power? The answer is, 'They will bring all your brethren from all the nations, as a gift to the Lord, on horses and in chariots and in coaches and on mules and on camels.'[23] Jews themselves will be the gifts that gentiles bring to the Messiah.

"But which Jews? After all, Jews who heard the sound of the *shofar*, Jews whose hearts were touched by fear of God or love of their people, will come of their own initiative. Only the most assimilated of the assimilated, the ones lost in the midst of the gentiles – Jews who might not even know they are Jewish – won't come on their own. That's why, when the rulers of all the nations seek to present the Messiah with a gift, they will search high and low for that kind of Jew, rejoice when they find one, and exclaim, "Aha! We have a Jew in our country!" And they will place him in a magnificent wagon, adorn him with flowers, and bring him as a gift to the Messiah. If a Jew like that can be a gift for the Messiah, how can we possibly ignore him?"

I'm speaking about these gifts, these lost Jews. In order to find them, one need not travel to the ends of the earth, or even to the lands of Assyria and Egypt. Jews like that can be found even "on the holy mountain of Jerusalem."

23. Isaiah 66:20.

THE DISEASED BODY OF THE JEWISH PEOPLE

Concern for the most distant of the distant of our brethren isn't merely about extracting "the noble from the worthless,"[24] although that, too, would be a great accomplishment. The concern stems, first and foremost, from understanding that they, too, entered into the covenant with God, that the covenant was made with the entire Jewish people.

Leprosy (identified, apparently erroneously, with the biblical *tzara'at*) is an illness that attacks the body and kills it slowly. The limbs of a person afflicted with leprosy decompose and fall off. One day a big toe falls off, a few days later an ear falls off, and so on. The limb has already decomposed at its core long before it falls off. With no nerves or blood vessels, for all intents and purposes it's no longer part of the living body; it is merely an appendage. Whether its nose or little toe falls off, the body afflicted with this terrible disease is in horrible shape.

All Jews are a part of the body of the collective Jewish people. Jews who have severed ties with the Jewish people and with their Jewish identity are like limbs that are shriveling and falling off.

Using a similar analogy, we can understand why it's important for us to feel for Jews who are gradually disengaging from the Jewish people. One of the indications that a limb still has some vitality is that the body can actually feel it. People suffering from muscular dystrophy, for example, lose the ability to feel parts of their body. It can begin in the legs and progress until the person is incapable of walking. Then it reaches his arms, and so on, until the person can't do much at all. He may even lose his ability to speak as the illness proceeds to paralyze his mouth.

The body of a person with this disease can seem fine; it may be difficult to know just how far the disease has progressed. To ascertain viability of the affected area, a doctor pricks the skin with a needle and asks the patient what he feels. If he feels nothing, the doctor pricks him in additional places until he reaches a place where the patient can sense the needle. If a person with this disease loses feeling at the bottom of his foot, the doctor is concerned about more than just the foot; the entire body as a whole is ill. When the patient no longer feels pain anywhere, he is in grave danger.

24. Jeremiah 15:19.

In the same way, if we don't feel pain about Jews who are gradually disengaging from their Jewishness, the body of the Jewish people as a whole is perilously ill. It's as if we were examined by a doctor who stuck a pin in a certain place and, finding no sensation, concluded, "This person is suffering from advanced muscular dystrophy and is likely to die soon." Not only is the little toe about to die, but the whole body, top to bottom. On the other hand, as long as a person feels any pain at all, he's not yet dead. Some hope remains, even if he's ill and suffering.

The Mishna relates that when a Jew is led to be executed for a grave transgression – which he committed despite having been forewarned and in the presence of two witnesses – the Divine Presence is distraught and says, "I am distressed about My head! I am distressed about My arm!"[25] If the Divine Presence sees fit to weep over a Jew wicked enough to have been sentenced to death, we certainly must show concern about our brethren.

CARING

The Lubavitcher Rebbe was emphatic about the importance of thinking about "those who are not here with us today" and seeing them as a relevant part of the big picture of who we are as a people. It's important to care about them, before we take any specific action in this regard – like helping them to don *tefillin* or to kindle Shabbat candles. The Rebbe's concern wasn't about winning their hearts but rather about making us feel a sense of responsibility toward them. The very fact that someone cares, feels their pain, and is aware of them has significance, even if one can't do very much to change the situation.

When a person hears that a friend who had been dating a gentile woman has converted to her faith, the news is particularly jarring. Stories like this are not unheard of, but when a friend is involved, the information becomes personal. One thinks, *I thought I knew him. He was a good friend of mine. We shared so much, yet he left Judaism for good!* When the story is about a stranger, one cares less. The Lubavitcher Rebbe believed that we must be capable of going to the ends of the earth in order to do something on behalf of a fellow Jew who is completely unknown to us.

25. *Sanhedrin* 6:5.

I'll conclude with a wonderful story about the Rebbe. One of the Lubavitcher Rebbe's hasidim, who was an emissary in a remote location, related that the Rebbe instructed him to bring matza to someone. He searched for the man, found him, and brought him matza. The man was profoundly moved and said, "Do you realize what you have done for me? I am alone. My entire family was killed in Europe; not one relative remains. I no longer have any connection to anything Jewish. I told myself that unless a sign to remain Jewish is revealed to me today, I will convert and be done with it. And today you brought me matza! There is still someone who thinks about me. There is still someone who is connected to me!"

That man returned to Judaism and his world was transformed.

I relate this particular story, rather than speaking of the great exploits the Rebbe performed, in order to raise our consciousness that Jews like that exist. Even if one feels unable to do anything practical on behalf of these Jews, it's important to reach out to them and touch their lives so that they have a sense that they are connected to the Jewish people. As long as we are aware of the existence of these Jews, and care about them, the Jewish body is still alive.

Leḥayim!

17

What Is Novel?

A NEW SONG

I have often said that almost all the characteristics thought to have been initiated by the hasidic movement, and to have identified with it, are not new to Judaism. It's possible to find novel practices here and there, but as a rule these elements have existed forever.

So let me ask a basic question: What is really novel? Is it only something that has never been seen before, like the drawing of a beast with the head of an elephant and the legs of a mouse? Not necessarily. It's possible for a drawing of flowers that look exactly like flowers, with no added faces or eyes and no added components, to be novel.

This is true not only regarding the realm of the arts but also in the realm of the intellect. A novel idea isn't always something that has never before been heard. Sometimes something that has been said more than once can be novel. It's the manner in which it is expressed is that makes it novel.

The verse "Sing to the Lord a new song"[1] appears in Psalms several times. In many of these instances the "new song" is structured like previous ones and is, in fact, not really new. And yet a song based on an old,

1. Psalms 96:1, 98:1, 149:1.

familiar theme – a theme that has been stated five, ten, or more times – can still be new.

The same thing is true about many hasidic customs and practices: They have existed forever. It is specifically those aspects that are truly ancient that may now seem new to us; they undergo a transformation when presented differently. To a great extent, the power of Hasidism – not the specific details, but the very essence of Hasidism – was in its ability to discover novelty in matters that had already existed for centuries.

NEW THAT IS OLD AND OLD THAT IS NEW

The question of the nature of the new is not merely a fundamental philosophical question, but it relates to every Jew, every day. Where and when is a person renewed? Where is he involved in the renewal of the world, together with the One who "continually renews in His goodness each day"? By contrast, when is he merely a faded copy of himself, not even in the category of recycled paper, not even a second copy, but a twelfth copy that becomes more and more faded every day?

One of the most enduring, profound, and fundamental challenges confronting the Jew is prayer. The problem isn't reciting the words written in the prayer book, nor the difficulty of understanding the words inside. There is a different problem. A person is likely to ask himself, *Why repeat the prayer three times every day? After all, the only thing new about this prayer is the number of times I say it!*

The Jerusalem Talmud discusses the question of whether a person is allowed to pray a new prayer, and states that Aḥitofel would pray three new prayers each day.[2] It turns out that with all his new prayers, he remained Aḥitofel who doesn't have a share in the World to Come. In any event, why don't we sing a new song or pray a new prayer each day?

The answer to these two questions is that a person can compose a song that he thinks is new but in fact has nothing new about it. Sometimes it's not even a song, no matter how well written and well recited. On the other hand, a person can express extremely old ideas that each time are a truly new song. In order to do so, one need not write new words or compose new melodies.

2. *Berakhot* 4:4.

Similarly, there are excerpts and passages that are recited consecutively several times. "The Lord is God" is recited seven times at the conclusion of Yom Kippur. Is that just one phrase that is recited again and again or is it seven different ones? In truth, different worlds of meaning can be ascribed to those four words with every utterance.

A certain American was once taken to the Western Wall. When later asked about the experience, he answered, "That western wall is no different from every other western wall in the world."

One who is able to discern newness can see the difference immediately. There is no need for additional examples to drive home the point.

A person with personality and vitality can find new meanings in old things. It is written of the manna that "its taste was like the taste of a cake moist with oil [*leshad hashamen*]."[3] The Midrash associates *leshad* with breast (*shad*) milk, in which a baby finds new tastes based on what his mother eats every time he nurses.[4]

I once gave a volume of my Talmud to a certain individual who said to me, "Thank you, but know that I will not study from it. I follow the custom of the son of the Baal Shem Tov who, when he grew older, studied just one tractate, *Berakhot*, over and over. Now that I have grown older, I, too, study only tractate *Berakhot*."

If a person renews himself, his world is new, and as a result, his prayer is new and his Torah is new. If he doesn't renew himself, nothing will change; everything will become one prolonged monotony.

Some things can appear to be a tremendous, unparalleled novelty, but in truth there's nothing new about them. A clear example of this can be seen with several political parties here in Israel. They may be touted as new, but in fact they are nothing more than recycled rags. This is generally true of all the parties, religious and nonreligious; they unite, split, separate, meet, and ostensibly renew themselves. They are, in fact, merely recycled.

This is all tied to one's daily work regimen and daily study regimen. There are people who are able to see new elements in familiar things,

3. Numbers 11:8.
4. See *Sifrei, Behaalotekha* 89; see also *Eiruvin* 54b.

while others will never identify anything new. Everything new seems old in their eyes.

RICH AND FRESH

God in His goodness continually renews the act of Creation each day, but it's not always possible to discern it. Sometimes one sees the novelty of each day very well, and sometimes a person must take the time to contemplate the world in order to discern novelty. Someone who sits in a garden all day, for example, can behold the appearance of two new leaves here, a new flower there.

Anyone who has had a baby knows that the baby before you today is a new baby compared to yesterday, even though his face hasn't changed. He renews himself each day. Adults are liable to become bored, but babies are never bored because they see a new world every day. This isn't because they are shown Asia one day and Europe, America, and the rest of the wonders of the world the next. It's because every time a baby looks at his hand, he suddenly understands something that he didn't understand before. He gains a new understanding about his hand. He also learns to do new things with it, which causes all sorts of other ideas to enter his mind. That's why he isn't bored. His older brother, on the other hand, who is twenty years old, is often bored, because he knows everything about his hands and feet, as well as about all the discoveries in science and philosophy. Nothing is new to him.

There is an awful disease called progeria, whose precise cause remains unknown. It causes children to age rapidly. Cognitively they develop as expected, but in terms of their physical development, they develop at a rate approximately seven or eight times faster than normal. When a child like that reaches the chronological age of three, he already has a moustache and a beard begins to grow. When he reaches the age of seven or eight, he is elderly and hunched over. This is a type of old age that is unrelated to his chronological age. In the corporeal realm, it's extremely rare, and to date there's no known treatment.

Sometimes this kind of illness befalls people in the spiritual rather than the physical realm. They don't grow a beard at age two, but by the time they are seven or eight, their spirits are as aged and feeble as a sixty-year-old. They've seen everything, they've heard everything, and they know everything. There are some among you whose balding heads and pot bellies I could sense when you were only fifteen. The balding head couldn't be seen because it was still covered with hair, but it is, in fact, there. The pot belly is also already there – not yet visibly, but still there.

One can also be at the other end of the spectrum. It's actually appropriate for a person to pray that he won't reach old age. I'm not speaking of chronological age, God forbid. I wish you all a long life, until one hundred and twenty years and beyond. I'm saying that a person should pray to remain intrinsically young, so that at the age of eighty and ninety he will still be able to look at things the way he did when he was two years old, to see a new world and new things.

I knew a Jew named Rabbi Avraham Sofer Schreiber, a Torah scholar who published almost all the commentaries of the Meiri. I could go on at great length about his life, his deeds, and his conduct, but it would be just a fraction of the praise he is due. I knew him when he was already advanced in years. We would meet at the *shtieblakh* in Katamon, the neighborhood where he lived. One day a Karliner hasid who was an erudite Torah scholar stopped in and shared a teaching or incident involving the Kotzker Rebbe. On hearing it, Rabbi Schreiber, then seventy years old at least, got up and danced enthusiastically in the middle of the synagogue. Imagine that: an elderly Jew jumping up to dance in the middle of the synagogue out of the sheer joy roused in him by a Torah insight.

Every so often, one can see a small child jumping for joy and dancing because of something that happened. It's less common to see an old man do so. Psalms states that this is how a *tzaddik* should be: "They will continue to yield fruit even in old age; they will remain rich and fresh."[5] Even in old age – rich and fresh.

I recommend that you all think about a new song – a song in which there is nothing new other than the novelty that you yourself give it. Perhaps in that way, you will acquire some of the ability to remain full of life even as you age.

5. Psalms 92:15.

The Essence of the Rebbe

THE DISTINCTION OF A TORAH SCHOLAR

I will now return to the topic I addressed before that introduction, and that is that most of the elements thought to be inherent qualities of Hasidism are not novel. The hasidim didn't invent *VeTatzmaḥ Purkanei, nusaḥ Sefard,* or the *gartel.*

One of the elements that is truly characteristic and central to Hasidism is the centrality of the *tzaddik* or the Rebbe. Some historians even called the hasidic movement "the tzaddikism movement" – the movement of those who follow *tzaddikim.* Is the *tzaddik* an invention of Hasidism? It turns out that even if Hasidism has given a different nuance to the meaning of *tzaddik* (in the sense of "sing to the Lord a new song"), it's an ancient concept. Essentially everything that hasidim say about their Rebbes has already been written about Torah scholars in the Gemara, the *Zohar,* the early commentaries and the later commentaries.

Several sources in the holy books make clear that Torah scholars are people of distinction, not only in Torah, but also in good deeds and fear of Heaven. One who doesn't possess these virtues is not considered a Torah scholar. A Torah scholar isn't someone who knows a certain number of chapters of Mishna or pages of Gemara by heart. A person like that is called (and not in praise) a "basket full of books" or "a donkey bearing books." A library is also full of books. The Sages considered Doeg and Aḥitofel among the great scholars, but still denounced them; they were not categorized as Torah scholars.

When the Sages, the *Zohar,* and other books praise Torah scholars, they don't include those who know only how to learn. The attitude is different regarding people of that sort. There is a long story in the Gemara about a young scholar who had a bad reputation. Rav Yehuda ostracized him. When Rav Yehuda was dying, he saw that scholar in his room and smiled. The person wondered aloud, "Is it not enough that you ostracized me? Do you also have to laugh at me?" Rav Yehuda answered, "I am not laughing at you. Rather, I am happy as I go to that other world that I did not flatter even a great scholar such as you, but instead treated you fairly in accordance with the *halakha*."[6]

Throughout the generations, much has been written about reverence toward sages that is similar to what is written about reverence toward Rebbes in hasidic literature. These exalted descriptions can be found in esoteric sources as well as in the *Zohar*. The following statement, for example, is from the Jerusalem Talmud: "'The Lord is in His holy Sanctuary'[7] – this is Rabbi Yitzḥak."[8] What greater reverence is there than that? This description is terribly sacrilegious and possibly heretical, yet it is written in the Jerusalem Talmud about Rabbi Yitzḥak.

Pirkei Avot has a list of all the virtues through which the Torah is acquired, which happen to be the same virtues that Torah instills in a person. On that long list, there is very little mentioned about scholarship, but a great deal is written about other qualities.[9] Most of them have little to do with whether or not a person is sufficiently knowledgeable to issue a halakhic ruling on the kashrut of a pot.

In any number of books written about the Vilna Gaon, one can find praises about him that in terms of content and style could have been written about any one of the hasidic Rebbes. In many ways the criticism of hasidim was ad hominem – opposition to a specific person. The argument was whether or not a specific person possessed all the virtues necessary to be considered a person of distinction, and even these arguments were nonsensical at times. The principle itself – that it is appropriate to esteem and praise a Torah scholar who possesses certain virtues – was never in doubt.

THE PRAYERS AND COUNSEL OF THE *TZADDIK*

Many years before the hasidic era, the Gemara stated that a person suffering from troubles should ask a Torah scholar to pray for him.[10] Since

6. *Mo'ed Katan* 17a.
7. Habakkuk 2:20.
8. *Bikkurim* 3:3.
9. *Avot* 6:6.
10. See *Bava Batra* 116a and the Meiri there.

a Torah scholar is a man of great merit, it makes sense to request that he pray on one's behalf. The Torah scholar could claim that his expertise is limited to the talmudic disputes of Abaye and Rava, but in truth, as a Torah scholar, he was esteemed for more than just scholarship. He was valued for his many virtues. One of those was his ability to pray.

Something akin to this is described as far back as the book of Genesis. When Avimelekh wept and complained about his troubles, God said to him, "Go to the Rebbe. Go to Abraham. 'He is a prophet, and he will pray on your behalf.'[11] The reason Avimelekh was told to ask Abraham to pray for him wasn't because Abraham was wise. It was because Abraham was holy. The notion that a Rebbe's prayers on behalf of others are heard by God can be found in the *Tanakh*, in the Mishna, a third time in the Talmud, and in many other books countless times.[12]

One of the items that appears on the list in *Pirkei Avot* that enumerates the qualities of a person who engages in Torah study for its own sake is "One benefits from his counsel and resourcefulness."[13] This evokes the descriptions with which hasidim describe their Rebbes. Logically, it may not seem worthwhile to seek counsel from someone who engages in Torah study for its own sake. He might seem out of touch, someone who knows nothing about people's physical or mental health. And yet the Sages taught, "One benefits from his counsel and resourcefulness." One may still question a specific individual's worthiness – has he attained a given level of holiness? – but the basic principle of the value of consulting with a holy person remains intact.

Even the Baal HaTanya, who strongly opposed turning to the Rebbe to ask his advice about worldly matters, claiming that this wasn't within the purview of a Rebbe, that people wasted his time with questions of that kind – even he, until his final day, was asked such questions and answered them.

When people approach a Torah scholar to consult with him, they don't do so because of his penetrating intellect and broad scope of knowledge. There are individuals who are renowned as Torah

11. Genesis 20:7.
12. See, e.g., Rashi on Job 36:32; *Alei Tamar, Mo'ed Katan* 1:2.
13. *Avot* 6:1.

luminaries and who are genuinely prominent in their field but know nothing relevant to understanding the practical world. There are Torah scholars who are incisive and others who are less so; there are Torah scholars who understand the world in fine detail and others who don't. Yet when a person asks a Rebbe's advice about business matters, he does so, not because the Rebbe is an expert on trading on the New York Stock Exchange or in analyzing the subject in *Bava Metzia*. These qualities are beside the point. The merits of Torah scholarship aren't limited to knowledge or intellectual attainments. Being a true Torah scholar encompasses personality and conduct; the individual is primed to be an instrument of Torah. A person like that is in the category of "Counsel and resourcefulness are mine; I am understanding; might is mine."[14] All of these characteristics accompany his status as a Torah luminary, and because of this, he is able to provide good advice even if he doesn't fully understand the question – because the counsel comes from above and not from below.

These side issues aren't the main points I wanted to speak about, but they do touch on certain nuanced aspects of the essence of a *tzaddik*.

THE CONNECTION TO THE REBBE

The primary distinctive quality of a Rebbe goes far beyond his being someone people go to for a blessing, prayer, or counsel. A Rebbe's essence is much greater than the sum of all the virtues that are written about sages in the Torah. A Rebbe is also not revered merely because of the importance of showing deference to authority, according honor where it is due, or financially supporting scholars, for example. The substantive feature – specifically the hasidic feature – of a Rebbe is the profound connection that exists between a Rebbe and his hasidim. The connection doesn't stem from the Rebbe's words or Torah insights. The connection is also unrelated to a person's need for counsel or for prayers on his behalf. For some reason, a profound sense of connection exists between a person and a particular Rebbe; the connection is not contingent on anything external. Perhaps along the way, the person will seek the Rebbe's counsel or ask him to pray on his behalf, but it's also

14. Proverbs 8:14.

possible that he won't ask for counsel or blessings. It is not on this that the connection is based.

Several hasidim once sat and spoke about the greatness of their respective Rebbes, each relating wonders and miracles performed by his Rebbe. A prominent Lubavitcher hasid who was sitting with them related the following miracle:

"I went to the Rebbe Rashab (Rabbi Shalom Dovber Schneerson) and asked for advice regarding a business matter. I followed the advice he gave me and proceeded to lose everything. That is the miracle."

They asked him, "What kind of miracle is that?"

The hasid answered, "The miracle is that I remained his hasid, just as I had been before."

What was that hasid trying to convey? He was trying to say that he wasn't the Rebbe's hasid because he needed a business adviser; he was his Rebbe's hasid because he needed something else. The fact that the Rebbe gave him advice that had a bad outcome could be attributed to a variety of external factors, but regarding his connection to the Rebbe, nothing had changed.

A prominent, esteemed, and wealthy hasid of the Belzer Rebbe would come to Belz from time to time, primarily in order to seek the Rebbe's counsel about matchmaking. He would go to the Rebbe and ask him, "They are offering my son or my daughter several matches. Which one should I choose?"

The Rebbe would ask him, "What does your heart say regarding this matter?"

The hasid would answer, "My heart says that so-and-so is worthy to be my son-in-law."

The Rebbe said to him, "Do so."

The next time, too, he asked a similar question and received a similar answer: "Toward whom does your heart lean? Then do so."

Sometime later, he arrived yet again to finalize a match and waited to consult with the Rebbe. A somewhat enlightened *mitnaged* who was present asked him, "What does the Rebbe advise you when you ask him?"

The hasid replied, "The Rebbe asks me where my heart is leaning, and then he tells me to act accordingly."

The man asked him, "If so, why do you need to travel to ask the Rebbe? After all, you know what he will say!"

The man's question made an impression, and the hasid stopped traveling to consult with the Rebbe. Sometime later, the hasid came back to the Rebbe with another question. In the course of the conversation, the Rebbe asked him, "Why haven't we seen you for some time?"

He told the Rebbe about his exchange with the *mitnaged,* and the Rebbe said to him, "His logic is sound, so why did you come back?"

The hasid answered, "Why did I come? Since he gave me that advice and I stopped coming, my heart no longer leans in any direction!"

AN ANCHOR TO GRASP

It is written that one should "make [*aseh*] a rabbi for yourself and acquire [*keneh*] a friend for yourself."[15] The advice to "acquire a friend" can be understood because even though making friends can be effortless, on occasion it can also require a sustained effort involving repeated attempts to pursue the friend in various ways. Sometimes in order to acquire a friend, one must pay. Hence the usage of the word *keneh,* "acquire," which connotes a transaction.

"Make a rabbi for yourself," on the other hand, requires a decision and action. Hence the usage of *aseh,* "make," which also means to act. A person must choose a rabbi for himself because "it is not good for man to be alone."[16] Apparently, a person needs more than just "a helper alongside him."[17] A person also needs someone above him.

The admonition to "make a rabbi for yourself" addresses a person's spiritual needs. In the course of my dealings with people, I've had the opportunity, for better or for worse, to meet many different types of people. One of the things I've noticed about people who are healthy as well as those suffering from various illnesses is that those who lack an anchor are in the most dire situation. A person with an anchor to grasp has hope. If he is ill, he will frequently recover; if he is suffering, he will usually find relief from his distress.

---

15. *Avot* 1:6.
16. Genesis 2:18.
17. Genesis 2:18.

Those who have lost their anchor, or who have never had one, wander the world with an overwhelming sense of unease and vulnerability; their situation is exceedingly dangerous. As long as life goes along uneventfully – for example, he has a job as a bank clerk, raises his children, sends them to a *yeshiva ketana* and then to a *yeshiva gedola* – then he doesn't hurt himself or others. But when he has a problem, without an anchor he has nothing to grasp.

WHO IS THE SUPREME AUTHORITY?

In recent generations, there have been people, and even entire communities, in the Jewish world who preferred on principle not to have a rabbi. This phenomenon is problematic; it created in those people and communities an illness of sorts. People and communities without a Rebbe lack an awareness that people who do have a Rebbe know with certainty: that ours is not a world of anarchy and that I'm not at its center. It's not all about me.

I was once acquainted with a very interesting Jew, the son of a great rabbi who was the head of a prominent yeshiva in Lithuania. Both he and his brother had stopped being observant, a phenomenon that was almost a built-in component of the zeitgeist of that time. They became leaders of the anarchist movement, one of the most powerful in the Soviet Union. A basic tenet of the movement was that everything begins and ends with the individual; society and the state are secondary. That is why the movement aspired to destroy, not only a regime, but the entire framework of the state – the mechanism itself.

The members of the movement used terrorism for that purpose and killed a significant number of people, many of whom were prominent individuals. Because of this, when the Bolsheviks came into power, the anarchist movement was earmarked for complete destruction and its members were dealt with harshly. In order to rid himself of the anarchists, Lenin invited them to convene in a large assembly and then proceeded to shoot them all. This Jew, this son of the Lithuanian rabbi, somehow escaped death. After he had been in and out of Soviet prisons, Lenin freed him, and he managed to leave the country and travel around the world. He ultimately settled in Herzliya, where he gave lectures on Judaism and anarchy. After all, he was the son of a great Torah scholar;

until a certain age he had studied Torah diligently. Only later did he learn Marx and Engels by heart.

In his book, this Jew wrote that anarchy is the essence of Judaism. His first proof was from the Ten Commandments: How does the first commandment begin? "I [*anokhi*] am the Lord your God."[18] One way or another, a person who has no Rebbe basically says, "Who is the supreme authority? I am. Who determines what is truth and what is falsehood? I do."

MAKE YOURSELF A RABBI

Occasionally a person has the privilege of encountering an individual of such great stature that it feels as though he is facing Mount Everest. When this occurs, the essence of their relationship becomes clear immediately. When every aspect of his knowledge and behavior, from every perspective, is superior to yours, no effort is required to make that person your rabbi. It's wonderful when that happens. But when it's not that clear, and when it doesn't happen easily, a person must still "make a rabbi for himself." Sometimes the decision is made with forethought, and sometimes the decision is arbitrary.

Some people go from one *tzaddik* to another, visiting holy men as if begging from door to door. Actually, seeking out saintly men is a worthy endeavor. I once sat with the elder Slonimer Rebbe and listened to his stories, some of which were about himself and his life. In his youth, he had been a loyal emissary of the previous Slonimer Rebbe who wanted to establish an organization that would unite *ḥaredi* Judaism long before Agudat Yisrael was formed. The Rebbe sent his young emissary to speak to virtually all of the Torah leaders of the generation. He told me that when he met with one of them, that Rebbe asked his hasidim to look at the guest because "happy are the eyes that saw the eyes that saw the eyes." Sometimes, the very fact that a certain person has had the privilege of seeing the Torah leadership of the generation eye to eye accords him a certain status.

On the other hand, wandering from one holy man to another has the potential for danger. When one seeks counsel from different

18. Exodus 20:2.

tzaddikim, and also attempts to act in accordance with that counsel, an impossible confusion can be created in a person's mind. This is not because any of the rabbis spoke falsehoods, but rather because their opinions and recommendations can't always coexist in harmony. The mandate to "make yourself a rabbi" demands determination and decisiveness.

THE KEY TO MY LOCK

When a person needs to decide who his Rebbe will be, he must at times search for the person who is suitable for him in particular. In a certain sense, finding a rabbi is like finding a spouse. When it comes to a marriage partner, matters are conducted not according to an absolute standard but according to suitability. When a man marries a woman, he does not necessarily think that there is no one more beautiful or smarter than she is, but he knows that she is the most fitting for him.

Choosing a Rebbe is also a private matter; one must find a Rebbe who is personally suitable. Once, when hasidim would travel to a certain Rebbe, they would be asked, "Isn't so-and-so" – a different Rebbe – "greater?" The hasidim would likely agree: "Yes, so-and-so is certainly greater than our Rebbe." Actually, in Ukraine it wasn't unusual for a Rebbe to travel to consult with another Rebbe of greater stature. This wasn't a secret; everyone knew about it. If so, why would hasidim settle for a second-rate Rebbe when they could be hasidim of the Rebbe's Rebbe?

It is because the relationship between Rebbe and hasid is similar to the relationship between a lock and a key. I have a lock, and so-and-so has the appropriate key. Perhaps the one with the key to my lock isn't the greatest, but still, he holds my key. Another person, who may be immeasurably greater, holds the key to the heart of my Rebbe, but not to mine. Conceivably, there is a person who has keys to all of the most secret rooms in the state, to all the most secure vaults in the land, and he's able to open the most secret of treasures, but he still may lack the key to my door. That's why, in a true search for a rabbi, one isn't searching for someone who is greatest in Torah, wisdom, and good deeds, someone of renown throughout the world, but rather for the one who holds the key to his heart.

If someone like that exists – he is his Rebbe.

The Departure of the Lubavitcher Rebbe

WHAT DOES ONE DO WHEN THE SUN SETS?

Here is where I reach the distinctiveness of the day. The passing of the Lubavitcher Rebbe resulted in immense darkness, as none of his hasidim searched for or found another Rebbe. This was because, among other reasons, the Lubavitcher Rebbe had overshadowed a great many people during his lifetime.

At first there was great light, then there were torches – lights on a smaller scale – and people knew that they could use a torch for light. Over time, all the torches were extinguished, and only one light remained. When that light set, when the light of the sun vanished, many were confronted with a substantive problem: They had no candle, and they didn't even know how to light a candle. They were groping in pitch darkness and were liable to enter a snake pit, and even want to remain there, because they were unable to get help from any light source.

The Gemara states, "The elders who were in that generation [the generation of the wilderness] said, 'The face of Moses was like the face of the sun; the face of Joshua was like the face of the moon. Woe for this embarrassment; woe for this disgrace [that we did not merit another leader with the stature of Moses].'"[19]

The sun had set, and although Moses had infused Joshua with his wisdom, understanding, and power, he couldn't do what Moshe had done. Joshua was a great light, even if he didn't become a Moses and didn't shine as bright. And what would have happened had Joshua not existed? What did happen when the light of Joshua set?

When the sun set, the people walked by the light of the moon for several years. Then the moon set. What happened then? Did people walk around groping in the dark? Who then saved us from stumbling blocks?

Throughout the generations, when a bright light was extinguished, people would light a candle or find a lamp. The light of a candle is a microcosm of the light of the sun. From a physics perspective, all energy sources found in the world (that do not involve atomic energy) are an aspect of sunlight. Sometimes sunlight shines through holes and cracks,

19. *Bava Batra* 75a.

and sometimes it illuminates by means of a wax candle. Either way the light is from the same source. Clearly, a lamp is not the sun, but it's possible to walk by its light, even if it only enables us to know, with some certainty, where we are going. We can walk by its light if only to keep from falling into the first pit we encounter on our path.

When God took the great *tzaddikim* from the Jewish people, he left them with lesser *tzaddikim*, even minuscule *tzaddikim*, in terms of their respective worth and prominence. People may prefer walking by the light of the sun, but the sunlight is intense and blinds them. There may also be those who are blinded by the light of the moon. They have no alternative but to walk by the light of fireflies, which, in all seriousness, also provide light.

THE LUBAVITCHER REBBE'S INSTRUCTIONS

Often questions are raised that require a decision, among them halakhic questions. One of the final and unusual instructions the Lubavitcher Rebbe gave to all of his hasidim was to "make yourself a rabbi" – to choose a rabbi to consult with regarding all matters of Torah and *mitzvot*. Beyond this general instruction, the Lubavitcher Rebbe gave advice that pertained to consulting with experts in specific areas. For medical problems, one should go to two or three doctors who are also friends, consult with them, and act in accordance with their advice. When there is a problem regarding commerce and business, one should turn to three friends with financial expertise and act in accordance with their counsel.

In effect, the Lubavitcher Rebbe was saying that it was no longer possible to receive guidance from above as before. Now one would have to light candles – a candle for this matter and a candle for a different matter. When there is no daylight, a person must kindle a lamp for himself and walk by its light.

Do hasidim want to accept this instruction? Most great hasidim don't. "A fool does not desire sagacity, but only the revealing of his heart."[20] Most seek to find someone who will confirm what is in his heart. In that sense, a Rebbe who is no longer with us is much more convenient for me than a living Rebbe, because I can attribute to him whatever I want.

---

20. Proverbs 18:2.

I will relate to you a story that seems humorous, but it's really not a joke. I was once a guest in a certain hasidic community outside Israel. The time for the *Mussaf* prayer on Shabbat arrived, and the *kohanim* went up to the podium to recite *Birkat Kohanim* Although in Sefardic synagogues, *kohanim* go up to the podium each day, in Ashkenazic synagogues outside the Land of Israel, they do so only a few times during the year. I'd never heard of a custom of Ashkenazic *kohanim* going up to the podium on an ordinary Shabbat outside of Israel. But a guest must be polite, so I didn't stand up and immediately protest. Although it goes against my nature, I remained silent.

Sometime later, after we had eaten and drunk and were merry, I asked – truly very courteously – what was the source of that custom I witnessed. The host immediately answered, "The Rebbe told me to do this." I thought to myself, *Nu, perhaps.*

Logically it's possible to find a very reasonable explanation for this. There were dozens, if not hundreds, of rabbis, of all affiliations and all ideologies, who wrote that if they had the authority, they would institute the recitation of *Birkat Kohanim* every day. The reasons this hasn't been done are very weak, but still the practice was never implemented.

Sometime later I calculated the year that this person came to that area and realized that he simply couldn't have heard such a statement from the Lubavitcher Rebbe in person. I understood that he probably opened the *Iggerot* and found the answer he wanted there.

The real problem with the *Iggerot* is that it doesn't have an index. If one wants, say, to find advice on finding a spouse, there are dozens of letters about matchmaking. After reading them all, one can get a pretty good idea of the Lubavitcher Rebbe's fundamental position on the topic. If one seeks to find answers to questions about earning a living, countless letters can also be found on that topic. But people tend to open the book to a random page when seeking the Rebbe's opinion. It's very possible that the Lubavitcher Rebbe may have expressed his opinion on the subject in a clear, explicit manner on a different page from the one that was opened. I assume that this man, who had a question regarding *Birkat Kohanim*, opened the book of *Iggerot*, found one letter stating, "It is proper to do so," and thought, *Wonderful – the Rebbe issued a ruling.*

It's very easy to get along with a Rebbe like that.

The *Zohar* states, "After passing away, a *tzaddik* can be found in all the worlds more than during his lifetime."[21] A *tzaddik* continues to have an influence in this world as well as in the higher worlds. All the holy books state that the shepherds of Israel, from Abraham through King David, continue to lead Israel after their departure. This is also true of prominent leaders who didn't attain the status of a shepherd of Israel. Having said that, there is a difference between the influence of a *tzaddik* in Heaven and that of a *tzaddik* who is alive and serving on earth, at least in terms of the clarity of advice. The words of the *tzaddik* who has passed from this world aren't always understood.

When a person relies absolutely on God's mercy, and prays with all his heart for guidance and resolution of a problem, it's possible that he will succeed in receiving an answer from Heaven. But answers that come from Heaven are similar to answers conveyed by *tzaddikim* who have passed away in that they are not always clear. After all, it's possible to see nature itself as an instruction from Heaven. This idea was expressed beautifully by someone who wrote, "What is nature? A book written by God, signed with a pseudonym: Nature." In this world, sanctity can be found in many forms; sometimes it appears with a signature and sometimes without.

There are times when one clearly sees eye to eye with his teacher, and there are times when a mentor or luminary is shrouded in fog and impossible to find. Even if a person may hear a voice, it can be difficult to identify. "Your teacher will no longer be concealed"[22] is a blessing that at times remains unfulfilled.

FORGOING THE IDEAL SOLUTION

When the sun has set, it may be possible to find another source of light, but if one doesn't look for it, he certainly won't find anything.

One time, the Yid HaKadosh, Rabbi Yaakov Yitzḥak Rabinowitz of Peshisḥa, was seen sitting with a concerned expression on his face. When asked why, he explained, "I'm gazing upon future generations. At first, the Jewish people were led by the prophets. Then came the *tanna'im*,

21. *Zohar* 3:71b.
22. Isaiah 30:20.

and after them the *amora'im*, then the *geonim*. After them came the rabbis, and after them the Rebbes. I see that their time, too, is about to end, but I can't see what will come after the Rebbes."

I'm emphasizing the concern of the Yid HaKadosh, because attempts to address it have been problematic. The verse "There is no longer any prophet, nor is there any among us who knows for how long"[23] can be seen as a justification for doing nothing. Presumably it was meant to instill a fear of Heaven and encourage reliance on faith, but in fact, it engenders inertia. Sometimes, great faith becomes a cover-up for inaction.

This problem recurs in each and every generation each and every day in different ways. When people became disconnected from a brilliant source of light, they searched for something that would be an ideal replacement. But some despair of finding a substitute, and do nothing, hoping the problem will somehow be resolved.

In principle, every problem of every kind has an optimal solution. The optimal solution for the problem of friction interfering with the effective movement of a car, for example, would be to make a car of ice that could glide on ice. That would result in the lowest possible drag coefficient. But it's impossible to create a car made of ice that can glide on ice. So one must make an ordinary car, and do what one can to minimize friction. The solution is far from optimal – one doesn't reach zero drag – but it's the best possible realistic solution. One can write on a blank ballot, "I vote for the Messiah son of David," and there is no doubt that the Messiah would be the optimal choice, but those ballots would be discarded and achieve nothing.

That's why I say that one must always keep trying whatever the circumstances. There are rare individuals who are able to perceive instructions of some kind from above (and I'm not referring to those who seek solutions to problems by trying to communicate with spirits). So what are good people who are unable to hear clear instructions from on high supposed to do? First of all, they must stop standing around and waiting until they hear a voice saying, "This is the way to proceed: First you go right and then you go left." My fervent hope is that by tomorrow

23. Psalms 74:9.

morning, in the streets of Jerusalem, we will hear the voice that will tell each and every one of us what is incumbent on us to do. But until then we must keep trying to conduct ourselves like those who write on a wedding invitation: "The wedding ceremony will take place, God willing, in the courtyard of the Temple in Jerusalem. If we have not yet earned that privilege, the wedding will be held on such-and-such street in Boro Park...."

I've spoken to you today about matters of great significance. I don't know what you'll do with this information. After all, even Moses, to whom God spoke directly, who was able to bring the Torah down from Heaven with one hand and make the ground open up to swallow his opponents with the other – even Moses, at the peak of his greatness and his glory, concluded his speech to the people of Israel by saying, "I know you. I know that you won't heed everything that I'm saying to you. I know that ultimately you will do whatever you feel like doing. But I'm telling you that if you don't heed what I say, so many troubles will befall you that you will begin to rethink the matter."

I'm nothing like Moses, and I don't share his abilities in any way, but I can only tell you that if you behave in a certain way, you may end up with broken legs, broken arms, and your head covered with wounds. If that happens, at least you will remember that you were warned, that you were told that there is another way, and perhaps you will even follow it.

Leḥayim.

12–13 Tammuz
The Festival of the Redemption of Rabbi Yosef Yitzḥak Schneerson

On the twelfth and thirteenth of Tammuz, Lubavitcher hasidim mark the release of the sixth Lubavitcher Rebbe, Rabbi Yosef Yitzḥak Schneerson, from Soviet Russian prison. Rabbi Yosef Yitzḥak was incarcerated by the authorities in the month of Sivan, in the year 1927, and was sentenced to death for his efforts to preserve the embers of the Jewish people throughout the Soviet Union. In the wake of international pressure, his punishment was reduced to exile, and he was ultimately deported from the country. His release was announced on the twelfth of Tammuz but was officially ratified on the thirteenth.

Even after Rabbi Yosef Yitzḥak Schneerson left Russia, the infrastructure that he left behind, as well as the multitudes of hasidim who remained in the anti-religious Communist regime, continued to preserve Judaism under almost impossible conditions over the course of many years.

In detailed diaries that were published in several volumes of *Likkutei Dibburim*, Rabbi Yosef Yitzḥak documented his incarceration, the interrogations he underwent, and his release. He also recorded what he was feeling and thinking during that period. Those descriptions provide a glimpse into the incredible personality of Rabbi Yosef Yitzḥak Schneerson, his absolute devotion to Jews and Judaism, and his courage in the face of mortal danger.

When Rabbi Steinsaltz spoke of Rabbi Yosef Yitzḥak, he always spoke of him as a paragon of self-sacrifice, as someone who loved the Jewish people, and as someone who attended to the material needs of the people no less than to their spiritual needs.

18

Self-Sacrifice for the Sake of Judaism

HEAD OF THE JEWISH PEOPLE

On the twelfth and thirteenth of Tammuz, a festival of redemption is celebrated in honor of Rabbi Yosef Yitzḥak Schneerson, who was released from Russian prison on that date. I would like to start by explaining the leadership philosophy of Rabbi Yosef Yitzḥak specifically and Chabad Rebbes in general. I must preface this by saying something that I may not be worthy of saying:

During the time period that Rabbi Yosef Yitzḥak was active, there were many other Rebbes who also engaged in Torah, prayer, and good deeds and encouraged their hasidim to do the same, but there was no other Rebbe who went beyond that, who considered himself to be responsible for addressing the troubles of all Jews. There were great Rebbes who had thousands of followers, but none of them addressed, comprehensively and fundamentally, the question of how their followers would earn a living. To the best of my knowledge, only the Lubavitcher Rebbes tried to see to the material needs of their adherents in a manner that dealt with the basics of their economic situations and the economic structure of their lives.

Even Rabbi Dovber Schneuri, the second Lubavitcher Rebbe, also known as the Mitteler Rebbe, did so, though he seems to have been a wholly spiritual person. He concerned himself with the productivity of

Jews and encouraged them to abandon professions like peddling and innkeeping and work the land instead. Undoubtedly, it wasn't easy to transform city-dwelling Jews who barely knew where to find a goat's tail into farmers. Rabbi Dovber also sought to help with the economic welfare of his followers by encouraging factory work and the like. He wasn't merely a "good Jew" residing on the periphery, but a person who felt the responsibility of leadership weighing heavily on his shoulders, deeply involved in the problems of his people.

Even today, with all of the great rabbis among us, which of them sits and tends to the troubles of the Jewish people? Some rabbis may promote organizations that provide interest-free loans; others actively encourage charity to relief organizations or soup kitchens. But is there anyone among them who concerns himself with the practical question of how a Jew will make a living?

One could claim that this is not the role of the Rebbe, not the role of the rabbi, not the role of the chief rabbinate, and not the role of the local rabbinate. But then, whose role is it? Who must concern himself with the livelihood of this person and the income of that person?

I'm not saying that the rabbi has to get involved in economics, but a leader of the Jewish people must involve himself with the problems of the Jewish people.

Rabbi Shneur Zalman of Liadi explains in the *Tanya* that a leader is the "head" of the Jewish people.[1] One of the characteristics of the head is that it feels the pain of the entire body. If it doesn't feel the pain of the whole body, one would need to suspect that perhaps it's not really the head. Although it's located in the correct place, it might not be the right body part.

Imagine a head that says, "I only know what happens above the diaphragm. I have no idea what goes on below that. I have never heard of what takes place in the stomach." There are heads today who apparently know many things, but they certainly don't know everything that's happening below. What kind of head doesn't know these things? It may not be proper to ask this question about a specific person, and I don't wish to disparage any particular leader. I'm merely trying to emphasize the

1. *Likkutei Amarim*, chap. 2.

uniqueness of those who do devote significant thought and attention to all issues facing the Jewish people.

THE COMMUNIST STATE AND CIVIL WAR

Rabbi Yosef Yitzḥak Schneerson was an only child. When he was fifteen, his father, Rabbi Shalom Dovber Schneerson, appointed him director general of the Lubavitch institutions. From then on, over the course of many years, he engaged in communal service and administration of the yeshiva. In 1920, Rabbi Shalom Dovber passed away, and Rabbi Yosef Yitzḥak succeeded him in the leadership. This didn't occur immediately because precisely at that time, he became ill with typhus and was bedridden for several months. When he recovered, the environment had changed completely: Russia had become a newly Communist state, steeped in ideology and ideologues.

The Communist party itself constituted a minority of the population, but over time it became organized and its ranks expanded. From the very beginning of Communist rule, a reign of extreme terror was unleashed, and Jews, among others, participated. Lenin, who headed the party at that time, said, "When one fells trees, chips fall." How many chips fell? One million, two, four million, good chips, bad chips, chips of all kinds.

It is said that the head of the secret police, Dzerzhinsky, personally signed one million death sentences. One would think that just signing one's name a million times would exhaust a person's hand; it turns out that Dzerzhinsky did so with great devotion.

When Rabbi Yosef Yitzḥak Schneerson ascended to Chabad leadership in 1920, the civil war in Russia hadn't yet ended and the situation was dire. There were places where the factions battled each other and places where power changed hands. But in all places, before anything else was done, Jews were attacked as capitalists, as reactionaries, as Communists, as supporters of Communism.

Someone who wrote a book about the Russian civil war described it in this manner: What is the difference between the White Russians (the Right), and the Communists? The difference is where they say "dirty Jew." The Communists say it at home, in private, and the White Russians say it straight to the Jew's face. All sides killed Jews – some for ideological reasons and some for no reason other than the fact that their victims were Jews. No one cared when a Jew was killed.

The new Communist state wasn't well organized. It was said of the Soviet constitution that it could have been fantastic if only someone had actually implemented it. The law provided for all sorts of rights and allowances, but in practice, none of it was realized. Theoretically, officially and legally, there was freedom of religion; any religion could be practiced. But from a practical standpoint, Communist agents in the Yevsektsiya, who were assigned to dealing with Jews, invested great effort into destroying and suppressing Judaism. The Communist state was characterized by terror that wasn't always regulated at that time. The Yevsektsiya terrorized the Jews, and it was never clear whether or not their activities were state-sponsored.

In his memoirs, Rabbi Yosef Yitzḥak Schneerson describes encounters that he had with Communists. They were riffraff of sorts, but they were in power and no one dared to oppose them. They not only acted crudely – for that, perhaps, it is possible to forgive them – but they also destroyed things they had no authority to destroy.

SOBRIETY, ORGANIZATIONAL ABILITY, AND COURAGE

Before World War I, Jewish life flourished in Belarus, Ukraine, and Eastern Europe in general. There were synagogues, ritual baths, and study halls everywhere, though they weren't particularly organized. Under Communist rule, it became very difficult to maintain Judaism because the regime supported an agenda promoting Judaism's total destruction. This policy didn't stem from anti-Semitism – more than a few Communists were Jews – but from hatred of the practice of Judaism. For example, the Communists would disseminate anti-religious propaganda before and after the holidays. This propaganda was diverse – from theoretical, philosophical, and scientific reasoning to dirty jokes. And it was always found in abundance, thanks to the support of the authorities. The local rabbi needed to stand firm against all that; very often he would do nothing more than moan and say, "*Nu, nu,* this is not so nice."

At that time, it was difficult to see the complete picture and understand it. There were people, among them good and righteous rabbis, who said, "*Nu,* okay, another day or two, a year or two, and it will pass."

They didn't think that the Communists would endure, but the Communists did endure. They grew stronger and stronger.

Sometimes it astounds me to think that people who had the ability to study the entire Talmud from cover to cover and understand it forward and backward were unable to understand what was befalling the Jewish people and Judaism.

Rabbi Yosef Yitzḥak Schneerson had the ability to see this reality. He saw that there were things that needed to be done, and he began to take action. He had outstanding organizational ability, and he worked with people, some of whom heeded him. In contrast to the great majority of rabbis who fled if someone merely frightened them, Rabbi Yosef Yitzḥak wasn't afraid. He took risks and did things that weren't completely legal, things that certainly didn't meet with the approval of the party apparatchiks.

EDUCATION BEFORE EVERYTHING

Rabbi Yosef Yitzḥak began to organize the Jewish institutions in general and, with even greater vigor, institutions of Jewish education in particular. From the beginning, he understood that this was a vulnerable element.

There is a widespread phenomenon that when Jews come from different places to a new city or a new country, segmentation takes place. Each acts in accordance with the customs of his place of origin. Lubavitchers will build a Talmud Torah. Sefardim will build a synagogue, place a Torah scroll in it, and adorn it. Others will open a kosher restaurant. Access to kosher food is, indeed, important, and one who provides it fulfills a great *mitzva* and keeps people from transgressing. One who builds a synagogue has also performed a great *mitzva*. But educational institutions are critically important because education addresses the question of our future.

In the realm of education, the situation in Russia wasn't simple at all. My mother-in-law grew up in a Lubavitch family in Russia. In her neighborhood, there were Jewish children like her who never attended school because the schools not only taught heresy, but the students were expected to practice it. On the other hand, refraining from sending children to school was very dangerous; it could lead to the parents' incarceration. The mission that Rabbi Yosef Yitzḥak Schneerson undertook – building educational institutions, whether they were perfectly legal, semilegal, or illegal – certainly involved great danger.

ORGANIZATION OF THE STRUGGLE

One of the first things Rabbi Yosef Yitzḥak Schneerson did was to mobilize his hasidim. He didn't succeed in mobilizing all of them, but he succeeded in mobilizing a number of people who were willing to devote their lives to Jewish education, no matter how much self-sacrifice it entailed.

Rabbi Yosef Yitzḥak also organized rabbis who weren't affiliated with Chabad. One of those rabbis who remained in Russia after Rabbi Yosef Yitzḥak's departure was Rabbi Yeḥezkel Abramsky.

Rabbi Abramsky was a truly great rabbi and a prominent *mitnaged*. Ideologically, he was as far removed from Chabad as possible, but he and others like him understood that the problem under Communism wasn't whether to pray *nusaḥ Sefard* or *nusaḥ Ashkenaz*. The problem was whether Jews would pray at all. The question wasn't whether to don *tefillin* of Rabbeinu Tam or *tefillin* of Rashi, but whether any Jew could don *tefillin*. The problem wasn't whether the word *dakka* should be written in the Torah scroll with an *alef* or with a *heh*,[2] but whether there would be Torah scrolls at all.

Years later, when I visited Russia, I was shown a Communist warehouse in which eight hundred Torah scrolls were stored. Apparently they had been confiscated during that period.

Rabbi Yosef Yitzḥak's organization was stable enough so that even after he left Russia, it continued to be run by local officials he had installed to lead his projects. Before he left, he reinforced the system that had worked until then, and it continued to function even after the people who headed it also left Russia.

Rabbi Yosef Yitzḥak never had an abundance of money, but he needed resources to organize classes, to transport people from place to

2. See Deuteronomy 23:2. In most Torah scrolls, *dakka* is written with a *heh*. In Yemenite Torah scrolls, the tradition is to write it with an *alef*. That is, likewise, the Chabad tradition based on the ancient Ashkenazi tradition.

place, and for many other activities. He would dispatch emissaries to raise funds and established good relations with the Joint Distribution Committee, among other organizations. Though board members of the JDC were, on the whole, good people, they didn't understand what was happening in Russia. They didn't grasp the significance of every sum that they sent him. As a result, their support was minimal.

Rabbi Yosef Yitzḥak spurred people to action, and also served as a role model for many. He didn't hesitate to openly denounce the Communist party, its policies and ideology, even though he knew that there were people in the synagogue documenting every word he said and that his words were liable to bring about his demise. As I said, he had a lot of courage.

With the passage of time, it became increasingly clear to the authorities that this Schneerson was not a small-town rabbi, merely a local phenomenon, but rather a personality who spearheaded movements. No totalitarian regime would tolerate a phenomenon of that kind, and the Soviet regime, with all of its Jews, certainly didn't. But Rabbi Yosef Yitzḥak continued to act, undeterred.

STANDING AGAINST A STATE FROM HELL

Everything Rabbi Yosef Yitzḥak Schneerson did in Communist Russia was for the purpose of constructing a force that could withstand not only a particular decree but a state from hell. It was a state that was unquestionably and blatantly opposed to Judaism, even if it denied being anti-Semitic. Rabbi Yosef Yitzḥak was committed to building a system within such a state that would have continuity, beyond its own particular time and place.

There was a great deal of cruelty in the Russian regime, and this wasn't necessarily cruelty for its own sake. The cruelty was in a philosophy that cared nothing for individual human life; the life or death of a person made no difference.

Here is an example: After hundreds of years of planning, a very important one-hundred-kilometer canal was constructed between the Volga River and the Don River. According to calculations, for each meter of canal, at least one person would die constructing it. So if the length of the canal was a hundred kilometers, one hundred thousand men would have to die. I'm not saying that the Russians set out to kill a hundred thousand people. They just deemed it necessary to build the canal, and they simply accepted the fact that people would die in the process.

My late uncle told me that he was in a convoy of people whose primary crime was that they fled to Russia from Poland when it was under Hitler's control. Everyone in the entire convoy was placed on trial as a spy because they all had entered the country without permission. This is how the judges conducted the trial: Three years, five years, three years, five years – that is to say, three years' exile in a remote place or five years of exile there. The judges didn't sentence them to death, God forbid, but they did sentence them to forced labor like chopping down trees. But if someone died while performing these labors, no one made a big deal out of it. I can relate to you many similar incidents. Even if the Russians had no interest in killing people, a human life was worth virtually nothing in their eyes.

Despite everything that the Russians managed to do, their bureaucracy was inefficient and had many flaws. The rabbi with whom I studied told me that he would go from place to place to serve local Jewish communities. In every city or village, the secret police would know he was there by the day after his arrival. But since officially there wasn't even one document of evidence against him, he could reside in a city for one month, two months, four or five months, until someone filed a complaint that he was engaging in religious propaganda. At that point, he was forced to escape and flee to another city.

The entire scenario repeated itself in the next city because the Soviets didn't inform officials of the arrival of this dangerous rabbi who must be incarcerated. The moment the police expelled him from their jurisdiction, from their perspective, the matter was closed.

For years, this bureaucratic inefficiency was advantageous to the Jews. The state wasn't efficient enough to eradicate Judaism. As a result, Jewish families stayed put despite ongoing terror and despite the fact that it was impossible to trust anyone and informers were everywhere. There were Jewish children studying Torah, and there were Jews fulfilling *mitzvot* to one degree or another, but everything was done under great duress, with great hardship and great suffering.

Jewish life and observance didn't organize itself. Someone needed to send a teacher to a place that had no teacher, someone needed to ensure that the teacher could actually teach there, and so on. Rabbi Yosef Yitzḥak Schneerson and a few people in his inner circle did all this. They maintained a framework that would enable children to study and families to sustain Jewish life. All this he did with great devotion, and he successfully transmitted that selfless commitment to others.

THE STORY OF THE LIBERATION

Before I elaborate on the extent of Rabbi Yosef Yitzḥak Schneerson's devotion, I will conclude the story of his incarceration and liberation. The story is replete with miracles – not miracles that split the heavens, but a confluence of incidents that were unquestionably miraculous. In *Reshimat HaMa'asar*, Rabbi Yosef Yitzḥak describes some of what he underwent, and he related additional stories about his ordeal orally. All are wondrous portrayals of what he experienced during interrogation and in prison.

When he arrived at the prison, he thought he would be executed within a day or two because that's what he was told by the jailers who took him into custody. It made no difference to them under which article of the law he would be sentenced – they would execute him first and fabricate a reason afterward.

Rabbi Yosef Yitzḥak relates that at a certain stage they ordered him to leave his cell, walk to one end of the corridor, and knock on the door of a room. He didn't remember in which direction he had been told to turn, so he said to himself, "All turns that you turn should be only to the right."[3] He turned right and continued through the corridor until he found a room, which was a registration office. From the perspective of the state, this was a disaster. His captors had intended for him to enter a room where twelve religious leaders had just been shot, one after another, and they were hoping to do the same to him. But since Rabbi Yosef Yitzḥak entered the registration office and had registered there, it became impossible to execute him in that way. Now they couldn't just claim that he had disappeared.

---

3. Based on *Yoma* 17b.

Rabbi Yosef Yitzḥak's registration delayed his execution. In the meantime, the hasidim publicized that they had incarcerated the Rebbe. The Jewish community at the time, including the Jewish community in the United States, didn't have enough influence to get him released, but it was strong enough to publicize the issue in the press and create a ruckus. The Soviets were also not that strong at the time, and the commotion surrounding the incarceration of a religious leader didn't help them. Their plan to execute Rabbi Yosef Yitzḥak was postponed for another two or three days.

By a very strange coincidence, a member of the Latvian Parliament had heard about Rabbi Yosef Yitzḥak's incarceration and had an outstanding opportunity to help facilitate his release. He wasn't a Lubavitcher hasid, but he was a religious Jew who was closely associated with Chabad. The ruling party in the Latvian government had a very tenuous majority at the time and needed this Jew to join the majority so they could remain in power. Because of this, he was in a position to make demands, and one of his demands was that the Latvian government intervene on behalf of Rabbi Yosef Yitzḥak to engineer his release. The Latvian government had leverage because the Soviets were completely isolated politically. They had no diplomatic ties with any country and were very interested in ties with Latvia. When the Latvians requested that the Soviets release Rabbi Yosef Yitzḥak, the Soviets agreed. That was the decisive factor in his liberation.

More and more pressure was exerted on the Soviets, and ultimately, on the third of Tammuz, they sentenced Rabbi Yosef Yitzḥak to three years of incarceration in exile. He no longer had a death sentence hanging over his head, and his hasidim immediately sought to build a place for the Rebbe to live while in exile.

Some people follow orders, and some people carry out many orders, but actions performed out of devotion are the most effective. That's how those hasidim acted.

One and a half weeks later, on the twelfth of Tammuz, which happened to be Rabbi Yosef Yitzḥak's birthday, the Soviets informed him that he was free. He was told that they would actually prefer that he leave the country, and though he didn't really want to leave, they didn't give him much of a choice. He tried to arrange for his departure to the best of his ability. He also arranged for his son-in-law, Rabbi Menaḥem Mendel, to leave Russia. But taking his family out of Russia was no simple task. For each one of the people Rabbi Yosef Yitzḥak wanted to take with him, he had to provide the Soviets with an explanation as to why. "This is my wife." "This is my daughter." "This is my personal secretary." "This one is to be my son-in-law."

The Soviets said to him, "Granted, you need a secretary with you, but why do you need your future son-in-law? Let your daughter find another groom."

Rabbi Yosef Yitzḥak answered, "I won't find a son-in-law like this one."

And so the Soviets allowed Rabbi Menaḥem Mendel to leave, too.

Ultimately, Rabbi Abramsky also managed to leave Russia, as did Rabbi Zevin, who was number two in the Chabad hierarchy after Rabbi Yosef Yitzḥak. As each one left, they entrusted their Jewish communal activities into the hands of people they appointed to continue their work.

Rabbi Yosef Yitzḥak's liberation was joyously celebrated. It was a victory of sorts over the evil empire. No one had ever heard of a person emerging intact from the claws of the wild beast that had exterminated so many of their own people. Millions had died like flies, but this one person, through strange and unusual coincidences, managed to be set free.

LIFE DEVOTED TO SANCTIFICATION OF GOD

It's impossible to overestimate the devotion of the Jews in Russia to Judaism. They withstood enormous difficulties and had to exert immense effort to observe Judaism in every aspect of Jewish life: eating kosher, praying, organizing a *minyan*, managing to have a farbrengen every so often – and primarily, educating children in Torah study. There were places where a ritual bath could be maintained, but it wasn't simple to do. Women would often drill a hole in the ice of a river and immerse themselves there.

An elderly Jew once told me about his life and experiences in a Soviet prison. He related how he managed to light Hanukkah candles in prison, something that was absolutely prohibited. He became creative, thinking that sections of an onion, with its peels within peels, could be used as a receptacles for oil. He prepared the onion, took oil from what remained in sardine tins, and made wicks from threads in the mattresses. As for the candle lighting itself, a miracle occurred: The inmates – all of them gentiles – created a human wall of sorts around him so the jailers wouldn't see that he was lighting candles. That is how he lit candles on the eight days of Hanukkah.

This person knew that he was all alone and didn't know what would become of him. He also knew that he could never trust other people because informers were everywhere. Yet still he struggled to continue living as a Jew.

People lived this struggle in all sorts of places and in all sorts of different ways. In Europe, in Belarus, in Moscow, in the Soviet satellite countries, they continued, time and again, to establish schools, to maintain synagogues, to take actions that would enable Jews to live as Jews. These heroic acts were much more challenging than the heroism of a person who jumps into a fire. Their heroism was more like that of a person who is willing to sit in the fire and continue sitting there for an extended period of time.

The main challenge that Rabbi Yosef Yitzḥak Schneerson's followers faced was to accomplish things that would last so that a simple Jew who resided wherever he resided would not only remember that he was a Jew, but he would also have the ability to endure as a Jew, day after day, year after year, in an evil empire. It was impossible to know how long that empire would last as it continued to grow and expand and it wasn't showing any signs of weakening. It was an empire whose end could not be foreseen, and it was understood that there was no leaving Russia.

Generation after generation had passed, and the evil regime remained in power. The Jews were repeatedly disgraced and defeated, yet despite it all, they continued to believe that God would not forsake them.

I met people who came from Russia. Most of them weren't Torah luminaries, but they all knew how to pray. Did they understand any word of the prayers? I don't know. Did they contemplate love and fear of God? I have my doubts about that, too. But they lived Jewish lives under difficult circumstances, not for one day and not for one year, but year after year.

The *Tanya* states that if forced to deny the existence of the God of Israel or be put to death, every Jew would choose to die rather than deny the existence of God.[4] The self-sacrifice required in Russia was different. It wasn't comprised of one fatal decision made at a critical moment. It was, rather, love and connection to God "with all your might"[5] – self-sacrifice based on love that was ongoing despite all the hardships from day to day and from month to month.

CREATING DEVOTED PEOPLE

One of the purposes of this festival of redemption is to remember those whom Rabbi Yosef Yitzḥak left behind in Russia. Rabbi Yosef Yitzḥak Schneerson managed to inspire in them love of the Jewish people, love of Torah, and love of God. Though some of these people appeared to have little or no connection to Judaism, Rabbi Yosef Yitzḥak enabled them to tap into whatever remained of their Jewishness so that all wouldn't be lost, so that all wouldn't die.

These people weren't all spiritual giants, but their actions were an expression of a love of God and a connection to God that was boundless. Influencing and motivating these people to act as they did wasn't a minor accomplishment. If I knew I had succeeded in inculcating these qualities in just one person, or in two people, or three, I'm sure I would be able to justify my place in the World to Come. If they tried to expel me, I could say, "But look, I made a lasting impact on another person, and it stood the test of time!"

Did Rabbi Yosef Yitzḥak's accomplishments change the big picture? Did he manage to overthrow Communism? No. But he managed to resist the Soviet machine and defied all odds in perpetuating Judaism among the pockets of Jews whom he influenced. He had the vigor, energy, and courage to withstand the reality that surrounded him, and it's still important to understand the origins of this strength. This endurance didn't stem from insanity; it stemmed from a decision that was, in certain respects, cold and calculated: "I'm going to do this to sanctify God's name." Rabbi Yosef Yitzḥak didn't have that many people working with him, but those he had took an oath to live for the sanctification of God.

---

4. *Likkutei Amarim,* chaps. 18–19.
5. Deuteronomy 6:5.

Most impressively, the organization he created lasted for many years. Rabbi Yosef Yitzḥak was active in it when he was in Russia, and he continued to participate in it even after he left. Even then, those inside Soviet Russia would attempt to contact him in order to seek counsel from "Saba" (his underground alias).

What Rabbi Yosef Yitzḥak Schneerson managed to accomplish in this world was nothing short of miraculous. He was more than just the engine that got people moving to perform specific tasks. His projects influenced people – be they prominent, be they great hasidim, be they simple folk – to continue to hold on to their Jewishness with dedication and devotion.

"ISRAEL IN WHOM I GLORY"

I'm speaking to you about this struggle because it's part of the history of the Jewish people.

In a city in Portugal, Jews lived clandestinely as Marranos over the course of four hundred and fifty years. When I think of those Jews, who for generations didn't know whether there were any other Jews in the world, who attempted to observe as many *mitzvot* as they could – preparing matza for Passover, praying on Rosh HaShana and Yom Kippur, and so on – I ask myself: What was the source of their strength? How did they keep this up, day after day, year after year, century after century after century?

In essence, they represent the true "pride of Jacob."[6] People like them are the glory of the Jewish people. Those who had the minds for it wrote books and became known through their books, while others sacrificed their lives in silence, with no one to tell their stories. I know several children of Russian Jews who were sent into exile at the time. Their fathers simply disappeared, never to be heard from again. This happened to many people; no one ever found out what happened to them in the end. They just vanished somewhere in the bureaucracy en route to cruelty. But the glory of the Jewish people is due to these simple Jews, who lived, sacrificed their lives, and died for the continuation of Judaism.

---

6. Amos 6:8.

The festival of redemption is not only about Rabbi Yosef Yitzḥak's redemption; it also celebrates what he managed to accomplish in Russia. Someone once wrote that the opponents of Hasidism created books, while hasidim created people. I don't know if this is true of hasidim in general, but it's certainly true of Rabbi Yosef Yitzḥak, who left people who were Jewish in the fullest sense of the word in Russia.

Not all of them were scholars or great philosophers, but the words "Israel in whom I glory"[7] apply to them. God glories in people who, with their very lives, declare, "For we are killed all day long for You."[8] These Russian Jews were prepared to sacrifice their lives for the sake of God, not with a decision made in an extreme situation – a single life-or-death moment – but as the defining characteristic of their day-to-day lives.

SELF-SACRIFICE TODAY

Our reality is very different. Is there anyone here who experiences this kind of ongoing struggle, not as a onetime battle, but as a daily ordeal? Is there anyone here who must consider, on a daily basis, what the future of his children will be in an environment that is aggressively hostile to Judaism? Is there anyone who has to decide what he must do so that they will receive an education that will teach them the values he wishes to instill in them, so they will know the *alef-beit*, so that if they were to be sent into exile – as was the case for so many Russian Jews – they would still know how to exist as Jews?

If our reality is so different from the Jews in Russia, then what self-sacrifice is required of us today? We must think about what we are transmitting to our children in the world as it currently exists. Among other things, do parents transmit to their children their outlook on what is truly important? That question itself involves a struggle.

People today may have more comfortable lives than they did in the past. People have careers and even go out and have a good time. Life may not be as violent as it once was, but it's no less aggressive and leads to the same results. The big question remains unchanged: What will I transmit to my children who I leave behind?

7. Isaiah 49:3.
8. Psalms 44:23.

Most of you are young men. Think about what you would like to transmit to your children, and how you will transmit it to them. A person can raise his children to be Torah scholars, but that's not enough. Even with scholarship, they could do what they want. There are corrupt Torah scholars of all kinds. Some of them not only cease being Torah scholars; they cease being human beings at all.

How do we ensure continuity of a truly Jewish way of life? How do we keep the flame burning?

When I think of Rabbi Yosef Yitzḥak Schneerson in the context of this festival, I think less about his release from prison than I do about his essence – his life's mission that focused on the question: How does one pass on the flaming nucleus to others?

"SO THAT HE WILL COMMAND HIS CHILDREN"

Here is what God says about why He loved Abraham: "I love him so that he will command his children and his household after him, so they will observe the way of the Lord."[9] Abraham devoted his life to the sanctity of God, waged war with kings, and even managed to join forces with five abhorrent kings without becoming nauseated in the process. But these weren't the reasons God loved Abraham. God loved Abraham "so that he will command his children."

In a certain sense, it is because of this that God waited for Abraham to come along. There were many righteous men who lived before Abraham. It is said that Methuselah was righteous, and Ḥanokh was certainly righteous, but their children were ne'er-do-wells. Noah's sons were also nothing more than the sons of Noah. By contrast, Abraham "commanded his children and his household after him." That's why his children are different. Stability begins here. The entire significance of Abraham's life is that what began with him has and will endure. That is what God is seeking. That is what Moses referred to many years later when praying on behalf of the people of Israel after the sin of the golden calf: "Master of the universe, You have constructed something so it would endure."

9. Genesis 18:19.

I'd like to share with you something I've read. In his *Critique of Pure Reason,* Immanuel Kant writes about antinomy – fundamental philosophical problems that are impossible to prove and impossible to disprove. These dilemmas remain unresolved because arguments can be made for and against. On his list of fundamental dilemmas he includes faith in the existence of God. He enumerates reasons for and against, but he doesn't reach a conclusion. I read that Kant, from his personal perspective (not as a philosopher), tended to believe in the existence of the Creator for two reasons. The first reason is the harmony he sees in the cosmos; astronomy gives the impression that there is a Creator. The second reason is the existence of the Jewish people.

In the book of Isaiah it is written, "You are My witnesses, the utterance of the Lord, and I am God."[10] The Midrash explains, "When you are My witnesses, I am God, and when you are not My witnesses – I am not God."[11] Our ultimate role is to be God's witnesses, and we must ensure that those who succeed us will continue to be witnesses. When God sends His Messiah, we will have less work to do in this regard, but there are no guarantees that this will happen speedily in our time.

I haven't tried to console you or tell you tales of wonders. I've attempted to speak to you about matters that I think are substantive: how we can ensure that nothing will destroy the very essence of who we are as Jews, and how can we take action so that the Jewish way of life will endure.

Leḥayim leḥayim!

10. Isaiah 43:12.
11. *Sifrei, Devarim* 346.

19

When It's Hard and Uncomfortable

PEOPLE WHO ARE A WONDER

We're having a farbrengen in honor of the festival of redemption of the sixth Lubavitcher Rebbe, Rabbi Yosef Yitzḥak Schneerson.

Rabbi Yosef Yitzḥak took up the mantle of Rebbe after the Communists had risen to power in Russia. At that time, the regime was in deliberately wicked, cruel hands whose objective – semi-officially, one-quarter-officially, or not officially – was to uproot everything. Rabbi Yosef Yitzḥak was against that regime, and he acted to secure the future of Judaism in Russia. In the wake of his activities, he was incarcerated, sentenced to death – a sentence that was subsequently commuted – sentenced to exile, then ultimately released from prison and expelled from Russia. Today we are celebrating this long, heroic story about Rabbi Yosef Yitzḥak Schneerson, part of which is recorded in his *Reshimot HaMa'asar*, but we are also celebrating the resolute stand taken by the people he left behind.

When Rabbi Yosef Yitzḥak was expelled from Russia, he left behind a relatively small group of several thousand people, who literally gave their lives for the sanctity of God's name. Some were exiled and sent to all sorts of places, and many of them never returned. Danger wasn't limited to those who worked in the labor camps; the Russians routinely killed people outside the camps as well. In any event, today I don't want to speak about those who died, but about those who sentenced themselves to unbearable Jewish lives under the Communist regime.

This wasn't a one-day exercise or a two-day demonstration. People lived that way for years without knowing what would be, with no idea what the future would bring. No one could promise them that things would improve in another five or ten years. In a certain sense, they lived this reality the way we Jews in exile live in general, and that is with the knowledge that the exile will last until the end of days. A Jew can anticipate the coming of the Messiah, but he can't prepare for his imminent coming. He has nowhere to go; he knows that life for him will go on as it always has. If he is poor and indigent, he will almost certainly continue to live a life of poverty and indigence. If he is getting beaten up, he will, in all likelihood, continue to receive beatings. How long can this go on? Apparently it can go on for the rest of his life, the lives of his children, and so on.

One aspect of the miracle celebrated on this festival of redemption is that the people didn't abandon their Jewishness under the Soviets; they held on to their faith and their connection to one another. When Rabbi Yosef Yitzḥak left Russia, these people stayed behind, and they were loyal in that place of deceit and betrayal. Those who stayed are the bigger miracle that we celebrate today.

In my library, I have memoirs written by a Jew who was a member of the Bund. This was a man who believed neither in God nor in His Messiah. Because of this, his writings are more credible about the greatness of Rabbi Yosef Yitzḥak's followers than the testimony of God-fearing Jews, since he is not an involved party. The Russians exiled him to camps and to all sorts of other places, which he describes in his book about life in Russia. He relates that people in and out of the camps stopped being human beings as a result of the regime's actions. The only people who maintained "the image of God" were the Lubavitcher hasidim.

There is a verse in Psalms that is sung in the context of release from incarceration: "He redeemed my soul in peace."[1] The redemption and salvation we celebrate today are based on what is written at the

1. Psalms 55:19.

conclusion of that verse: "For there were many with me." That conclusion is not about the single individual who experienced a personal miracle, but about the thousands of partners to the miracle. Even those among them who may not have been great in terms of their Torah knowledge were exalted because they served God "with all their might" – because they relinquished all kinds of comfort in order to cleave to God.

At this farbrengen, our focus is on a person's ability to bear all kinds of suffering in order to continue to maintain his Judaism. We are speaking about people who wake up in the morning with the knowledge that the new day will be hard and that they will need to attempt to live through it, to attempt to maintain their faith as well as some sort of family structure.

I would like to address a point that is significant to this entire story. What happens when a person realizes that he is part of a minority that the majority is seeking to eradicate? What happens when he knows that if he protests, there is a distinct possibility that his arms and legs will be broken or that he will be shot and killed?

THE ABILITY TO SUFFER

This was the situation in Russia. People were routinely shot and killed, and if there was a trial, it would be held after the fact. What does a person do when he lives in that kind of environment? How can he survive and bear it?

I know that your lives here are completely different from the lives of Jews who were trapped in Communist Russia. But a person must still have the ability to take on challenges and do things even when the outcome remains uncertain, when it's not clear that these actions will lead to the realization of a dream of having a home and a family in five years. I'm speaking of a willingness to manage without the Mitsubishi, the dishwasher, and all sorts of other items that improve one's comfort and one's quality of life. This ability to endure, even in uncomfortable situations, is a serious matter. Quite a bit depends on it.

This is true in general. Someone claimed, correctly, that in modern-day wars the country capable of absorbing the most blows wins, even if's not the more powerful country. The question isn't who is more powerful, but who is willing to suffer more, who is willing to pay more.

This issue stands at the center of our lives. When I'm willing to pay a high price for something, I'm the stronger one. The more I'm willing to suffer for things, the stronger I am.

The lack of willingness to bear hardship to achieve a greater good weakens and destroys a community, while a group of people who are willing to suffer have a powerful ability to act.

STUDYING LIKE A MADMAN

Most of you sit and study in a yeshiva. When a person sits and studies Torah, he must attempt to devote as much energy to it as possible. One could play around during study sessions, play around in yeshiva, play around when it comes to anything that requires serious effort. By contrast, a person can realize that he is part of an infrastructure where he must sit and study Torah, and that it is his mission and duty to do so properly. Ideally, the army ought to seem like a vacation from the perspective of a yeshiva student. If a student worked like a madman in yeshiva and didn't even stop to eat and drink, then the army, or any other place for that matter, would feel like a vacation.

In actuality, it often seems like a student only learns how to live a life of comfort during the many years that he sits in the yeshiva. It doesn't have to be that way. It's possible to learn with manic intensity. Although you are now sitting in yeshiva rather than participating in basic training, you are still capable of working like crazy.

Each of you can and should study Torah topics of interest. One student might decide to complete the entire Talmud over the course of a year. Another could decide to write an essay about the *halakhot* of ritual hand washing, and a third could, perhaps, decide to learn all six orders of Mishna by heart. But each must be absolutely devoted to what he is doing and work at it day and night. Even a student who is not gifted, even one who can't stop yawning during intensive Gemara lectures, even one who can't understand the Gemara and looks upon *Tosafot* like a rooster at people – he can still learn material by heart. To do that, a person only has to have the ability to sit. A person can learn the book of Psalms, even if he has to review it fifty, sixty, or eighty times until he is successful.

Do important things. There are many examples of people your age who have accomplished great things. The Shakh, for example, wrote his commentary when he was only about twenty-four years old. He may have been a genius, but in order to write a commentary, being a genius is not enough; one must also learn something. I mention the Shakh, not because I expect you to do what he did, but because he, and others like him, devoted their lives to achieving their goals without considering their personal comfort.

Not everyone can achieve great things. God, for better or for worse, didn't create all heads the same size. He also doesn't make the same demands on all people. Having said that, people can achieve quite a bit if they invest quite a bit. Even if someone is incapable of becoming the leader of a generation, he is certainly capable of studying Torah on a level that suits him. A person who can't innovate can still become an expert in what he has been taught. If he can't become an expert, he can still learn the material by heart – anyone can do that. With patience and persistence, it's even possible to teach fleas to jump and roaches to swim.

The truth is that it's possible to train fleas because no one is concerned about their well-being. Training yeshiva boys is more difficult because everyone is concerned about their well-being. Yeshiva boys are told, "Eat, drink, and rest, and if you're tired, rest a little more. And if, God forbid, your head hurts from so much Torah study, take it easy and relax a bit." The end result of this kind of coddling is obvious.

One can appreciate the value of Torah, but the question is, how much is one willing to pay for it? If one is unwilling to sacrifice his material or inner comfort for it, he won't get very far.

"IF YOU SEEK IT LIKE SILVER"

My objective here is not specifically to encourage Torah study, but to emphasize that in order to accomplish anything, one must, among other things, be prepared to sacrifice one's comfort. The necessity of hard work and effort in order to achieve a goal applies to everyone, not only to yeshiva students studying Torah.

I had a cousin who studied at the Zeitlin religious high school in Tel Aviv. One day she decided, on her own, that she also wanted to study in the Beit Yaakov Teachers Seminary. Somehow she was able to convince the school to accept her. She studied in both the high school and the seminary until she graduated from both institutions. She was quite young when she completed her studies and began teaching. After a month teaching first graders the *alef-beit*, she was disappointed to see that some of her students still didn't know how to read. She felt that she had failed as a teacher, and because she was young, she didn't know that some children still couldn't even read by the second grade. She proceeded to work harder and put her soul into teaching, and by Hanukkah every single child in the class was able to read. How did this happen? Her success stemmed from the massive effort she invested in accomplishing her goal.

Any teacher can achieve similar things. It only depends on how one performs the job. A perfectly good teacher can enter a classroom, sit patiently with a cup of tea in his hand, teach the required lesson, listen to the children's questions, and answer them to the best of his ability. At the end of the day he can relax, and he leads an altogether pleasant life. The assumption behind this style of teaching is that even though some work must be done in order to achieve a life of comfort, one can perform a minimal amount of work in a maximum period of time. By contrast, even the *alef-beit* can be taught with relentless energy and passion by a teacher who devotes time and attention to every single student until the subject matter is absorbed by all.

In the book of Proverbs, it is written, "If you seek it like silver and search for it like for hidden treasures, then you will understand fear of the Lord."[2] If a person searches and digs – be it with a hoe, with his teeth, or with his fingernails – and is determined to find something, he will find treasure. On the other hand, if he digs half-heartedly, as part of a group assigned to a small excavation, he won't unearth anything significant.

I often hear people say, "With diligence and effort, one can accomplish anything," but it's not true. With diligence and effort, a person can accomplish what exists in his potential. With great effort, he can even reach a bit beyond that, but he can't become three heads taller than he is now. Having said that, I still believe that people can achieve more than they actually achieve in practice. The reason they don't accomplish more is because they don't expend the effort. Even a Jew can strive to become

2. Proverbs 2:4–5.

no more than a *ben noaḥ* – part of the group of people who live lives of comfort [*noḥut*]. It is certainly uncomfortable to work hard, but people who do exert themselves can at times, without noticing, realize their full potential.

HAPPY ARE YOU IN THIS WORLD

Everything that I'm saying relates not only to life in the World to Come but also to life in this world. It is written, "When you eat of the labor of your hands, you are happy, and it is good for you."[3] Our Sages explain: "You are happy" – in this world; "and it is good for you" – in the World to Come.[4] It's self-evident that life will be good for a person in the World to Come if he studies Torah and performs *mitzvot* in this world. But our Sages emphasize that hard work also has a beneficial effect on a person in this world.

Some of the problems in this world come about specifically because people aren't prepared to suffer. This reluctance to bear a yoke diminishes their share in the World to Come, as well as their experience in this world. A certain eighty-five-year-old Jew whom I know has lived a life of misfortune. I think the reason for this is because he inherited a large fortune from his father and never had to work. Had he worked, he wouldn't have been so unfortunate.

It's possible to accomplish a lot in this world, but one can't be idle. A person who wants to remain one of the *benei noaḥ* is simply lazy. There are people who have an aptitude for writing – why don't they write? There are people with the ability to sing – why don't they sing? There are people with an aptitude for other things – why don't they do them? It's because they are lazy. God weeps over people who go to waste; He gave them a mind and abilities, but they don't use them.

A person can accomplish many things, but in order to do so, he must invest effort. He must work hard and exert himself. A person can achieve quite a bit in forty-eight, twenty-four, or even twelve hours. He can accomplish a whole world of things if only he expends the effort and is a little crazy. I'm not saying that he must be a madman, but he must be

---

3. Psalms 128:2.
4. Mishna *Avot* 4:1.

a little crazy. The question is whether a person is capable of tapping in to a point of truth, a point of life, a point of madness within himself. If he is capable of accessing these characteristics – then he is happy in this world, and it is good for him in the World to Come.

There are people who want the diametric opposite. Their ideal is to maintain mediocrity. I can more easily understand a person who decides to become absolutely wicked. I don't approve of that kind of person, but I can say that when he ultimately incurs Gehenna, at least he will have incurred it honestly. But what can be said of a person who manages to stay out of Gehenna only because he was circumcised as a Jew? After all, it is written in the Midrash that Abraham sees to it that the circumcised will not enter Gehenna. What, then, is the ultimate fate of a person whose dreams are neither black nor white, neither hot nor cold? There is a Yiddish saying that describes a middling person as "neither a little idiot nor a great sage." This same thought has also been expressed with the words "Mediocrity is neither 'turn away from evil' nor 'do good.'"[5]

The verse states regarding Sinai before the giving of the Torah, "Beware of ascending the mountain or touching its edge."[6] This admonition can be explained as follows: If you have already decided to ascend the mountain, even though you've been warned not to, ascend all the way, to the place "that God is there."[7] Why are you just sitting there, scratching yourselves with sacred stones?! If a person wishes to conquer the world, he will attempt to do everything he can to succeed, even though it's highly unlikely that he will achieve his goal. On the other hand, a person who is satisfied with mediocrity reconciles himself to failure from the outset.

WHAT CAN BE DONE WITH THE REMNANTS?

Sometimes a person reaches the conclusion that he will remain a ne'er-do-well, and he consoles himself by saying that his children will achieve more. The problem is that his children will say the same thing, and the situation continues for generation after generation. A person could also

5. Psalms 34:15.
6. Exodus 19:12.
7. Exodus 20:18.

think differently. Even if he sees that many years have passed and he hasn't become the man he thought he would be, he can still change. He can resolve to do things that he's able to do in the proper way. Even if it's not in the realm of Torah scholarship, a person who puts in the effort can accomplish great things.

A person might think, *I don't have a good brain. What can I possibly accomplish?* Know that it is possible to accomplish quite a bit even if you "don't have a good brain." The most simple people, the simplest of the simple, can achieve something of value.

A certain United States champion of track and field races was a fascinating person. He contracted polio as a child, and since his muscles weren't strong enough to bear weight, he had to wear iron braces on his legs. With the help of those braces, he trained and became the champion of ten-thousand- and fifteen-thousand-meter races. It turns out that with motivation and effort, even a child afflicted with polio can become a champion runner.

When I was a child myself, there was an unfortunate Jew who worked as a water carrier in our neighborhood. His four brothers were all rabbis, each in a different city. He had apparently suffered a blow to the head as a child and was mentally challenged all his life. He had the intellect of an eight-year-old and did what he could as a water carrier.

This man was known for his exceptional honesty. One day someone hired him to take a barrel of water from the Beit Yisrael neighborhood to Katamon. He was a small-boned man and not particularly strong. He rolled the barrel as far as he could until he realized that he didn't have the strength to finish the job, and he rolled the barrel back. The Jew who had hired him wanted to pay him because, after all, he had worked the entire day. The water carrier wouldn't accept the money under any circumstances. "I was hired to do a job," he said, "and I didn't do it. I don't deserve anything."

This Jew had a custom. If he would receive, say, five pennies for each jug of water he delivered, he would set aside one penny for charity. At the end of his life, he left behind piles of coins, all of which he had designated for charity.

This person was mentally challenged, yet God-fearing. He did what he could with his limited intellect. He was someone who "walks with integrity and acts with righteousness."[8] I know many people who aren't mentally challenged, but aren't so steadfast when it comes to charity or good deeds. A person can be mentally challenged and live a life of sanctity and devotion to God, while a person who has no mental deficits is liable to be absolutely worthless.

One can't demand that a person do more than he is capable of doing, but it's possible to demand that he do some of what he is capable of doing. It's not always simple to take action; it's always easier to sit and do nothing. There are always excuses and explanations as to why something couldn't be done, but a person who works hard, who makes a concerted effort, can accomplish quite a bit.

"SPEAK TO THE CHILDREN OF ISRAEL AND LET THEM TRAVEL"

I don't mean to depress you. Nothing of what I've said so far is meant to be pessimistic. On the contrary, my remarks are wholly optimistic. Granted, they aren't as comforting as caresses or pink flowers, but they do contain much faith and hope.

You might be familiar with the Partisan's Song: "Do not say, 'Behold this is my final path.'" It was sung by Jewish partisans whose families had been killed, and they couldn't be certain that the gentile partisans weren't going to kill them, too. Death accompanied these Jewish partisans – not as a possibility but as a virtual certainty – and still they sang an optimistic song. Much can develop from this type of optimism.

One time, instead of a giving a sermon before the sounding of the *shofar*, I read "Unknown Soldiers," a poem by Avraham Stern. It's a very religious and optimistic poem. Every Jew should know the words of this poem: "We are unknown soldiers without uniforms, with terror and the shadow of death surrounding us. We have all been conscripted for our entire lives; only death will liberate us from the ranks." This is an anthem that every Jew could stand by.

The Torah states that before the splitting of the Red Sea, Moses stood and prayed. God said to him, "Why are you crying out to Me?"[9] But

8. Psalms 15:2.
9. Exodus 14:15.

what was Moses supposed to do? "Speak to the children of Israel and let them travel." So they began to walk. When they asked, "What will be?" the answer was, "When we reach the sea, we will cross it." When a person wants to walk and begins to do so, he will succeed in getting somewhere. Instead of sighing about the things one didn't accomplish, it's imperative to say, "I have to do this!"

Sometimes the problem is that a person says, "Tell me what I have to do and I'll do it." A person shouldn't wait for another to impose obligations on him. After age two or three, does anyone need to be told to eat? It turns out that people remember to eat. If so, then why not remember to do other things? Why do people need to wait for someone else to tell them what to do?

Leḥayim! *Leḥayim*!

3 Av
The Birthday of Rabbi Steinsaltz

The third of Av is Rabbi Steinsaltz's birthday. Birthdays have a significant place in Hasidism. They are considered days of personal reflection when a person reviews his own life and reevaluates where he is standing. In view of this, hasidim hold a farbrengen on their birthdays, and in keeping with this hasidic custom, Rabbi Steinsaltz would likewise have a farbrengen on his birthday. Among other things, it was an opportunity for him to think out loud about his own perception of what he had and hadn't accomplished in the past year.

Rabbi Steinsaltz always made a *siyum* of some kind on his birthday. Sometimes he would conclude the Babylonian Talmud, sometimes the Jerusalem Talmud, sometimes both. As a rule, he spoke very little about himself, but the *siyum* was a window into a private aspect of his life, and during these farbrengens, one had a sense of being a part of his personal life, when he usually revealed only its external aspects. He would share personal thoughts about things he wanted to accomplish, feelings he had about not having done enough, and thoughts about what he sought to achieve in all his actions.

Sometimes he would also share personal thoughts about the students who had gathered to be with him on that day. These tended to be thoughts about what disappointed him, what satisfied him, what he would he like to see us become, and what he wanted us to accomplish in this world.

20

Reckonings

Typically, when the verse "And the living will take it to heart"[1] is quoted, it refers to the day of one's death. But the truth is that this verse is much more relevant to one's birthday, a time for reckoning and self-reflection. It's actually necessary to conduct this kind of reckoning quite often, but there isn't always time. Certain days and events prompt it, and one of them is a person's birthday.

It seems to me that a birthday is like a personal Rosh HaShana. Just as a year in the history of the world begins on Rosh HaShana, so does a personal Rosh HaShana begin and end on one's birthday. That's why one must conduct a reckoning on one's birthday. Having said that, there is a difference between these two reckonings.

THE RECKONING OF ROSH HASHANA

Rosh HaShana is said to be "the day of the beginning of Your works, a remembrance of the first day."[2] Even though Rosh HaShana is not the actual day that the world began, it is a birthday in the precise sense of the word: the birthday of mankind. That's why, on Rosh HaShana, we don't review the status of mountains, stones, or horses. There is

1. Ecclesiastes 7:2.
2. Introduction to the verses of *Zikhronot*; see *Rosh HaShana* 27a.

primarily a reckoning of a human being. Where does he find himself and what must he do?

At the same time, there is another meaning to the creation of mankind. One of the great philosophical questions is whether it's possible to speak of the time before mankind existed. Many contend that time had no significance before there was man. It's not that time didn't exist in an objective sense, but that it had to be acknowledged in order to be significant, and before man, no creature had the mental capacity to relate to time.

Incidentally, even physicists speak about the difference between measured time and our sense of time, and about the question of whether there is time at all without a sense of time. Actual physical time began with the creation of the world and the onset of events that enabled the measurement of time to a certain extent. Acknowledgment of time began only with the existence of man. That is why on Rosh HaShana, the day of the creation of man, we engage in a reckoning of man, in a reckoning of time – which could be acknowledged when man was created – and essentially, in a reckoning of the entire world.

The reckoning of the world is based on one question that we must ask ourselves since the reality of the world began on Rosh HaShana: What have we done and what are we doing to repair the world and its essence? Alternatively: To what degree is the sovereignty of God apparent in the world? This is the reckoning we conduct on Rosh HaShana, and all of the prayers and *shofar* blasts of Rosh HaShana address it. Even if a person engages in his own personal reckoning on Rosh HaShana, the question that he must still address is, over the course of this past year, how much did I contribute to glorifying the kingship of God in this world and how much did I detract from it?

THE GRAVITY OF THE JUDGMENT

When Rosh HaShana arrives, a person sometimes thinks to himself, *If God wishes for His kingship to rely on me – He doesn't have very much upon which to rely.* Perhaps, since we are required to look upon others positively, a person must think, *Even though I may have sinned and transgressed, my neighbors are certainly righteous; it is they who sustain the world.* This points to the kind of exacting reckoning that occurs on Rosh HaShana.

Last night I heard about a woman who is twenty-five years old and suffering from cancer. Because she demanded it, she was treated with powerful anti-cancer drugs – poisons that are designed to kill cells and so have terrible and painful side effects. This woman says that her suffering atones for her sins. But what sins could such a God-fearing woman have?

Here I must point out that we can't know the tally of our sins from Heaven's perspective. We can't know the extent of the liability incurred by our actions. We can't know exactly to what degree we must atone, to what degree we deserve punishment. When a person rebels against a mortal king, he is imprisoned for a specific number of years. But when a person rebels against the King of kings, perhaps there is no remedy at all. If a God-fearing young woman who is so afflicted is fearful of her ultimate day of judgment in the next world, what of a person who can't boast such merit?

This understanding can be found in a variety of other sources. The Gemara recounts that when the strap of Rav Huna's *tefillin* was found to have been turned over – by itself – he fasted for forty days.[3] If Rav Huna did that to atone for an accident, what would be required of a person with a long list of willfully wicked deeds?!

It turns out that there is a tally in the holy books of the number of fasts a person is required to observe to atone for each transgression he committed in a given year. The sum can be greater than the number of days in a year. If he lost his temper twice during the year, he is required to fast for more than a year. He can therefore lose his temper no more than one and a half times a year.

It is told of Reb Elimelekh of Lizhensk that although he prohibited others from engaging in fasting and self-abnegation, he would inflict all kinds of mortifications on himself. One time he repented and engaged in self-abnegation to atone for having possibly scratched his mother when he was nursing as a baby. If he repented and fasted for something like that, what must people with more obvious transgressions do?

Here is another example: The Cossack riots of 1648 were horrific events. The murder of Jews that took place at that time was, in a certain

3. *Mo'ed Katan* 25a.

sense, as egregious as the Holocaust, not in terms of absolute numbers, because it involved fewer Jews, but in terms of percentages. The author of *Tosefot Yom Tov* asks: Why did God do this?

In the period preceding the riots, there were prominent Torah scholars throughout the world, and the Jewish people as a whole were Torah observant, even if they weren't all absolutely righteous. Why did they receive this great punishment?

His answer was that the riots were a punishment for talking in synagogue during prayer. He also instituted a *Mi Sheberakh* prayer on behalf of everyone who did not talk during the prayers and Torah reading. (This prayer appears in the more comprehensive prayer books.) Apparently, he saw a connection between the murder of so many Jews in all sorts of awful deaths and talking during the prayers. If this is the punishment incurred by one who speaks during prayer, what can an ordinary person, who may have committed all sorts of other sins, say?

EXTENUATING CIRCUMSTANCES

There is, however, another side to this reckoning. It is told of Rabbi David of Lelov that he was late for a meeting with his Rebbe. When asked about the nature of his delay, he replied that he had stopped to observe a person who was extremely God-fearing. When asked who it was that he saw, he related that as he was walking in the forest, he passed a small house where a father and son were having an extremely impassioned quarrel. The son held an ax in his hand and said, "Father, if I did not fear God, I would chop off your head with this ax!"

This story might sound like a joke, but the truth is that given this person's anger, it would have been simple in his eyes to kill his father. Only his fear of God restrained him; he was an exceptionally God-fearing Jew.

Rabbi Levi Yitzḥak of Berditchev was a defender of Jews and did so in many different ways, and he did so sincerely and authentically because he assessed others based on different standards than those he applied to himself. It is told that he once saw a Jewish wagon driver adorned with *tallit* and *tefillin* while spreading tar on his wagon wheel. Rabbi Levi Yitzḥak remarked, "See what Jews there are in this world! This Jew prays even while spreading tar on his wagon wheels!"

This anecdote is also not a joke. The wagon driver didn't skip the prayer even though finding time to pray was difficult for him. His livelihood depended on functioning wheels and he had to maintain them. If you understand a person's situation, you can see how the very fact that he prays attests to his fear of God.

It is written in many books that if one is going to assess people, one must consider their situation, their life circumstances, the strength of their evil inclination, and the education they received. Only if all these variables are taken into account can one know the extent to which a person can be seen as sinful as opposed to unfortunate.

A GENERATION OF COARSE SOULS

From this perspective, perhaps Heaven will absolve all sinners in our generation except the religious from most punishments. What claim can be made against a Jew who desecrates Shabbat? The great majority of Jews who desecrate Shabbat have no connection to Shabbat and are ignorant of its laws and its significance. At most, if they happen to live in Israel, they see Shabbat observance as a custom observed by pious Jews, a custom that has nothing to do with them. A person like that still sees himself as a good Jew, just one who simply doesn't adhere to all the dictates of Judaism.

Even according to the civil penal code, a person who violates the law can be held liable for the crime he committed only if he knows that it is a violation. To convict him, the court must show intent to break the law. An insane man could be very intelligent, and could even be familiar with criminal law, but if he can't distinguish between good and evil, he is absolved of punishment. Juveniles are also held to different standards and absolved of punishment, or given lighter sentences, for similar reasons.

In our generation, many indecent things that in the past never would have even entered one's mind, let alone acted upon, are done frequently. Because these behaviors are seen and done widely, they penetrate reality and influence one's consciousness. Even if a person doesn't intend to do them, they become part of a reality that he knows and sees.

This is one of the problems encountered by religious young men who enter the army. It's not that the army forces people to sin – that rarely happens. The problem is that a religious young man comes from an environment where certain behaviors would never even enter his mind. In the army, the atmosphere is immeasurably different. He is exposed to phenomena – in realms of thought, speech, and action – that wouldn't have occurred to him otherwise. Even if these things don't involve him directly, they still enter into the reality of his life, into his consciousness, and it's inevitable that he will be influenced by them.

This is the simple reason that God prohibited Adam from eating of the tree of knowledge, which would result in his knowing about good and evil. A person can't know evil without becoming somewhat involved in it. That's one of the differences between a person and an angel. The knowledge of good and evil has no impact on angels whatsoever. In that sense, they are like computers. It's possible to write awful things on a computer, but even if the computer analyzes and corrects the grammar of what was written, it won't be outraged. An angel is likewise not influenced by the things he knows; knowledge doesn't have an impact on his behavior.

An angel can know a person's repulsive statements and know the disgusting thoughts the person harbors, record all of these statements, and say, "Okay, now we must lop off someone's arms and legs in accordance with section 28a." But none of this has any effect on the angel. The angel doesn't care. That is an aspect of his nature as an angel.

By contrast, a person can't escape the influence of things he knows. When a person begins to know evil, even if he doesn't recognize it as evil, he is already involved in evil, and this involvement is liable to increase.

Unlike generations of Jews in the past, our generation's exposure to indecent matters has become common. As a result, most of the souls of our generation have become coarse, and because of this, they don't deserve numerous and harsh punishments. The coarse souls exist on such a low level that even the basest standards of evaluation don't pertain to them.

A RIGHTEOUS MAN IN HIS GENERATION

On the other hand, a righteous person with an elevated soul might think he deserves all the punishments in the world because of one minor flaw or slight transgression. He accepts whatever terrible suffering he might experience as expiation for his sins. For most people who are not made that way, personal shortcomings work in their favor. Their souls function at a low level, and their lack of awareness of sin makes them undeserving of punishment. In this generation, people who are sensitive and aware of their own transgressions are the exception rather than the rule.

The Yid HaKadosh said that in the generation before the messianic era, life will be bad for sensitive people both materially and spiritually. For coarse people, on the other hand, life will be good both materially and spiritually. In some generations, life is hard for sensitive souls; the entire world causes them pain and torments them. A person like that sees what is happening in the world and is unable to sleep at night. By contrast, a thick-skinned person is unmoved and unaffected by abhorrent occurrences in this world.

According to the *halakha,* if a man interrupts his prayers between the blessings of *Yishtabaḥ* and *Yotzer Or,* he is exempt from serving in war, because he falls into the category of "a man who is fearful and fainthearted."[4] It's assumed that he would be so upset about his interrupted prayers that he would see himself as deserving of death in combat as punishment for his sin. The question is whether this *halakha* applies only to the righteous. Only a righteous person, for example, could be distraught by the thought that two strings of his *tzitzit* were torn. It is those Jews who are unaware of these types of wrongdoings who go off to war, because they don't fear dying as punishment for those transgressions.

I once knew a Jew who repented wholeheartedly. Every so often he would come to my Jerusalem neighborhood of Reḥavia on vacation and share his private journals with me. In one of them he wrote, "Just as I was leaving the synagogue on Shabbat eve, filled with feelings of peace and tranquility, a motorcycle roared passed me. Its noise ripped my Shabbat serenity to shreds. I felt like picking up a stone and throwing it at him." This Jew didn't grow up in any religious enclave, but his soul had become as sensitive as if it had been pure from birth. Of course, he

4. Deuteronomy 20:8.

would not have actually thrown any stones, but seeing the desecration of Shabbat tore his heart to shreds.

That kind of sensitivity hardens over time. It has been said that the first time a beggar extends his hand for a donation, the coin he is given burns a hole in his palm. But once the hole is there, there is room for many more coins to flow in without causing pain.

A righteous person might think he deserves to have his hands severed because he wasn't scrupulous enough in ritual hand washing. In truth, in our generation, when the deeds that people perform and don't perform are totally different from the deeds of previous generations, perhaps one who doesn't engage in murder can be considered righteous. This is one interpretations of "These are the generations of Noah. Noah was a righteous man; he was faultless in his generations."[5] In his generation, Noah was considered righteous, but had he lived in Abraham's generation, he wouldn't have been considered extraordinary.

It is written, "Your righteousness is like mighty mountains; Your judgments are a fathomless deep"[6] – that is, Your judgments are meted out with the deepest understanding of true justice. In a generation like ours and in a world like ours, ordinary people won't be punished with suffering because they are vulnerable and coarse by nature and can't be expected to overcome temptations.

As stated above, this downward trend in the level of our souls stems from the decline of the generations over time, and from the fact that, unfortunately, it's impossible to remain completely isolated from the goings-on of the world, as if in a hermetically sealed glass box. But it's also impossible to isolate the human consciousness. Sometimes it's possible to distance a person from direct contact with negative forces, but it's impossible to distance him from indirect contact. If he doesn't learn about these things on his own, he knows about them second- or third-hand. Because of this, one can advocate on behalf of the Jewish people, on behalf of us and other Jews who live in our generation. We deserve leniency; because our souls are vulnerable and we are coarse by nature, we don't deserve to be punished.

5. Genesis 6:9.
6. Psalms 36:7.

I'm not saying that this is a good thing; it's simply a part of reality. This can exonerate us and other Jews who live in this generation.

KNOWING THAT THERE IS HEAVEN

A person who is always functioning at a low level can imagine that the whole world is like him, that there is no alternative way to live. But it's important for a person to know that there is an alternative. This is one of the reasons it's good to hear tales of *tzaddikim*. A person might think, *What does this have to do with me, given the level on which I live my life?* But it's still good for him to at least have an idea of the heights an individual is capable of reaching.

This is, after all, the difference between human beings and beasts. Someone once explained the words "God made man upright"[7] by pointing out that man is the only creature who stands upright, and his virtue lies in the fact that he is the only creature who can see Heaven. Even if it is beyond his reach, it's good for a person to set his sights above his own level. This way he will at least know that there is a Heaven, and some thoughts of regret about his own behavior will be aroused in him from time to time.

A person who perpetually lives in the mud is liable to forget that there is Heaven. He may begin to think that all of existence is found in that murky swamp, and that the only distinction one can possibly make is between thick mud and watery mud. The very knowledge that there is Heaven helps a person from sinking into the mud.

THE RECKONING OF A BIRTHDAY

So far we have spoken about Rosh HaShana. When someone conducts an inspection of his own virtues and transgressions, this is part of the reckoning of the world. He asks himself: What has the world gained from my actions this past year? Rosh HaShana is the time for a person to consider that question, to undertake all the appropriate remedies, and to renew his dedication to God and everything that comes along with it to the best of his ability.

---

7. Ecclesiastes 7:29.

On one's birthday, a personal Rosh HaShana, a person should also review his own behavior and conduct in a kind of personal reckoning. This isn't a tally of *mitzvot* and transgressions. There are other times designated for calculating *mitzvot* and transgressions, such as the custom to observe a Yom Kippur Katan – a mini Yom Kippur – every month on the day before Rosh Ḥodesh. There are places and times when people would conduct daily reviews, and the holy books state that it's appropriate to conduct reviews of that kind. This is reflected in the nightly recitation of *Shema* that, in some prayer books, includes the confession.

On one's birthday, in contrast to the focus on tallying one's *mitzvot* and transgressions that is made on Rosh HaShana, a person should ask himself: What is the relationship between what I'm capable of accomplishing and what I've actually accomplished? Did I live up to my potential? This pertains to tasks that are incumbent on a given individual to perform, and includes those imposed on him from without as well as those he imposes on himself.

On Rosh HaShana, each person must assume universal responsibility for the welfare of the entire world. In that context, a personal review of one's individual accomplishments isn't important. By contrast, on a person's birthday, the central question is about what he achieved during the previous year. This is a very private reckoning that revolves around the question of the actualization of a person's potential in all areas, with *mitzvot* and transgressions being merely one aspect of that. Just as a person can, for example, regret not having cleaned his yard, a person can hold himself accountable for not having accomplished certain things he might have done, even if they are things he wasn't obligated to do. The birthday is not a day of judgment; it's a day of introspection and review.

THE FREQUENCY OF THE RECKONING

Why does one perform this kind of review only once a year on one's birthday? It's because in order to assess behavior, a longer period of observation is more accurate than a brief observation. One doesn't calculate how long it should take to get from one place to another based on speed at just one point along the way. One looks at the average of speeds at different points on the trip. Then it becomes possible to determine whether a given trip took too long or was fast enough. Similarly, when a person looks back at one week in his lifetime, it's conceivable that one particular week was unsuccessful for a variety of reasons, and that it's not representative of the person's life as a whole. That's why one must look back at a longer period of time, and evaluate the mean.

In practice, a comprehensive reckoning that takes a person's entire life into account occurs on the day of his death. I'll tell you a story that admittedly seems to contain a degree of callousness, and I also can't vouch for its veracity, but it illustrates my point. In the city of Dvinsk, two rabbis lived: the Rogotchover Gaon, Rabbi Yosef Rosen, who was a proponent of Hasidism and had close connections to Chabad and their rebbes, and the Or Same'aḥ, Rabbi Meir Simḥa HaKohen, who was an opponent of Hasidism. Despite their opposing outlooks on Hasidism, there were very good relations between the two men. It is told that when the Or Same'aḥ passed away, the Rogotchover passed by his corpse, pulled on his ear, and said, "Meir Simḥa, Meir Simḥa, you have finally begun to learn a little, and you are already dead?!"

In any event, there are people who conduct a comprehensive review of their lives on the day of their death. This review isn't limited to a tally of *mitzvot* and transgressions. A person is born and lives his life and has the opportunity to accomplish all sorts of things – sometimes because of his talents, sometimes because of his inheritance, sometimes because of his station. Given all that, what did he actually manage to accomplish? A person conducts this kind of review of the previous year on his birthday.

PERSONAL RECKONING

Above I explained that when conducting a reckoning of his sins, every person must be judged based on his own particular circumstances. It's impossible to compare one person to another. The review that is done on one's birthday is also subjective and one person can't be held up against another.

Even in the business world, there is a difference between a large company, a small company, and a private business. A large company that had a profit of a hundred thousand dollars in one year is in big trouble, but a private person who earned that much in one year isn't in bad shape. The personal review performed on one's birthday is similar to a personal ledger of expenditures and earnings. The gap between what I could have accomplished and what I accomplished is, in a sense, my annual deficit. It differs for each person, and there is no room for comparisons.

RATIONALIZATIONS

Regarding the reckoning on one's birthday, we can quote the Kotzker Rebbe: "Rationalizations, one tells the police."

When reviewing one's good deeds and transgressions, there is some room for rationalizations: "Such and such obstacles prevented me from performing the *mitzva*," or "I stumbled in such-and-such place, and that's why I violated such-and-such transgression," or "The situation in which I found myself did not allow me to perform any good deeds." When God conducts His tally of *mitzvot* and transgressions, He takes these excuses into consideration.

This is the meaning of "The reward is commensurate with the effort."[8] Ostensibly, no one in the world is rewarded in accordance with his effort. The opposite is often the case. The salary of a laborer who digs a foundation is lower than the salary of the high-ranking engineer who planned it but whose efforts require less exertion. The carpenter whose hand hurts and as a result is unable to work effectively won't be paid. If he does continue working despite the pain, his salary doesn't increase accordingly.

By contrast, God takes a person's pain and suffering into account. If a person overcomes pain and suffering and fulfills a *mitzva* despite it all, his reward is greater. God can give a person who studied a single page of Gemara the same reward He would give to a person who studied ten pages in the same amount of time, if the first person exerted himself greatly and the second person learned with minimal effort. God's calculations aren't necessary calculations of performance. Rather, they are calculations of the essential value of the deed, which certainly varies based on effort, pain, and suffering.

8. Mishna *Avot* 5:22.

God knows more than just our thoughts. The thoughts themselves are part of the currency with which He conducts His assessment. Virtue, temptations, inclinations, obstacles, difficulties, and moods are also taken into account. That's why a person who spent all his days in sin can still be judged leniently by God. The impediments that were placed in his way are taken into consideration. God can decide that this person achieved what he was able to achieve. By contrast, in this world, none of these considerations are taken into account. A person is only asked, "Did you or did you not accomplish the task?"

It's not only that God sees into the heart. The assessment of each *mitzva* and each transgression is complex, because considerations of the degree of suffering involved and the difficulties experienced in carrying out the deed, for example, are taken into account. How the *mitzva* was done, whether it was performed properly, a person's intent, and ultimately, how much was invested in it are all important. It's possible to objectively assess the beauty and superior quality of an *etrog*, for example, but the beauty of the *etrog* is just a small consideration in the calculation of the *mitzva*. Other considerations like effort, heart, intent, and so on, all matter. In this world, for the most part, no value is placed on any of these factors. The impediments, stumbling blocks, and intent – these are all considerations that are factored into the heavenly calculations, but not the earthly calculations.

On Yom Kippur, a person could say, "Master of the universe, you know that my evil inclination is powerful and that it's an impediment for me in many ways." So we say in our prayers, "For He knows our inclinations; He is mindful that we are but dust."[9] God can say of an individual, "I know this person. If he were an exalted, noble creature, he would deserve a certain punishment, but he is, in effect, a coarse, vulgar person. He can't be held to the same standard as someone with a more refined soul."

Someone once questioned why truth is one of the thirteen attributes of mercy considering that truth tends to be an extremely unmerciful quality. Let us imagine a rabbi with a long beard and an unblemished past. Based on his appearance and comportment, one would think he

9. Psalms 103:14.

deserves to be judged as a righteous Torah scholar and receive a severe punishment for any transgression he commits. But God knows that beneath this façade, beneath this *tallit,* stands a very ordinary person, and He judges him accordingly: as an ordinary person. This is the attribute of truth at work.

But rationalizations and excuses that may be effective on Yom Kippur are not effective in the personal review that occurs on one's birthday. At times, when a person is subject to God's reckoning, there is room to rationalize. The review that occurs on a person's birthday, on the other hand, is a self-assessment, an earthly evaluation that seeks to answer the simple question: Did I or did I not achieve? Did I or did I not transgress? Did I or did I not fulfill my obligations? In that kind of reckoning, there is no room for excuses.

One also doesn't take rationalizations into account in the stock market, for example. If a company is unsuccessful, it plummets. If it doesn't succeed a second time, it plummets further. The company can claim that a natural disaster occurred and its executives did everything they should have, but that changes nothing. The company has already lost all its value. Similarly, when a person evaluates his past year, rationalizations are irrelevant and ineffective.

The reckoning on a birthday can be compared to Belshatzar's writing on the wall: "*Mene mene tekel ufarsin*"[10] – Count and weigh, but you did not reach the correct weight. There was a reckoning and you were found lacking. Even if there are a thousand reasons for the fact that you are deficient, that's the reality, and nothing can be done to change it.

If a person participates in a long jump tournament and doesn't succeed in jumping to the target distance, but does manage to jump ten centimeters short of his goal, perhaps two points will be deducted from his score, and he'll lose a medal or trophy. But if a person is required to jump over a chasm between two mountains, and he misses by ten centimeters, two points won't be deducted from his score. He'll simply fall into the abyss. Those are the consequences, whether or not they seem fair.

10. Daniel 5:25.

By the way, an annual review on a birthday isn't the same as making a financial balance sheet. Sometimes, even if the general balance sheet is sound, the personal ledger is not, because I could have achieved twice as much as I actually did. I could have made a bigger profit. Even if I can't be blamed from a business perspective – on the contrary, it could be said that I worked hard and I deserve accolades and a bonus – I didn't do enough by my personal standards and goals. Therefore, I deserve nothing.

Years ago I met a prominent Jew who told me that it's possible to repent for everything except for the *mitzvot* a person didn't perform because of poor health. True, the sick person wasn't able to perform the *mitzva* because of his limitation, yet the *mitzva* remained unobserved. How can a person repent for that?

Theoretically, one could have demonstrated penitence by being more vigilant in trying to get well, but that's not always dependent on the person himself. When a person's health is so compromised that he's really unable to fulfill his obligations, it's impossible to repent. Though no transgression was committed, a shortcoming remains a shortcoming.

SELF-FORGIVENESS

A person will often forgive himself for his transgressions and shortcomings as he makes his self-evaluation since he is, after all, witness, judge, accused, advocate, and prosecutor. An American judge was once caught speeding. He went to court and said to himself, "So-and-so, you are accused of driving over the speed limit. How do you plead?"

He answered, "Guilty."

"Do you have any justifications?"

"I don't have sufficient justification."

"Alright then, I will fine you such-and-such sum."

Although this sounds like a joke, people conduct themselves this way all the time. A person judges himself: "Today you prayed like a baboon. How do you plead?"

"What can I say? Guilty!"

"Can you justify yourself?"

"I didn't get enough sleep."

"I was in a hurry."

"My neck was itching."

Then the person says, "All good reasons. I will reduce your fine to three dollars, and you'll pay it when you have the opportunity, when you have the time."

The problem is that in most cases, the verdict exonerates the accused: "Every way of a man is right in his own eyes, but the Lord measures hearts."[11] When a person judges himself, he finds excuses. If one excuse isn't effective, he tries harder and finds another excuse.

This sort of self-forgiveness is a problem that's related to the essence of repentance. Years ago I wrote, in the context of the High Holy Days, that there is no such thing as forgiveness and atonement in this world. Whoever fails has failed, and whoever loses out loses out. The concepts of forgiveness or atonement are irrational. If a person slaps another person in the face, then asks for forgiveness and is forgiven, how does that change anything? The slap can't be rescinded.

The truth is that only God can really forgive. He, and only He, can say, "I have wiped away your transgressions like a thick cloud."[12] There were transgressions, but they are now gone; the wind carried them away. It's as if God is able to film a new version of a person's life. When a person performs full-fledged repentance, God takes the film of his life, and just as videographers do, He splices the film and edits out the transgression or introduces changes. He will eradicate the transgression or change intentional misdeeds into inadvertent ones. Sometimes He even transforms intentional misdeeds into merits. It's as if He is saying, "You see the film of your life as you remember it, but that's not the real film. The film I have reflects the truth and is completely different from your version."

That people are capable of forgiving has great significance, but forgiving doesn't necessarily remedy the harm that has been done. If I damaged another person's car and he forgives me, the car is still in need of repair. Even if I ask for forgiveness sixty times, the car will still be in need of repair.

---

11. Proverbs 21:2.
12. Isaiah 44:22.

It's also easier to forgive than to forget. A person may no longer be angry with whoever harmed him, but the memory of the event remains. The damage that was done may no longer cause emotional trauma or physical distress, but it is not forgotten. A person who wronged another and begs for forgiveness may alleviate his own intense pain, but the person who was wronged remembers his pain very well. People have the ability to forgive, and that's something we shouldn't take for granted, but human beings are unable to rewrite the screenplay of their own lives. When a person forgives, it's as if he is saying, "I may be unable to create a new world, but I can still imagine that an event never happened. I can try to visualize a new world."

In other words, even if we seek to remedy events that took place in the past, we can't do so perfectly. We can forgive others, and that's a good thing, but in our own personal reckoning, we have neither the ability nor permission to forgive ourselves – not in terms of our reckoning to God and not in evaluating our personal accomplishments. If a person built a warped wall, even if he forgives himself, the wall will remain warped. Even if he were to claim that he didn't really know how to construct a wall and wasn't expert at building and so on, these rationalizations will be ineffective. Since the reckoning of one's birthday relates to what a person has actually accomplished or failed to accomplish in reality, forgiving oneself will be ineffective and certainly won't result in positive change.

CONSIDERING THE POSSIBILITIES

There are times when a person has the ability to accomplish more and times when he's unable to accomplish anything. When a person has the ability to accomplish quite a bit, his responsibility to do so is much greater.

A person may justifiably claim that other people think he is much more qualified than he actually is. That's why, when he is accused of not having done something, he doesn't admit guilt. He knows that he lacks the talent to do it. Generally, when other people make various demands on a person, it's based on their calculations. The reckoning that a person conducts with himself relates to what he knows he is actually capable of achieving.

Every so often when I was a child, I engaged in all sorts of reckonings with myself. I would compare myself to others, and as a result, I was sometimes able to feel quite arrogant. It seemed to my uncle that I was a bit full of myself, so he showed me a newspaper clipping about a child about my age, eleven years old, who was tested and proven to know a thousand pages of Gemara by heart. My uncle asked me, "*Nu*, and what do you know?" In truth, I shouldn't have been too ashamed, because even had I studied for that entire year, there is no way I would have been able to learn a thousand pages of Gemara. My car isn't engineered to travel at a speed of five hundred miles an hour, so there's no reason to question why it doesn't go that fast.

THE SIGNIFICANCE OF A RECKONING OF ACCOMPLISHMENTS

Unfortunately, people don't typically mark their birthdays in this way. They celebrate, but no one turns to a small child on his birthday and says, "How is it possible that you are now seven years old and you still don't know how to read?" In reality, this is the essential purpose of a birthday – to assess even a seven-year-old child and determine whether he has achieved the milestones he was supposed to achieve.

One doesn't say this to a child even on other days, and I think that this is an educational problem. I know that this kind of criticism isn't nice and it goes against the bylaws and provisions of the Department of Education. But a child must know, or at least his parents should know, that there is a problem when he doesn't achieve the milestones that can be expected of him.

This can happen even to a good child who sits in class without being disruptive and attempts to do his homework. He may deserve a good grade for industriousness, he may receive a good grade for not being disruptive in class, but the fact is that in terms of achievement he is underperforming. Someone must be reprimanded, but that doesn't always happen.

In other areas, appraisals are continually conducted. When a child is small and doesn't grow, he is evaluated by the doctor who seeks to diagnose the problem and treat it. No one is at fault and no one is guilty because the problem is one of measurement. But the child's achievements should also be measured. If a child in the third grade doesn't perform at grade level, something must be done about it.

It's not really my business and it's not my job, and it's certainly not pleasant to do, but occasionally I will say to a person, "Look, I'm not assessing your tally of *mitzvot* and transgressions, but I can say that your accomplishments are not in keeping with your potential. It's true that you've tried and that your efforts are fine and good and ascend on high and are taken into account in the reckoning conducted in Heaven. But in this world, it's not about effort. It's about whether you are realizing your potential."

And sometimes I say to a person, "You're twenty-one years old. What have you accomplished in the past twenty-one years? It's possible to calculate approximately how much bread you've consumed in this lifetime. It's possible to approximate how much Coca-Cola you drank and how much meat and fish you ate. But other than the fact that you succeeded in sustaining yourself by eating and drinking, and that food and drink passed through your esophagus, what have you accomplished?"

A story is told about two people who came before the heavenly court and waited in line. One of them was given precedence over the other. The second one complained: "Why was he given precedence? I've been waiting much longer."

They said to him, "He is greater than you are."

"What does that mean? I was his *sandak*!"

"It's true that chronologically you are older, but in terms of achievements, he became a fully grown man and you remained a small child. Therefore, be so kind as to wait."

WHEN THERE IS A DEFICIT

Fortunate is one who can say each year that he had the potential to accomplish such and such, but he pushed himself and was able to accomplish twice as much. If a person performs three tasks simultaneously, he may end up with a surplus at the end of the year. He was supposed to perform one task, but he succeeded in performing three.

What does a person do when his birthday arrives and he discovers that he has a deficit? What happens when a person discovers that three months have gone to waste? If year after year passes in this way, the deficit grows. One year he has a deficit of one month; the following year the deficit is liable to increase and continue growing throughout his life. He can make excuses, but they'll find their way to the excuses column; they won't appear in the column of actions. Excuses will be treated precisely the way anything that doesn't work properly is treated. If someone buys a car and it turns out to be defective, he must repair it or junk it.

A person can make an effort to shrink the deficit instead of doubling it by working faster and studying harder the following year. Since I frequently fly in airplanes, I've noticed something interesting that is relevant to this topic. When a flight departs a half hour late – sometimes through no fault of the airline – one would expect it to arrive a half hour late. But a late arrival would present a bigger problem than the mere inconvenience of having to sit around and wait: People might miss connecting flights. If a plane lands two hours late, a person may actually lose an entire day. This delay can be prevented by injecting more fuel into the jet engine so that the plane can go faster and arrive on time.

I once asked, "If an airplane can travel, say, a distance that usually takes ten hours, in nine and a half hours, why doesn't it always fly at that speed?" It turns out that it costs too much money and the airlines don't want to incur the expense of paying for extra fuel on a regular basis. But when it's necessary to accelerate to keep to a schedule, more fuel can be injected into the engine so that the plane can arrive on time. This is what a person must do when he discovers that he is behind. Whether he actually does so depends on the depth of his regret and the profundity of his thoughts.

Perhaps there are people who rejoice on their birthdays because they conducted a comprehensive review and determined that, thank God, their ledger is balanced. It's also conceivable that there are people who celebrate their birthdays fearlessly, proudly, and with a good feeling because they can pride themselves on the number of deeds they managed to perform that year. I, on the other hand, am overcome with melancholy when my birthday arrives. My review depresses me; it doesn't help if I compare myself to others. The question of whether my speed is faster or slower than the speed of others is irrelevant. The question is whether I reached my own potential given my particular reality.

Be that as it may, I'm glad that you are here with me. Maybe you feel you should be expressing your condolences rather than celebrating, but at least you have come to be with me.

May we all be able to reduce our deficits in the coming year.

Leḥayim!

21

The Seventy-Fifth Birthday of Rabbi Steinsaltz

What is the significance of a birthday? What does one do on a birthday?

A birthday relates to the private life of a specific person. In that sense, it's different from general, communal days – days that are tied to the nation or to the entire world. The year marked by a birthday is a private one, similar in a sense to the Torah's description of "a sheep in its first year."[1] Each sheep has its own year that begins on the day it is born; it is not a universal year. It is also not significant for the rest of the world. By contrast, the year that begins on Rosh HaShana is a universal year.

There is a difference between a personal birthday and the universal New Year in terms of the reckoning conducted on that date. On Rosh HaShana, a person conducts a reckoning about the year that has just ended. Although it is his own personal reckoning, it relates to what he did in terms of *mitzvot* and good deeds that benefit or damage the world at large. All these matters relate to the universal year that begins on Rosh HaShana, and it is appropriate to conduct such a reckoning on that date. Similarly, people review their financial accounts on the date that the fiscal year begins, be it the first of January or the first of April.

1. Numbers 6:12.

On Rosh HaShana, one focuses on transgressions and deeds, and at the beginning of the fiscal year, one examines his finances. There are also specific dates for reviewing other matters. What review, then, must be conducted on one's birthday?

The review conducted on a birthday can't be measured by objective criteria. *Mitzvot* and transgressions are matters that exist in the world, and money, too, is something that exists in the world. On a birthday, one's own personal New Year, one reviews his past year and everything that transpired in it. I would say that this kind of review is not at all simple and straightforward. It's not about a tally of *mitzvot* and transgressions. It addresses the question, what could I have done over the course of the year, and what did I actually do?

This review is undertaken on one's birthday because it is subjective; a person conducts it with himself, and about himself. It is unrelated to what others think. They can say and think whatever they want. A person may have been lauded during the year, or demeaned; both are based on the assessments of others. His personal review doesn't relate to his relative standing vis-à-vis another person or society, but to his standing vis-à-vis himself.

In this review, an individual doesn't confront questions about the level of his pure and holy soul; it is also not an objective tally of his *mitzvot* and transgressions. The questions that must be addressed are, What did I do with the hours I was given? What did I do with the days I was given? What good did I do? What did I accomplish? This review isn't a trial. It simply asks the question: Given what you could have accomplished in the course of the year, how much did you actually do?

If, in the course of the year, I could have accomplished two, three, or four times as much as I did, then the result is pathetic and a failure. On my birthday, I probably deserve a slap in the face.

That's why, for me, my birthday has been a day of greater or lesser melancholy for many years now. It's not because my birthday falls in the month of Av; it's because of this review. I would be happy if, when I reached my birthday, I could say, "Thank God, this year was successful for me." Unfortunately, that doesn't happen.

The melancholy arrives on every birthday. On milestone birthdays, like this one, it is much more discouraging, much more depressing, and much murkier. Seventy-three is not as bad as seventy-five, which seems to be a more significant number.

If I could, I would simply take fifty of my years and toss them over to somebody else. I would feel a bit better if I were now twenty-five years old instead of seventy-five. The fact that so much time has passed isn't what frightens me. Time that has passed, has passed. All it means is that I'm able to tell stories from seventy years ago. What frightens me is the thought of what has happened over the course of all that time. What occurred in those years? Again, I could sit and measure myself relative to others, but that wouldn't help me. Those measurements are worthless.

I've already spoken about the saying "The day is short, the task is great, the laborers are lazy, the reward is great, and the employer is prodding."[2] This prodding isn't a nationwide or countrywide prodding. The employer prods me personally: "The time is short. The task is great. *Nu*, what have you accomplished?" What can I say? Excuses: "Today is Shabbat." "Today is Passover." "Today is a festival." "I went on a trip today." "Today I had a meeting with a very important person." "Tomorrow I have a meeting with a not so important person," and so on. I wish I could at least say, "A meeting I had today with so-and-so totally revolutionized his life. He became a new person." But I can hardly even say that I left a small mark on him.

If I could discard fifty years, I could begin to work now. If I had another fifty years, I would be able to have a pretty good plan about what to do with them. (I am not saying that I do not have plans of that kind; I make plans without paying attention to my doctors' assessments about my medical condition.) Another problem is that fifty years wouldn't give me enough time to do everything that needs to be done based on the pace that I work. Sometimes I'm envious when I see how much another person manages to accomplish in the course of the year and how much I'm unable to accomplish in the course of ten years. Were I promised another hundred years, I would certainly be able to make serious plans. The fact that I might die in the meantime wouldn't deter

2. Mishna *Avot* 2:16.

me. It's not that I'm asking, "Let me dwell in Your tent forever"[3] – to live forever. It's just that plans must be made; there are a great many things that need to be done.

I'm not speaking about deducting fifty years because I haven't accomplished anything useful to date. I've managed to accomplish some useful things here and there, mistakenly or intentionally. And don't think that I didn't have good intentions. I had a great many good intentions, but the realization of those good intentions occurred only with great difficulty. This is what I'm thinking about now. Seventy-five is a frightening number because of the question it brings up: What have I truly accomplished in all those years?

That's why I'm saying that a birthday is a day of melancholy. On another day, say, the day after tomorrow, I will forget all about this and continue to do what I do, as I have no alternative. I would rejoice if I were to receive a note signed by God that says, "Do such and such." But to my disappointment I've never received such a note, not with that signature nor with any other signature. So what am I supposed to do?

What I can say is that even if I look upon myself like a sheep, I can see that, based on its tail and legs and the smudges of dirt on its body, that it is still trying to accomplish something.

What am I trying to accomplish? There are things that I accomplish alone, but the question is, what am I attempting to accomplish beyond that?

Something else I do is write books. I've written quite a bit, but that's still not enough. It's not enough because I can create a long list of all the books that I'm thinking about writing – not only those that I haven't started yet, but also those that I have started and am halfway or three-quarters of the way through. Since I'm somewhat of a lazy person, I don't write at a good pace.

Moreover, even when my books are published, and even when they are read, some questions remain: Were my thoughts conveyed to the reader? Did he internalize anything? Only if that happens, have I accomplished something good. But that hasn't happened, not even a small fraction of it. I've written all sorts of things, some more significant and

3. Psalms 61:5.

some less. An entire forest or several forests of trees were undoubtably chopped down for all that paper. And I ask myself: How much good resulted from this? After all, the forest grew and it could have grown pine cones, nuts, or other things. What did the books grow? I would have liked for something to have happened because of those books other than the fact that they were placed on a bookshelf.

I envy writers whose every word emerges from a diamond mine. I'm envious when I hear of a person who fought with his editor for two weeks over the placement of a comma in a sentence. Happy is one who feels that his every word is a gem. What can I do? I don't have that feeling. That's not to say that I wouldn't want it to be so. Believe me, I'd like to sit and write three sentences that would inflame the hearts of anyone who reads them. If only I could write a sentence that would have the power to keep any person who read it awake all night. If that were the case, I would be able to say, "Thank God, I have accomplished something this year!" But I can't write a book, or even half a book, that would have that effect on people. Even if I were to expend greater effort, could I succeed in accomplishing that?

I write words of wisdom, and I feel as though they are just lines taking up space. It's as if the words themselves feel the need to fill up and sully blank pages, as if they were ordained from Heaven to do so, like those worms whose role it is to consume the dead. What is the point of it?

There are people who claim that the world doesn't recognize their genius, that people don't know that they are great, wise, righteous, pious, and God-fearing, that people don't understand that every word they write is hewn from onyx stones.

I know that if my words lack impact, it's not the world's fault.

I'm not here to complain about the cruelty of my fate. I could take comfort in the fact that God created a creature like this, like me. But I know that this creature can do better. This sheep could weigh twenty more pounds. It could have more wool. It could be fairer.

I take action, I try, I expend effort, and after all that, I hear a divine voice that is not encouraging, that utters a statement that we recite each day in prayer. I know that this statement also appears in your prayer books. It's just that in my prayer book, it seems to cry out specifically to me: "That we will neither toil in vain nor emerge in panic." A person could be doing all sorts of things that are nothing more than toiling in vain and emerging in panic.

Another area in which I have made achievements is in institutions. Most of the people who are here belong to institutions to which I am in some way connected. What emerged from this? One can count students – a certain number of heads, a certain number of *kippot*. Some of those heads also happen to lack *kippot*. But one thing that I really want to accomplish, which is my objective whenever I deal with people, be they children or adults, is to help them to feel the fear of God within them.

When I speak about the fear of God, I'm referring to a person being truly authentic in his religious observance. I say this because some of you here teach children. But this also pertains to yourselves. This is something that really concerns me.

Once, when I was in some remote place in the middle of Siberia, I was summoned by the district governor, who is a quasi-king in his territory. When he summons you, you go, if only for reasons of courtesy. When I was standing before him, he questioned me: "What are you doing here?"

I answered him truthfully: "I came to visit my family."

He heard me, then we spoke. No harm befell me. I spoke the truth – I really did come to visit my family. All Jews, after all, are my brothers and sisters.

Ultimately I seek to accomplish two things that are really one and the same. These two aspirations are expressed in a statement recited in the prayers: "Guardian of Israel, guard the remnant of Israel, and let Israel, who recite, 'Hear, O Israel,' not perish."

I'm not talking about my *shtiebel*, my friends, or even my immediate family. I'm speaking of the remnant of Israel; it is they who concern me. Perhaps that's a mistake. Perhaps I should be thinking only about those residing in the German Colony, the neighborhood in which I live, or perhaps only about those residing on Graetz Street, the street where I live. There is enough work to do there. And yet my thoughts are on the remnant of Israel.

What would I like to do for the remnant of Israel? "Guard the remnant of Israel" – I want the remnant of Israel to endure.

I have tried to explain to gentiles that the existence of the world depends on the Jewish people. Just as there are some radioactive elements – less than one percent of all of the other elements, in fact – that are needed for the world at large, the Jewish people are also essential to the continued existence of the world. As long as radioactive elements are active and emitting energy, they sustain the world. This is also true of the Jewish people. If we are destroyed, the world cannot endure; it, too, will be destroyed shortly thereafter.

When I recite, "Guard the remnant of Israel," I'm not merely praying that we remain alive and that our enemies don't kill us, but rather, "Guard the remnant of Israel who recite, 'Hear, O Israel.'" This is the outcome I always strive for – whether I am writing books, giving talks, or even visiting a remote location unfit for human habitation. What am I doing there? I'm there because of my family. What am I trying to do for my family? Everything that I can to enable them to say, "Hear, O Israel" – *Shema Yisrael*. I want to succeed in doing this to the best of my ability for everyone I meet, be they child or adult. I want to enable them to say *Shema Yisrael* – to roar *Shema Yisrael* – so that *Shema Yisrael* will exist in their midst.

Have I accomplished this? I've enabled the education of a certain number of children who wear *kippot*, a certain number of children who don *tzitzit*, and a certain number of girls who didn't go astray. But am I able to say that they also say *Shema Yisrael*? Whether I'm sitting with a child in the first grade or with a yeshiva student, I ask myself: Have I conveyed this point to him? Granted, the student sits and studies Gemara, but Gemara can be forgotten. In half a year he can forget all the Gemara he learned over the course of twenty years. The question is whether he will continue to say *Shema Yisrael* and whether it will inspire him.

I will say something else that as far as I'm concerned doesn't contradict what I've been saying. I would also like to be able to feel that the people whom I've met will have more than a spark and a flame within their hearts, that each one will be a person of value. This doesn't mean that I want everyone to be equal to one another; I just want them all to be worth something.

Rabbi Naḥman of Breslov once said to his hasidim that he wanted better hasidim. The hasidim thought that their Rebbe and *tzaddik* must have a good explanation for his statement, and when they asked what he meant by "better hasidim," he answered, "Wealthier, more learned, and with better lineage." He wasn't seeking people who could meditate in solitude for hours. He wanted hasidim who were wealthier, more learned, and with better lineage.

I, too, would like the learned, the wealthy, and those with lineage to study my teachings. It's not necessary for everyone to have all those qualities, but each person should have at least one of them – one would be wealthy, another learned, and a third, possess lineage.

A year has passed since my last birthday. Then, too, we gathered together. I'm still attempting to accomplish what I wanted to accomplish then. A year has passed, seventy-five years have passed, and I am still sitting here and aspiring.

Someone asked me if I could share some memories. "What is there to tell?" I told him. "I never climbed Kilimanjaro, the highest mountain in Africa, but I do have a sword in my house that can be used to kill lions. In a certain tribe, when a boy reaches the equivalent age of a bar mitzva, he is given a sword of this kind and told to enter the jungle and either kill a lion or be devoured by it. He must choose: Either bring the lion's tail back home, as proof that he killed the lion and cut off its tail, or have the lion show the tail of the young man to its family. I have a sword like that, but I myself have never killed a lion. I did, though, at age ten, on my own personal great expedition, succeed in taking a curl from a lion's mane. I know it's hard to believe, but I did it, among other reasons, to compare the color of the lion's hair to mine."

At the time, we had the same exact color hair. I'm sure you agree with me that this isn't something to be proud of. It's not worthy of praise or merit in this world or in the World to Come.

So what is appropriate to be proud of? Imagine my coming here next year – perhaps to half or a quarter of the number of people present given all the insults and awful things I've said to you. But maybe, perhaps in the merit of things I've written or things I've said, or even because of some blow that I struck, I will see people with a flame burning within them. Not a three-dimensional rendering of fire, but a real flame.

Perhaps I will be able to see people about whom I can say, "Israel in whom I glory."[4]

Perhaps I will be able to say, "Ah," and sigh with pleasure.

There have been several people – some no longer in this world – whom I helped emerge from a troubled world to a Jewish world. Because of them, I know that I won't end up in Gehenna, even if I justifiably belong there. Those people will stand at the entrance and say, "This man is our teacher and you want to cast him into Gehenna? We won't allow it."

I know that I have some protection. I'm not asking for much – just that there will be at least some people on whom I can rely to keep me out of Gehennna. I would like to be able to say, "I left them behind me. They will protect me and take some pity on me if need be."

It's not that I'm particularly afraid of the fire of Gehenna. I'm just thinking about what kind of actions have real value. I'm thinking about the remnant of Israel.

Someone brought me a bottle of whiskey today for my birthday. The whiskey is good, but I don't drink whiskey very often, and I don't drink for pleasure. What matters is that the person who gave me the whiskey loves me very much, and that despite the fact that he walks with a cane and it was hard for him, he went to the trouble of personally bringing me a bottle of whiskey. I look at this person, a Jew who is ninety-four years old and still walks about, and I think, *I have hope*. That is a beautiful gift. Not the whiskey, but the fact that he brought it himself, the mere fact that he came.

If next year I can see a person here (and he doesn't necessarily have to be ninety-five years old) about whom I could say, "Ah! Master of the universe, look. There's a person like this here, and I had a hand in it," well, then, let them send me wherever they send me. *Reshit Ḥokhma* has detailed descriptions of Gehenna. Those descriptions don't interest me. What interests me is that I will be able to say, "I did something of value" – that I will be able to say, "Look, I built a soul."

4. Isaiah 49:3.

There are people about whom I think, "*Nu*, okay, they've just begun. Next year they will bear fruit."

Thank God, I am content with my lot. But perhaps I can also say, "Ah! Look at what emerged from this man! I sat with him and didn't know whether I was wasting my time, but apparently something stuck."

This connection is what really touches me: seeing something emerge that is truly worthwhile, something that is "glory in the eyes of the one who performs it and glory in the eyes of others."[5] When a person emerges with fire in him – that is "glory in the eyes of the one who performs it." When a person emerges with some value in this world – that is "glory in the eyes of others." Who could ask for more?

For now, commiserate with me on my melancholy birthday. Perhaps things will be better next year.

Leḥayim tovim, and thank you for taking the trouble to come. It is conceivable that if I were to tell you all how delightful you are and how beautiful you are, each of you would bring another five people with you next year to hear the compliments. Instead, I screamed at all of you, even if my screams were only implied.

I'm a Jewish optimist, and this is what a Jewish optimist says: The world is dark and ugly, but there is hope. If someone sees the world differently, he has a problem with his vision – he is colorblind or needs new glasses. I do think I see the right colors, and this is the way the world looks. It is black and malodorous. But it need not remain that way, and it is by the strength of this hope that I live.

Leḥayim!

---

5. Mishna *Avot* 2:1.

Glossary

aggada: Nonlegal rabbinic literature, including stories, parables, and homiletical teachings that appear in the classical rabbinic literature of Judaism, particularly the Talmud and Midrash

Al Ḥet: Literally, "for the sin"; confession prayer said on Yom Kippur

alef: The first letter of the Hebrew alphabet

alef-beit: The Hebrew alphabet

am ha'aretz: Someone who is unlearned in Torah

Amida: Silent prayer recited three times daily

amora'im: Sages of the Talmud who lived from approximately 200 to 500 CE

Arba Bavot: The melody of Four Stanzas composed by Rabbi Schneur Zalman of Liadi

Arvit: Evening prayer service

Ashkenazim: Jews who originated from northern and eastern Europe, primarily Germany and its environs

bar mitzva: Coming-of-age ceremony for Jewish boys when they turn thirteen

baraita: A teaching of the Sages that was not included in the Mishna

Bava Kamma: First tractate of talmudic civil law

Beinoni: Literally, "intermediate"; one who is on a level where he is neither wicked nor righteous

Beit Hillel: Literally, "House of Hillel"; a school of thought named after the mishnaic Sage Hillel, who founded it

Beit Shammai: Literally, "House of Shammai"; a school of thought named after the mishnaic Sage Shammai, who founded it

Birkat Kohanim: The priestly blessing

Chabad: An acronym of the three cognitive divine attributes, *Ḥokhma, Bina,* and *Da'at*; the name attributed to Lubavitch Hasidism, founded by Rabbi Shneur Zalman of Liadi

davening: Yiddish term for Jewish prayer

dinar: A coin that was common in the times of the Talmud; the term attributed to several coins

Ein Yaakov: A sixteenth-century compilation of all aggadic material in the Talmud together with commentaries

Elul: The twelfth month of the Jewish year

etrog: Citron, one of the four species waved on the festival of Sukkot

farbrengen: A hasidic gathering, which may consist of explanations of general Torah subjects, the telling of hasidic stories, and lively hasidic melodies, with refreshments served

gadol hador: Leading rabbi of the generation

galut: Exile

gartel: Belt worn during prayer by some hasidim

Gemara: Another name for the Talmud

geonim: The presidents of the two great Babylonian talmudic academies of Sura and Pumbedita who were generally accepted as the spiritual leaders of the Jewish community worldwide in the early medieval era

haftara: The passage from the Prophets or Writings that is read after the weekly Torah portion

Haggada: Book that tells the story of the exodus to be related at the Seder on the first night of Passover

halakha: Jewish law

ḥaredi: Ultra-Orthodox Jew

hasid (pl. hasidim): Literally, "pious individual"; a follower of Hasidism

Hasidism: Hasidic movement initiated by the Baal Shem Tov

heh: The fifth letter of the Hebrew alphabet

hilula: Anniversary of a *tzaddik*'s passing

Ḥumash: The Five Books of Moses

Jerusalem Talmud: Written in the Land of Israel, an extensive work built upon the foundation of the Mishna like its better-known counterpart, the Babylonian Talmud

Kabbala: The mystical teachings of the Torah

Kaddish: A Jewish prayer in Aramaic praising God's name and affirming divine sovereignty

kashrut: The set of Jewish dietary laws that define which foods are fit (kosher) or unfit (non-kosher) for consumption

kelippa (pl. kelippot): Literally, "husk"; the aspect of the universe that is unholy and conceals the Divine

Kiddush: Benediction and prayer recited over a cup of wine immediately before the meal on Shabbat or a festival

kippa (pl. kippot): Also known as a yarmulke, a traditional head covering worn by men

Kislev: The third month in the Jewish calendar, which falls out during winter

Kitzur Shulḥan Arukh: A condensed version of the *Shulḥan Arukh,* the authoritative code of Jewish law, authored by Rabbi Shlomo Gantzfreid (1804–1886)

Lag BaOmer: A Jewish holiday celebrated on the thirty-third day of the period between Passover and Shavuot, commemorating the passing of Rabbi Shimon bar Yoḥai

leḥayim: Toast meaning "to life"

Likkutei Dibburim: A series of books containing the teachings of the sixth Lubavitcher Rebbe, Rabbi Yosef Yitzḥak Schneerson (1880–1950)

Likkutei Moharan: The magnum opus of Rabbi Naḥman of Breslov (1772–1810) containing all of his primary teachings

lulav: Palm frond, one of the four species waved on the festival of Sukkot

matza: Unleavened bread eaten on Passover

megilla: Scroll, particularly the Book of Esther

mezuza: A parchment scroll on which four passages from the Torah are inscribed and affixed to the doorpost of a Jewish home

Midrash Tanḥuma: Midrash comprising a collection of homiletic teachings expounding the Torah

Midrash: Collection of homiletic interpretations of the Bible by the Sages of the Talmud

mikve (pl. mikva'ot): Bath used for ritual immersion

Minḥa: Afternoon prayer service

minyan: Prayer quorum of ten Jewish adult men

Mishna: A concise summary of the teachings of the Sages on all topics of Torah, which was redacted in the beginning of the third century CE by Rabbi Yehuda HaNasi

Mishne Torah: Code of Jewish law composed by Rambam (1138–1204), containing fourteen books, including *Sefer HaMadda* (the Book of Knowledge), which addresses fundamentals of Judaism

mitnaged: Opponent of Hasidism

mitzva (pl. mitzvot): A Torah commandment

Mussaf: Additional prayer service recited on special days

mussar: Literally, "reproof"; ethical instruction and self-improvement

Nei'la: Closing prayer service of Yom Kippur

niggunim: Hasidic melodies, typically sung using simple syllables rather than actual words believed to help connect with the Divine in ways that transcend language

Nisan: Seventh month of the Jewish calendar

nusaḥ: The traditional order, text, and melodic pattern of Jewish prayers that varies among different Jewish communities

nusaḥ Sefard: A specific prayer tradition developed by hasidic Jews that combines both Ashkenazic and Sefardic elements and is commonly used by hasidic communities

Oraḥ Ḥayim: The section of the *Shulḥan Arukh* that addresses daily life, encompassing laws about prayers, Shabbat, holidays, blessings, and other rituals and practices that are part of everyday Jewish observance

Otzar Iggerot Kodesh: A collection of letters written by the Lubavitcher Rebbe, Rabbi Menaḥem Mendel Schneerson

parasha: Torah portion

Peirush HaMishnayot: Rambam's commentary on the Mishna

Pesukei DeZimra: Preliminary morning prayers

peyot: Sidelocks worn by Jewish males

Pirkei Avot: Literally, "Chapters of the Fathers"; a tractate of the Mishna dealing with ethics and piety

Rabbeinu Tam tefillin: The head *tefillin* containing the four passages from the Torah in the order arranged by Rabbeinu Tam, which differs from the commonly used version

Rashi tefillin: The head *tefillin* containing the four passages from the Torah in the order arranged by Rashi, which is the commonly used version that places the passages in the order they appear in the Torah

Rebbe: Leader of a hasidic sect

Reshit Ḥokhma: Work of Kabbala, ethics, and morality written by sixteenth-century scholar Rabbi Eliyahu de Vidas based largely on the *Zohar*

Rosh HaShana: Jewish New Year

Rosh Ḥodesh: The beginning of a new Jewish month

Sambatyon: Legendary river beyond which the ten lost tribes of Israel were exiled, described in the Talmud as unnavigable on weekdays

sandak: One who holds the baby during a circumcision

Seder: Order that follows the recitation of the Passover Haggada, which includes a festive meal and the telling of the story of the exodus, on the first night of Passover

Sefardim: A Jewish population associated with the Iberian Peninsula (Spain and Portugal), but can also refer to the Jews of the Middle East and North Africa

Sefer HaHafla'a: Novellae on the tractate *Ketubot*, written by Rabbi Pinchas HaLevi Horowitz (1731–1805)

Sefer Ḥasidim: A foundational work containing ethical, ascetic, and mystical teachings by Rabbi Yehuda of Regensburg (1150–1217), also known as Rabbi Yehuda HeḤasid

Sefer HaZikhronot: A work that contains descriptions of places, historical events and biographies, and fragments of the history and origins of hasidic teachings, based on the notes of Rabbi Yosef Yitzḥak Schneersohn of Lubavitch

seuda shelishit: The third Shabbat meal

Shabbat: The Jewish Sabbath celebrated on Saturday

Shabbat HaGadol: The Shabbat before Passover

Shabbetai Tzvi: A Jewish mystic and self-proclaimed Messiah (1626–1676) who gained a massive following across the Jewish world before converting to Islam under Ottoman pressure, causing widespread disillusionment and theological crisis.

shamash: Attendant

Shavuot: A major Jewish festival celebrating the giving of the Torah at Mount Sinai, observed seven weeks after Passover with customs including all-night Torah study, eating dairy foods, and reading the Book of Ruth

shefa: Divine flow of blessing

Shema: Prayer recited three times daily in which one declares one's faith in the oneness of God

shofar: Ram's horn sounded on the festival of Rosh HaShana

shtiebel (pl. shtieblakh): A place used for communal Jewish prayer, which, in contrast to a formal synagogue, is fairly small and approached more casually

shtreimel: Fur hat worn by hasidic men on Shabbat and Jewish holidays and other festive occasions

Shulḥan Arukh: The codification of Jewish law compiled by Rabbi Yosef Karo (1488–1575)

siddur: Prayer book

Sukkot: The harvest festival celebrated in the fall during which Jews leave their houses to live in temporary shelters

tallit: Prayer shawl

Talmud Torah: Religious Jewish elementary school for boys

Tammuz: The tenth month of the Jewish year

Tanakh: An acronym for *Torah, Nevi'im, Ketuvim* (Torah, Prophets, Writings), comprising the twenty-four books of the Bible

tanna (pl. tanna'im): Sages who lived in the period spanning 332 BCE to 220 CE whose views were recorded in the Mishna

Tanya: The foundational work of Chabad, written by Rabbi Shneur Zalman of Liadi, the founder of Chabad Hasidism, first published in 1796

tefillin: Leather boxes worn on the arm and forehead containing certain biblical passages that declare the unity of God and the miracles of the exodus from Egypt

Teharot: Tractate of the Talmud that deals with the laws of ritual purity

Tevet: The fourth month of the Jewish year

tisch: Hasidic gathering around the Rebbe's table

Tishrei: The first month of the Jewish year

tosafists: Medieval talmudic commentators

Tosefot Yom Tov: Commentary on the Mishna written by Rabbi Yom Tov Lipmann Heller (1579–1654)

Tur: An important halakhic work composed by Rabbi Yaakov ben Asher (1270–1340), who is also referred to as Baal HaTurim

tzaddik (pl. tzaddikim): Righteous individual

Tzefat: Safed, city located in northern Israel known as a center of Kabbala

tzitzit: Strings that are affixed to four-cornered garments

U'Netaneh Tokef: One of the most stirring and evocative Jewish prayers recited on the High Holidays

yartzeit: Anniversary of a death

yeshiva (pl. yeshivot): An academy dedicated to the study of Torah

Yevamot: The first talmudic tractate in the section of *Nashim*

Yom Kippur: The Day of Atonement, when the Jewish people engage in fasting, prayer, and repentance

Zohar: One of the fundamental texts of Kabbala that consists of the teachings of the talmudic sage Rabbi Shimon bar Yoḥai, as transcribed by his close disciples

Personalities Who Appear in This Work

Arizal: Rabbi Yitzḥak Luria of Tzefat (1534–1572), the most influential kabbalist of modern times.

Rabbi Avraham Dov of Avritch: Rabb Abraham Dov (1765–1840), was a rabbi in Zhitomir. In 1830 he moved to Tzefat and became it's Ashkenazi rabbi. His books *Bat Ayin* on the Torah, are well respected in hasidic circles

Rabbi Avraham HaMalakh: Rabbi Avraham Friedman (1739–1776), son of the Maggid of Mezeritch, known for his ascetic lifestyle earning the moniker "HaMalakh," which means "the Angel." His teachings were mostly oral, but he did publish the book *Ḥesed LeAvraham,* a Torah commentary that also discusses teachings of the Talmud and the Jewish holidays.

Baal Shem Tov: Rabbi Yisrael ben Eliezer (1698–1760), founder of the hasidic movement.

Baal HaTanya: Rabbi Shneur Zalman of Liadi (1745–1812), the founder of Chabad Hasidism. Rabbi Shneur Zalman's Torah discourses are found in a number of works, chiefly the *Tanya, Torah Or,* and *Likkutei Torah.* He also wrote the halakhic masterwork *Shulḥan Arukh HaRav.*

Rabbi Barukh of Medzhibozh: A grandson of the Baal Shem Tov (1753–1811) and author of *Botzina DiNehora.*

Rabbi David of Lelov: A disciple of the Chozeh of Lublin, he became an early hasidic master (1746–1814) known for his love of his fellow Jews and was the first Rebbe and founder of the Lelov hasidic dynasty.

Reb Elimelekh of Lizhensk: A student of the Maggid of Mezeritch, Reb Elimelekh (1717–1787) is known for his work *Noam Elimelekh,* which consists of lessons on the weekly *parasha* and the festivals based on hasidic teachings and kabbalistic thought.

Elisha ben Avuya: Known as Aḥer, the "Other," Elisha ben Avuya was a talmudic Sage who lived in the second century CE and became a heretic.

Rabbi Eliyahu de Vidas: Jewish mystic and ethicist (1518–1587) from Tzefat who wrote *Reshit Chochmah,* an influential work combining Kabbala with practical ethical teachings.

Rabbi Ḥanina ben Dosa: A talmudic sage who lived in the first century CE known for miracle stories.

Rabbi Ḥayim Vital: A master kabbalist (1543–1620) from Tzefat and Damascus, he was a primary disciple of the Arizal.

Hershele of Ostropoli: Famous Jewish storyteller and wit (1725–1800), his stories were collected in various compilations.

Ḥida: An acronym for Rabbi Ḥayim Yosef David Azulai (1724–1806), a prolific writer and a legal scholar. His major works include *Shem HaGedolim,* a biographical dictionary, and *Birkei Yosef.*

Reb Leibele Eiger: Reb Leibele (1816–1888) was the grandson of Rabbi Akiva Eiger and a disciple of Rabbi Menaḥem Mendel of Kotzk. He was the founder of the Lublin hasidic dynasty and is known for his works *Torat Emet* and *Imrei Emet.*

Rabbi Levi Yitzḥak of Berditchev: Rabbi Levi Yitzḥak (1740–1809) served as the rabbi of Zelechov, Pinsk, and Berditchev. His work, *Kedushat Levi,* contains sermons on the weekly *parasha* and the festivals. He was known as the defender of Israel due to his overwhelming love for the Jewish people.

Maggid of Mezeritch: Rabbi Dov Ber (d. 1772), a disciple of the Baal Shem Tov and the teacher and mentor of Rabbi Shneur Zalman of Liadi.

Maggid of Turisk: Rabbi Avraham Twersky (1806–1889), who founded the Turisk hasidic dynasty and became its first Rebbe. He was also known for his halakhic work, *Magen Avraham.*

Maharal of Prague: An acronym for Rabbi Yehudah Loew of Prague (1525–1609), one of the outstanding scholars and Jewish leaders of the sixteenth century.

Meiri: Rabbi Menaḥem HaMeiri (1249–1315), whose major work is *Beit HaBeḥira* on the Talmud, which clearly reviews the opinions brought in the Mishna and the Talmud, by Rashi and *Tosafot*, as well as the halakhic rulings of the Ashkenazic, Provençal, and Sefardic authorities. He also wrote *Kiryat Sefer* and *Magen Avot* on various halakhic topics.

Rabbi Menaḥem Azarya de Fano: A kabbalist, a great talmudist, and a halakhic scholar (1548–1620), he is known for his works, which include *Asara Ma'amarot* and *Kanfei Yona*.

Rabbi Menaḥem Mendel Morgenstern of Kotzk: Known as the Kotzker Rebbe (1787–1859), he established a hasidic court that was known to be a fierce critic of self-deception and falsehood. His Torah discourses were compiled in the works titled *Ohel Torah* and *Emet VeEmuna*. He did not write any books himself, but many incisive statements, some of which are quite radical, have been quoted in his name.

Rabbi Menaḥem Mendel of Vitebsk: Born in Vitebsk, Rabbi Menaḥem Mendel (1730–1788) spread hasidic ideas in Belarus and Lithuania. He moved to Tzefat, where he established the hasidic community in the Land of Israel, and then to Tiberias, where he died. . He is the author of *Peri HaAretz*, which contains discourses on the weekly *parasha* and the festivals.

Rabbi Mordekhai of Chernobyl: Also known as Reb Mottele (1730–1797), he would wander from town to town giving sermons and later established a hasidic court in the city of Chernobyl. His book, *Me'or Einayim*, consists of discourses on the weekly *parasha* and festivals. At the end of the book there is a short composition called *Yismaḥ Lev*, which consists of hasidic novellae on the Talmud.

Rabbi Moshe Cordevero: Also known by the acronym Ramak (1522–1570), he is one of the most prominent kabbalists of Tzefat in the sixteenth century. He was also the author of kabbalistic works such as *Pardes Rimmonim* and *Tomer Devora,* which influenced the teachings of the Arizal.

Rabbi Moshe Leib of Sassov: Rabbi Moshe Yehuda Leib Erblich (1745–1807) was one of the early hasidic Rebbes in eighteenth-century Europe who founded the Sassov hasidic dynasty.

Rabbi Naḥman of Breslov: Rabbi Naḥman (1772–1810) was the founder of the Breslov hasidic movement. He was particularly known for his creative parables.

Rabbi Naḥum of Chernobyl: Rabbi Menaḥem Naḥum Twersky, also known as Reb Naḥumke, (1730–1787), was a disciple of the Baal Shem Tov and the Maggid of Mezeritch and the founder of the Chernobyl hasidic dynasty. His book, *Me'or Einayim,* was one of the first published works of hasidic thought.

Reb Noson of Breslov: Reb Noson (1780–1844) was the primary disciple of Rabbi Naḥman of Breslov and he is famously known for transcribing and compiling Rabbi Naḥman's teachings under the title *Likkutei Moharan,* as well as the halakhic work *Likkutei Halakhot.*

Rambam: Also known as Maimonides, Rabbi Moses ben Maimon (1138–1204) was a leading halakhic authority and philosopher.

Rashi: An acronym for Rabbi Shlomo Yitzḥaki (1040–1105), one of the foremost commentators of the Torah and Talmud.

Shakh: An acronym for his work *Siftei Kohen,* Rabbi Shabbetai ben Meir HaKohen (1621–1662) was a noted seventeenth-century talmudist and halakhist.

Rabbi Shimon bar Yoḥai: Also known by the acronym Rashbi, Rabbi Shimon bar Yoḥai was a second-century talmudic Sage and one of the most eminent disciples of Rabbi Akiva. The *Zohar,* a thirteenth-century foundational work of Kabbala, is ascribed to him by kabbalistic tradition.

Rabbi Shlomo Eiger: Rabbi Shlomo Eiger (1786–1852) was the son of Rabbi Akiva Eiger and served as the chief rabbi of Kalisz and Posen. Among his other writings, he is known for his work *Gilyon Maharsha.*

Rabbi Simḥa Bunim of Peshisḥa: Also known as the Rebbe Reb Bunim (1765–1827), Rabbi Simḥa Bunim was one of the key leaders of Hasidism in Poland. A disciple of Rabbi Yaakov Yitzḥak Rabinowitz, he served as the second Rebbe of Peshisḥa.

Sochatchover Rebbe: Rabbi Avraham Borenstein (1838–1910) was a leading *posek* in late-nineteenth century Europe and founder of the Sochatchover hasidic dynasty. He is also known as the Avnei Nezer, after the title of his set of Torah responsa.

Rabbi Tzadok HaKohen of Lublin: Rabbi Tzadok (1823–1900) was a talmudist, thinker, kabbalist, and one of the most prolific writers of hasidic teachings. He is most known for his works *Tzidkas HaTzaddik* and *Pri Tzaddik*.

Rabbi Yaakov Yitzḥak Horowitz: Famously known as the Ḥozeh of Lublin (1745–1815), he was a leading figure in the early hasidic movement in Poland, as well as a disciple of the Maggid of Mezeritch. His works have been compiled under the title *Torat HaḤozeh MiLublin*, where his commentaries are arranged alphabetically according to topics and according to the weekly Torah portion.

Rabbi Yaakov Yitzḥak Rabinowitz of Peshisḥa: Also known as the Yid HaKadosh (1766–1813), he was the founder of the Peshisḥa hasidic dynasty and an important figure of Polish Hasidism, as well as the primary disciple of the Ḥozeh of Lublin. He wrote no works of his own, but many of his teachings were transmitted orally and published posthumously.

Rabbi Yeḥiel Meir of Gustinin: Also known as the *Tehillim Yid* (1816–1888), his reputation for righteousness was such that even in his youth he was called one of the thirty-six hidden *tzaddikim*.

Rabbi Yehuda HaNasi: A *tanna* (135–217 CE) of the fifth generation and chief redactor of the Mishna.

Rabbi Yehuda Leib of Shpola: Also known as the Shpoler Zeide (1725–1811), he was a disciple of the Maggid of Mezritch and the Baal Shem Tov and served as a hasidic Rebbe who was known as a miracle worker and faith healer.

Rabbi Yitzḥak Meir Alter: Also known as Ḥiddushei HaRim after his work that contains teachings on the Torah, Talmud, and *Shulḥan Arukh,* he served as the first Gerrer Rebbe (1799–1866). He was known to be sharp-witted and erudite and wrote several works, including a book of responsa.

Reb Zusha of Anipoli: A brother of Reb Elimelekh of Lizhensk and a disciple of the Maggid of Mezeritch, he was known for his extraordinary piousness.